# Human Tissue in Transpl

C000061878

Deficiencies and shortfalls in the supply of human organs for transplantation and human tissue for research generate policy dilemmas across the world and have often given rise to major and deleterious controversies. They also create an environment in which illegitimate commercial activities flourish. At the same time, patients are denied the therapy they desperately require and researchers are impeded from carrying out vital work into the causes of, and efficacious treatments for, major illnesses and diseases.

David Price sets out a clear and integrated legal and policy framework which emanates from the tissue source but protects the interests of donors and relevant professionals through tailored property entitlements, but without presupposing rights to trade in 'original' materials.

**David Price** is Professor of Medical Law at De Montfort University, Leicester, where his research focuses on areas relating to human tissue for medical purposes. He was very recently a member of the Secretary of State's Organ Donation Taskforce examining presumed consent and previously a member of a World Health Organisation Taskforce on Organ Transplantation. He is a member of the European Expert Group Relating to Ethical, Legal and Psychosocial Aspects of Organ Transplantation and a member of the Editorial Board of the *Medical Law Review*.

*Cambridge Law, Medicine and Ethics*

This series of books was founded by Cambridge University Press with Alexander McCall Smith as its first editor in 2003. It focuses on the law's complex and troubled relationship with medicine across both the developed and the developing world. In the past twenty years, we have seen in many countries increasing resort to the courts by dissatisfied patients and a growing use of the courts to attempt to resolve intractable ethical dilemmas. At the same time, legislatures across the world have struggled to address the questions posed by both the successes and the failures of modern medicine, while international organisations such as the WHO and UNESCO now regularly address issues of medical law.

It follows that we would expect ethical and policy questions to be integral to the analysis of the legal issues discussed in this series. The series responds to the high profile of medical law in universities, in legal and medical practice, as well as in public and political affairs. We seek to reflect the evidence that many major health-related policy debates in the UK, Europe and the international community over the past two decades have involved a strong medical law dimension. Organ retention, embryonic stem cell research, physician-assisted suicide and the allocation of resources to fund healthcare are but a few examples among many. The emphasis of this series is thus on matters of public concern and/or practical significance. We look for books that could make a difference to the development of medical law and enhance the role of medico-legal debate in policy circles. That is not to say that we lack interest in the important theoretical dimensions of the subject, but we aim to ensure that theoretical debate is grounded in the realities of how the law does and should interact with medicine and health care.

*General Editors*
Professor Margaret Brazier, *University of Manchester*
Professor Graeme Laurie, *University of Edinburgh*

*Editorial Advisory Board*
Professor Richard Ashcroft, *Queen Mary, University of London*
Professor Martin Bobrow, *University of Cambridge*
Dr Alexander Morgan Capron, *Director, Ethics and Health, World Health Organization, Geneva*
Professor Ruth Chadwick, *Cardiff Law School*
Professor Jim Childress, *University of Virginia*
Dame Ruth Deech, *University of Oxford*
Professor John Keown, *Georgetown University, Washington, DC*
Dr Kathy Liddell, *University of Cambridge*
Professor Alexander McCall Smith, *University of Edinburgh*
Professor Dr Mónica Navarro-Michel, *University of Barcelona*

Marcus Radetzki, Marian Radetzki and Niklas Juth
*Genes and Insurance: Ethical, Legal and Economic Issues*
978 0 521 83090 4

Ruth Macklin
*Double Standards in Medical Research in Developing Countries*
978 0 521 83388 2 hardback    978 0 521 54170 1 paperback

Donna Dickenson
*Property in the Body: Feminist Perspectives*
978 0 521 86792 4

Matti Häyry, Ruth Chadwick, Vilhjálmur Árnason and Gardar Árnason
*The Ethics and Governance of Human Genetic Databases: European Perspectives*
978 0 521 85662 1

Ken Mason
*The Troubled Pregnancy: Legal Wrongs and Rights in Reproduction*
978 0 521 85075 9

Daniel Sperling
*Posthumous Interests: Legal and Ethical Perspectives*
978 0 521 87784 8

Keith Syrett
*Law, Legitimacy and the Rationing of Health Care*
978 0 521 85773 4

Alastair Maclean
*Autonomy, Informed Consent and the Law: A Relational Change*
978 0 521 89693 1

Heather Widdows and Caroline Mullen
*The Governance of Genetic Information: Who Decides?*
978 0 521 50991 6

David Price
*Human Tissue in Transplantation and Research*
978 0 521 88302 3

# Human Tissue in Transplantation and Research

## A Model Legal and Ethical Donation Framework

David Price

CAMBRIDGE UNIVERSITY PRESS
Cambridge, New York, Melbourne, Madrid, Cape Town, Singapore,
São Paulo, Delhi

Cambridge University Press
The Edinburgh Building, Cambridge CB2 8RU, UK

Published in the United States of America by
Cambridge University Press, New York

www.cambridge.org
Information on this title: www.cambridge.org/9780521883023

First published 2009

Printed in the United Kingdom at the University Press, Cambridge

*A catalogue record for this publication is available from the British Library*

ISBN 978-0-521-88302-3 Hardback
ISBN 978-0-521-70954-5 Paperback

This is book is dedicated to my 'special girls' –
Charlotte, Amelie, Isabelle and Lily.

# Contents

# Preface

This book is the culmination of many years of working in the fields of organ tissue transplantation and research in an academic and policy advisory context, leading me to a conviction of the urgent need for a unifying legal and ethical donation framework incorporating various central concepts and principles. The necessarily complex policy-making in this sphere is a function of the fact that humans themselves *are* the 'therapy' or 'research material' here, involved in a uniquely human activity. These are consequently areas which not only preserve but also reflect our humanity.

I am very grateful in the making of this book for the assistance received from the staff at Cambridge University Press, and in particular Finola O'Sullivan, Brenda Burke and Richard Woodham, and to Martin Wilkinson for his hugely helpful remarks in regard to two of the most substantial parts of the book. Mostly of course, my thanks and love are directed to my long-suffering wife Arlene, whose support is profoundly appreciated.

# Cases cited

## DOMESTIC AUTHORITIES

*AB* v. *National Blood Authority* [2001] 3 All ER 289

*Airedale NHS Trust* v. *Bland* [1993] 1 All ER 821

*B* v. *Islington Area Health Authority* [1992] 3 All ER 832

*The Creutzfeldt-Jakob Disease Litigation* (2000) 54 BMLR 1

*Director of Public Prosecution* v. *Smith* [2006] 2 All ER 16; [2006] EWHC 94

*Dobson* v. *North Tyneside Health Authority* [1997] 1 WLR 596

*Gillick* v. *West Norfolk Health Authority* [1986] AC 112

*HM Advocate* v. *Dewar* (1945) SC 5

*In re Organ Retention Group Litigation* [2005] QB 506

*Kennedy* v. *Lord Advocate and Scottish Ministers; Black* v. *Lord Advocate and Scottish Ministers* [2008] ScotCS CSOH 21 (5 February 2008)

*Leigh and Sillivan Ltd* v. *Aliakmon Shipping Co Ltd* [1986] AC 785

*R* v. *Bentham* [2005] UKHL 18; [2005] 1 WLR 1057

*R* v. *Bristol Coroner, Ex parte Kerr* [1974] 1 QB 652

*R* v. *Brown* [1994] AC 212

*R* v. *Cooke* [1995] 1 Cr. App. Rep. 318

*R* v. *Department of Health, ex parte Source Informatics* [2001] QB 424

*R* v. *Herbert* (1960) 25 *Journal of Criminal Law* 163

*R* v. *Kelly* [1999] QB 621

*R* v. *Rothery* [1976] RTR 550

*R* v. *Welsh* [1974] RTR 478

*R (on the application of Pretty)* v. *DPP* [2002] 1 All ER 1

*Re T (Adult: Refusal of Treatment)* [1993] Fam. 95

*St George's Healthcare NHS Trust* v. *S, R* v. *Collins, ex parte S* [1998] 3 WLR 936

*Sidaway* v. *Governors of the Royal Bethlem Hospital* [1985] 1 All ER 643

*Stevens* v. *Yorkhill NHS Trust and Anor* [2006] ScotCS CSOH 143 (13 September 2006)

*Williams* v. *Phillips* (1957) 41 Cr. App. Rep. 5
*Yearworth* v. *North Bristol NHS Trust* [2009] EWCA Civ 37


## OVERSEAS AUTHORITIES

*Brotherton* v. *Cleveland* 923 F 2d 477 (6th Cir. 1990)
Bundesgerichtshof, Urteil 9. November 1993, Aktenzeichen VI ZR 62/93
*Carter* v. *Inter-Faith Hospital of Queens* 60 Misc. 2d 733, 304 NYS 2d 97 (1969)
*Colavito* v. *New York Organ Donor Network Inc.* 356 F Supp. 2d 237 (EDNY 2005); *Colavito* v. *New York Organ Donor Network Inc.* 438 F 3d 214 (2nd Cir. 2006); *Colavito* v. *New York Organ Donor Network Inc.* 6 NY 3d 820 (NY CA 2006); *Colavito* v. *New York Organ Donor Network Inc.* 8 NY 3d 43 (NY CA 2006); *Colavito* v. *New York Organ Donor Network Inc.* 486 F 3d 78 (2nd Cir. 2007)
*Cornelio* v. *Stamford Hospital* 717 A 2d 140 (Conn. 1998)
*Devlin* v. *National Maternity Hospital* [2007] IESC 50
*Doodeward* v. *Spence* (1908) 6 CLR 406 (HCA)
*Georgia Lions Eye Bank, Inc.* v. *Lavant* 335 SE 2d 127 (Ga. 1985)
*Gray* (2000) 117 Australian Criminal Reports 22
*Greenberg* v. *Miami Children's Hospital Research Institute Inc.* 264 F Supp. 2d 1064 (SD Fla. 2003); 208 F Supp. 2d 918 (ND Ill. 2002)
*Hawkins* v. *McGee* 146 Atl. 641 (NH, 1929)
*Hecht* v. *Superior Court* 20 Cal. Rptr. 2d 275 (1993)
*In the* Matter *of X* [2002] JRC 202
*Kaiser Aetna* v. *United States* 444 US 164 (1979)
*Kohn* v. *United States* 680 F 2d 922 (2d Cir. 1982)
*Mansaw* v. *Midwest Organ Bank* LEXIS 10307 (US Dist. Ct. WD Mo. 1998)
*McFall* v. *Shimp* 10 Pa. D & C (3d) 90 (1978)
*Moore* v. *Regents of the University of California* [1988] 249 Cal. Rptr. 494 (Cal. Ct. App.)
*Moore* v. *Regents of the University of California* 51 Cal. 3d 120, 793 P 2d 479, 271 Cal. Rptr. 146 (Cal. Sup. Ct. 1990)
*Newman* v. *Sathyavaglswaran* 287 F 3d 786 (US Ct. App., 9th Cir. 2002)
*O'Connor and Tormey* v. *Lenihan* , unreported, 9 June 2005
*Pecar* v. *National Australia Trustees Ltd* BC9605678
*Perlmutter* v. *Beth David Hospital* 123 NE 2d 792 (1954)
*PQ* v. *Australian Red Cross Society* [1992] 1 VR 19
*Prune Yard Shopping Center* v. *Robins* 447 US 74 (1980)
*R* v. *Ladue* (1965) 4 CCC 264
*R* v. *Stillman* [1997] SCR 607 (Supreme Court of Canada)
*Roche* v. *Douglas* (2000) 22 WAR 331 (WA SC)

# Selected statutory sources

DOMESTIC

Anatomy Act 1832
Human Tissue Act 1961
Anatomy Act 1984
Human Organ Transplants Act 1989
Human Tissue Act 2004
Human Tissue (Scotland) Act 2006

OVERSEAS

AUSTRALIA

Transplantation and Anatomy Ordinance 1978 (Australian Capital
    Territory)
Human Tissue Transplant Act 1979 (Northern Territory)
Transplantation and Anatomy Act 1979 (Queensland)
Transplantation and Anatomy Act 1983 (South Australia)
Human Tissue Act 1983 (New South Wales)
Human Tissue Act 1985 (Tasmania)

AUSTRIA

Federal Law of 1 June 1982

BELGIUM

Law of 13 June 1986

BULGARIA

Law of 30 July 2003

CANADA

Uniform Human Tissue Donation Act 1990

CHILE

Law No. 19451 of 29 March 1996

COSTA RICA

Law No. 7409 of 12 May 1994

DENMARK

Law No. 402 of 13 June 1990
Law No. 432 of 29 May 2001

ESTONIA

Human Genes Research Act 2000
Law of 30 January 2002

FINLAND

Law No. 101 of 2 February 2001
Law of 11 May 2007

FRANCE

Law No. 94–654 of 29 July 1994
Law No. 2004–800 of 6 August 2004

GERMANY

Law of 5 November 1997

ISRAEL

Organ Transplant Law 2008

LITHUANIA

Law No. VIII-1484 of 21 December 1999
Law No. VIII-1985 of 10 October 2000

NETHERLANDS

Law of 24 May 1996
Decree of 5 March 2004

Law of 23 June 2006
Law of 21 December 2006

NEW ZEALAND
Human Tissue Act 2008

NORWAY
Law No. 12 of 21 February 2003

POLAND
Law of 1 July 2005

PORTUGAL
Law No. 12/93

SPAIN
Law No. 30 of 27 October 1979

SWEDEN
Law 297 Biobanks in Medical Care Act 2002

SWITZERLAND
Federal Law of 8 October 2004

UNITED STATES
Uniform Anatomical Gift Act 1968
Uniform Anatomical Gift Act 1987
Uniform Anatomical Gift Act 2006

EUROPEAN UNION
EU Blood Directive 2002/98/EC
EU Tissues and Cells Framework Directive 2004/23/EC

STATUTORY INSTRUMENTS

Blood Safety and Quality Regulations 2005 SI 2005 No. 50
Human Tissue Act 2004 (Ethical Approval, Exceptions from Licensing
and Supply of Information) Regulations 2006 SI 2006 No. 1260

# Introduction

This is a book about policy, aimed at professionals, academics and strategists. It aspires to map out a broad, transferable contemporary 'model' framework to govern human organ and tissue donation for transplantation and research. It is my contention that existing systems, whilst well-meaning and considered, often serve – on account of deficiencies and anomalies – to defeat the very objectives which they have set out to achieve; to the detriment of patients, subjects and society in general. Deconstruction is consequently crucial, especially in the light of the controversies surrounding such activities and the ever-increasing challenges presented by them. Of course, differences of view are inevitable in spheres touching so closely upon intimate areas of human activity, but this is a field riven not only by divergence of perspective and emphasis, but also by misconception. These are areas of policy which have invariably developed in pragmatic, customary fashion, being science-, technology- and practice (and hence largely demand-) driven, partly by dint of necessity, but which require in the modern age a sure footing which can survive critical scrutiny.[1] To be sure, legal and ethical principles will inevitably operate in a 'fuzzy' way in the real world, but there is nonetheless a need for clear concepts to cut through the increasing 'noise'. The challenges here are great, but so are the prizes. The need for human organs and tissues is one of the hallmarks of contemporary society and the gateway to interventions of incalculable benefit to mankind, either as forms of therapy or as precursors to the development of preventive, therapeutic and diagnostic strategies.

Whilst there are an increasing number of published works touching on the topics dealt with in this book, and including ethical analyses of the central issues, there are few which attempt to develop a modal framework

---

[1] In relation to post-mortem practice, the system was said to have operated over the previous thirty years on a 'custom and practice' basis; see Chief Medical Officer, *The Removal, Retention and Use of Human Organs and Tissue from Post-mortem Examination*, 2001, at www. doh.gov.uk/orgretentionadvice/orgretcmoadv2.htm. See also V. S. Leith, 'Consent and nothing but consent? The organ retention scandal' (2007) 29(7) *Sociology of Health & Illness* 1023 at 1032.

which cashes out these legal and ethical 'conclusions' and translate them into a workable and coherent form able to adequately guide practice. Indeed my own previous book in this sphere fell short of a wholly normative enterprise, being principally analytical in parts.[2] In this current work some of the areas of detailed discussion in that earlier work are omitted, and it is intended that the present volume 'build' upon the earlier one in normative terms.

## An ethico-legal skeleton

The book seeks to knit together ethical and legal perspectives relating in particular to autonomy, consent, justice and property. The issue of consent has come to dominate contemporary debates with respect to the donation of human material, albeit without any shared or unifying vision as to what constitutes 'consent', or what interests consent is designed to protect. As Brazier notes, 'Consent is such a simple word' and is the more beguiling and elusive for that.[3] Moreover, it has historically by no means been the norm. The perceived or actual failure to obtain proper consent has been at the heart of many controversies in the transplantation and research spheres, most visibly in the postmortem organ and tissue retention scandals which have lately arisen around the globe, and in particular in the UK,[4] and in other analogous

[2] D. Price, *Legal and Ethical Aspects of Organ Transplantation* (Cambridge University Press, 2000) [Price, *Legal and Ethical Aspects*].

[3] M. Brazier, 'Organ retention and return: Problems of consent' (2003) 29 *Journal of Medical Ethics* 30 at 30.

[4] See Bristol Royal Infirmary Inquiry Interim Report, 2001, at www.bristol-inquiry.org.uk/ interim_report/index.htm (hearts of 170 dead children retained); Redfern Inquiry into the Liverpool Children's (Alder Hey) NHS Trust, at www.rlcinquiry.org.uk/download/index. htm (organs of 3,500 children retained); HM Inspector of Anatomy, Investigation of events that followed the death of Cyril Mark Isaacs, May 2003, at www.doh.gov.uk/cmo/ isaccsreport/ (24,000 brains in storage in Britain in 2003). A Census in England in 2000 revealed that 54,300 organs, body parts, still-births or foetuses were held following postmortem examinations carried out since 1970; see Chief Medical Officer, *Report of a Census of Organs and Tissues Retained by Pathology Services in England*, London: The Stationery Office, 2001. See also the Scottish Report, *Final Report of the Independent Review Group on Retention of Organs at Post-Mortem in Scotland*, 2000, and the Northern Ireland, Organ Retention Report, Belfast, 2001. Abroad, see the Madden Report on Post Mortem Practices and Procedures (2006) in Ireland, at www.dohc.ie/publications/pdf/madden. pdf; D. Tilmann, 'German prosecutor investigates the removal of dead babies' organs' (2000) 320 *British Medical Journal* 77; *Organs Retained at Autopsy*, Advice of the Australian Health Ethics Committee, NHMRC, 2001, Commonwealth of Australia, Canberra; U. Jensen, 'Property, rights, and the body: The Danish context' in H. Ten Have, J. Welie and S. Spicker (eds.), *Ownership of the Human Body* (Dordrecht: Kluwer Academic Publishers, 1998), 173 at 174 (retention of brains of thousands of psychiatric patients at Aarhus).

contexts.[5] The perceived benefits of such activities have often led to practice blinkered to wider ethical perspectives, and the possibility of profit from human body parts has in some other instances been the motivation for the witting or reckless failure to obtain necessary consent for removal and use.[6] Human bodily resources are increasingly acquiring value and utility either in themselves or as the basis for the development of further biological materials, or merely as sources of biological or genomic information *per se*. This 'value' enhances the vulnerability and prospectability of our bodies and the need for donor, and indeed often community, interests to be properly protected.[7] By virtue of their nexus to 'self', the retention and use of human material raises profound issues pertaining to the relationship between bodies and personal identity, and generates fundamental questions about who we are and what sort of society we wish to live in.

There is an ever-present tension between the imperative to generate sufficient body parts for societally and ethically crucial goods and the rights of individuals or their families to control the use of such materials. It is argued here that the need to satisfy the relevant demands for body parts cannot entirely justify a donation policy in itself, although it is recognised that a failure to satisfy the needs (of patients and professionals, respectively) is not only a major moral deficiency *per se* but will invariably fuel more and more extreme means of dealing with the deficit; which, in turn, produces a further policy dimension. Whilst a requirement for consent is becoming ubiquitous, different notions of 'consent' prevail in

---

[5] Body parts from deceased former workers at nuclear power plants have allegedly been non-consensually retained and tested in both the UK and the US (Los Alamos) over many years; see O. Dyer, 'Inquiry will study claims that Sellafield workers' body parts were-removed without families' consent' (2007) 334 *British Medical Journal* 868; *The Times*, 18 April 2007, 19 April 2007, 20 April 2007 and 27 April 2007; L. Andrews and D. Nelkin, *Body Bazaar: The Market for Human Tissue in the Biotechnology Age* (New York: Crown Publishers, 2001), p. 20 [Andrews and Nelkin, *Body Bazaar*]. Body parts have frequently been merely 'retained' post-mortem; see, e.g., C. Abraham, *Possessing Genius: The Bizarre Odyssey of Einstein's Brain* (Cambridge: Icon Books, 2001); N. Stafford, 'German medical schools respond to claim they have stored Namibian skulls from colonial times' (2008) 337 *British Medical Journal* 1047.

[6] Of course, the exploits of graverobbers and others supplying anatomy schools with whole corpses for profit were the catalyst for the passing of the anatomy legislation in the early nineteenth century. For a contemporary analogue, see http://news.bbc.co.uk/1/hi/world/africa/3039513.stm.

[7] The interests of indigenous populations such as Native American Indians and Aborigines are being increasingly protected, e.g. Native American Graves Protection and Repatriation Act 1990 and the Aboriginal Heritage Act 1988 (South Australia) and the Heritage Conservation Act 1991 (Northern Territory). See R. Tsosie, 'Native American genetic resources and the concept of cultural harm' (2007) 35(3) *Journal of Law, Medicine and Ethics* 396.

official policies, and widely varying laws, practices and perceptions exist around the world. In particular, presumed consent is a concept which, despite being a widespread legal phenomenon, continues to draw trenchant criticism from various quarters.

The relationship between 'donation' and the allocation or permitted use(s) of organs and tissues to patients or users is a crucial one. Especially contentious is the extent to which the latter should be controlled by donors, professionals, or by society, with issues of justice, equity and utility juxtaposed against individual rights of disposition and control. This again introduces issues pertaining to the relationship between the donor and his or her (separated) body parts. The US President's Council on Bioethics has stated that 'In dramatic ways, the question of who, if anyone, *owns* a part of the body that is brought out of the body's interior and into the light of the laboratory or clinic has become a meaningful one'.[8] The jurisprudence in common law jurisdictions has been loathe to recognise the existence of private property rights in human materials, especially in tissue sources themselves.[9] But as Magnusson observes 'To hold categorically that human tissue cannot be the subject of proprietary rights suggests that, in the absence of specific empowering legislation, such tissue could not be gifted, bought or sold, stolen or converted, bailed or patented. In a rapidly developing biotechnological age, a legal vacuum such as this would be very curious indeed.'[10] A lack of a network of property rights emanating initially from the tissue source is unsustainable in the context of a true 'donation' scheme. This by no means necessarily implies a right to trade in such material, however. This is a separate and further matter beyond rights of exclusion, use and transfer *per se*.

There is a perceived conflict between sufficiently protecting donors' interests and the smooth and efficient running of the various services dependent upon the human material emanating from them. This is especially patent in the US jurisprudence relating to the use of human tissue for research but similar tensions can be seen in relation to the secondary use of tissue from living individuals for research across the board, e.g. archived pathology samples, newborn screening cards, etc.[11]

---

[8] President's Council on Bioethics, *On the Body and Transplantation: Philosophical and Legal Context*, Staff Discussion Paper, 2006/7 at 8–9.

[9] The decision in *Yearworth* v. *North Bristol NHS Trust* [2009] EWCA Civ 37 (4 February 2009) is a very welcome recent exception.

[10] R. Magnusson, 'Proprietary rights in human tissue', in N. Palmer and E. McKendrick (eds.), *Interests in Goods* (London: Lloyds of London Press, 1993) 237 at 237.

[11] Research on pathological specimens has led to important discoveries such as helicobacter pylori bacteria as the cause of peptic ulcers. The distinction between further pathological examination and 'research' is itself blurred. Their conflation has historically been

The post-mortem organ retention scandals in the UK and elsewhere likewise generated the perception of professional and public interests being at odds,[12] but this must be seen in the light of either the professional failure to adhere to contemporary ethical or legal standards or the failure of the prevailing standards to comport with appropriate present-day values.[13] Whilst in many situations there was a failure to comply with the mandates of the law, in others both law and existing ethical standards supported the retention and subsequent use of tissues removed at post-mortem for various purposes, including research, without proper consent.[14] There was apparently no evidence of any general unwillingness to allow such (research) practices, however, where consent was first obtained. Subject to some necessary accommodations, conflict is not inevitable if openness and transparency exist and a shared, partnership approach is adopted. As the Retained Organs Commission (ROC) remarked 'If adequate ethical principles govern organ retention enforced by effective laws and regulations, neither medicine nor science should suffer.'[15]

## Ambit

This book focuses on the use of human material for transplantation and research rather than for 'treatment' purposes more broadly. It thus

considered good practice and is to some degree unavoidable. The ability to look back at retained autopsy material has helped to define vCJD, AIDS and the causes of cot death, cerebral palsy and epilepsy.

[12] The majority apparently support the retention of organs and tissue for research post-mortem provided informed consent had been obtained; see Retained Organs Commission, *Qualitative Research to Explore Public Perceptions Regarding Retention of Organs and Tissue for Medical Practice, Teaching and Research*, Research Report, London, 2002.

[13] Whilst in some instances such practices were lawful, 'staying within the law is not enough – practice needs to reflect what the community regards as acceptable in the environment in which autopsies are now performed'; see Australian Health Ministers' Advisory Council, *The National Code of Ethical Autopsy Practice*, Australian Department of Human Services, 2002 at 5.

[14] The Chief Medical Officer's Report remarked that 'The law governing organ retention is unclear, ambiguous and ageing. It was poorly understood and, as a result, not well applied'; see Chief Medical Officer, *The Removal, Retention and Use of Human Organs and Tissue from Post-Mortem Examinations*, Stationery Office, London, 2001. By contrast, in various jurisdictions, including many Australian States and Territories, consent for hospital post-mortem examination was by law explicitly stated to be sufficient to permit the retention and use of body parts for transplantation or research, e.g. section 28, Transplantation and Anatomy Act 1983 (South Australia). See also *Report Into the Retention of Body Parts After Post-Mortems*, Solicitor General South Australia, August 2001, Adelaide; and *Interim Report into the Retention of Tissue and Organs Following Post-Mortems in NSW*, New South Wales Health Department, February 2001, Sydney.

[15] Retained Organs Commission, *Remembering the Past, Looking to the Future*, NHS, 2004, para.1.19.

excludes the use of substances of human origin as aspects of medicinal products or *in-vitro* diagnostic devices. The rationale for such exclusion hangs on the need to focus attention on core common issues and avoid the need to consider discrete and specific areas of regulatory activity.[16] The use of organs and tissues from animals for transplantation ('xenotransplantation') or research are not considered here either, in view of the broader issues they raise and the fact that the former is not yet generally even considered to be an experimental therapy (principally on account of issues relating to physiology, disease transmission and public health).[17] They require detailed scrutiny in their own right which cannot be afforded here.

At first glance, to focus solely upon transplantation and research may seem arbitrary and selective. Human biological materials have a plethora of other uses, such as forensic purposes, education and training, cadaver identification, infertility treatment, etc. However, quite apart from constraints of space, both of these chosen activities may be broadly seen as part of the 'therapeutic endeavour'. Although the UK Organ Donation Taskforce Supplement Report remarked as regards transplantation that 'Rarely in health is there such a direct and rapid link between the action to address a problem and its resolution to save lives',[18] medical research has been appropriately dubbed 'indirectly therapeutic',[19] focusing on better and more accurate diagnoses, development of new therapies, better understanding of disease, etc. Sanner's research found that both autopsy and anatomical dissection are regarded by individuals as beneficent activities in the longer term, although not regarded as altruistic acts in the same way as organ donation, which has a direct immediate, potentially life-saving consequence.[20]

Moreover, they are not discrete spheres. Organs and tissue not suitable for transplantation – which takes priority – may be used instead for

---

[16] Medicines are governed by a discrete regulatory regime under the Medicines Act 1968 and *in-vitro* medical devices by the Medical Devices Regulations 2002 SI 2002 No. 618 as amended.

[17] It is anticipated that xenotransplant trials will be initiated in the UK in the near future. Lord Winston has announced that pig organs could be available for transplantation within ten years; see *The Times*, 7 November 2008. See also www.dh.gov.uk/en/Publicationsandstatistics/Publications/PublicationsPolicyAndGuidance/DH_06307. See generally S. McLean and L. Williamson, 'The demise of UKXIRA and the regulation of solid-organ xenotransplantation in the UK' (2008) 34 *Journal of Medical Ethics* 373.

[18] *Organs for Transplant: A Report from the Organ Donation Taskforce: Supplement Report*, Department of Health, 2008 at 6 [*Supplement Report*].

[19] Nuffield Council on Bioethics Working Party Report, *Human Tissue: Ethical and Legal Issues*, 1995, Nuffield Council, at para. 6 [Nuffield Council].

[20] M. Sanner, 'People's attitudes and reactions to organ donation' (2006) 11(2) *Mortality* 133 at 143.

research, e.g. livers converted to liver hepatocytes for drug function tests, etc. Transplant organ and tissue donor retrieval teams work alongside research tissue retrieval teams in many healthcare institutions.[21] Moreover, research on human tissue is the very source of many developments in transplantation therapies.[22] Most importantly, though, the ethical and conceptual underpinnings have very significant commonality, so that whilst they are usually considered discretely the discussion is better informed by considering issues as between them. Indeed, this work centres on *donation* policy rather than broader aspects of either transplantation or research.[23] This is not, however, to deny the very significant contemporary importance of some of these other matters, e.g. the treatment of the potential donor prior to death and non-heart-beating donation, etc.[24]

## Replacement therapies

At present there are generally no substitute 'permanent' therapies to transplantation available for end-stage organ failure. Research is continuing apace to develop stem cell and tissue engineering techniques to 'grow' tissues for replacement,[25] either from pluripotent/totipotent stem cells or from adult cells.[26] Whilst the use of human totipotent embryonic stem cells as a source for transplantation is being investigated to replace diseased or damaged tissue,[27] it is estimated that in order to avoid graft rejection from poor tissue (HLA) compatibility, a bank of at

---

[21] Some forms of tissue to be used for transplantation are actually removed by pathologists at post-mortem examination.

[22] Although it has been alleged that research in Britain is being unnecessarily hindered by bureaucracy, including Lord Winston's research on growing replacement organs inside genetically modified pigs (which was allegedly moved to the US as a result); see 'Organ research being hindered by red tape, says professor', *Guardian*, 11 September 2007.

[23] My previous book considered transplantation in slightly broader fashion. See, e.g., Price, *Legal and Ethical Aspects*, chapters 4, 5 and 10.

[24] See *Organs for Transplant: A Report from the Organ Donation Taskforce*, Department of Health, 2008, at 33 [*Organs for Transplant*].

[25] EU Regulation (EC) No. 1394/2007 governing tissue engineered products which have potential therapeutic application to humans has been issued. Currently some of these products fall outside the definition of either medicinal products or medical devices.

[26] Such as the use of artificial livers to provide pieces of liver to repair damaged livers and potentially entire liver transplants (see 'British scientists grow human liver in a laboratory', at www.thisislondon.co.uk/news/article-23372701-details/British+scientists +grow). Work is also ongoing to re-grow damaged bones and cartilage using patients' stem cells; see *The Times*, 18 February 2008.

[27] In somatic cell nuclear transfer a nucleus from an adult cell is inserted into a recipient egg cell from which its own nucleus has been removed. At present, however, its efficiency for stem cell derivation is very low.

least 150 HLA-typed human embryonic stem cells would be required in order to generate an acceptable match for the large majority of patients.[28] Cloned embryos created by using cell nuclear transfer, on the other hand, are likely to be immunologically compatible with the donor. However, quite apart from the scientific challenges, research using embryos (which will thereafter be destroyed) is highly controversial, and under attack from the Roman Catholic Church in particular.[29] The news that it may be feasible to generate induced pluripotent stem cells from skin cells rather than embryos is therefore highly significant.[30] However, much of this research is still at a very early, unrealised stage, and the potential of such therapies has been subject to much overblown hype and misinformation.[31] In theory, in so far as these are 'master' cells, stem cells could be caused to differentiate into any of the tissues or organs of the body. They are also self-renewing, so that the entire demand for such materials could be theoretically met. However, due to their anatomical and functional complexity renewing human organs is only a longer-term potential reality. Nonetheless, stem cells can already be induced to form the insulin-producing cells of the pancreas and it is anticipated that heart valves and muscles might soon be grown by such methods.[32] Patients' stem cells may also be used to re-grow damaged tissue where a scaffold can be formed using donated tissue.[33] A patient recently had a windpipe transplanted in Barcelona which had been constructed using the patient's own re-engineered bone marrow stem cells.[34]

---

[28] C. Taylor *et al.*, 'Banking on human embryonic stem cells: Estimating the number of donor cell lines needed for HLA matching' (2005) 366 *The Lancet* 2019.

[29] See *The Times*, 26 November 2007. In the US, embryonic stem cells have apparently been produced by stimulating unfertilised eggs, see www.medicalnewstoday.com/articles/75700.php. Embryonic stem cells have also been produced in mice without destroying embryos in the process.

[30] See *The Times*, 21 November 2007 and 1 December 2007.

[31] The scandal surrounding Dr Hwang's false claims regarding the creation of human embryonic stem cell lines from somatic cell nuclear transfer in South Korea led to much re-appraisal and even a US Congressional Hearing. See http://olpa.od.nih.gov/hearings/109/session2/testimonies/koreaclone2.asp.

[32] See *The Times*, 11 April and 3 September 2007. Whilst the growth of whole replacement organs still remains a distant vision, injections of stem cells into organs may, with nature doing the rest, allow repair *in situ*, e.g. heart attack patients' own stem cells being injected to repair organ damage; see *The Times*, 8 November 2006. President Obama has recently lifted restrictions upon federal funding of the therapeutic use of stem cells.

[33] Tissue may also be created from existing material. Bladders, cartilage and skin (from foetal skin tissue) have already been grown, the latter for the use of paediatric patients with burns; see J. Hohlfeld *et al.*, 'Tissue engineered fetal skin constructs for pediatric burns' (2005) 366 *The Lancet* 840.

[34] See *The Times*, 19 November 2008.

### Tissue issues

Despite the overwhelming attention of clinicians, the media and politicians upon *organ* transplantation, tissue transplantation occurs on an even larger scale, although deceased patients are assessed less routinely. In some instances, these are equally as 'life-saving' as some forms of organ transplantation, e.g. heart valve replacement procedures, although they are generally life-enhancing rather than life-saving.[35] Heart valves, tendons, cartilage and bone, skin, corneas and other tissues have been routinely transplanted for many years – some, such as skin and corneas, even longer than organs. Tissue donors need not always be as healthy as organ donors, and in so far as such tissue is avascular, the compatibility of donor and recipient is less important. There is also typically less urgency with the transplantation of tissue, such as skin, corneas and tendons, than with organs, as there is no need for the heart to be still beating at retrieval, and thus continued ventilation is unnecessary (retrieval may take place several hours or even longer after a death has been certified).[36] There are specific psychological issues which attach to certain types of tissue transplantation. For instance, *composite* tissue, such as hand and face, transplants generate particular issues relating to 'self' and personal identity. Isabelle Dinoire, the first face transplant patient, has spoken of the 'other woman inside her', and the difficulty of living with her new 'features'.[37] This book does not consider the specific issues raised here for reasons of space.[38]

As with much tissue that is used for research, tissue intended for transplantation is typically 'banked', where it is cleaned, sterilised and tested for certain types of infection, by contrast with most forms of organ transplantation where any substantial storage period remains elusive. It is this longer-term storage of tissue and the routine intermediate processing of

---

[35] This alters the ethical calculus, as health risks generated by immunosuppression therapy need to be outweighed by the benefits which attach exclusively to improved quality of life.

[36] For more detail, see B. Kent, 'Tissue donation and the attitudes of health care professionals', in M. Sque and S. Payne (eds.), *Organ and Tissue Donation: An Evidence Base for Practice* (Maidenhead: Open University Press, 2007) 102 [Sque and Payne (eds.), *Organ and Tissue Donation*]. Organs are also removed from non-heart-beating donors for transplantation in many instances, although removal must take place very soon after pronouncement of death.

[37] 'Face transplant "made me human again"', *The Times*, 7 July 2007; 'Face patient tells of "the woman inside her"', *The Times*, 1 October 2007. See generally R. Hartman, 'Face value: Challenges of transplant technology' (2005) 31 *American Journal of Law and Medicine* 7.

[38] See D. Dickenson and G. Widdershoven, 'Ethical issues in limb transplants' (2001) 15 *Bioethics* 110. The first hand transplant was performed in Lyon, France, but was removed in 2001 as the patient could not psychologically adjust to it and stopped taking his immunosuppression.

such material (and potential vending of such end-products) which distinguish it from organ transplantation. Tissue banks are proliferating. As well as specific disease-based banks and registries (e.g. the UK Children's Cancer Study Group tumour bank; the Canavan disease registry, etc.) and small hospital-based collections typically linked to one type of tissue (such as bone or eye banks), much more extensive multi-tissue banks supplying research as well as therapeutic needs have come into being, at arm's length from treatment providers.[39] In addition to sperm and brain banks, we have witnessed the recent growth of public and private peripheral cord blood banks containing stem cells able to be used in the treatment of leukaemias and anaemias, etc.[40] In addition, 'purpose-built' or converted 'biobanks' or 'genebanks' are being created to facilitate population-based disease research, for instance in Estonia, Iceland and the UK (UK Biobank), consisting of biological samples linked to personal data relating to health, lifestyle, etc.[41] Such tissue bank repositories are vital to satisfy the needs of clinicians, researchers, biotechnology and pharmaceutical companies, academic institutions, etc.

## A pound of flesh

Both profit and not-for-profit enterprises play a part in the process of transition from donated to transplantable tissue and tissue suitable for research. In the US, tissue transplantation is a billion-dollar industry.[42] Since the Nuffield Council on Bioethics advocated the growth of non-profit medical intermediaries in tissue collection and distribution – to connect the market and non-market structures – commercial tissue banks have proliferated around the world.[43] There is also a trend toward the commercialisation of existing public tissue collections.[44] The

---

[39] The United Kingdom Human Tissue Bank based at De Montfort University is one such example in the research arena.

[40] In the UK the public Kingscord cord blood bank has been established. A two-year-old with leukaemia recovered after receiving a transplant from a donor who was discovered from tracing umbilical cord blood frozen in Tokyo; see *The Times*, 6 February 2008.

[41] UK Biobank hopes to collect blood and urine samples from 500,000 individuals; see www.ukbiobank.ac.uk/about/what.php. Generation Scotland is another UK-based genetic database.

[42] See R. Katz, 'The re-gift of life: Who should capture the value of transplanted human tissue?' (2006) 18(4) *The Health Lawyer* 14. He notes that the government makes little or no attempt to stop intermediaries earning 'super-normal' profits, at 15.

[43] Nuffield Council, at paras. 6.38–6.40. For-profit enterprises process such tissue to produce materials such as bone and hips for therapeutic application.

[44] See G. Lewis, 'Tissue collection and the pharmaceutical industry', in R. Tutton and O. Corrigan (eds.), *Genetic Databases: Socio-Ethical Issues in the Collection and Use of DNA* (Oxford: Routledge, 2004) 181 at 191 [Tutton and Corrigan (eds.), *Genetic Databases*].

co-mingling of not-for-profit and for-profit enterprises in tissue procurement, tissue banking, tissue processing and tissue application is evident everywhere. An investigation in the US in 2000 revealed that 70 per cent of the fifty-nine Organ Procurement Organisations (OPOs) sold body parts directly to for-profit firms and another 18 per cent sold body parts (such as hearts, veins, tendons and bones) to other not-for-profit tissue banks who then shipped the tissues to for-profit companies.[45]

Laws routinely proscribe reward being offered to or provided to organ and tissue sources themselves, but other actors in the process may be subject to different rules. Under the National Organ Transplant Act 1984 in the US, for instance, therapeutic tissue banks are permitted to charge 'reasonable fees' for their services.[46] Whilst the involvement of for-profit enterprises processing tissue and distributing it to end-users arguably enhances the value of such materials to recipients, to some it commoditises human material and undermines donor altruism. Healy observes that 'The public conception of exchange in human goods, and especially organ donation, is at odds with the rapidly growing and increasingly lucrative secondary markets in human tissue'.[47] It has been noted that tissue donation for transplantation has invariably taken place 'under the radar of public awareness', but as the veil is drawn back there is increasing hostility towards the industry from some quarters.[48] Indeed, it has been suggested that if providers were routinely made aware of the profits procured by the tissue industry, donations would reduce.[49] Andrews and Nelkin have commented 'But the proliferation and diversity of disputes over body tissue are symptomatic of a much larger problem – a growing divide between scientific and social views of the body in the commercial context of the biotechnology age'.[50] At the least, greater transparency is required.

The effect of the increasing commercial influences involved in tissue retrieval and use and the tendency to 'cutting ethical and legal corners'

---

[45] See M. Goodwin, *Black Markets: The Supply and Demand of Body Parts* (Cambridge University Press, 2006), p. 179.

[46] The costs of storing, preserving and preparing materials are permissible under section 32 (5)–(6), Human Tissue Act 2004.

[47] K. Healy, *Last Best Gifts* (University of Chicago Press, 2006), pp. 20–1.

[48] V. Perlman, review of S. Youngner, M. Anderson and R. Schapiro (eds.), *Transplanting Human Tissue: Ethics, Policy and Practice* (Oxford University Press, 2004), in (2005) 33 *Journal of Law, Medicine and Ethics* 163 at 163.

[49] See President's Council on Bioethics, 'Appendix', at www.bioethics.gov/background/organs_and_tissue_appendix.html. In *Greenberg* v. *Miami Children's Hospital Research Institute Inc.* 264 F Supp. 2d 1064 (SD Fla. 2003), for instance, the plaintiffs claimed that they would not have agreed to donate their tissue if they had been aware that the defendants intended to 'commercialise' the results of their contributions.

[50] L. Andrews and D. Nelkin, 'Whose body is it anyway? Disputes over body tissue in a biotechnology age' (1998) 351 *The Lancet* 53 at 53.

can be seen in the scandal attending the use of Alistair Cooke's bones and other related US practices (involving funeral directors, embalmers, medical schools, crematoria staff, etc.).[51] It is reported that some of the more than forty British patients who received implanted contaminated tissue derived from body parts allegedly 'stolen' (obtained without consent) in the US[52] are intending to sue.[53] Abuses have occurred in the research as well as therapeutic sphere, involving whole corpses as well as parts of corpses. Surplus cadavers from 'willed body' programmes have been illegally sold to private research firms in the US, and even to the military for use in anti-mine footwear tests.[54]

Such practices draw attention to the need for minimum quality and safety standards to be met. The potential risk of disease transmission from tissue transplantation is much greater than from organ transplantation as over 100 tissue transplants can derive from a single donor.[55] The European Union (EU) has now adopted various initiatives based on its mandate under Article 152(4)(a) of the EC Treaty, which enables the European Parliament and Council to adopt harmonised health measures by setting high standards of quality and safety of organs and substances of human origin, blood and blood derivatives.[56] Article 152(5), however, states that such measures 'shall not affect national provisions on the donation or medical use of organs and blood', which is designed to deny jurisdiction

---

[51] His bones were allegedly sold for $7,000 to two tissue provider companies. See 'FDA shuts down human tissue company' (2006) 332 *British Medical Journal* 507. See also *Whaley* v. *County of Tuscola* 58 F 3d 1111 (6th Cir. 1995). Such scandals are not exclusive to the US. See, e.g., S. Olsena, 'A Latvian case: The removal of tissue from 400 deceased persons', in W. Weimar, M. Bos and J. Busschbach (eds.), *Organ Transplantation: Ethical, Legal, and Psychosocial Aspects* (Lengerich: Pabst Publishing, 2008) 64 [Weimer *et al.* (eds.), *Organ Transplantation*].

[52] See http://news.bbc.co.uk/1/hi/england/staffordshire/5368620.stm. The company Biomedical Tissue Services allegedly exported body parts without prior consent. Bone graft tissue is used as a filler in orthopaedic surgery such as hip replacements and jaw construction.

[53] See *The Times*, 19 October 2006 and 6 October 2007. Some of the tissue sources suffered from HIV, hepatitis C and cancer.

[54] See *The Times*, 10 and 12 March 2004, *Guardian*, 20 March 2008, 'US trade in body parts' (2004) 199 *Bulletin of Medical Ethics* 4 and http://news.bbc.co.uk/1/hi/world/americas/6064692.stm.

[55] In 2002, five US recipients contracted hepatitis C from the same tissue donor. There are also reports of CJD transmission from corneas and dura mater, clostridium contracted from implanted knee tissue, etc.; see J. Warner and K. Zoon, 'The view from the Food and Drug Administration', in S. Youngner, M. Anderson and R. Schapiro (eds.), *Transplanting Human Tissue: Ethics, Policy and Practice* (Oxford University Press, 2004) 71 at 73 [Youngner, Anderson and Schapiro (eds.), *Transplanting Human Tissue*]. Moreover, tissues from various patients may be combined to produce a treatment for a specific patient, e.g. bone grafts.

[56] This article was introduced into the original Treaty by the Treaty of Maastricht in 1993. The Council is required to act in accordance with the co-decision procedure pursuant to Article 251 EC.

in relation to national donor consent laws, by virtue of the subsidiarity principle.[57] Following on from the Blood Directive 2002/98/EC it issued the Tissues and Cells Framework Directive 2004/23/EC in 2004. These have both been implemented in the UK and other Member States.[58]

### Regulatory and policy initiatives

There have been a plethora of major recent legislative changes, including in the UK where both the Human Tissue Act 2004 and the Human Tissue (Scotland) Act 2006 came into force in September 2006, replacing the Human Tissue Act 1961, Anatomy Act 1984 and the Human Organ Transplants Act 1989. These were both a product of the organ retention controversies mentioned earlier and apply to both transplantation and research, although the Scottish statute applies only to research involving tissue from deceased persons. In the US, legislative activity has been primarily driven by the Uniform Anatomical Gift Acts (UAGAs) drawn up by the National Conference of Commissioners on Uniform State Laws. The earliest version, formulated in 1968, was promptly implemented in all states. Another version was drawn up in 1987, but thereafter state laws ceased to be homogeneous or harmonious, as a result of which a further, substantially modified, version was generated in 2006, which has already been enacted in thirty-four states and introduced in various others.[59] These Acts apply only to deceased donation, though, leaving living donation governed by either the general law or other statute law. Organ and tissue retention following autopsy in the US is also governed by state law. Whilst most states' laws are silent on this issue, some states permit organs and tissues (although usually just corneas and/or pituitary glands) removed at post-mortem examination to be retained and used for research purposes without consent, as do many Australian jurisdictions.[60] Across Europe in particular there have been a raft of recent statutes relating to transplantation but specific laws relating to the use of tissue for research are less universal.[61]

---

[57] See T. Hervey and J. McHale, *Health Law and the European Union* (Cambridge University Press, 2004), p. 80. Also excluded from the jurisdiction of the EU is the medical use of substances of human origin.

[58] See Blood Safety and Quality Regulations SI 2005 No. 50 and the Human Tissue (Quality and Safety for Human Application) Regulations SI 2007 No. 1523.

[59] For enactment details, see www.anatomicalgiftact.org/DesktopDefault.aspx?tabindex=2&tabid=72.

[60] See D. Sperling, *Posthumous Interests: Legal and Ethical Perspectives* (Cambridge University Press, 2008), pp. 99–100.

[61] E.g. Estonian Law of 30 January 2002; Bulgarian Law of 30 July 2003; Swiss Federal Law of 8 October 2004; Dutch Law of 21 December 2006; Finnish Law of 11 May 2007.

### Transplant activity

There have been very significant organisational and resource initiatives in the domestic transplant sphere. In England and Wales, substantial resources have been invested in various programmes through UK Transplant, notably in the areas of living organ donation and non-heart-beating donation. A policy, *Saving Lives, Valuing Donors*, was launched in 2003 (the Transplant Framework) setting ambitious targets in England, now including the objective for 20 million people to be signed up to the Organ Donor Register by 2010 and 25 million by 2013; and there has been substantial activity in Scotland also. In the US, the Organ Breakthrough Collaborative driven by federal government has achieved outstanding results, even in its early stages.

Moreover, the regulation of transplantation and the need to increase organ donation rates has moved steadily up the political agenda at both national and international level. In the UK, a Ministerial Organ Donation Task Force reported in 2008 on measures to ameliorate or remove current barriers to meeting the organ shortage within the constraints of the existing legal framework, and a similar Government Taskforce has been operational in Australia.[62] In addition, the Chief Medical Officer, Liam Donaldson, nominated the chronic lack of organs for transplantation as one of the two most pressing contemporary UK public health issues.[63] This led to the Organ Donation Taskforce (ODT) being re-convened and re-constituted to consider the possibility of introducing presumed consent, which advised, negatively, in November 2008, concerned that whilst there were real potential benefits there were also significant risks of worsening current donation rates.[64] Such high-level attention is mirrored in the US, where the President's Council on Bioethics has examined, fairly expansively, organ transplantation matters, following upon the Institute of Medicine's Report *Organ Donation: Opportunities for Action*.[65] Within Europe, the Dutch Health Council and the German National Ethics Council have been particularly active in recent years.

The first ODT Report focused on organisational, structural and systemic factors. It asserted that increases in donation rates were dependent

---

[62] *Organs for Transplants*; *National Clinical Taskforce on Organ and Tissue Donation: Final Report: Think Nationally, Act Locally*, Department of Health and Ageing, February 2008.

[63] Annual Report of the Chief Medical Officer 2006, Organ Transplants: The Waiting Game 27–33 [CMO, Organ Transplants].

[64] *The Potential Impact of an Opt Out System for Organ Donation in the UK: An Independent Report from the Organ Donation Taskforce*, 2008, para. 1.14.

[65] Institute of Medicine Report, *Organ Donation: Opportunities for Action* (Washington, DC: National Academies Press, 2006) [Institute of Medicine, *Organ Donation*].

on three spheres of activity: donor identification and referral; donor co-ordination; and organ retrieval arrangements. Culturally, it emphasised the need for organ donation to be regarded as the 'usual event' after death. It recommended, *inter alia*, minimum notification criteria for potential organ donors, the monitoring of rates of donation activity in all Trusts with the creation of a Trust Donation Committee reporting to the Trust Board,[66] that brain death testing should be conducted in all cases where it is a likely diagnosis (even if organ donation is unlikely), that the current network of transplant co-ordinators be substantially expanded and strengthened and that a UK-wide network of dedicated retrieval teams be established for all organs. Assuming that the recommendations as a whole were put in place, it was argued that it was possible to see a 50 per cent increase in organ donation after death in the UK within five years (an additional 1,200 transplants per annum).[67] At present the UK has one of the lowest deceased organ donor rates (13.2 per million population (p.m.p.) in 2007) and deceased kidney transplant rates (23.5 p.m.p.) in Europe. This compares with figures of 34.3 p.m.p. and 45.9 p.m.p. in Spain and an EU average of 16.8 p.m.p. and 29.2 p.m.p., respectively.[68] The Report was accepted by the UK Government and all of the devolved administrations.[69] It is stressed that clear political leadership and commit-ment is required in order to realise such goals, similar to that demonstra-ted by Secretary of State Tommy Taylor in the US, where the Organ Breakthrough Collaborative has achieved a 30 per cent increase in the volume of deceased organ donation in the past five years (compared with a 1–2 per cent increase over the previous decade).[70] The US experience, but even more notably that in Spain and countries which have followed the 'Spanish model', highlight the impact that an integrated, planned and well-resourced system can have in improving 'conversion rates' – i.e. the

---

[66] *Organs for Transplants*, para. 1.32. Reports should be regarded as part of the assessment of Trusts generally through the relevant healthcare regulator.

[67] This assumed that sufficient resources were made available and was based on extrapolat-ing organ donation rates from the best 20 per cent of performing hospitals, to produce a 40 per cent increase, coupled with an estimate of a further 10 per cent based on experience obtained abroad using such systems, such as in Spain, the US, Tuscany and certain South American nations, e.g. Argentina and Uruguay.

[68] Council of Europe Newsletter 2008, *International Figures on Organ Donation and Transplantation 2007*, Council of Europe, 2008.

[69] Amongst the specific recommendations in the Report are the setting up of a UK-wide Organ Donor Organisation under the responsibility of the existing special health authority NHS Blood and Transplant, see *Organs for Transplants*, para. 1.18.

[70] The Health Resources and Services Administration estimates that 4,000 additional annual transplants have been attributable to such initiatives; see T. Shafer *et al.*, 'US Organ Donation Breakthrough Collaborative increases organ donation' (2008) 31(3) *Critical Care Nursing Quarterly* 190.

number of potentially suitable donors who die and go on to become actual donors.[71]

## Global perspectives

Historically, international regulatory and political attention relating to organ transplantation has focused very largely upon issues relating to commercialisation. Recently it has broadened considerably into general matters affecting public health. Highly significantly, the EU has increased its activity in this sphere, although its intervention and legislative competence is constrained by the principle of subsidiarity, i.e. it is only permissible to regulate where the goal concerned can be achieved better on a European than a national scale, resulting in overall European benefit.[72] Safety and quality issues provide the basis for the EU's Framework Directives which Member States are obliged to implement into their law. The Commission is developing an EU Action Plan to strengthen cooperation between Member States and formulating proposals for a forthcoming directive relating to organs. It is also considering the potential introduction of a European organ donor card.[73] The House of Lords Select Committee on the European Union recently issued a report supporting a directive on organ donation and the implementation of an Action Plan, although expressing scepticism as regards the merits of a European-wide donor card.[74] The EU institutions all recognise though that the most pressing European public health issue relating to *organs* for transplantation is scarcity, and that greater sensitivity is required in this context.[75] Not only are there some very specific quality and safety issues affecting human organs, e.g. relating to disease transmission (infections, cancers, for

---

[71] In Tuscany, rates have improved from 9–10 donors per million population (p.m.p.) to 42. See also F. Filipponi, P. De Simone and E. Rossi, 'The Tuscany model of a regional transplantation service authority: Organizzazione Toscana Trapianti' (2007) 39 *Transplantation Proceedings* 2953.

[72] Article 5(2) European Treaty.

[73] The European Parliament has endorsed these measures; see European Parliament, Resolution of 22 April 2008 on organ donation and transplantation: Policy actions at EU level (2007/2210(INI)), at 2 [European Parliament, Resolution]. See also Council Conclusions on Organ Donation and Transplantation, 15332/07. See also A.-M. Farrell, 'EU governance of organ Donation and Transplantation', in A.-M. Farrell, M. Quigley and D. Price (eds), *Organ Shortage: Ethics, Law and Pragmatism* (Cambridge University Press, forthcoming, 2010).

[74] House of Lords European Union Committee, *Increasing the Supply of Donor Organs within the European Union*, Volume 1: 17th Report of Session 2007–08, HL Paper 123–1 [House of Lords, *Increasing the Supply*].

[75] The European Parliament has stated that the organ and donor shortage is 'the main challenge that Member States face with regard to organ transplantation', see European Parliament, Resolution.

example),[76] but in so far as organ transplantation is often a matter of life and death, safety cannot always be the overriding priority. The shortage of donors has led to increased expanded donor criteria – so-called 'marginal' donors – in particular the use of older donors. The difficulties and tensions are evident in the media surprise and scepticism in the UK attaching to the information that drug addicts are sometimes used as sources of deceased donor organs,[77] contrasted with calls in the US for the *greater* use of 'high-risk' donors, including intravenous drug users, to meet the shortfall.[78]

Within Europe, rates of donation differ markedly, with deceased donor rates ranging from 1 to 35 million donors p.m.p. The scarcity of human organs itself contributes to the trafficking carried out by organised criminal groups, tracking down and removing organs in developing countries and supplying them to recipients within the EU, as well as encouraging patients to travel elsewhere to purchase organs.[79] Thus, organ shortages and safety issues are linked and the first priority is to address the organ shortage. The European Parliament has equated the trafficking of organs and tissues with the trafficking in human beings which undermines fundamental human rights.[80] Trafficking of organs *within* the EU itself seems at present to be a limited problem,[81] although world-wide illegal 'transplant tourism' is regarded by the World Health Organisation (WHO) as being on the wax not the wane, becoming wholly global in character.[82] It

---

[76] Deaths have occurred in the US as a consequence of receiving organs from donors who had cancer; see *The Times*, 4 April 2008; rabies and West Nile fever have both been transmitted via organ transplants; see (2004) 364 *The Lancet* 648 and B. Dietzschold and H. Koprowski, 'Rabies transmission from organ transplants in the USA' (2004) 364 *The Lancet* 648. In Europe, transmissions of HIV, HTLV, malaria, rabies and malignant neoplasms have all been reported.

[77] 'Drug addicts used as organ donors', 10.12.2007, at http://news.bbc.co.uk/1/health/7136005.stm.

[78] E.g. R. Veatch; see 'USA confronts looming organ-shortage crisis' (2006) 368 *The Lancet* 567.

[79] The European Parliament has estimated that there are 150–250 cases annually within the EU; see European Parliament, Resolution, at 18. Moldova appears to have been a significant source of vendors.

[80] *Ibid.*, at 16. It called on Member States to sign, ratify and implement the Council of Europe Convention on Action Against Trafficking in Human Beings.

[81] See Commission Staff Working Paper, *Fifth Report to the European Parliament and the Council on the Implementation of the Title VI Programmes*, 2001 at 3, and Council of Europe, *Trafficking in Organs in Europe*, at www.coe.int. In 2005, a Romanian man was charged with illegally selling an organ for transplant into an Austrian man; see (2005) 365 *The Lancet* 1918. In 2006, a Bulgarian hospital admitted to involvement in at least twenty illegal organ transplants, linked to organ trading from patients flown in from parts of Eastern Europe; see (2006) 367 *The Lancet* 461. Moreover, there have been allegations that Kosovan Albanian guerrillas traded in the body parts of their captured Serbian prisoners following Nato bombings in 1999; see *Guardian*, 12 April 2008.

[82] See www.who.int/bulletin/volumes/82/9/feature0904/en/print.html. In 2004 police broke a ring involving Israelis intending to receive kidneys from poor Brazilians in South Africa.

estimated that in 2004 such trafficking accounted for around 10 per cent of all kidney transplants performed.[83] There is an increasing trend for patients from the UK, Germany and other European states to travel to Asian countries such as India or Pakistan to purchase kidneys for trans-plantation,[84] prompted by the shortage of domestic organs for transplant and the consequent extended waiting times generated.[85] Some medical insurance programmes (e.g. in the US) are even encouraging organ tour-ism in order to save costs and reduce waiting times,[86] despite often greater risks (e.g. of infection) and poorer post-transplant care.[87] A global state-ment, the Declaration of Istanbul on Organ Trafficking and Transplant, signed by clinicians, lawyers and ethicists from seventy-eight countries, has called on all Governments to outlaw transplant tourism.[88]

The WHO has been an influential body in this sphere, having issued Guiding Principles on Human Organ Transplantation in 1991 which emphasised voluntary donation and non-commercialisation, and a pref-erence for deceased rather than living donors, and genetically related living donors to non-genetically related donors.[89] These have now been recently revised in the light of changing ethical and situational perspec-tives and attitudes.[90] At a European level, the Council of Europe has historically been the most active in the transplant sphere. Its intervention

In view of its negative effects, it has been argued that 'transplant tourism' is a misleading euphemism here; see L. Turner, 'Let's wave goodbye to "transplant tourism"' (2008) 336 *British Medical Journal* 1377.

[83] See the World Health Organisation's Global Knowledge Base on Transplantation, and Editorial, 'Legal and illegal organ donation' (2007) 369 *The Lancet* 1901.

[84] Between twenty and thirty patients travel abroad for a transplant each year and return to the UK for follow-up care; see Evidence of Chris Rudge to the House of Lords Select Committee on the European Union: *Increasing the Supply of Donor Organs within the European Union, Volume II: Evidence* (HL Paper 123-II) at 38.

[85] See, e.g., R. Higgins *et al.*, 'Kidney transplantation in patients travelling from the UK to India or Pakistan' (2003) 18 *Nephrology, Dialysis, Transplantation* 851.

[86] See K. Bramstedt and J. Xu, 'Checklist: Passport, plane ticket, organ transplant' (2007) 7 *American Journal of Transplantation* 1698. A 'blind eye' has been similarly turned in Israel, but see now the Israeli Organ Transplant Law 2008.

[87] A national audit identified twenty-three UK patients who had received transplants in Asia; 35 per cent died shortly after return and short-term organ failure was 56 per cent; see CMO, Organ Transplants at 31. In Germany, two patients died from severe post-operative septic shock after receiving an organ from a paid donor in India; see (1996) 313 *British Medical Journal* 1282. See also N. Inston, D. Gill, A. Al-Hakim and A. Ready, 'Living paid organ transplantation results in unacceptably high recipient morbidity and mortality' (2005) 37 *Transplantation Proceedings* 560.

[88] The declaration was supported by the Transplantation Society, the World Health Organisation and the International Society of Nephrology. It calls for surgeons partic-ipating in such activities to be stripped of their medical qualifications.

[89] World Health Organisation, Guiding Principles on Human Organ Transplantation, 1991, WHO, Geneva.

[90] See World Health Organinsation, Guiding Principles on Human Cell, Tissue and Organ Transplantation, 2008, available at www.who.int/entity/transplantation/TxGP08-en.pdf.

dates back to the 1970s,[91] and culminated in an Additional Protocol to the Council of Europe's Biomedicine Convention concerning the transplantation of organs and tissues of human origin, which came into force in May 2006.[92] Unlike the Convention itself, it has provisions relating to deceased donation.[93] The UK has yet to sign or ratify either document. Whilst these instruments currently have no direct legal effect, they are nonetheless important and influential.[94]

### Scientific and technological developments

In addition to reports and policy developments, there have been a host of important scientific and clinical initiatives and 'breakthroughs' since the new millennium, in addition to improved clinical outcomes and prognoses across the board. In November 2006 the first (partial) face transplant was performed in France, followed by the performance of an 'almost total' face transplant in America in late 2008, leading to preparations being made for similar procedures to also be performed in the UK.[95] More than twenty hand transplants have been performed, and knees, nerves, the flexor tendon apparatus of the hand and the forearm have all been transplanted. The first double arm transplant was recently carried out in Germany.[96] Other important innovative procedures include the recent birth of babies born following an ovary transplant,[97] and the injection of cells from the islets of Langerhans tissue (pancreatic tissue producing insulin for sufferers from type 1 diabetes) as an alternative to whole-organ pancreas transplants.[98] There have additionally been major advances in alternatives to organ

---

[91] Resolution on harmonisation of legislation of Member States relating to removal, grafting and transplantation of human substances, Resolution 78 (29).

[92] Council of Europe, Additional Protocol concerning the Transplantation of Organs and Tissues of Human Origin, 2002. It entered into force upon the fifth ratification by Slovenia in May 2006.

[93] Council of Europe, Convention for the Protection of Human Rights and Dignity of the Human Being with regard to the application of biology and medicine, 1997. It is presently in force in twenty-two Member States.

[94] They may perhaps influence interpretation of the European Convention on Human Rights itself.

[95] See 'First US face transplant complete', at news.bbc.co.uk/2/hi/americas/7786236.stm and 'UK gets face transplant go-ahead', at news.bbc.co.uk/1/hi/health/6083392.stm. See also Working Party Report of the Royal College of Surgeons, *Facial Transplantation*, 2006. Another face transplant was carried out in China in 2006.

[96] See Editorial, 'Extending the boundaries of transplantation' (2003) 326 *British Medical Journal* 1226; *The Times*, 2 August 2008 and http://news.bbc.co.uk/2/hi/health/7537897.stm.

[97] *Daily Telegraph*, 15 November 2008. See also 'US woman gives birth to daughter after transplant of ovarian tissue from her twin' (2005) 330 *British Medical Journal* 1408.

[98] This procedure has recently been approved for treatment on the NHS in the UK; see *Guardian*, 12 February 2008.

replacement therapy by way of artificial devices or prostheses, either as temporary or permanent measures, including the use of implantable ventricular assist devices and the 'first' fully implantable artificial hearts,[99] wearable battery-powered artificial kidneys,[100] sensory bionic limbs, etc.[101] Artificial corneas, spinal discs, retinas, teeth and skin are all either currently available for implantation, or are under development.

As regards deceased organ donation, non-heart-beating donor programmes have mushroomed in many regions, including in the UK (where there has been a fall of 9 per cent in the number of heart-beating donors since 2001–2), and new technology has facilitated the first 'beating-heart' heart transplantations.[102] With respect to living organ donation, living organ donor nephrectomy procedures are now performed by laparoscopic (rather than open surgical) means in many centres, living paired 'swap' and anonymous donations have started to take off in a substantial way, individuals have become donors of new types of tissue, etc. The shortage of deceased donors itself is the primary impetus for the increasing use of living donors even in regions with well-established deceased donor transplant programmes, e.g. the UK, Germany, the Netherlands and Switzerland. However, the increasing and heavy reliance upon living donation is itself an ethical issue which needs to be addressed. In other situations, the considerable use of living donors is an unavoidable or unsurprising consequence of either cultural, resource, or clinical obstacles. A lack of acceptance of the concept of brain death has hindered the development of heart-beating donation in countries such as China and Japan, although both nations now formally endorse the concept.[103] In India, despite the existence of

---

[99] See 'Boy beats odds with Berlin Heart', *The Times*, 25 August 2007. The French claim to have developed the first implantable heart; see www.telegraph.co.uk/health/article3269354.ece.

[100] See *Daily Mail*, 14 December 2007.

[101] See *Guardian*, 27 November 2007. Work is also on-going in the development of hybrid devices, such as an artificial pancreas combining insulin pumps with encapsulated pancreatic beta-cells that sense glucose levels.

[102] NHS Blood and Transplant, *Bulletin* Autumn 2006, Issue 60 at 14. The process was enabled by the use of a new storage and perfusion medium. A similar transplant occurred at Bad Oeynhausen in Germany in January 2006. See also M. Bouek *et al.*, 'Pediatric heart transplantation after declaration of cardiocirculatory death' (2008) 359 *New England Journal of Medicine* 709.

[103] See J. Parry, 'Doctors hope consensus on brain death in China will boost transplants' (2008) 336 *British Medical Journal* 581. In July 2007, new regulations came into effect which banned organ trafficking and required foreigners seeking transplants in China to obtain the approval of the Ministry of Health; see (2007) 335 *British Medical Journal* 961. Around the world, there is generally a high degree of consensus relating to brain death; see E. Wijdicks, 'Brain death worldwide' (2002) 58 *Neurology* 20, although there are many who still oppose it – see, e.g., R. Truog and F. Miller, 'The dead donor rule and organ transplantation' (2008) 359 *New England Journal of Medicine* 674.

laws facilitating deceased donor transplantation and incorporating the concept of brain death, the deceased donor programme is extremely modest, with an annual donor rate of only 0.05 per cent p.m.p.[104]

## Need

Transplantation and human tissue research rely upon public support for their viability. In the US as of August 2009, 111,000 patients were waiting for an organ, rising by approximately 5,000 per annum. It is estimated that by 2010 there will 100,000 patients on the waiting lists for a kidney alone, and that the average waiting time will be nearly ten years.[105] In Europe, there were 58,000 persons on waiting lists in 2006 (40,000 patients waiting for a kidney transplant), in addition to which it must be borne in mind that many people become too sick to appear on the waiting list, coupled with the fact that demand is suppressed in many regions by virtue of the shortage of organs itself – i.e. they are not listed for transplants when, if more organs were available, they might be.[106] Mortality rates whilst waiting for a heart, liver, or lung transplant usually range between 15 and 30 per cent. Every day some ten people die waiting for an organ in Europe and nineteen people in the US. In the UK, more than 1,000 people per year are dying for lack of a transplant, in addition to which average waiting times for a kidney transplant are now more than two years for adults.[107] The situation will undoubtedly worsen in most regions as demographic trends take effect, such as an ageing population and growing rates of diabetes and other conditions resulting in renal failure, such as cardiovascular disorders. These may be especially pronounced amongst certain population sub-groups.[108] The same may be said as regards increasing rates of hepatitis and the need for liver transplantation. Yet the costs of transplantation, kidney transplantation at least, greatly undercut the costs of alternative (dialysis) treatment over the longer term.[109]

---

[104] It is hoped that a recent widespread scandal relating to organ trafficking will invigorate the process of establishing a nation-wide programme. See G. Mudur, 'Indian doctors hope kidney scandal will spur cadaver donation programme' (2008) 336 *British Medical Journal* 413.

[105] See www.chfpatients.com/tx/txrules.htm.

[106] Sir Liam Donaldson, Oral Evidence to the Select Committee on the European Union (Sub-Committee G) of the House of Lords, December 6 2007. See also House of Lords, *Increasing the Supply*, para. 5 [Donaldson].

[107] Donaldson, *ibid*. See House of Lords, *Increasing the Supply*, para. 4. The percentage of the waiting list operated on fell by 5 per cent between 2003 and 2007. See *Supplement Report* at 21.

[108] In the UK, demand for renal transplantation is anticipated to rise by 2 per cent per annum; see *Supplement Report* at 28. The incidence of renal failure is three to four times higher in Afro-Caribbean, African, or Asian patients than amongst Caucasian patients.

[109] The Organ Donation Taskforce calculated that for each cohort of renal patients in the UK that have received a transplant the cost savings over a thirty-year period were estimated to be at least £100 million. See *Supplement Report* Appendix 1.

Human tissue for research is also required on an ever-growing scale, with animal replacement models in increasing demand and genomics research proceeding apace. Pharmaceutical companies are heavily involved in researching genes and biological markers that correlate with disease states and in pharmacogenetics – i.e. the relationship between genetic profile and drug response (based usually on blood samples). The latter is an aspect of a new promised era of patient-centred treatment, aimed at tailoring drugs to each individual's genetic constitution.[110] Such research projects are frequently global in dimension and regularly require large volumes of raw materials or data. Biotechnology companies are becoming increasingly interested in more complex areas of research, such as stem cell research, tissue engineering and proteomics.

I implicitly accept for the purposes of this book that the activities considered here are public goods which should be supported and promoted. This is not, however, to imply a missionary zeal to advance transplantation or medical research. It is essential that provisions governing the procurement of organs and tissues for such ends are not wholly utility-driven. Reliance upon the bodies of humans for the treatment and cure of other humans is not an ideal situation in itself. There is a pressing need for an increased emphasis upon prevention and public health, rather than therapies themselves. There are also admittedly greater immediate priorities in some societies, such as enhanced primary care and cures for epidemics such as the HIV/AIDS pandemic in the developing world.[111]

The profile as well as the quality of the ethical and policy debate has been raised in recent years, with significant attention afforded also to the psychological, sociological, anthropological, theological and economic aspects of the subject.[112] In particular, important theses and collections have been published relating to transplantation,[113] human tissue collection and banking,[114] property rights in the human

---

[110] E.g. personalised medication based on the genetic cause of diabetes; see *The Times*, 7 June 2008.

[111] S. Benatar, 'Blinkered bioethics' (2004) 30 *Journal of Medical Ethics* 291. He also draws attention to the lack of access to healthcare of many citizens around the world.

[112] See, e.g., K. Healy, *Last Best Gifts* (University of Chicago Press, 2006); M. Lock, *Twice Dead: Organ Transplants and the Reinvention of Death* (Berkeley, CA: University of California Press, 2001).

[113] For example, Weimar *et al.* (eds.), *Organ Transplantation*; Sque and Payne (eds.), *Organ and Tissue Donation*; T. Gutmann, A. Daar, R. Sells and W. Land (eds.), *Ethical, Legal, and Social Issues in Organ Transplantation* (Lengerich: Pabst Publishers, 2004); D. Price (ed.), *Organ and Tissue Transplantation* (Aldershot: Ashgate, 2006).

[114] For example, R. Weir and R. Olick, *The Stored Tissue Issue: Biomedical Research, Ethics, and Law in the Era of Genomic Medicine* (Oxford University Press, 2004); Youngner, Anderson and Schapiro (eds.), *Transplanting Human Tissue*.

body,[115] commerce in human body tissues,[116] consent,[117] etc. The literature is now voluminous and increasingly multi-disciplinary. But translating ideas and thoughts into actions and policies is enormously challenging and problematic at a time when public opinion is unprecedentedly fickle and crucial, and where the media spotlight glares ever more brightly.

I shall set out here the structure of the book and the central ideas and concepts advanced. Whilst contentious, the model offered here is by no means radical and draws on many existing accepted tenets and practices. The crucial fulcrum of my thesis is the idea of 'donation' and the need to locate the focus around the true *donor*, the tissue source. I wish to re-emphasise the idea of 'donation' and of the 'gift', whilst avoiding the baggage and connotations that these notions frequently carry with them. In the context of research, the gift metaphor has been attacked for demanding altruism, ceding of control from donors, obscuring the potential value of tissues[118] and rendering the body 'an open source of free biological material for commercial use'.[119] In the sphere of transplantation it is accused of burdening recipients and failing to maintain adequate donation rates. But, as Gillett has articulated, the notion of the 'gift of oneself' parallels the highest ideals of most moralities, both secular and religious, *in abstracto* (general ethical dialogue) and *in concreto* (at the bedside). He states 'I have suggested that the concept of a gift, particularly as exemplified in the Christian eucharist, is eminently suited to inform our ethics in this area. The Eucharistic image that symbolizes (among other things) a sacrificial giving of self to another is so central to our highest

---

[115] For example, R. Hardcastle, *Law and the Human Body* (Oxford: Hart Publishing, 2007); D. Dickenson, *Property in the Human Body: Feminist Perspectives* (Cambridge University Press, 2007); D. Sperling, *Posthumous Interests: Legal and Ethical Perspectives* (Cambridge University Press, 2008); N. Nwabueze, *Biotechnology and the Challenge of Property: Property Rights in Dead Bodies, Body Parts and Genetic Information* (Aldershot: Ashgate, 2007) [Nwabueze, *Biotechnology*].

[116] For example, J. S. Taylor, *Stakes and Kidneys: Why Markets in Human Body Parts are Morally Imperative* (Aldershot: Ashgate, 2005); S. Wilkinson, *Bodies for Sale: Ethics and Exploitation in the Human Body Trade* (Oxford: Routledge, 2003); M. Cherry, *Kidney for Sale by Owner: Human Organs, Transplantation, and the Market* (Washington, DC: Georgetown University Press, 2005).

[117] P. Westen, *The Logic of Consent* (Aldershot: Ashgate, 2004); D. Beyleveld and R. Brownsword, *Consent in the Law* (Oxford: Hart Publishing, 2008).

[118] See M. Dixon-Woods *et al.*, 'Tissue samples as "gifts" for research: A qualitative study of families and professionals' (2008) 9 *Medical Law International* 131 at 132. The metaphor appears, for instance, in guidance issued by the Medical Research Council; see *Human Tissue and Biological Samples for Use in Research*, London: Medical Research Council, 2001.

[119] C. Waldby and R. Mitchell, *Tissue Economies: Blood, Organs and Cell Lines in Late Capitalism*, (Durham, NC: Duke University Press, 2006), p. 24.

moral ideas that it can serve outside the particular faith and doctrine that specifically celebrates it.'[120] This would appear to be as equally apposite in the context of human tissue donation for research as in relation to transplantation.[121] Whilst I have already rejected any essential connection between the idea of property and commercialisation, there is no reason why the notion of the 'gift' should not be equated with 'property'. Although some maintain that the donation of body parts is too personal in nature to be regarded as a transfer of property, gifts in fact 'imply' and are 'inexorably connected to' property.[122] These notions can properly co-exist in harmony.

It is my contention therefore that it is the wishes of donors, including deceased persons, that are the central ethical and legal imperative in organ and tissue donation by virtue of the prerogative and entitlement of the tissue source to determine such matters. This central assertion may seem uncontroversial, but then one must appreciate that in very many jurisdictions, including the UK, the US and many others, the norm after death has been *family* decision-making. To adopt a different emphasis is consequently to alter the status quo ante. The wishes of the tissue source (the 'donor') are typically evidence upon which relatives may then base *their* decision. Allowing relatives the power of decision-making seems perhaps to flow logically from their common role as guardians of the corpse, linked to their potential duty of disposal, and is frequently perceived as a part of the bereavement process itself. There has recently been a new donor-oriented emphasis in the UK and the US in particular.[123] Whether this will amount to more than rhetoric when compared to practice remains to be seen. In the past this was typically mere lip service. Quite apart from such a change in orientation *per se*, there are infrastructural issues raised by any such change which require addressing. Arising out of this, the following questions emerge: (1) how are such wishes to be gleaned, (2) what do we do in the face of an absence of direct evidence of such wishes and (3) what impact does the volume of organ and tissue procurement have on

---

[120] G. Gillett, 'Ethics and images in organ transplantation', in P. Trzepacz and A. Dimatini (eds.), *The Transplant Patient: Biological, Psychiatric and Ethical Issues in Organ Transplantation* (Cambridge University Press, 2000) 239 at 252.

[121] See R. Tutton, 'Persons, property and gift', in Tutton and Corrigan (eds.), *Genetic Databases* at 19.

[122] G. Laurie, *Genetic Privacy: A Challenge to Medico-Legal Norms* (Cambridge University Press, 2002), p. 317 and Nwabueze, *Biotechnology*, p. 188. McHale observes that the links between the language of the 'gift' and the notion of property in one's own human material has 'not gone unnoticed' in the academic literature; see J. McHale, 'Regulating genetic databases: some legal and ethical issues' (2004) 12 *Medical Law Review* 70.

[123] See Institute of Medicine, *Organ Donation* at 175.

this stance? These are weighty matters to the extent that in most juris-dictions we do not directly know the wishes of the deceased.

The final plank of my proposal is the need to protect legitimate interests in human tissue (the generic expression I have chosen to employ here) involved in medical research or transplantation. It is my contention that this unavoidably implicates the need for recognition of property interests in tissue sources themselves to protect and ensure their 'gifts', property interests in transplanters and researchers to ensure proper protection and use of materials donated for such ends, and property interests allowing the appropriate 'exploitation' and use of tissue for scientific and clinical ends, etc. Such interests are inadequately protected at the present time. Such rights principally protect the right of possession, exclusion, control and transferability ('donation') of tissue, rather than its commerciality. Whether trading in such material should be permitted is an *additional* severable matter which requires separate consideration. Unfortunately the very terminology of 'property' has become fused in the popular mind with permissible trading in human material. But such material is initially just that, 'human', and in virtue of its uniqueness may require separate and discrete regulation. Whilst property rights generate strong entitlements to control the disposition and use of tissue, they are not absolute and may be subject to legitimate constraints.

# 1    Human biological materials

This chapter is concerned with the language and concepts applied to 'human biological materials' for transplantation and research within the practice and policy arena, and the ambit(s) of legal regulation. The language and dialogue historically employed in this sphere has often hindered rather than assisted adequate and clear communication between professionals and lay persons. This can be seen in the repeated misapprehension attaching to the use of the term 'tissue' in the context of post-mortem examination and retention for research, revealed in the recent inquiry reports in the UK ('tissue' typically being taken by families to exclude whole organs or brains, yet having a broad generic meaning for clinicians and pathologists).[1] Moreover, there is a need to be sensitive to the inappropriate or irreverent use of language applied to activities relating to human body parts, which might even negatively impact on rates of donation, e.g. 'harvesting', 'products', 'cadavers', etc. Even the expression 'human material' proved controversial to some consultees during the lead-up to the Human Tissue Bill being presented to Parliament, on account of the 'objectification' allegedly implied by the expression.[2]

A legislative framework governing the (removal and) use of human material for medical purposes generally is currently to be found in some jurisdictions.[3] There is, for instance, a comprehensive framework governing the use of human material for research, transplantation and other

---

[1] See www.bristol-inquiry.org.uk/interim_report/index.htm (Bristol Inquiry); rlcinquiry. org.uk/download/index.htm [Liverpool Children's Inquiry]. Parry remarks, 'One of the most important outcomes of the Alder Hey and Bristol enquiries was the recognition that there was a very serious disjunction or lack of correspondence between pathologists' and the general public's perception of what might constitute "a sample of tissue"', B. Parry, 'The new Human Tissue Bill: Categorization and definitional issues and their implications' (2005) 1(1) *Genomics, Society and Policy* 74 at 75 [Parry, 'The new Human Tissue Bill'].

[2] Department of Health, *Summary of Responses to the Consultation Report Human Bodies, Human Choices*, Department of Health, London, 2003, at para. 2.4.

[3] E.g. New Zealand.

medical purposes across most of the UK,[4] replacing the patchwork of legislative provisions previously applying to different spheres.[5] Quite apart from the need for explicit legal authority to take, hold, or use the material itself, especially as regards deceased persons, there are concerns that need to be addressed relating to the safety and quality of material, potential limitations on use and commerciality, suitability of the personnel and premises connected with the material, etc. Other jurisdictions have discrete statute laws governing specific activities, such as transplantation (e.g. Belgium, Germany, the Netherlands), or research, even sometimes specifically relating to bio-banking (e.g. Norway and Sweden).[6] Laws have also been enacted specifically to implement the EU Tissues and Cells Directives.[7] Legislation is generally more extensive with regard to the dead than the living, notably in relation to research.[8] The US Uniform Anatomical Gift Acts (UAGAs), for instance, apply only to the removal and use of material, for transplantation and research, from deceased persons. Specific laws governing the retention and use of human material following post-mortem examination are more sporadic. Moreover, even the Human Tissue Act 2004 does not apply to consent to the *removal* of tissue from the living. Such issues are typically governed by the general law.[9]

### Fitness for purpose

Legal terminology should be able to effectively communicate with relevant professionals and agencies. The definition of 'organ' in the context of

---

[4] The Human Tissue (Scotland) Act 2006 does not apply to research relating to living persons. State legislation in Australia has generally been fairly comprehensive; see, e.g., Queensland's Transplantation and Anatomy Act 1979, as is the New Zealand Human Tissue Act 2008.

[5] For instance, anatomical examination was governed exclusively by the Anatomy Acts 1832 and 1984.

[6] Norwegian Law No. 12 of 21 February 2003. Swedish Law 297 Biobanks in Medical Care Act 2002.

[7] For example, Human Tissue (Quality and Safety for Human Application) Regulations SI 2007 No. 1523; Netherlands Decree of 5 March 2004. Only Cyprus, Ireland and Malta still have no legislation relating to deceased donor transplantation, and Ireland is currently consulting over draft legislation.

[8] Although federal regulations in the US, and provisions relating to research in general, are more extensive with regard to the living.

[9] The 2004 Act, and the analogous legislation in Scotland, however, contain offences relating to both the *removal* and use of materials taken from living individuals for transplantation unless certain conditions are satisfied; see section 33(1)–(2), Human Tissue Act 2004; section 17, Human Tissue (Scotland) Act 2006. These are designed principally to ensure that certain conditions are satisfied, including an absence of reward given or to be given.

the federal offence of interstate commerce in the National Organ Transplants Act 1984 (NOTA) in the US, which includes bone marrow, bone, etc., has been criticised for being inconsistent with the use of the term in general scientific and medical quarters, thus generating confusion.[10] It even jars with the terminology of the US UAGAs themselves (see below). There is a tension, though, in so far as legal language must also faithfully and accurately reflect and implement the policy intended to be encapsulated. This imperative can seen, for instance, in the definition of a 'genetically related' person under the previous Human Organ Transplants Act 1989 in the UK which, seemingly anomalously, excluded spouses and even some individuals *with* a clear genetic relationship to the donor/recipient. However, the definition was intended to further the principal objective of the legislation, to eradicate trading in human organs for transplantation.

Permissive legislation ordinarily employs an expansive generic term to apply to the human materials within its ambit, at least with regard to the pre-requisites for donation and use. The Human Tissue Act 2004, for instance, applies to 'relevant material' which, subject to some specific exceptions, includes any human materials comprising (consisting of or including) cells. The previous 1961 Human Tissue Act spoke of 'parts' of bodies and the Human Tissue (Scotland) Act 2006 now adopts this same terminology. The tendency is to avoid either crude or fine distinctions between different materials.[11] Whilst the 2006 Act does not define 'parts of bodies', the 2006 version of the UAGA describes an 'anatomical gift' as 'a donation of all or part of a human body', and defines a part of a human body as meaning an 'organ, an eye, or tissue of a human being'.[12] Despite the problems it has previously generated (see above), the term 'tissue' is intended in this work to be used in a broad generic fashion, coterminously with 'human (biological) materials', unless otherwise stated or the context makes clear.[13] After all, the 2004 and 2006 Acts in the UK are themselves entitled the Human *Tissue* Act(s) and there are many other similarly titled statutes around the world, e.g. New Zealand.

---

[10] 'Human organ' is defined for this purpose as including bone marrow, corneas, eyes, bone and skin, as well as orthodox organs such as lungs, hearts, kidneys, pancreata and livers.

[11] The 2004 Act itself eschews terms such as 'organ' and 'tissue', ostensibly by virtue of the historical issues attaching to them. The ambiguously drafted definition of the term 'organ' under section 7(2), Human Organ Transplants Act 1989 created uncertainties with respect to parts of organs such as livers, and as regards certain tissues such as bone. See D. Price and R. Mackay, 'The trade in human organs' (1991) 141 *New Law Journal* 1307.

[12] Uniform Anatomical Gift Act 2006, section 1. Tissue is defined as 'a portion of the body other than an organ or an eye'.

[13] 'Tissue' usually refers to all constituent parts of the body formed by cells – see, e.g., the EU Tissues and Cells Directive 2004/23/EC, Article 3(b).

Laws therefore employ sub-categories of materials, or distinctions, for the achievement of various ends. The Human Organ Transplants Act 1989 distinguished 'organs' from other human material as it was not thought necessary at that time to criminalise commercial dealings in other materials. The 2004 legislative framework now includes human material in general within its ambit, but distinguishes between organs and other human materials for licensing and other purposes. A licence is required for storage for both research and transplantation, other than with respect to ethically approved research (i.e. holdings for specific research projects do not require licences) or the storage of organs or parts of organs for transplantation, or where the storage of the materials for transplantation is for less than 48 hours.[14] The long-term storage potential of tissues explains their discrete handling in such regulatory contexts, e.g. tissue banking.[15] The Human Tissue (Scotland) Act 2006 distinguishes between organs and other materials for the purposes of retention of material removed at post-mortem.[16] With respect to *non-forensic* post-mortems, any parts of the body other than an organ which are removed during the performance of an author-ised post-mortem examination automatically form part of the decea-sed's medical record and may be retained and used for various purposes, including research.[17] An organ, on the other hand, may be used only for research, training, or educational purposes with an appro-priate authorisation. The distinction between organs and tissues was intended to reflect the different emotional significance they allegedly have in this context.[18]

There may also be legal distinctions drawn between materials based on the risks to (living) donors from removal, including the protection

---

[14] Human Tissue Act 2004 (Ethical Approval, Exceptions from Licensing and Supply of Information) Regulations 2006 SI 2006 No. 1260, reg. 3(3). For the purposes of these Regulations, an 'organ' is defined as meaning 'a differentiated and vital part of the human body, formed by different tissues, that maintains its structure, vascularisation and capacity to develop physiological functions with an important level of autonomy', reg. 3(5).

[15] As a consequence, 'end-users' do not require a licence for approved research whereas general research tissue banks do. In 1994, the Committee of Ministers adopted a defi-nition of tissues as 'All constituent parts of the human body, including surgical residues, but excluding organs, blood, blood products as well as reproductive tissue such as sperm, eggs and embryos. Hair, nails, placentas and body wastes are also excluded'; see Recommendation No. R (94) 1 of the Committee of Ministers to Member States on human tissue banks.

[16] 'Organs' are not defined in the statute although section 60 states that 'tissue' includes skin, corneas and bone marrow, and a 'tissue sample' includes any derivative of skin.

[17] Sections 23 and 28.

[18] Human Tissue Authority, *Human Tissue (Scotland) Act 2006: A Guide to its Implications for NHSScotland*, at para. 35, at www.sehd.scot.nhs.uk/mels/HDL2006_46.pdf and www.hta.gov.uk/_db/_documents/Information_about_HT_(Scotland)_Act.pdf.

of vulnerable persons, i.e. minors and adult individuals unable to give consent. The Council of Europe Biomedicine Convention states that no organ or tissue removal may be carried out on a person lacking capacity unless the removal is of *regenerative* tissue and satisfies various other pre-conditions.[19] Many jurisdictions have laws to this effect, such as Belgium, France, Portugal, Lithuania and Scotland.[20] By contrast, whilst organ donation by a minor or mentally incapacitated adult would occur, as the Human Tissue Authority (HTA) Code of Practice states 'only in extremely rare circumstances',[21] it is nonetheless a theoretical possibility in the remainder of the UK apart from Scotland.

Whilst the Human Tissue Act 2004 prescribes comprehensive regulatory oversight of living donor transplantation procedures, which is itself rare elsewhere apart from in Germany,[22] a discriminating approach can be seen in the varying levels of review of 'transplantable material' required. The regulations passed under the statute are tailored to the body materials involved, the vulnerability of the individual and the risks and invasiveness attached to the procedure.[23] They define transplantable material for such

---

[19] Article 20, Council of Europe Convention for the Protection of Human Rights and Dignity of the Human Being with Regard to the Application of Biology and Medicine, 1997, Orviedo, stipulates the following conditions: (i) there is no compatible donor available who has capacity, (ii) the recipient is a brother or sister of the donor, (iii) the donation has life-saving potential for the recipient, (iv) an authorisation within the terms of the Convention has been given in writing in accordance with the law and the approval of the competent body and (v) the potential donor does not object [Council of Europe Convention]. The Additional Protocol applies to organs, tissues and cells, including haematopoietic stem cells. Article 14 states that the limitation to regenerative material does not apply to *cell* removal, however, by virtue of the qualitatively different level of risk associated with the removal of a few (e.g. skin) cells, Council of Europe, Additional Protocol to the Convention on Human Rights and Biomedicine Concerning Transplantation of Organs and Tissues of Human Origin, ETS No.186, 2002, Article 2.

[20] For example, Portugal Law No. 12/93. See section 17(1), (2) and (4), Human Tissue (Scotland) Act 2006 and the Human Organ and Tissue Live Transplants (Scotland) Regulations 2006 SSI 2006 No. 390. Similar laws are to be found in many Australian states.

[21] Human Tissue Authority, Code of Practice on Donation of Organs, Tissues and Cells for Transplantation, July 2006, para. 30.

[22] Living Donor Commissions exist in Germany. Court approval is, however, required in some jurisdictions.

[23] See the Human Tissue Act 2004 (Persons who Lack Capacity to Consent and Transplants) Regulations 2006 SI 2006 No. 1659, and the HTA Code of Practice, Donation of Allogeneic Bone Marrow and Peripheral Blood Stem Cells, July 2006, paras. 22–30 and 45–52. Regrettably, the regulations fail to cater for potential conflicts of interest relating to persons with parental responsibility for both patient and potential donor, nor for the potential for pressure to be exerted by parents on competent minors. See J. Fortin, *Children's Rights and Developing Law*, 3rd edn. (Cambridge University Press, 2009).

purposes as meaning an organ,[24] or part of an organ that is to be used for the same purpose as the entire organ in the human body, bone marrow and peripheral blood stem cells.[25] However, bone marrow and peripheral blood stem cells fall within the definition only where the person from whom the material is removed is either an adult or a child who lacks capacity.[26] It was not deemed necessary for the HTA to monitor bone marrow or peripheral blood stem cell donations from *competent* adults or minors. Where monitoring is necessary, an Independent Assessor must report to the HTA having interviewed the parties.[27] Enhanced review by a panel of at least three members of the HTA is required in the case of novel procedures such as paired or pooled living donation, and in instances where the intended donor of an *organ or part of an organ* is a child or an adult who lacks capacity.[28]

The 2004 Act has been criticised for its plethora of terms and definitions relating to human materials, but it must be appreciated that they serve particular functions, leading to the need for separate or overlapping concepts.[29] Parry remarks upon the difficulty the drafters had trying to accommodate the very different relationships that different constituencies have to bodily materials when in different forms.[30] Complexity is to some extent inherent in the exercise.

Certain materials may fall outside the jurisdictional ambit of different institutions or agencies.[31] In particular the reach of organisations may not extend to organs. The Federal Food and Drug Administration (FDA), for instance, has a role in ensuring the safety and effectiveness of tissue transplants in the US, including avoidance of the spread of communicable disease.[32] Establishments that recover, process, store, or distribute banked human tissue are subject to FDA oversight. The FDA originally

---

[24] 'Organ' is defined in the same way as in relation to licensing, see Human Tissue Act 2004 (Ethical Approval, Exceptions from Licensing and Supply of Information) Regulations 2006 SI 2006 No. 1260, reg. 3(5).

[25] The Human Tissue Act 2004 (Persons who Lack Capacity to Consent and Transplants) Regulations 2006 SI 2006 No. 1659, reg. 10. Domino procedures fall outside the compass of the definition as they are a bi-product of the treatment of the patient (reg. 10(2)).

[26] Reg. 10(3).     [27] Reg. 11.     [28] Reg. 12.

[29] The 2004 Act refers to 'qualifying consent' and 'appropriate consent', 'controlled material' and 'relevant material', etc.

[30] Parry, 'The new Human Tissue Bill' at 81.

[31] For example, gametes and embryos fall outwith the 2004 Act and are governed instead by the Human Fertilisation and Embryology Acts 1990 and 2008.

[32] See J. Warner and K. Zoon, 'The View from the Food and Drug Administration', in S. Youngner, M. Anderson and R. Schapiro (eds.), *Transplanting Human Tissue: Ethics, Policy, and Practice* (Oxford University Press, 2004) 71. The FDA first attempted to regulate after reports in 1993 of brokers attempting to sell tissue from Russia, Eastern Europe and Central and South America to US tissue banks.

monitored only tissue banks, but whilst its regulatory ambit now extends to human cells, tissues and cellular and tissue-based products, it excludes organs.[33] The EU's jurisdiction and competence is limited by the EC Treaty. Although it has broad powers in relation to human materials, it has chosen to regulate blood, tissues and cells, and organs, discretely, in so far as issues of safety and quality play out differently in these contexts and specific issues apply. There are a variety of different legal regulatory frameworks bearing on human material or items derived wholly or partially from human material. In the UK, medicinal products and medical devices are governed by the Medicines and Healthcare Products Regulatory Agency, which is also the competent authority under the EU Blood Directive.[34] Medical devices include artificial organs but not natural organs, tissues or cells for transplantation or research.[35]

## Human Tissue Act 2004

The 2004 Act generally governs 'relevant material',[36] which covers organs, tissues and other cellular material, but not sub-cellular material such as cytological specimens, acellular serum and plasma, or DNA and RNA.[37] The legislation has been criticised for overbreadth and adopting a blanket approach to human material across the board, 'wholly unnuanced' in Parry's parlance,[38] and a failure to reflect the mischief the legislation was designed to remedy, i.e. the post-mortem retention scandals.[39] Parry states 'Each were to be treated commensurably under the new law despite the fact that, in general, the interests (both personal and legal) that individuals have in these materials is mediated by factors such as the nature of the material (what type it is, its size, etc.); the manner

[33] The Health Resources Services Administration instead governs the transplantation of vascularised organ transplants.

[34] See Blood Safety and Quality Regulations SI 2005 No. 50 and Amendment (No. 2) Regulations SI 2005 No. 2898. In relation to tissues and cells it is the HTA, which is also responsible for the safety and testing of autologous and allogeneic tissue engineered products containing human tissues or cells.

[35] Medical Devices Regulations 2002 SI 2002 No. 618 as amended.

[36] This definition is applicable to the consent and licensing elements in particular.

[37] It would also exclude cultured cells which have divided outside the body, artificially created embryonic stem cells, extracted DNA and plasma extracted DNA, see Human Tissue Authority guidance at www.hta.gov.uk/guidance/licensing_guidance/definition_of_relevant_material.cfm.

[38] Parry, 'The new Human Tissue Bill' at 76. The New Zealand Human Tissue Act 2008 also applies to material which is or includes cells, section 7(1)(b).

[39] Research appears to show that people generally have a different attitude toward their own tissues as opposed to those of others after death; see C. Womack and N. Gray, 'Human research tissue banks in the UK National Health Service: Law, ethics, controls and constraints' (2000) 55 British Journal of Biomedical Sciences 250.

in which it was collected; and the prospective uses to which it might be put.'[40] She states that the first draft of the Bill was 'underwritten by a presumption that individuals have an undifferentiated relationship to their extracted body parts'.[41] The 2004 Act even applies its consent regime to (cellular) waste products excreted from the body, such as urine, sputum and faeces. Whilst this may seem excessive, it is apparently promoting a point of principle – that individuals should generally have a right to control the use of tissues emanating from their bodies.[42]

The context and motivation are crucial here. Whilst discardable tissue such as nails and hair from the living do not require consent for their use for scheduled purposes,[43] certain applications to even the minutest of quantities of tissue may threaten great harm, such as by way of (direct or indirect) genetic testing, e.g. paternity testing. The results of such genetic analysis could have significant implications for relatives, or even their communities, as well as tissue providers. As has been stated in another context 'one person's waste can be another person's raw material'.[44] Section 45 of the 2004 Act makes it an offence to have in one's possession any 'bodily material' intending that any human DNA in the material be analysed without (qualifying) consent and that the results of the analysis be used otherwise than for an excepted purpose.[45] 'Bodily material' for these purposes includes *any* material which consists of or includes human cells, *including* hair or nails.[46] Thus, although extracted DNA is not 'relevant material', the non-consensual keeping and handling of any bodily material for the purpose of extracting and analysing DNA may be. As Dr Ladyman stated in the House of Commons Standing Committee, 'Acellular materials are not themselves within the scope of the Bill, but the control of cells from which they come is within the scope of consent'.[47] But why was isolated DNA not itself generally included? Was this simply out of a desire not to unduly extend the reach of the

---

[40] Parry, 'The new Human Tissue Bill' at 76.     [41] *Ibid.*, at 77.

[42] This was a matter underscored by parliamentary spokespersons on the Bill; see, e.g., Dr Ladyman, House of Commons Hansard Debates, Standing Committee G, col. 65, 29 January 2004.

[43] Section 53(2) Human Tissue Act 2004. Whilst the root of a hair and the sheath consists of living cellular tissue, dead tissue above the scalp does not (although consisting of acellular keratin); see Glidewell J. in *R* v. *Cooke* [1995] 1 Cr. App. Rep. 318 at 325–6.

[44] S. Ball and S. Bell, *Environmental Law*, 4th edn. (London: Blackstone Press, 1997), p. 382.

[45] Such an offence was recommended by the Human Genetics Commission in *Inside Information*, 2002, at para. 3.60. Excepted purposes include, *inter alia*, the prevention and detection of crime, medical diagnosis, or treatment; see Schedule 4, 2004 Act.

[46] Section 45(5).

[47] Dr Ladyman, House of Commons Hansard Debates, Standing Committee G, col. 58, 27 January 2004.

regulatory framework? If so, it generates an ostensible anomaly in so far as DNA is as much a 'biosample' as cellular tissue such as blood from which DNA may be derived, and they may well be stored alongside each other in a 'genetic database' or 'gene/bio bank' of some sort.[48] Or may be biological materials become increasingly less part of our humanness the more molecularised they become?[49]

Perhaps one explanation is that sub-cellular genetic material is principally conceived of *as* information rather than material *from which* information may be obtained. It is instrumentally but not intrinsically significant, and therefore something over which there need not be any direct right of control. Unlike the sphere of transplantation, where it is the organ or tissue *per se* which is of central importance in terms of use, in the field of research and pharmaceutical product development it is the informational potential of the human tissue, rather than the material form *per se*, which is of crucial value to the user.[50] Barton remarks that 'As biotechnologists are increasingly likely to look to global genomic databases rather than to the underlying organisms from which the information is derived ... genetic resource issues may soon be outflanked by genomic information issues'.[51] Some commentators have even argued that biotechnology should simply be seen as a new form of information technology. Palmer asserts that 'Rather than thinking of blood, DNA, cell lines, etc., solely in terms of their materiality – assets subject to control – I propose that these specimens (whether derived from humans, animals, plants) be viewed as *data* with the potential to become useful knowledge'.[52] Different legislative structures ordinarily apply to the material and informational domains, though. Whether they *should* is another matter.

---

[48] This would be especially problematic if isolated DNA might be removed directly from the body for analysis.

[49] See I. Ellis, 'Justice versus utility in the ethics of research on: "human genetic material"' (2001) 1(5) *Genetics Law Monitor* 1 at 2.

[50] See G. Lewis, 'Tissue collection and the pharmaceutical industry', in R. Tutton and O. Corrigan (eds.), *Genetic Databases: Socio-Ethical Issues in the Collection and Use of DNA* (Oxford: Routledge, 2004) 181 at 184.

[51] J. Barton, 'The Biodiversity Convention and the flow of scientific information', in K. Hoagland and A. Rossman (eds.), *Global Genetic Resources: Access, Ownership, and Intellectual Property Rights* (Washington, DC: Association of Systematics Research Publishers, 1997), p. 55. It has been forcefully pointed out, however, that *all* human tissue, not just 'genetic material', may provide a basis for genetic analysis; see S. Gevers and E. Olsthoorn-Heim, 'DNA sampling: Dutch and European approaches to the issues of informed consent and confidentiality', in B. Knoppers (ed.), *Human DNA: Law and Policy* (Dordrecht: Kluwer Law International, 1997) 109 at 118.

[52] L. Palmer, 'Should liability play a role in social control of biobanks?' (2005)(Spring) *Journal of Law, Medicine and Ethics* 70 at 70. Jones likewise asserts that if such samples are anonymised they have the status of epidemiological data; see D. Jones, *Speaking for the Dead: Cadavers in Biology and Medicine* (Aldershot: Ashgate, 2000), p. 77.

## Dematerialisation

An evolutionary process occurs from analysis to end-point in a great deal of research upon human tissue; a gradual *dematerialisation*. Parry comments that advanced biotechnologies have rendered genetic and biochemical resources a variety of progressively less corporeal and more informational forms, 'as cryogenically stored tissue samples, as cell-lines, extracted DNA, or even as gene sequences stored in databases'.[53] The gradual deconstruction or disaggregation of human materials into lesser and lesser constituent elements ('biological derivatives') has itself resulted in 'autonomous commodities',[54] to which issues of control and ownership attach. However, whilst a metamorphosis of sorts can be seen to accompany many of the processes alluded to, there is an inevitable fuzziness connected to these 'stages'. Parry remarks 'However, ..., boundaries of many sorts – between "natural" and "artificial," "organism" and "machine," between "humans" and "animals," "material" and "information" – are blurring, making it difficult to discern where one ends and another begins'.[55]

The existence of biobanks housing an amalgam of tissue samples, DNA, genetic data and other personal information generates challenges for appropriate legal regulation. The Australian Law Reform Commission explicitly recognised that human tissue samples can 'yield' genetic information rather than being genetic information *per se*, but nonetheless asserted that 'A uniform approach to the regulation of samples and information is preferable, to avoid complexity, inconsistency and further fragmentation of such privacy laws'.[56] It recommended regulating genetic samples by way of an extension to privacy laws.[57] Indeed, Estonia has sometimes been held up as a model in the sphere of genetic databases, for having one piece of legislation governing both genetic tissue and data. The Human Genes Research Act 2000 applies to 'gene banks' defined as databases consisting of 'tissue samples, descriptions of DNA, descriptions of state of health, genealogies, genetic data and data enabling the identification of gene donors'.[58] However, despite the allure of simplicity,[59] it is

---

[53] B. Parry, *Trading the Genome: Investigating the Commodification of Bio-Information* (New York: Columbia University Press, 2004), p. 44 [Parry, *Trading the Genome*].

[54] *Ibid.*, p. 43.    [55] *Ibid.*, p. 65.

[56] Australian Law Reform Commission, *Essentially Yours: The Protection of Human Genetic Information in Australia*, ALRC Report 96, Sydney, 2003, at paras. 20.1 and 20.49.

[57] See generally J. McHale, 'Regulating genetic databases: Some legal and ethical issues' (2004) 12(1) *Medical Law Review* 70.

[58] Under the 2000 Act ownership of donated samples passes to the processor, although the processor has no powers to transfer its rights of property over the samples.

[59] There is no denying the current complex regulatory interaction in the UK, though. See J. Kaye and S. McGibbons, 'Mapping the regulatory space for genetic databases and biobanks in England and Wales' (2008) 9 *Medical Law International* 111.

necessary to recognise the different interests at stake with regard to human materials *per se*,[60] which may not be effectively and adequately catered for by way of privacy laws alone.[61] Where these are conflated, as arguably in a 2004 German National Ethics Council Opinion, notions of harm and utility tend to override issues of individual designation and control.[62] In particular, notions of property rights are especially problematic as regards information.[63]

Whilst Gere and Parry deny that there is any sharp ontological distinction between bodily 'material' and (potential) medical 'information', they nonetheless endorse its existence and note that privacy legislation and protection has no relevance unless the resources concerned are 'legible', i.e. can be understood in that form by another party.[64] The contrast between *informational* and *spatial* privacy arises here.[65] Gere and Parry remark, 'In the wake of the Alder Hey scandal it might seem legislatively pragmatic to define tissue blocks and slides as texts, thus draining them of the emotional significance attached to physical samples. We hope to have shown ... that is neither possible nor desirable.'[66] We should not ignore the connection between human materials and their 'personal' origins.

### Exclusions

The requirement for consent is applicable to all 'relevant material' which, as we have seen, is very widely defined.[67] Nevertheless it excludes embryos and gametes and hair and nails from a living person, the latter seemingly on the basis of its discardability and tenuous link to personal identity.[68] Kant apparently distinguished *organs* of the body and *parts* of the body to justify the removal of human materials for certain purposes. He implicitly suggested that some parts of the body are aspects of 'selves'

---

[60] See S. Alpert, 'Privacy and the analysis of stored tissues', in *Research Involving Human Biological Materials: Ethical Issues and Policy Guidance*, National Bioethics Advisory Commission, Rockville, MD, 2000 at 15–16.

[61] By virtue of the fact that data is information on identifiable persons, genetic samples *per se* may initially fall outside data protection regimes.

[62] German National Ethics Council Opinion, *Biobanks for Research*, Berlin, 2004 at 46.

[63] Moreover, the application of property concepts to information is additionally problematic in so far as information is not always 'individual' in character, especially genetic information. See also G. Laurie, *Genetic Privacy: A Challenge to Medico-Legal Norms* (Cambridge University Press, 2002), pp. 301–4 [Laurie, *Genetic Privacy*].

[64] C. Gere and B. Parry, 'The flesh made word: Banking the body in the age of information' (2006) 1 *Biosocieties* 41 [Gere and Parry, 'The flesh made word'].

[65] See Laurie, *Genetic Privacy*, pp. 250–1.    [66] Gere and Parry, 'The flesh made word' at 46.

[67] In Scotland, the analogous concept of authorisation is employed instead.

[68] Section 53(2)(b). Some arbitrariness may nevertheless be apparent, in so far as waste products such as faeces are within the statutory remit whereas hair and nails are not.

whilst others are not.[69] Indeed, as Cohen states 'We do not ordinarily consider that hair, spit, or fingernail parings carry human dignity and worth, for these generally function as inessential human bits and pieces unrelated to what it is that makes human beings of special value'.[70] Not only may this suggest that non-consensual use of some human materials is legitimate, but such differences may even permit trading. Campbell states (in the US context) 'Indeed, the loss of hair, the spilling of blood, or the emission of sperm seems a common enough experience in life that it does not threaten the sense of identification of self with body. This may account for why we allow for both sales and donation of such materials.'[71] However, as Gillett notes, these are highly complex issues, 'touching upon some of the most basic features of our moral belief systems about human beings as embodied individuals'.[72]

Not only may there be legal nuances relating to types of tissues, but also to their *mode of acquisition*. For instance, there are exceptions in the 2004 Act to the need for consent with respect to *surplus* material taken from *living* persons for various (scheduled) purposes. Firstly, with regard to 'non-identifying' tissue used in ethically approved research.[73] Secondly, tissue to be used for various scheduled purposes, i.e. clinical audit, quality assurance, education or training relating to human health, performance assessment and public health monitoring.[74] The exceptions derive partially from the fact that the tissue was originally removed as part, or a by-product, of a legitimate clinical procedure, and will typically be 'diseased'. No substantial relaxations were made as regards tissue from deceased persons, though, not even (although the position is different in Scotland, see below) in respect of preserved tissue in blocks or slides residual to post-mortem examination. There might be ethical differences between tissues taken from deceased as opposed to living individuals, but the

---

[69] See M. Miyasaka, 'Resourcifying human bodies – Kant and bioethics' (2005) 8 *Medicine, Health Care and Philosophy* 19 at 23.

[70] C. Cohen, 'Selling bits and pieces of humans to make babies: *The Gift of the Magi* revisited' (1999) 24(3) *Journal of Medicine and Philosophy* 288 at 291 [Cohen, 'Selling bits and pieces']. Hair already severed from the head was regarded as being of little intrinsic significance in *Yearworth* v. *North Bristol NHS Trust* (12/3/08, Judge Griggs).

[71] C. Campbell, 'Body, self, and the property paradigm' (1992) 22(5) *Hastings Center Report* 34 at 36. However, whilst buying and selling gametes is permitted in the US, it is broadly regarded as impermissible across Europe. Policies relating to blood also differ considerably.

[72] G. Gillett, 'Ethics and images in organ transplantation', in P. Trzepacz and A. Dimatini (eds.), *The Transplant Patient: Biological, Psychiatric and Ethical Issues in Organ Transplantation* (Cambridge University Press, 2000) 239 at 239.

[73] Section 1(9). This was a concession eventually wrung out of the Government.

[74] Schedule 1 Part 2. There are also exceptions for 'existing holdings'; see sections 9 and 10.

legislative disparities in the 2004 Act may be best explained by the sensitivities and features of the recent organ and tissue retention scandals.

### Tissue blocks and slides

Tissue blocks and slides are within the ambit of the 2004 Act but, for limited purposes, outside the 2006 Act in Scotland. Tissue blocks are generated from small pieces of tissue or tissue from organs and placed in small plastic cassettes,[75] 80 per cent of the volume (water and fat) is replaced by paraffin wax, prior to being cut into extremely thin sections.[76]

The 2006 Act essentially adopts the recommendations of the Scottish Independent Review Group.[77] The Report of the Group asserted that the preparation of tissue blocks and slides is an important part of a thorough post-mortem examination, and that in the absence of a specific objection they should be seen as an integral part of the authorisation for the post-mortem itself.[78] The process has potential value for members of the family now or in the future, as well as conceivably being of major public health importance.[79] The Group drew on the endorsement of such a position in the Nuffield Council on Bioethics Working Party Report, *Human Tissue: Ethical and Legal Issues.*[80] The Act regards tissue samples and tissue blocks and slides as forming part of the medical record which may be used for research in the case of a non-forensic post-mortem without further authorisation. The Review Group drew an analogy between slides and X-rays.[81] This accords with the traditional perception of clinicians. In England and Wales, the Retained Organs Commission (ROC) conducted a consultation exercise relating to the status of tissue blocks and slides and ultimately issued a report and recommendations to the Department of Health as part of its review of

---

[75] Where blocks or slides are preserved there is ordinarily no need to also store organs or major pieces of tissues over the long term.

[76] In fact ten times thinner than a hair.

[77] Final Report of the Independent Review Group on Retention of Organs at Post-Mortem, 2000 [Final Report].

[78] Final Report, Summary of Recommendations, para. 33. It opined that it was unfortunate the brain (the brain must be fixed in formalin for around two weeks) and heart typically took longest to analyse, as they tended to have the most emotional significance to loved ones.

[79] Guidance has noted the role of the post-mortem in providing continuous NHS care even beyond the death of the individual, e.g. retrospectively influencing assessment of the cause of death; see 'Human Tissue (Scotland) Act 2006: A Guide to its Implications for NHSScotland', para. 33.

[80] Nuffield Council on Bioethics Working Party Report, *Human Tissue: Ethical and Legal Issues*, 1995, para. 4.5.

[81] Final Report, section 2, para. 70.

the reforms of the law in this area.[82] It observed, by contrast, that a 'record' is usually information about something or a copy of an item, not the actual parts of the thing itself. It preferred the phrase 'being related to the medical record'.[83]

A fundamental question posed by the Commission was whether there is any fundamental difference between tissue blocks and slides and other human organs and tissues. Has the process of replacing water and fat with paraffin wax changed the intrinsic character of the material? The Scottish Review Group had stated 'We have chosen to deal with tissue blocks and slides separately because we believe that they raise personal and professional issues which may be quite distinct from those associated with organs and major tissues',[84] and opined that 'the tissue is transformed so that it is well-nigh impossible to regard the material on the slide as meaningful human tissue'.[85] The Alder Hey Children's Hospital Inquiry Report also advocated 'a more liberal attitude with regard to the retention and use of tissue, particularly in the form of wax blocks and slides'.[86] ROC was much less sure, however, that tissue blocks and slides should be treated as a 'special case' and ultimately the Human Tissue Act 2004 drew no distinction between them and other forms of human cellular ('relevant') material.[87] This was principally on account of the fact that some relatives reacted angrily and with substantial grief to the knowledge that even minute amounts of material were retained without their specific consent.[88] Gere and Parry allude to the fracture of perceptions here: 'So it seems that, on the one hand, for many of the parents whose children's organs had been retained at Alder Hey, tissue blocks and slides were unambiguously parts of the body, corporeal entities endowed with all the spiritual and emotional significance carried by the human remains of beloved family members. For most members of

---

[82] Retained Organs Commission, *Tissue Blocks and Slides: A Consultation Paper*, November 2002 [ROC, *Tissue Blocks and Slides*]. Retained Organs Commission, *Tissue Blocks and Slides: A Consultation Note*, November 2002. Retained Organs Commission Recommendations on the Legal Status of Tissue Blocks and Slides. Advice Paper, June 2003.

[83] ROC, *Tissue Blocks and Slides*, para. 38.     [84] Final Report, section 2, para. 63.

[85] *Ibid.*, para. 70.

[86] Liverpool Children's Inquiry; see rlcinquiry.org.uk/download/index.htm, chapter 11, para. 3.3.

[87] The fact that such blocks might contain very small babies or whole or substantial parts of major organs was identified as a factor requiring attention. Moreover, it was felt that even if consent was not explicitly necessary for such retention, that some mechanism to take into account religious and cultural reservations might have to be put into place in any event. ROC, *Tissue Blocks and Slides*, para. 49.

[88] See Parry, 'The new Human Tissue Bill' at 75. Second and even third burials or cremations of remaining tissues were conducted by families of young children. The Cremation Regulations had to be amended to facilitate this.

the medical establishment, on the other hand, "blocks and slides constitute a medical record", something to be filed with case notes and temperature charts.'[89]

## Property and commerce

By contrast with the previous Human Organ Transplants Act 1989, which had only proscribed such activities in the context of organs, the 2004 Act seeks to ban commercial dealings in *all* cellular material for transplant ('controlled material'), a policy essentially replicated in the Human Tissue (Scotland) Act 2006.[90] In some countries a wider prohibitory ambit has been in effect for some while. We have seen already that the federal offence relating to interstate commerce in NOTA in the US defines 'human organ' very widely for this purpose. Some jurisdictions nevertheless do still apparently have proscriptions pertaining only to solid organs.[91]

Materials which are the subject of property because of an application of human skill are not however 'controlled' materials within the 2004 Act, generating the notion that some human material is either no longer human material or at least no longer human material *per se* (albeit having been derived from human material), in the same way perhaps as cell lines, which are exempted under the Act.[92] Cell lines are regarded as different from the cells which initially went into their development,[93] and human biological materials generally may therefore *become* some other material entity distinct from their original form; 'technological artefacts' as Parry dubs them.[94]

Parliament is by inference conveying its view that human tissue is *not*, ordinarily, property. There are various issues raised by this, but suffice it for the present to observe that where human cellular material has been the subject of the application of human skill it may be traded freely, and thus the notion of 'property' is being made to do some serious moral and legal work. Human material may not be traded; property derived from human material may be. However, as Parry opines, specifically in

---

[89] Gere and Parry, 'The flesh made word' at 43.
[90] Section 32(8)–(10). Regarding Scotland, see section 17, 2006 Act.
[91] Such as Spain, see section 2, Law No. 30 of 27 October 1979.
[92] Section 54(7). Cell lines are typically created by being infected with a virus, thereby 'immortalising' the cells.
[93] The majority in *Moore* v. *Regents of the University of California* 51 Cal. 3d 120, 793 P 2d 479, 271 Cal. Rptr. 146 emphasised that the cell line developed from Moore's cells was a different item from those cells themselves.
[94] Divested of their original organic form, they are, in Parry's words, 'bio-informational proxies'; see Parry, *Trading the Genome*, p. 72.

the research context, 'While this exemption is designed to place tech-
nologically produced human materials – such as cloned cells and cell
lines – beyond the jurisdictional reach of the Bill, it is not clear that there
will be widespread public support for exempting materials that are
derived from the human body (such as human cells) simply because
they are produced by a technological process. If the general public
consider it unacceptable to profit from a commercial use of a person's
cells they are unlikely to agree that it is acceptable to profit from the use
of their cloned cells.'[95]

The present broad legal position is piecemeal and anomalous.
Generally only commercial dealings in the context of transplantation
and/or artificial reproduction are legally proscribed.[96] The original
Human Tissue Bill would have extended to the research context as well,
but the Government was persuaded following substantial lobbying that
the pragmatic needs of researchers for brokers to source certain tissues
would be materially undermined by a broader prohibition. This exclusion
was made despite the sweeping proscriptive statement relating to financial
gain from body parts in Article 21 of the Council of Europe Biomedicine
Convention.[97]

In the US, although paying blood donors was halted in the 1970s,
plasma donors continue to be paid, in addition to which egg donors are
often very lucratively rewarded.[98] But not only are there arguably
potential balances and compromises necessary to secure an adequate
supply of human materials for some purposes,[99] it is not obvious that all
such materials should be treated alike anyhow. There is, as previously
mentioned, considerably less antipathy to the sale of discarded material
such as hair than to, say, a kidney, suggesting a complex intuitive
conception of the body. As Cohen remarks 'The reason we are reluctant to exchange money for human kidneys is that this would deny
something distinctly valuable about human beings – their dignity and
human worth ... Our body has special value because it is the medium
through which we express ourselves. Thus, our special value as human

---

[95] *Ibid.*, p. 83.
[96] See section 12, Human Fertilisation and Embryology Act 1990. In the US, the prohibitions in the UAGAs also apply only to transplantation.
[97] Council of Europe Convention, Article 21.
[98] Up to $8,000 per collection; see A. Friedman, 'Payment for living organ donation should
be legalised' (2006) 333 *British Medical Journal* 746 at 747. In the UK, egg-sharing
schemes whereby clinic fees are wholly or partially waived in return for donation of
spare embryos to other infertile couples have been endorsed by the Human Fertilisation
and Embryology Authority.
[99] In the UK, Parliament was persuaded that it was necessary to allow for-profit activities
linked to the procurement of certain difficult-to-source tissues for research.

beings extends to our bodies.'[100] Cherry argues that the more the
conceptual distance between persons and their body parts is increased,
the more body parts become like other objects in the world to be
possessed, given away, or sold.[101] This is suggestive of the (il)legiti-
macy of trading being linked to some notion of the closeness of various
body parts to identity and 'self'. Ironically though, some of the parts of
our bodies which we would identify as most precious to our integrity
and selfhood are the most needed and scarcest, e.g. organs for
transplantation.

---

[100] Cohen, 'Selling bits and pieces' at 291. Kant similarly based his view on the fact that it
was not conceivable to imagine a life not mediated by the body; see I. Kant, *Lectures on
Ethics*, trans. Louis Infield (New York: Harper & Row, 1963), pp. 147–8.

[101] M. Cherry, *Kidney for Sale by Owner: Human Organs, Transplantation, and the Market*
(Washington, DC: Georgetown University Press, 2005), p. 26.

# 2    Interests in the living body and corpse

This chapter critically considers the interests that living individuals have in their bodies whilst they are still alive and once they are dead, and those of the next of kin of deceased persons, and the relative weights of such interests compared with the needs of those requiring body materials for transplantation or of society in researching and developing knowledge of human conditions and their effective treatments. Where such interests exist then compelling reasons are required to override the normal respect which they warrant. This is a subject at the very heart of this work as it points to the proper system of donation which a society should adopt, in terms of whether it is necessary to obtain consent for donation, and from whom. Where an individual interest is infringed this constitutes a legal/moral harm to that person.[1] However, whilst no harm will accrue to an individual who has consented to it, at least not from a liberal or rights perspective, even consented-to acts may constitute *public* wrongs, proscribed by the criminal law.

Whilst such issues are problematic with regard to the taking and use of human material from the living, the issue of what interests exist with respect to the dead human form is hugely more contentious and the subject of considerably diverse opinion. This diversity manifests itself in varying attitudes to conscription, presumed consent, mandated choice, directed donation, required request and a host of other matters. Inconsistency and confusion in this regard has been harmful to both transplantation and research, and substantial deconstruction is essential. I entertain the interests of the living only, as the dead themselves are not in possession of interests capable of being affected by the actions of others. Nonetheless, prior to their deaths individuals have interests which are capable of being affected by the actions of others *after* their deaths, including with regard to decisions to donate or not

---

[1]  The civil law of torts (delict in civil law jurisdictions) reflects the underlying interest in the individual not being harmed.

to donate organs or tissues for therapy or research.[2] McGuinness and Brazier maintain that 'the living have interests in what happens to their dead bodies',[3] and declare that respecting the living means also respecting the dead. It is therefore the ante-mortem rather than the post-mortem person with whom we are concerned, and references to the 'deceased' are henceforward intended to refer only to the former. I propose for present purposes to gloss over the exact criteria that should be employed to distinguish the living and the dead and will simply accept that in this context the distinction is of crucial moral and legal relevance, whilst recognising the fact that there is no universal consensus on this matter.[4]

## Conscription

'Conscription', by which is meant the (routine) *removal* and use of organs and tissues for the requisite purpose(s) without the necessity for consent, is sometimes advocated as a means of overcoming the substantial shortage of organs for transplantation which exists in most jurisdictions. It is justified on the basis that such materials are needed by the living and that neither the living/deceased person, nor his/her surviving relatives in the case of the dead, have any overriding rights which are infringed by such routine removal and use.[5] Whilst such schemes are generally proposed with respect to body parts after death, some commentators similarly advocate it with regard to the living.[6] Such a policy is less often advanced in connection with tissues, which would appear to be largely a function of the general absence of shortage of tissues

---

[2] The failure to inquire into a death occurring in certain circumstances may even constitute a breach of the deceased person's European Convention rights; see, e.g., *Kennedy* v. *Lord Advocate and Scottish Ministers*; *Black* v. *Lord Advocate and Scottish Ministers* [2008] ScotCS CSOH 21 (5 February 2008).

[3] S. McGuinness and M. Brazier, 'Respecting the living means respecting the dead too' (2008) 28(2) *Oxford Journal of Legal Studies* 297.

[4] Commentators such as Truog, Youngner and Arnold have, however, questioned the relevance of the dead donor rule and suggested that reliance upon the ethical principles of autonomy and non-maleficence would serve us better. There are, however, difficulties in applying concepts with specific meaning for living entities to those without the essential qualities of living beings.

[5] See generally W. Glannon, 'The case against conscription of cadaveric organs for transplantation' (2008) 17 *Cambridge Quarterly of Healthcare Ethics* 330 and A. Spital and J. S. Taylor, 'In defense of routine recovery of cadaveric organs: A response to Walter Glannon' (2008) 17 *Cambridge Quarterly of Healthcare Ethics* 337.

[6] See, e.g., J. Harris, *Wonderwoman and Superman: The Ethics of Human Biotechnology* (Oxford University Press, 1992), pp. 100–3 [Harris, *Wonderwoman*].

for transplantation.[7] It is even occasionally suggested that there is such a duty in the context of research, although in this context it is wrapped up in the general notion of a duty to be a research participant.[8] Such proposals are radical and unlikely to curry much political favour in the short to medium term. Notwithstanding, discussion usefully focuses attention on the merits of the supportive and countervailing arguments. We should consider the living and the deceased separately.

### Living tissue banks

A duty to participate in medical research may appear less compelling than with regard to transplantation. Whilst the risks and harms associated with the use of tissue for research are less significant than those attaching to the removal of organs for transplant, at the same time the potential benefits are less immediate and certain. Harris nonetheless argues that we have a duty to put something back and to sustain social practices that benefit us, as well as to provide potential rescue to sufferers in the future, which might sometimes justify mandatory participation.[9] However, arguments from 'free riding', moral debt and rescue are ethically problematic in themselves, imposing demands upon individuals without the presence of clear moral obligations.[10] Whilst such participation is a moral good, the duty of rescue is an *imperfect* one, incorporating a discretion as to which means one wishes to pursue in order to help others.[11] This is quite apart from the potential additional 'costs' involved in taking human tissue from the body for such ends, as compared with participation in medical research in general.

In the context of transplantation, Harris advocated a survival lottery for the living as long ago as 1975.[12] This was similarly based on the notion of moral obligation or responsibility, and beneficial consequentialist considerations. Fabre analogously offers a rights-based theory of justice which requires individuals to give up organs to those in need,

---

[7] Although consent has not been universally required with respect to the further *use* of surplus tissues, i.e. tissue originally removed for therapeutic ends; see chapter 6.

[8] See, e.g., J. Harris, 'Scientific research is a moral duty' (2005) 31 *Journal of Medical Ethics* 242.

[9] *Ibid.*

[10] We could, for instance, meet a potential duty to rescue those who are suffering by various other means apart from involvement in research. See I. Brassington, 'John Harris' argument for a duty to rescue' (2007) 21(3) *Bioethics* 160.

[11] S. Shapshay and K. Pringle, 'Participation in biomedical research is an imperfect moral duty: A response to John Harris' (2007) 33 *Journal of Medical Ethics* 414.

[12] J. Harris, 'The survival lottery' (1975) 50 *Philosophy* 81. For a consideration of different types of lottery, see G. Overland, 'Survival lotteries reconsidered' (2007) 21(7) *Bioethics* 355.

in the same way that we are obliged to pay taxes for such monies to be distributed to those in financial and material need. The right to the resources one needs in order to live a minimally flourishing life (the principle of sufficiency) allegedly applies equally as against living as deceased persons, although confiscation of body parts from living persons would only be permissible to the extent that the person's autonomy (to pursue their conception of the good) was not unacceptably compromised. She states 'In so far as those who might need our body parts and personal services sometimes have a right to them, our right to personal integrity does not include a right to the exclusive use of our person'.[13] But such an uncompromising egalitarian position and analogies between body parts and one's 'external' material resources are unconvincing to many. Liberals, for instance, generally draw a boundary around the human body so that it does not form part of social resources at all.[14]

Even where it is considered there is a *moral* duty to give human material whilst alive to another needy, perhaps related, individual, the law will typically refuse to *compel* such a donation. In *McFall* v. *Shimp*, a Pennsylvania court refused to require a cousin to undergo bone marrow testing even though the relative's life was potentially at risk.[15] Although Flaherty J opined that the cousin's refusal was morally reprehensible, he declined to order it to be done, commenting on the unacceptable nature of a judicial order requiring an intrusion into a body and the concern as to where this might subsequently lead. Picking up on this, Judge LJ stated in his judgment in the English Court of Appeal in *St George's Healthcare NHS Trust* v. *S, R* v. *Collins, ex parte S* that any such order would irremediably damage the principle of self-determination.[16]

With regard to the living, consent for removal ensures not only protection of autonomy interests but those relating to respect for bodily integrity and physical welfare. It also indirectly protects the person's informational interests in so far as consent ensures that information with the potential for psychological harm may not be obtained from

---

[13] C. Fabre, *Whose Body is it Anyway?* (Oxford: Clarendon Press, 2006), p. 2 [Fabre, *Whose Body*]. The corollary as she sees it is that such persons should have a right, under some circumstances, to sell some of their body parts.

[14] See, e.g., R. Dworkin, 'Comment on Narveson: In defence of equality' (1983) 1 *Social Philosophy and Policy* 24 at 39.

[15] *McFall* v. *Shimp* 10 Pa D & C (3d) 90 (1978).

[16] *St George's Healthcare NHS Trust* v. *S, R* v. *Collins, ex parte S* [1998] 3 WLR 936 at 953D (CA).

collected human tissue without permission.[17] Andrews and Nelkin assert that 'A person's control over what is done to his or her body, or its parts, is important to his or her psychological development and well-being. It is a way of establishing personal identity and conveying values to others'.[18]

### Human recycling

Supporters of conscription from deceased donors note that existing schemes place a higher value on respecting individual and/or family autonomy than on maximising the recovery of organs and relieving suffering, whereas they would reverse this priority.[19] Harris, for instance, states 'it seems clear that the benefits from cadaver transplants are so great and the reasons for objecting so transparently selfish or superstitious, that we should remove altogether the habit of seeking the consent of either the deceased or relatives'.[20] He notes, as others have done, that societies allow post-mortem examinations to be conducted for forensic purposes without the need for any prior individual consent. Advocates point to the additional advantages of conscription in terms of cost, efficiency, avoidance of delays (which may compromise organ quality),[21] and the obviation of stress on healthcare staff who would otherwise have to request donation and on families who currently have to make such decisions at a traumatic time, i.e. to the promotion of effective and maximised organ recovery. It is undoubtedly the only policy which, theoretically at least, could come close to achieving a recovery rate of near 100 per cent.

Whilst some advocates argue that with respect to the dead there are no interests at all in the deceased which are capable of being defeated,[22] they maintain that in any event whatever interests exist are *outweighed* by the compelling and immediate interests of those requiring such

---

[17] However, such information may be more directly protected by data protection and confidentiality laws.

[18] L. Andrews and D. Nelkin, *Body Bazaar: The Market for Human Tissue in the Biotechnology Age* (New York: Crown Publishers, 2001), p. 13.

[19] A. Spital, 'Conscription of cadaveric organs for transplantation: Neglected again' (2003) 13(2) *Kennedy Institute of Ethics Journal* 169.

[20] Harris, *Wonderwoman*, p. 102.

[21] See A. Spital and J. S. Taylor, 'Routine recovery: An ethical plan for greatly increasing the supply of transplantable organs' (2008) 13 *Current Opinion in Organ Transplantation* 202 at 203; A. Spital and J. S. Taylor, 'Routine recovery of cadaveric organs for transplantation: Consistent, fair, and life-saving' (2007) 2 *Clinical Journal of the American Society of Nephrology* 300 at 301 [Spital and Taylor, 'Routine recovery'].

[22] Spital, Taylor, Erin and Harris all maintain that the notion of posthumous harm to a (pre) deceased person is a fallacy. See e.g. J. S. Taylor, 'The myth of posthumous harm'

materials for their welfare. Spital and Taylor, for instance, state 'But even if we are mistaken in our skeptical view of the concept of posthumous harm, this would not change our belief that routine removal of usable cadaveric organs is the way to go'.[23] Harris apparently concedes that 'deceased' persons do retain interests after death, but describes them as 'artificial' and of little consequence, easily outweighed by the needs of the sick. He states 'She is dead and past being harmed, *except in the relatively trivial sense* in which people possess interests that persist beyond their death and which can in some sense be harmed' [my emphasis].[24] The denial of any (significant) persisting interests of the deceased person might perhaps suggest that the family should be the appropriate decision-makers, based on their own interests or rights. Not only may the strong tendency in practice toward respecting the wishes of surviving relatives reflect such an intuition, but the right to respect for private and family life under Article 8 of the European Convention on Human Rights may be deemed to generate some autonomous sphere of decision-making here.[25] Spital, Taylor and Erin all admit that surviving relatives may have interests in avoiding distress and offence, but nevertheless claim that these are also overshadowed by the needs of the ill.

Whilst the key advocates of conscription typically prefer a mandatory system without 'exceptions', they sometimes declare themselves prepared to offer an 'opt-out' to those with 'the strongest reasons' for not wishing to become sources of organs after their deaths; notably those with 'conscientious objections'.[26] This reflects the utilitarian position of many of these proponents and recognition of the existence of exceptional individual interests in some instances, e.g. profound objections based on religious or other beliefs. Indeed, the right to respect for private life and for religious beliefs protected by Articles 8 and 9 of the European Convention on Human Rights, and by the First and

---

(2005) 42 *American Philosophical Quarterly* 311, A. Spital and C. Erin, 'Conscription of cadaveric organs for transplantation: Let's at least talk about it' (2002) 30 *American Journal of Kidney Diseases* 611.

[23] Spital and Taylor, 'Routine recovery' at 302.

[24] J. Harris, 'Organ procurement: Dead interests, living needs' (2003) 29 *Journal of Medical Ethics* 130 at 131.

[25] See A. Garwood-Gowers, 'Extraction and use of body materials for transplantation and research purposes: The impact of the Human Rights Act 1998' in A. Garwood-Gowers, J. Tingle and T. Lewis (eds.), *Healthcare Law: The Impact of the Human Rights Act 1998* (London: Cavendish, 2001) 295 at 308.

[26] E.g. Harris, see C. Hamer and M. Rivlin, 'A stronger policy of organ retrieval from cadaveric donors: Some ethical considerations' (2003) 29 *Journal of Medical Ethics* 196 at 196 [Hamer and Rivlin, 'A stronger policy'].

Fourteenth Amendments to the United States Constitution, may suggest the necessity for some latitude to be given.[27]

The policy of routine taking from the dead is frequently tied to the notion of easy rescue and individual responsibility, namely that one has an obligation to surrender body parts for necessary purposes after death on the basis that the benefits far exceed the normal burdens.[28] This rationale – if one accepts the premises and views contained within it – might also very plausibly apply to the taking of organs and tissues for medical research. This is, however, a conception of *moral* duties which, as we have already noted, do not always translate easily or straightforwardly into legal duties. Moreover, proponents may have undervalued the interests at stake for the donor/family, albeit that the tissue source is no longer alive, so that the rescue is not so 'easy' after all.[29] Another philosophy supporting routine removal here is distributive justice. Whilst Erin and Spital allude to this argument, it appears to be their secondary rather than primary rationale. Not so, however, for Fabre, who describes the duty to rescue as a duty of justice.[30] 'Routine removal' is often bolstered by the view that corpses are under the ownership or at least control of the state, to be used as appropriate.[31]

### State ownership/control

Glannon states that 'The idea that the sick have a right to cadaveric organs is grounded partly in the belief that these organs are no longer of any use to the dead. Viable and therefore useful body parts can be treated as state property.'[32] Calabresi has argued that the state already exercises the right to possess the bodies of individuals by way

---

[27] See, e.g., *Kohn* v. *United States* 680 F 2d 922 (2d Cir. 1982).

[28] R. Howard, 'We have an obligation to provide organs for transplantation after we die' (2006) 6 *American Journal of Transplantation* 1786.

[29] Where there are strong religious beliefs, for instance.

[30] See Fabre, *Whose Body*, p. 42. There may be little between these philosophical underpinnings. Fabre alludes to such duties generating rights in the sick to such body parts, see Fabre, *ibid.*, p. 100. However, she rejects a utilitarian focus.

[31] Harris contends that cadavers should be considered to belong to the state; see Harris, *Wonderwoman*, p. 102. Conscription need not necessarily be based on the notion of state ownership, though; see G. den Hartogh, *Farewell to Non-commitment: Decision Systems for Organ Donation from an Ethical Viewpoint*, Monitoring Report Ethics and Health, Centre for Ethics and Health, The Hague, 2008 at 43–4 [Den Hartogh, *Farewell to Non-commitment*].

[32] W. Glannon, 'Do the sick have a right to cadaveric organs?' (2003) 29 *Journal of Medical Ethics* 153 at 153 [Glannon, 'Do the sick have a right'].

of, *inter alia*, the military draft.[33] Whilst people seemingly regard organs and tissues as personal property when the person is still alive, they often regard them as societal resources after death.[34] Various commentators have alleged that our dead bodily remains are not our own to give and thus we have no rights of disposition over them. It may be seen that the body belongs to no one at all or that it belongs only to a supreme deity. Alternatively, some insist that we move away from notions of private ownership of the cadaver and argue that the current individual focus has resulted in a neglect of the importance of communities and relationships. Herring and Chau, for instance, argue that 'our bodies are not just ours', and stress the interconnectedness, interdependency and interaction of our bodies.[35] Indeed, some commentators have argued that the corpse should be seen as subject to some broader view of cultural or moral ownership, as part of what is required in terms of respect for living indigenous communities.[36]

Some societies deny the existence of private property at all and regard all property as vesting in the state (i.e. public ownership). State/collective ownership amounts to 'quasi-ownership' only, though, and is constrained by pre-determined uses, duties and limitations in the interest of the public as a whole.[37] Heller states that

State property, also called collective property, can be defined as a property regime in which 'in principle, material resources are answerable to the needs and purposes of society as a whole, whatever they are and however they are determined, rather than to the needs and purposes of particular individuals considered on their own. No individual has such an intimate association with any object that he can make decisions about its use without reference to the interests of the collective.'[38]

These constraints in the context of human materials for transplantation can be regarded as rooted in obligations owed to specific (sick) members

---

[33] G. Calabresi, 'Do we own our own bodies?' (1991) 1 *Health Matrix* 5 at 7.

[34] R. Truog, 'Are organs personal property or a societal resource?' (2005) 5(4) *American Journal of Bioethics* 14. The US Task Force on Organ Transplantation, *Organ Transplantation: Issues and Recommendations*, Washington, DC: Department of Health, Education, and Welfare, 1986, considered that after death donated organs belong to the community.

[35] J. Herring and P.-L. Chau, 'My body, your body, our bodies' (2007) 15(1) *Medical Law Review* 34 at 35.

[36] See K. McEvoy and H. Conway, 'The dead, the law, and the politics of the past' (2004) 31 (4) *Journal of Law and Society* 539.

[37] See J. W. Harris, 'What is non-private property?', in J. W. Harris (ed.), *Property Problems: From Genes to Pension Funds* (Dordrecht: Kluwer Law International, 1997) 175 at 180–3.

[38] M. Heller, 'The dynamic analytics of property law' (2001) 2 *Theoretical Inquiries in Law* 79 at 85.

of the community.[39] Emson's perception is of a process of natural recycling of human body parts into future generations through decay, decomposition and transference, and that the 'right of control over the cadaver should be vested in the state as representative of those who may benefit from organ donation'.[40] He rejects the idea that the person has a right to govern disposal of their body after death, when separation of body and soul is irrevocably complete.[41]

By contrast, many egalitarian liberals and libertarians agree that we have a right to control what happens to our bodies and that others lack a right to any of our body parts, no matter how great their need, even after death.[42] Sperling remarks 'More generally, it will be argued that members of the human community have elementary interests which must not be sacrificed or overridden for the sake of collective welfare or other goals in society. One such interest is the interest in having one's body left alone unless proper authorization is given.'[43] To some observers societal ownership of organs conjures up impressions of the totalitarian state. The British Organ Donor Society (BODY) contends that 'It would be wrong to say a body belongs to the nation to do with whatever it likes. It would be completely alien to the culture of the land',[44] a remark equally apposite to many other nations and societies.[45] The idea of the 'gift' is an essential and intrinsic element of donation and is incompatible with body parts belonging to another, whether the state or a specific (sick) individual. The entitlement to give (and to withhold) provides the basis for the notion of consent.

### Interests of the living

There is generally no dispute that, with respect to the removal of organs or tissues from adult individuals either for transplantation or research, it is the interests and wishes of the individual living donor him/her self that are exclusively determinative. This is reflected universally in official

---

[39] As some have noted, individuals get (medically) sick, societies do not.
[40] H. Emson, 'Is it immoral to require consent for cadaver organ donation?' (2003) 29 *Journal of Medical Ethics* 125 at 125.
[41] *Ibid.*, at 126.
[42] Fabre, *Whose Body*, p. 2. It has been asserted that there is a 'special tie' between individuals and their bodies; see Den Hartogh, *Farewell to Non-commitment* at 23.
[43] D. Sperling, *Posthumous Interests: Legal and Ethical Perspectives* (Cambridge University Press, 2008), p. 117 [Sperling, *Posthumous Interests*].
[44] See http://news.bbc.co.uk/hi/english/health/newsid_281000/281404.stm.
[45] See the remarks of the German National Ethics Council in its Opinion, *Increasing the Number of Organ Donations: A Pressing Issue for Transplant Medicine in Germany*, Berlin, 2007 at 36.

policies. In order to protect such interests, the donor's consent in such circumstances is invariably perceived to be a 'given', as a reflection of respect for persons and their right to self-determination. The views of relatives, family members and friends are of no formal relevance as regards living adults with decision-making capacity (however defined in the relevant legislation), although those with parental responsibility may make donation decisions on behalf of their minor offspring, or at least such minors lacking decision-making capacity.

This stance is principally driven by the potential invasion of physical integrity involved in removal, rather than any broader conception of autonomy. The further 'use' of the material following its removal becomes somewhat subsumed by this imperative. Yet, with respect to medical research in particular it is very often the *subsequent use* which is the crucial moral and legal issue.[46] It was this concern which arose in *Moore* v. *Regents of the University of California*.[47] Whilst the California Supreme Court considered that John Moore should have been told about the intended further (research/commercial) use of his cancerous spleen – as a function of the fiduciary duty and duty of informed consent owed to him – it held that he had no property interest in the tissue which had been surgically removed, and thus no continuing interests in or control over it. The interests protected were thus tied to the point of 'removal' as opposed to the subsequent use and retention. The outcome was, however, heavily influenced by policy considerations relating to the availability and utility of tissues for medical research, and may therefore have been context-specific and potentially inapplicable in the context of living donor transplantation.[48]

Some of the reasoning in *Moore* was endorsed by the Nuffield Council on Bioethics Working Party Report in the United Kingdom in 1995,[49] which based its preferred view with respect to surplus tissue upon the concept of abandonment.[50] This approach was rejected in the Human Tissue Act 2004, which incorporates a general requirement for 'appropriate consent' by living persons to the storage and use of their biological

---

[46] Analogous issues arise with respect to tissue originally removed for different research purposes.

[47] *Moore* v. *Regents of the University of California* 51 Cal. 3d 120, 793 P 2d 479, 271 Cal. Rptr. 146.

[48] See B. Dickens, 'Living tissue and organ donors and property law: More on *Moore*' (1992) 8 *Journal of Contemporary Health Law and Problems* 73.

[49] Nuffield Council on Bioethics Working Party Report, *Human Tissue: Ethical and Legal Issues*, 1995, Nuffield Council, London. It asserted that the Court had appeared to find that the patient had abandoned his tissue in that case, see para. 9.12 [Nuffield Council, *Human Tissue*].

[50] *Ibid.*, at para. 9.14.

material for either research or transplantation.[51] It was asserted by Government spokespersons during the Parliamentary debates on the Bill that the provisions were premised on the right to control the use of such material, even surplus material.[52] However, the Bill subsequently came to include an exception with respect to the use of non-identifiable surplus material from the living in research ethics committee-approved research studies.[53] This sizeable vacuum in the consent requirements generates the perception that the interests being protected here are those relating only to physical/psychological harm, and informational privacy.[54] However, as Gitter remarks

> It is incorrect to assume that because the sources cannot be identified they cannot be harmed or wronged … Individuals have an interest in avoiding uses of their tissues they regard as morally impermissible or objectionable. Thus, were their materials to be used in research that they would consider objectionable, it is possible that some individuals could be wronged, if not harmed.[55]

This is a matter to which I shall return in chapter 6.

## Interests pertaining to deceased donation

We shall examine here the interests of the dead; but who or what is the 'dead person' for these purposes? Is this not a contradiction in terms? Jonsen states 'consent is ethically important because it manifests and protects the moral autonomy of persons … [and] it is a barrier to exploitation and harm. These purposes are no longer relevant to the cadaver, which has no autonomy and cannot be harmed.'[56] On this view, to require the consent of (now) dead people to protect their existing interests is

---

[51] There are provisions catering for individuals lacking decision-making capacity to be 'donors' of organs or tissues for therapy or research; see section 6. In some instances, such use would be in their own best interests. See Human Tissue Act 2004 (Persons who Lack Capacity to Consent and Transplants) Regulations 2006 SI 2006 No. 1659.

[52] See Dr Ladyman, House of Commons Hansard Debates, Standing Committee G, col. 65, 29 January 2004.

[53] Section 1(9).

[54] The German National Ethics Council also appears to have reduced the significant individual interests in anonymised tissue down to those in informational privacy and confidentiality; see German National Ethics Council Opinion, *Biobanks for research*, Berlin, 2004 at 46.

[55] D. Gitter, 'Ownership of human tissue: A proposal for federal recognition of human research participants' property rights in their biological material' (2004) 61 *Washington and Lee Law Review* 257 at 287.

[56] A. Jonsen, 'Transplantation of fetal tissue: An ethicist's viewpoint' (1988) 36 *Clinical Research* 215. Iserson also comments that 'corpses no longer are individuals, and so they cannot be the basis for either autonomy or informed consent. They are merely symbols'; K. Iserson, 'Life versus death: Exposing a misapplication of ethical reasoning' (1994) 5 *Journal of Clinical Ethics* 261 at 262.

nonsensical. The Law Reform Commission of Canada (LRC) has, however, asserted:

[T]he utter disregard of one's burial wishes, or the failure to honour one's express wishes on the post-mortem uses of one's body, lend credence to the claim that people have interests that survive their deaths and that they may be harmed when the interests are violated. What remains refractory is providing a coherent philosophical explanation of this intuition.[57]

I argue that this is not mere pre-theoretic intuition but a view grounded in straightforward ethical principles. The sentiments expressed by the LRC are seemingly reflected in widespread official policies and laws relating to transplantation and research. Thus, when we speak of the autonomy of dead people we are, instead, alluding to the autonomy of the once living person who has now died. Sperling asserts 'The act of organ donation should be regarded as enhancing the autonomy and self-expression of the donor and expanding – not abolishing – the self'.[58] The idea that one's self and the desire for aspects of one's *person* to be emphasised after death are bound up with donation decisions relating to body parts is both pervasive and persuasive. It is our last *personal* legacy. Unlike experiential interests, 'critical' interests (to use Ronald Dworkin's terminology) can be defeated after death; and surviving interests after death can be an integral part of one's life plan.[59] Wicclair urges that we should not regard death as signifying the total annihilation of all 'moral traces' of the person who once was.[60] And as the Retained Organs Commission (ROC) remarked

In a number of faiths, the treatment of the dead is as important as the treatment of the living. The values by which the deceased lived deserve respect just as society respects their wishes as to disposal of property by honouring last wills and testaments.[61]

---

[57] Law Reform Commission of Canada, *Procurement and Transfer of Human Tissues and Organs*, Working Paper 66, Law Reform Commission of Canada, 1992 at 45 [LRC of Canada, *Procurement and Transfer*].

[58] D. Sperling, 'Me or mine? On property from personhood, symbolic existence and motivation to donate', in W. Weimar, M. Bos and J. Busschbach (eds.), *Organ Transplantation: Ethical, Legal, and Psychosocial Aspects* (Lengerich: Pabst Publishing, 2008) 463 at 470.

[59] See Glannon, 'Do the sick have a right' at 154.

[60] R. Dworkin, *Life's Dominion* (London: Harper Collins, 1993), pp. 199–217. Belliotti notes that one may considerably orient one's existence toward the legacy one will leave for one's loved ones, especially toward the end of one's time; see R. Belliotti, 'Do dead human beings have rights?' (1979) *The Personalist* 201 at 206 [Belliotti, 'Do dead human beings have rights']. See also M. Wicclair, 'Ethics and research with deceased patients' (2008) 17 *Cambridge Quarterly of Healthcare Ethics* 87 at 88 [Wicclair, 'Ethics and research with deceased patients'].

[61] Retained Organs Commission, *Remembering the Past, Looking to the Future*, NHS, 2004, para.1.21 [ROC, *Remembering the Past*].

It has already been noted that even those who support organ conscription frequently offer 'concessions' to those with profound religious views militating against donation.

Some commentators nevertheless maintain that all that we are concerned with here is the fact that *prior to death* such individuals (or individuals in general) may be affected by the knowledge that their bodies may (not) be dealt with in a particular way after death,[62] that even as regards the willing of property after death it is merely pre-posthumous contentment and/or the proper and efficient ordering of things that is reflected in official policies, i.e. prudence or utility, as opposed to any *moral* entitlement. But whilst this may be a part of why they should be respected, it is not the principal reason. I argue that this not merely understates the significance and nature of the interests at stake,[63] but also fails to appreciate their *persisting character* beyond death.

There are, notwithstanding, some who maintain that the dead, *whilst dead*, possess interests.[64] There are various constructions of this view, based on existence in an alternative form (e.g. in an afterlife), timeless existence or some other analogous construct. Hamer and Rivlin contend that 'Clearly the dead person cannot be harmed: all that remains of him is his material body. To avoid this problem we must think of the person not simply in terms of his present condition but from an objective and timeless perspective.'[65] But this is counter-intuitive to the extent that the person is not perceived to be rooted in any particular time or space. Other formulations also require beliefs not universally shared. Sperling advances the notion of a 'subject holding interests' after death, which is a different *conceptualisation* of the form in which one exists.[66] He argues that even after death organ and tissue donation represents a manifestation of *the interest in the recognition of one's symbolic existence*, in immaterial, second-order, terms. The 'human subject' maintains a link with the living person and 'holds' all human interests belonging to the former person whose interests they are. Sperling appears to be driven by a problem-solving imperative to

---

[62] Belliotti rejects this notion that what happens to us posthumously affects only how we think about things whilst we are still alive. He suggests this is a confusion of thinking one's interests will be fulfilled after one dies and such interests actually being then fulfilled; see Belliotti, 'Do dead human beings have rights?' at 206.

[63] See M. Wicclair, 'Informed consent and research involving the newly dead' (2002) 12(4) *Kennedy Institute of Ethics Journal* 351.

[64] See, e.g., F. Feldman, *Confrontation With the Reaper – A Philosophical Study of the Nature and Value of Death* (Oxford University Press, 1992); H. Silverstein, 'The evil of death' (1980) 77(7) *Journal of Philosophy* 401.

[65] Hamer and Rivlin, 'A stronger policy' at 198.     [66] Sperling, *Posthumous Interests*.

overcome the inherent philosophical and jurisprudential difficulties connected to the absence of an existing moral or legal 'person' after death. But even for him, existence after death is essentially 'symbolic', and it is unclear how the 'human subject' in such a form is capable of 'holding' the person's interests, or what nexus must exist with that (original) person. Whilst death fails to sever emotional, biological and psychological links with surviving kin and loved ones, the dead can only *represent* the previous person, not reflect the same or analogous moral or legal status as the once living person. Whilst it is not possible to formulate a definitive ontological status of those who are dead, I maintain the orthodox view that the dead themselves have no interests. They are not persons in their own right and are not themselves directly part of the moral community.[67]

The same procedures may, however, have different moral and legal connotations depending upon whether they are performed upon a living person or a corpse. Whilst we do still regard the integrity of the cadaver as of importance, for various reasons, these are not connected to physical or psychological harms or present well-being and therefore have different implications. Wilkinson remarks 'The interest in bodily integrity is clearly changed by death, even if it does not disappear, as we can see when we consider that while people cannot consent to being dismembered while alive, they can consent to being dismembered after death'.[68]

### Posthumous harms

To many, the idea of posthumous harm is illusory. Its acceptance necessarily forces confrontation with two central interrelated philosophical problems: the 'no-subject' and 'backward-causation' objections.[69] One requires actual harm to a proper subject occurring at a specific point in time. Firstly, it is argued that there is 'no subject' in whom interests may vest, and thus anyone able to be harmed, after death. Partridge, for instance, maintains that the notion of interests surviving death is

---

[67] Other have, however, disputed this; see, e.g., B. Brecher, 'Our obligations to the dead' (2002) 19(2) *Journal of Applied Philosophy* 109 at 113 [Brecher, 'Our obligations']. He argues that as a 'person' is a moral construction dead 'persons' are capable of being the locus of moral obligations and part of the moral community. See also A. Baier, 'The rights of past and future persons', in E. Partridge (ed.), *Responsibilities to Future Generations* (Buffalo, NY: Prometheus Books, 1980).

[68] T. Wilkinson, 'Last rights: The ethics of research on the dead' (2002) 19(1) *Journal of Applied Philosophy* 32 at 34 [Wilkinson, 'Last rights'].

[69] Martin Wilkinson convincingly asserts that these issues all relate to the question of who the subject is (personal communication). However, I will consider them separately here for (supposed) clarity.

incoherent, as there is no ... one who can be harmed at the point that any wrongful setback of interest occurs.[70] Secondly, even if a person had interests *prior* to death which might be set back by actions taking place after death, no harm can occur retrospectively. Waluchow remarks

Similarly, when I do whatever it is that sets back the interest of the antemortem person (perhaps I break the promise or violate the conditions of his will), I do not make it true that his interests *were* set back. Rather, I make it true that the interests he had are *now* set back. The setting back takes place now, not then. At most we can say that back then it was true that the interests were going to be set back.[71]

These perceived temporal and causal lacunae suggest that there are only flimsy reasons for respecting the wishes of the pre-posthumous (living) person. Yet, we do seemingly perceive harms as befalling individuals *themselves* by way of various posthumous events, such as the unauthorised organ retention practices of previous years. As Hamer and Rivlin have remarked 'The idea that posthumous events can institute harms has enormous intuitive plausibility'.[72]

### No subject

There are two connected matters here: the identity of the potentially harmed subject and the nature of any potential 'harm' which might accrue. It has already been denied that dead individuals may be harmed by posthumous events, which necessitates a focus upon potential harm to the once living person by events occurring after death. But can individuals be harmed by having their interests thwarted or set back when they lack the ability to contemporaneously 'experience' such harm? And what interests may living persons have which survive their deaths?

A satisfactory explanation of how even the wrongful causing of someone's death may harm them has eluded very many commentators. Yet most people undoubtedly perceive a harm to have occurred, possibly the worst harm that can befall one. Indeed, a harm *to that person*, not merely to society in general. For both Feinberg and Li, if a person can be harmed by their own death then necessarily they can be harmed by certain posthumous events.[73] Similar philosophical obstacles are

---

[70] E. Partridge, 'Posthumous interests and posthumous respect' (1981) 91 *Ethics* 243.

[71] W. Waluchow, 'Feinberg's theory of "preposthumous" harm' (1986) 25 *Dialogue* 727 at 731 [Waluchow, 'Feinberg's theory'].

[72] Hamer and Rivlin, 'A stronger policy' at 198.

[73] See J. Li, *Can Death be a Harm to the Person who Dies?* (Dordrecht: Kluwer, 2002), p. 7 [Li, *Can Death be a Harm*].

encountered here. The first challenge is from those who regard death as not being a harm because it is not experienced. Epicurus stated 'Death ... the most awful of evils, is nothing to us, seeing that, when we are, death is not come, and, when death is come, we are not'.[74] It is then problematic to explain how an instantaneous and painless wrongful killing can be a harm to the person who is rendered no more by that very same action. However, mental state accounts of harm are unconvincing, as many commentators have shown.[75] One can, for instance, steal property from, and harm, a person who is blissfully unaware that this has occurred. In the Court of Appeal in *Airedale NHS Trust* v. *Bland*, Lord Justice Hoffmann stated

I think the fallacy in this argument is that it assumes that we have no interests except in those things of which we have conscious experience. But this does not accord with most people's intuitive feelings about their lives and their deaths. At least part of the reason why we honour the wishes of the dead about the distribution of their property is that we think it would wrong them not to do so, despite the fact that we believe that they will never know that their will has been ignored ... We pay respect to their dead bodies and to their memory because we think it an offence against the dead themselves if we do not.[76]

Feinberg distinguishes want satisfaction and want fulfilment, arguing that even if unaware whether a wish is fulfilled or not, a harm can occur by virtue of its non-fulfilment *per se*.[77] A non-experiential conception is able to capture the essence of failures to respect the previously expressed autonomous wishes of living individuals (i.e. advance decisions) who presently lack any awareness, such as those in a permanent vegetative state. It is the wishes of the once mentally competent person which have been defeated. Such rights 'survive' the individual's loss of capacity, sentience and awareness. However, whilst the entitlement to have such wishes respected has transcended time, the (legal) person is still in existence in such scenarios; albeit that some regard the later non-competent individual to be frequently lacking personhood, or to be morally a different 'person', or to have a different personal identity; which would infer that it was the *former*

---

[74] Epicurus (341–270 BC), *Letter to Menoeceus*, in G. Russell (trans.), *Letters, Principal Doctrines and Vatican Sayings* (New York: Macmillan, 1964). J. Fischer (ed.), *The Metaphysics of Death* (Stanford, CA: Stanford University Press, 1993) at 95.

[75] See Sperling, *Posthumous Interests*, p. 11 and S. Kagan, *Normative Ethics* (Boulder, CO: Westview Press, 1998), pp. 34–5 [Kagan, *Normative Ethics*].

[76] *Airedale NHS Trust* v. *Bland* [1993] 1 All ER 821 at 829.

[77] J. Feinberg, *The Moral Limits of the Criminal Law*, Vol. I, *Harm to Others* (Oxford University Press, 1984), p. 84 [Feinberg, *Harm to Others*].

person/self rather than the later person/self that was the subject of the harm.[78]

In so far as death is the first moment that the person ceases to exist, there is then no person in existence at the requisite moment in time to be harmed.[79] Thus, it is argued that no one exists who dies, and death cannot be a harm to a living individual. If we see harm or loss in causal physical terms alone the difficulty is self-evident. We cannot 'know' our own loss. The most convincing explanation of how death may harm a person lies however in the *deprivation* thesis, i.e. that death deprives the living person of all the goods that they might otherwise have achieved, including the fulfilment of some of their previously formulated, future-oriented desires.[80] Feinberg states 'To extinguish a person's life is, at one stroke, to defeat almost all of his self-regarding interests: to ensure that his on-going projects and enterprises, his long-range goals, and his most earnest hopes for his own achievement and personal enjoyment, must all be dashed'.[81] Desires regarding the use of one's cadaver after death are future-oriented and capable of being, only being, thwarted after death, i.e. when one has ceased to be. Steinbock states that 'The fulfilment of these wants is as much a part of their good as the fulfilment of wants while they are alive'.[82] Whilst generally subjective wishes and desires may not always be sufficient to ground moral interests, where the non-fulfilled desire is in our objective interests a harm may have arisen. But in the (posthumous) context under consideration there is little or no daylight between desires and objective interests, as our wishes are other-regarding in any event and there are no contemporaneous issues of well-being implicated. Li in any case argues that desires can in some circumstances be the basis of harms in themselves, i.e. future-oriented dependent unconditional desires.[83]

---

[78] See A. Buchanan, 'Advance directives and the personal identity problem' (1988) 17(4) *Philosophy and Public Affairs* 277; H. Kuhse, 'Some reflections on the problem of advance directives, personhood and personal identity' (1999) 9(4) *Kennedy Institute of Ethics Journal* 347.

[79] Levenbook attempts to navigate the problem by redefining harm in terms of 'loss' at the moment of death, rather than interests; see B. Levenbook, 'Harming someone after his death' (1984) 94 *Ethics* 407. However, Callahan describes this as mere 'loose talk', remarking that if death is the first moment of non-existence then at that moment there is also no longer a person; see J. Callahan, 'On harming the dead' (1987) 97 *Ethics* 341 at 343 [Callahan, 'On harming the dead']. See also 'Death' in *Stanford Encyclopaedia of Philosophy*, at http://plato.stanford.edu/entries/death/ at 2.2 [Death].

[80] See, e.g., T. Nagel, 'Death', in T. Nagel (ed.), *Mortal Questions* (Cambridge University Press, 1979).

[81] Feinberg, *Harm to Others*, p. 82.

[82] B. Steinbock, *Life Before Birth* (Oxford University Press, 1992), p. 25.

[83] Li, *Can Death be a Harm*, p. 69.

Glannon, however, contends that 'states of affairs that do not affect the body or mind cannot harm the person whilst alive'.[84] He contends that harming involves *comparison* between earlier and later states of body and mind, and alleges that interests which survive death are merely impersonal and cannot result in harm. On this view, any 'change' which occurs in the individual after death is at most what is known linguistically as a 'Cambridge change'; one that does not cause any *real* change, i.e. one which affects no intrinsic property of the person and thus is not 'person affecting'.[85] I nevertheless believe that we *can* make sense of harming someone after her death. The ante-mortem harm for our purposes is the defeating of the right to exercise control over the disposition of one's cadaver. The so-called 'wound model' of harm is too limited.[86] Although commentators such as Glannon consider that a person cannot be affected by events which have no 'impact' upon them, this would appear to be founded upon a notion of well-being consisting of existing mental or physical states. However, there are alternative conceptions of well-being, wherein a person's well-being can be measured as a function of the achievement of desires or preferences.[87] These are immune to criticisms relating to absence of contemporaneous effect on physical or psychological well-being.[88]

### Backward causation

The counterintuitive concept of backward causation raises its head in this connection. To many, it is concerns relating to retroactivity which are the primary stumbling blocks to recognition of posthumous harms.[89] Feinberg and Pitcher, however, argue that one does not *cause* harm to the ante-mortem person by thwarting a relevant interest after death. Pitcher asserts, 'On my view, the sense in which an ante-mortem person is harmed by an unfortunate event after his death is this: the occurrence of

[84] W. Glannon, 'Persons, lives, and posthumous harms' (2001) 32(2) *Journal of Social Philosophy* 127 at 128. He distinguishes between the goodness or badness of a person's life and things which affect *persons*.

[85] See P. Geach, *God and the Soul* (South Bend, IN: St. Augustine's Press, 1969), pp. 71–2. See also D. Hillel-Ruben, *Action and its Explanation* (Oxford University Press, 2003).

[86] See 'Death' at 3.1.

[87] See Kagan, *Normative Ethics*, pp. 36–7. See also 'Death', *ibid.*

[88] Belliotti observes that 'A human being's interests can be analyzed in two ways: to say X has an interest in Y may mean (i) that Y, on balance, improves X's well-being (or opportunity from well-being) or (ii) that X desires, wants or seeks Y'; see Belliotti, 'Do dead human beings have rights' at 201.

[89] Wilkinson states 'We can make sense of harming someone after her death in the same way that we can make sense of remembering someone after her death'; see Wilkinson, 'Last rights' at 34. However, we typically regard harming as affecting *the* individual.

the event makes it true that during the time before the person's death, he was harmed – harmed in that the unfortunate event was going to happen'.[90] It is nonetheless counterintuitive to see a person as 'harmed all along'.[91] Feinberg alludes to *logical* as contrasted with *physical* causation. This would appear to be entirely apposite in so far as non-satisfaction of one's wishes would not, even in the normal course of things, necessarily result in any physical loss or intrinsic change in the person. He states

All interests are the interests of some person or other and a person's surviving interests are simply the ones that we identify by naming *him*, the person whose interests they were. He is of course at that moment dead but that does not prevent us from referring now, in the present tense, to his interests. If they are still capable of being blocked or fulfilled, just as we refer to his outstanding debts or claims, as if they are still capable of being paid. The final tally book on a person's life is not closed until some time after his death.[92]

He maintains that it is absurd to think that once a promisee has died, the status of a broken promise made to him whilst alive suddenly ceases to be that of a serious injustice to a victim, and becomes instead (only) a more diffuse public harm.[93] Brecher notes that there is nothing awry or counterintuitive, or even controversial, about such a view.[94] We merely need to take into account events occurring after death in determining whether the person's surviving interests were properly respected. This seems compelling.

On the choice theory of rights, a failure to respect choices relating to the subject-matter of one's rights is in itself the basis for the wrong. Whilst one cogent reason for denying certain choice-based rights after death is the inability to waive or demand the performance of duties after death,[95] the ante-mortem person might be capable of doing so prior to death. Indeed, Sperling, whilst preferring the interest view of rights, states 'In principle, there should be no conceptual difficulty for the choice theory to acknowledge the exercise of such powers, thereby validating the holding of rights

---

[90]  G. Pitcher, 'The misfortunes of the dead' (1984) 21(2) *American Philosophical Quarterly* 183 at 187. He refers to the casting of a 'shadow of misfortune backward over the person's life'.

[91]  It implies, for instance, that the fact that one's football team loses at a weekend means that even before the weekend it was true that that team would lose. See B. Magee, *Confessions of a Philosopher* (London: Phoenix, 1997), pp. 5–6.

[92]  Feinberg, *Harm to Others*, p. 83.

[93]  *Ibid.*, p. 95. Even Aristotle accepted that these failures to respect wishes expressed prior to death are not mere 'public wrongs', although he considered the harm involved to be fairly negligible; see Aristotle, *Nicomachean Ethics*, trans. J. Thomson (Baltimore, MD: Penguin Books, 1953), I.10 para. 1.

[94]  Brecher, 'Our obligations' at 111.

[95]  See C. Fabre, 'The choice-based right to bequeath' (2001) 61 *Analysis* 60 at 64.

by the dead'.[96] It would seem that the right to control the use of one's body, even after death, is quite sufficient to ground such a right, although one must distinguish 'mere choices' from choice-protected rights. In addition there is a rights-based argument from interests here, although again, as Sperling asserts 'A distinction needs to be made between having an interest in the realization of a state of affairs and having a legal or moral claim to the realization of that state of affairs'.[97] Feinberg insists that the thwarted desire which gives rise to harm be a desire in which the person has an 'investment'.[98] Although individuals no longer have any surviving welfare interests after death, our previously formulated desires regarding the posthumous use of the corpse would appear to be intimately connected to our essential 'selves' in the broadest sense. Indeed, in so far as our corpses are our property after death for these purposes, as I shall later maintain, our desires clearly link to our interests and our right to control our bodies after death.

One central problem relates to the idea of interests persisting when the holder of such interests no longer does. Whilst we are concerned with rights, we can appropriately view such rights as triggering surviving *duties* which persist beyond death, even though the holder of such rights has now ceased to exist. Sperling suggests that it is internally inconsistent to endorse persisting duties but not persisting rights.[99] Wellmann, however, alludes to 'rights that impose future duties', and argues that whilst individual *rights* cannot survive the right-holder's death, duties generated by such rights can persist thereafter in order to impose on-going, future obligations on others.[100] He states 'But this need not be to ascribe rights to the dead; it can and should be to assert that the rights of the living continue to impose duties even after the persons who possessed those rights have ceased to exist'.[101] Perhaps this can be seen in the survival of certain contractual duties following the death of the other contracting party (promisee).[102]

---

[96] Sperling, *Posthumous Interests*, p. 69. He argues that this view is not plausible, however, where decision-making on behalf of the deceased is *objective*, p. 71.

[97] *Ibid.*, p. 10. Penner contends that our interests, unlike our desires, are necessarily related to a critical understanding of values; see J. Penner, *The Idea of Property* (Oxford University Press, 1997), p. 10. According to Raz, an interest generates rights when it is sufficiently important enough to place another under a duty; see J. Raz, *The Morality of Freedom* (Oxford: Clarendon Press, 1988), p. 166. See also Wilkinson, 'Last rights' at 32.

[98] Feinberg, *Harm to Others*, p. 33.

[99] Sperling, *Posthumous Interests*, p. 61. He suggests that posthumous duties *imply* posthumous rights.

[100] C. Wellmann, *Real Rights* (Oxford University Press, 1995), p. 156 [Wellmann, *Real Rights*].

[101] *Ibid.*

[102] Apart from with respect to 'personal' contracts, contractual rights and liabilities are automatically assigned to personal representatives on the death of a promisee.

Waluchow rightly remarks that harmed conditions and harmful events are usually temporally co-incident.[103] Li nevertheless notes that the question of when the harm event occurred is a different and conceptually separate one from the question 'when was the person harmed by it?'.[104] He notes that harm itself, as opposed to suffering, is an abstract idea not located in either space or time.[105] Moreover, assessments of causation *in law* are inherently flexible in order to accommodate intended policy. Harms might be attributed retrospectively to once living persons as opposed to being projected forward onto future persons at the moment of their first existence, as analogously occurs in the context of liability for pre-natal injuries at common law.[106] Alternatively, perhaps, laws might justifiably adopt 'fictions' to reflect the same outcome, in the same way that the civil law traditionally utilises them to ascribe harms to newborns resulting from events occurring prior to birth and to confer respect for testamentary wishes *vis-à-vis* unborn children.[107]

## Crimes against the dead

As Veatch once remarked, 'The dead body has unlimited use for the imaginative living'.[108] The common, as well as the civil, law has nevertheless been extremely vague regarding the legality of acts or procedures performed upon the dead, including those for societally useful purposes such as research or therapy. So much so that it is invariably accepted as necessary for legislation to be enacted setting out an explicit authorisation for such procedures to be performed. Legislation authorising anatomical examinations, post-mortem examinations, transplantation, research, etc., are legion around the world, dating back in the former case to the early nineteenth century, e.g. Anatomy Act 1832. Such legislation was and is *permissive* in character, clarifying the conditions for its legality, providing confidence to professionals and society as a whole that procedures conducted according to such conditions are legitimate. This explains the decidedly piecemeal development of many laws affecting procedures performed upon the cadaver. But whilst performing such procedures

---

[103] Waluchow, 'Feinberg's theory' at 730.
[104] Li, *Can Death be a Harm*, p. 93.      [105] *Ibid.*, p. 89.
[106] See, e.g., *B* v. *Islington Area Health Authority* [1992] 3 All ER 832 (CA).
[107] See I. Kennedy and A. Grubb, *Medical Law*, 3rd edn. (London: Butterworths, 2001), p. 1503 and R. Paisley, 'The succession rights of the unborn child' (2006) 10(1) *Edinburgh Law Review* 28.
[108] R. Veatch, 'The newly dead: Mortal remains or organ bank?', in R. Veatch (ed.), *Death, Dying and the Biological Revolution* (New Haven, CT.: Yale University Press, 1989) 197 at 199.

without satisfying the legislative pre-conditions (e.g. consent) typically constitutes a specific offence, this does not serve to clarify what wrongs are committed where they are not. How are the dead, or others, harmed thereby? Why is any procedural (i.e. consent), or other substantive, justification required at all?[109]

It is often remarked that there is no wrong committed where actions are directed towards a corpse. Whilst some jurisdictions have general offences of mistreatment of the cadaver many, including the UK and various jurisdictions in the US, do not.[110] During the debates on the Human Tissue Bill the Health Minister remarked that the new legitimating provisions, allowing for cooling and preservation procedures to be carried out on the corpse immediately after death where no consent could be solicited at that time, were strictly unnecessary as no wrong would result in any event.[111] However, if so, this begs the question why there would be any need for consent for removal and use for research, transplantation and analogous uses themselves. Spencer highlights a major anomaly under existing UK law. He notes that the Human Tissue Act 2004

will make punishable, with substantial prison terms, doctors, medical research-workers and similar enemies of society who, without appropriate consent store or use bodies or parts of them in the course of activities such as medical research, medical treatment and training doctors ... they will leave unpunished, as before, those who mutilate or desecrate human bodies for other and less savoury ends; such as black magic, perverted sexual pleasure, malice, or a desire to shock or offend.[112]

In other words, whilst it is an offence to carry out extremely societally useful activities using body parts without proper consent, it is not unlawful at all to do many things to corpses without any social utility or even

---

[109] Veatch argues that any intrusive procedure carried out on the corpse without consent is *prima facie morally* wrongful. R. Veatch, 'Consent for perfusion and other dilemmas with organ procurement from non-heart-beating cadavers', in R. Arnold, S. Youngner, R. Shapiro and C. M. Spicer (eds.), *Procuring Organs for Transplant: The Debate over Non-Heart-Beating Cadaver Protocols* (Baltimore, MD: Johns Hopkins University Press, 1995) 195 at 201.

[110] The US Model Penal Code 1962, section 250.10, contains the offence of 'abuse of a corpse', which has been enacted in some form in at least fourteen states; see T. Ochoa and C. Jones, 'Defiling the dead: Necrophilia and the law' (1997) 18 *Whittier Law Review* 539 at 560 [Ochoa and Jones, 'Defiling the dead'].

[111] R. Winterton MP, House of Commons Hansard Debates, Standing Committee G, col. 238, 5 February 2004.

[112] J. Spencer, 'Criminal liability for desecration of a corpse' [2004] 6 *Archbold News* 7 at 9. Although the 2004 Act creates offences relating to improper storage or use of body parts, there is no such crime committed if such body parts are maliciously destroyed; see R. Nwabueze, 'Donated organs, property rights and the remedial quagmire' (2008) 16(2) *Medical Law Review* 201 at 207 n. 28.

contrary to the public interest.[113] Even some of the more egregious types of conduct either remain legitimate or have only recently been declared illegal. In the US, necrophilia is still not explicitly unlawful in most jurisdictions and became an offence in England and Wales only with the passing of the Sexual Offences Act 2003.[114] Cannibalism seemingly still remains lawful after death in many jurisdictions to this day. Only a few jurisdictions have general offences relating to the mistreatment of the dead. The incongruence of the current legal patchwork is both amazing and indefensible. Herring has remarked that 'there is no coherent approach to the nature of the wrongs that are committed when the bodies of the dead are maltreated'.[115] There is certainly a widespread view that at least certain forms of conduct involving corpses are not only immoral but should be illegal. As Quay remarks 'Something at the roots of our own being demands that we treat the corpse with reverence'.[116] Is the law simply deficient and lacking in some jurisdictions, then, or is it that an absence of such offences points to the typical absence of harm resulting from most or all forms of conduct relating to the deceased?

Both the Nuffield Council on Bioethics Working Party Report, *Human Tissue: Ethical and Legal Issues*,[117] and the Dutch Health Council Report, *Proper Use of Human Tissue*,[118] recognised that the central ethical principle was respect for human lives and the human body and that the nature and utility of the activity are factors which bear on its ethical acceptability. The former stated that some uses of human tissue, such as cannibalism (except *in extremis*) and use for the production of human leather or soap, were ethically unacceptable *per se*, whether the person is dead or alive.[119] Thus, it is an *a priori* question whether the activity is ethically appropriate in the first place. Only if it is do other potential conditions of legitimacy, such as consent, arise.

The Nuffield Council Report stated that 'Removal of tissue from a corpse may constitute degradation unless it is *either* governed by a direct

---

[113] It was reported, for instance, that a Muslim woman's corpse was wrapped in bacon. See 'Desecrated body family could sue', 6 April 2004, BBC Newsonline, 2004.

[114] See Section 70, Sexual Offences Act 2003 and Ochoa and Jones, 'Defiling the dead'. It is expressly an offence in only thirteen states. In Canada, it would seem to fall within the general offence of offering indignity to a dead body under section 182(b) of the Criminal Code; see *R* v. *Ladue* (1965) 4 CCC 264 [CA].

[115] J. Herring, 'Crimes against the dead', in B. Brooks-Gordon, F. Ebtehaj, J. Herring, M. Johnson and M. Richards (eds.), *Death Rites and Rights* (Oxford: Hart Publishing, 2007) 219 at 219.

[116] P. Quay, 'Utilizing the bodies of the dead' (1984) 28 *Saint Louis University Law Journal* 889 at 902 [Quay, 'Utilizing the bodies of the dead'].

[117] Nuffield Council, *Human Tissue*, chapter 6.

[118] Health Council of the Netherlands Report, *Proper Use of Human Tissue*, 1994.

[119] Nuffield Council, *Human Tissue*, para. 6.2.

or indirect therapeutic intention *or* part of accepted funerary rites'.[120] But what 'wrong' results when there is no therapeutic objective and the activity is not related to accepted funerary rites? The LRC states that 'The duty to respect the dead body is a duty not to violate its intrinsic dignity and humanity'.[121] The Nuffield Report similarly stated, with regard to inherently unacceptable uses, that 'The most widely accepted reasons, however, often stress that these sorts of action fail to respect others or to accord them dignity, that they injure human beings by treating them as things, as less than human, as objects for use'.[122] This equates with Kantian notions of persons being inappropriately used as 'mere means' and translates into a duty not to violate the corpse without good cause. Beyleveld and Brownsword distinguish the notion of dignity as *empowerment* from that of dignity as *constraint*, with the dignitarian position linked to the latter.[123] It is no answer to the view that such persons are being used only instrumentally that consent has been given, as the dignitarian duty-based perspective regards such actions as *essentially* instrumental. Jones has alluded to the idea that 'the human race is demeaned when one of their kind (even though now dead) is treated in a less-than-human way'.[124] Thus, whilst societies do not penalise immoral conduct *per se*, they uphold a baseline concept of respect. Addressing the objection that moralism is typically regarded as an insufficient rationale for criminalisation, Beyleveld and Brownsword state that 'if we recast the terms of this debate, we can say that Devlin's position is that, even in secular societies, there will be a collective understanding of human dignity; and that, where particular forms of conduct seriously compromise human dignity as understood in a particular society, then that society legitimately takes steps to regulate the offending conduct'.[125]

---

[120] *Ibid.*, para. 6.29. Public revulsion, for instance, recently occurred in the US with the news that a crematory in Georgia had dumped corpses in the grounds to decompose. See generally Wicclair, 'Ethics and research with deceased patients' at 90. Religious beliefs and tenets and other intra-societal factors may influence such matters. For instance, whilst cremation is regarded as the appropriate form of disposal for Hindus, it is burial that is the appropriate method for Muslims.

[121] LRC of Canada, *Procurement and Transfer* at 182.

[122] Nuffield Council, *Human Tissue*, para. 6.7. Some commentators, however, argue that the independent concept of dignity is vacuous; see, e.g., R. Macklin, 'Dignity is a useless concept' (2003) 327 *British Medical Journal* 1419.

[123] D. Beyleveld and R. Brownsword, *Dignity in Bioethics and Biolaw* (Oxford University Press, 2002) [Beyleveld and Brownsword, *Dignity*].

[124] D. Jones, *Speaking for the Dead* (Aldershot: Ashgate, 2000), p. 87. Chadwick states that 'Our treatment of the corpse symbolises not only respect for the individual whose corpse it is but also for human life in general'; R. Chadwick, 'Corpses, recycling and therapeutic purposes', in R. Lee and D. Morgan, *Death Rites* (Oxford: Routledge, 1994) 54 at 62.

[125] Beyleveld and Brownsword, *Dignity*, p. 35.

Indeed, some jurisdictions have broad offences couched in terms of either 'indignity' or 'disrespect', such as the offence in section 182(b) of the Canadian Criminal Code of offering 'any indignity to a dead human body or human remains'.[126] With respect to the dead there is the perception that these offences are principally designed to protect the interests of society in general. The LRC stated that 'Concern over the moral integrity of the community has been a traditional basis in definitions of criminal mistreatment of the dead body or human remains'.[127] The US Model Penal Code, however, sees the essence of the general offence of abuse of a corpse as based upon the potential effects on families. It states that 'Except as authorized by law, a person who treats a corpse in a way that he knows would outrage ordinary family sensibilities commits a misdemeanour'.[128] It is suggested below, though, that the wrongs done to relatives are derivative from the wrong done to the predeceased person whose corpse it represents, although remedies may sometimes be properly available to relatives based on the causing 'profound offence'.[129]

### Interests of relatives

In practice, family members and others close to an adult deceased person are the central actors in the decision-making process. Similarly, parents of minors. The organ and tissue retention scandals at British hospitals testify to the ferocity with which relatives, especially parents (and spouses), jealously protect their role(s) in this sphere. We should thus enquire what moral and legal interests relatives possess in this context.

It may be argued that the body of the deceased person *belongs* to close relatives. Giordano, for instance, refers to 'shared others' who can be seen as 'part' of the surviving relatives.[130] Apart from the distinctly unsettling prospect of individuals, albeit dead persons, being able to be utterly owned by others, the uncertainty generated as a consequence should be disquieting. Do relatives have 'collective' powers or does the corpse belong only to certain close relatives, or *a* close relative alone? If the former, decision-making could be cumbersome and unwieldy, and if the

---

[126] The Canadian Criminal Code states in section 182(b) that 'Everyone who ... improperly or indecently interferes with or offers any indignity to a dead human body or remains, whether buried or not, is guilty of an indictable offence'.

[127] LRC of Canada, *Procurement and Transfer* at 109.

[128] Section 250.10 US Model Penal Code (1962).

[129] J. Feinberg, *Offense to Others* (Oxford University Press, 1985), pp. 50–96 [Feinberg, *Offense*].

[130] S. Giordano, 'Is the body a republic?' (2005) 31 *Journal of Medical Ethics* 470. Hyde notes that the implication of a 'body' is its separateness; see A. Hyde, *Bodies of Law* (Princeton, NJ: Princeton University Press, 1997), p. 9.

latter, questions would be raised as to who the particular individual's 'close relatives' might be. One could draw up a legislative hierarchy, as in the case of the Human Tissue Act 2004 and comparable Australian legislation, but the potential open-endedness of such powers should give pause for thought. Kamm is of the opinion that only ownership could yield a moral and legal right to donate, yet she is properly dubious about any rights of ownership vesting in relatives.[131]

A recent Dutch Report opined that the strongest justification for giving relatives a power to decide is that they have the greatest interest in the decision, but concluded that this would suggest that they should also be able to overrule the deceased's explicit consent, when this is not formally permitted by legislation, including in the Netherlands.[132] The Report ultimately asserted that the relatives' power to decide where the deceased has not made any decision cannot be justified under any of the moral starting points considered, including that underpinning the Dutch legislative policy, unless it has been explicitly delegated to them prior to death. It remarks 'The Organ Donation Act system is bankrupt: there is absolutely no justification whatsoever for making delegation to the next of kin the default, and this deficit is not even compensated by an adequate yield'.[133] Whilst relatives have interests linked to their special ties to the deceased, it concludes that although the next of kin are entitled to have their interests taken into consideration they cannot claim any authority to decide on these grounds.[134] Kamm likewise argues 'Neither caring most, nor the fact that they will be comforted by keeping or giving an organ, would seem to be a strong enough basis for a moral and legal right to decide'.[135] Indeed, she notes that such relatives may not in fact care enough.

The decision to defer to relatives may perhaps be seen as a utilitarian strategy to maximise the procurement of organs and tissues, i.e. a means of ensuring minimally adequate levels of donation, bearing in mind that deceased persons generally fail to make their own decision before their demise and the absence of effective mechanisms available for directly recording their wishes.[136] This is plausible to the extent that reliance

---

[131] F. Kamm, *Morality, Mortality. Volume 1* (Oxford University Press, 1993), p. 211 [Kamm, *Morality, Mortality*].

[132] Den Hartogh, *Farewell to Non-commitment* at 14.    [133] *Ibid.*, at 71.

[134] *Ibid.*, at 54. He argues that relatives have no entitlement to 'gift' parts of the deceased after death which the individual himself declined to do prior to death; *ibid.*, at 38.

[135] Kamm, *Morality, Mortality*, p. 211.

[136] Den Hartogh, *Farewell to Non-commitment* at 25. Kamm states 'A policy that allows the family to override an original owner's desire to donate may seem to exhibit a willingness, out of respect for family wishes, to tolerate loss of some organs. However, if it is known

upon only the expressed wishes of deceased persons to donate in an explicit consent system would undoubtedly result in a substantially reduced volume of donated materials for both purposes. It is broadly conceded that a greater percentage of individuals are willing to donate their organs or tissues after death than have explicitly stated this wish prior to their demise. Of course, such a rationale could cut both ways, though, as deferring to family *might* perhaps result in a lower volume of donation than would otherwise be the case. In any event, such a rationale fails to embed such interests in any moral entitlement.

The broad decision-making role of relatives afforded in practice appears to flow at least partially from their protective role towards the corpse in ensuring its respectful treatment, and their duty – where this legally exists – to dispose of the dead body.[137] Richardson notes that the protection of the physical body is a pervasive feature of popular death customs, i.e. that the corpse is treated with due care and reverence out of respect for the person whom the corpse now represents.[138] A failure to permit this role to be exercised was emphasised by some of the parents of affected children at Alder Hey Children's Hospital, with one parent stating that 'I feel like I failed to protect him even in death'.[139] This function is particularly associated with parents but extends to relatives in general. Quay, however, retorts that the only rights that relatives have with respect to the corpse 'are those that stem from common safety, common decency and interfamilial solidarity – none of which creates any independent basis for giving or donating the cadaver, still less for utilizing it or selling it'.[140] The 'right' of disposal is in any case strictly speaking a duty rather than a right. As Sperling comments 'However, a closer examination of this situation reveals that what is at issue is not X's rights, but rather X's *claims* vis-à-vis third parties such as the state, physicians or the coroner not to interfere with the duty that X owes to Y'.[141] It would therefore appear to be a *non sequitur* to derive *personal* dispositional rights from obligations to handle the corpse for a specific end, in the same way that we do not allocate such powers to coroners despite their duty to conduct post-mortems in specific instances. The perceived protective role of relatives cannot be analogised

---

that families are more likely to donate than original organ owners, giving the family power is really, over all, a policy for increasing organs donated'; Kamm, *Morality, Mortality*, p. 202. See also p. 223.

[137] In jurisdictions such as the UK and Canada such a duty vests as regards adults in the executors or, failing that, the administrators, but in some other jurisdictions, including the US, relatives have primacy in this matter.

[138] R. Richardson, *Death, Dissection and the Destitute* (University of Chicago Press, 2000).

[139] See *Daily Mail*, 26 November 1999.

[140] Quay, 'Utilizing the bodies of the dead' at 906.

[141] Sperling, *Posthumous Interests*, p. 96.

with the best interests function of those concerned with the interests of *living* persons without decision-making capacity either, as the deceased has no present welfare interests in need of protection. The role of relatives is better seen as a limited stewardship function linked to the disposal of the corpse.

Notwithstanding, where decision-making powers are conceded to relatives, there is no doubting the difficulty and potential sensitivity of a relative's decision to permit donation. Such decisions not only come at a time of profound grief but also when the bereavement process has already begun. Relatives may find it difficult to accept the death,[142] especially where it is unexpected or sudden, which may make focusing on such an issue hugely problematic.[143] In addition, because death may seem incongruous to many even where it has been confirmed by brain death testing – on account of the pink and respiring character of the corpse[144] – agreeing to the removal of organs for transplantation in particular may seem itself to confer a finality that is otherwise absent.[145] Based on their empirical work, Sque, Payne and Clark observed that 'Families appeared, at great emotional cost to themselves, reluctant to "let go" and relinquish their guardianship and ability to protect the body, even if it meant offering a lifeline to recipients'.[146] They state that families of organ donors should be firstly seen as *bereaved* families.[147] This highlights the fact that ordinarily this

---

[142] Indeed, Callahan argues that we are only able to identify with pre-mortem states; see Callahan, 'On harming the dead'.

[143] Research with families revealed that most often families make decisions collectively. They want decisions to be shared and do not wish the onus to fall on any single individual. See M. Sque, T. Long, S. Payne and D. Allardyce, *Exploring the End of Life Decision-making and Hospital Experiences of Families Who Did Not Donate Organs for Transplant Operations. Final Research Report for UK Transplant.* University of Southampton, 2006 at 25 [Sque *et al*, *Exploring the End of Life Decision-making*].

[144] Kellehear argues that medical and societal perspectives of the time of death are in tension; see 'Call to revamp death definition' at news.bbc.co.uk/2/hi/health/6987079. stm.

[145] See M. Sque, 'A dissonant loss: The bereavement of organ donor families', in M. Sque and S. Payne (eds.), *Organ and Tissue Donation: An Evidence Base for Practice* (Maidenhead: Open University Press, 2007) 59 at 68.

[146] M. Sque, S. Payne, and J. Clark, 'Gift of life or sacrifice? Key discourses for understanding decision-making by families of organ donors', in M. Sque and S. Payne (eds.), *Organ and Tissue Donation: An Evidence Base for Practice* (Maidenhead: Open University Press, 2007) 40 at 49 [Sque, Payne and Clark, 'Gift of life or sacrifice?']. Co-ordinators in England and Wales report the need to protect the body of the deceased as the most common reason for family members declining to agree to organ donation; see Mr Roy Thomas (Kidney Wales Foundation) and Ms Jayne Fisher (Chair of the UK Transplant Co-ordinators' Association), giving oral evidence to the House of Lords European Union Committee, see *Increasing the Supply of Donor Organs within the European Union, Volume II: Evidence* (HL Paper 123-II) at 59 and 120.

[147] Sque *et al*, *Exploring the End of Life Decision-making* at xiii.

decision is a very testing and emotional one. It has been suggested that it more closely approximates to a 'sacrifice' than an ordinary 'gift'.[148]

Whilst the most plausible basis for allowing relatives to decide is on the basis of potential and serious distress, Wilkinson points out that if this were a persuasive rationale across the board it should enable relatives 'to donate' even despite the deceased's own objection, where distress would be caused to the relatives by *not* donating.[149] Yet, neither officially nor in practice does such a view hold sway. It solely provides a ground for a veto. Whilst it is illuminating to consider why relatives are not permitted to override a deceased's *objections* no matter how vigorously they may react to such a decision,[150] realistically distress would be unlikely to result from a *failure* to remove material for such purposes.[151] Such a rationale *is* consequently plausible in the context of a (weak) presumed consent scheme where the deceased had not opted out (indeed the British Medical Association would allow a relative to veto donation where severe distress would otherwise result),[152] and might just possibly even justify a veto in an explicit consent jurisdiction where the deceased had explicitly consented to donate, although the latter is more contentious in view of the explicit assertion of the right to self-determination here.[153] Hence any sweeping decision-making power afforded to relatives would be too broad for the protection of these (allegedly) legitimate interests, i.e. where it extends to a power to positively donate material as well as to veto a removal. The responsibility of professionals to facilitate families coming to terms with the death of loved ones should not automatically subsume the right to make the donation decision. Indeed, severing such a responsibility may itself assist rather than hinder the grieving process.

Nonetheless, close relatives and family have interests in promoting the autonomous wishes of the deceased. In a society where deceased persons

---

[148] Sque, Payne and Clark, 'Gift of life or sacrifice?' at 40. See also A. Mongoven, 'Sharing our body and blood: Organ donation and feminist critiques of sacrifice' (2003) 28 *Journal of Medicine and Philosophy* 89.

[149] T. M. Wilkinson, 'Individual and family consent to organ and tissue donation: Is the current position coherent?' (2005) 31 *Journal of Medical Ethics* 587 at 588 [Wilkinson, 'Individual and family consent'].

[150] After all, the same rationale for permitting refusal by relatives cannot apply to the deceased. The deceased cannot suffer *distress* as a consequence of donation being permitted.

[151] Wilkinson draws attention to the important distinction between positive and negative rights in this context; see Wilkinson, 'Individual and family consent'.

[152] See www.bma.org.uk/health_promotion_ethics/organ_transplantation_donation/Organ Donation1108.jsp.

[153] Indeed, in Belgium the law provides that although organ donation is lawful where the deceased had not opted out relatives are nonetheless entitled to veto donation, but that where the deceased had explicitly opted in no such power of veto exists.

are seen as having the primary 'say' in whether and how their organs and tissues are used after death, relatives' interests are potentially implicated derivatively in relation to consent. Where relatives are afforded decision-making powers in the donation context, these *derive* from the rights of the deceased person. Kamm asserts

> But we seem not to be justified in locating in the next of kin a fundamental right to make donation decisions, other than those based on the principle of substituted judgment, especially decisions that override an original owner's dominant will to donate.[154]

Assuming for the present that the wishes of the deceased person are the crucial determinant of the legitimacy or otherwise of donation, relatives may have a role as either *the*, or at least *a*, conduit for the transmission of information regarding such wishes. Where there is an absence of a registry or donor/non-donor card or other mechanism for formally recording one's wishes prior to death, the family will generally be *the* mechanism by which such wishes may be made known and potentially respected, and even where one or both exist they may have an essential role as a *supplementary* source of information. In such circumstances, if relatives are permitted to decide as regards donation they should decide on the basis of such known wishes. Indeed, as stated above, to permit donation in the face of a refusal by the deceased person is universally unlawful. However, in most jurisdictions relatives are allowed in practice to decide such matters and to decide to refuse to donate on any basis whatever, whether this accords with the wishes of the deceased or otherwise. There is no legal obligation to reflect the deceased's wishes. Relatives should, however, be required to decide on the basis of the principle of substituted judgement, as is the case in Germany, where there is a duty to decide this matter according to the 'presumed wishes' of the deceased person.[155]

Feinberg argues that, consistent with a rights-based liberal system, one can accommodate criminal offences based on 'offence' as well as harm. He states that 'profound offence' offends because the conduct that occasions it is believed to be wrong, it is not believed to be wrong simply because it offends someone. The offence is parasitic on the harm done to the now deceased. Thus, we are not dealing with wounded feelings *per se*. Regarding a scenario where a woman's dead husband's face was smashed to bits during a scientific experiment conducted in the absence of consent, he comments

> Her grievance is personal (voiced on her own behalf) not simply because her moral sensibility is affronted (she has no personal *right* not to have her moral sensibility affronted) and she cannot keep *that* out of her mind, but rather because it is *her*

---

[154] Kamm, *Morality, Mortality*, p. 223.     [155] Law of 5 November 1997, section 4(1).

husband, and not someone else. In this quite exceptional kind of case, the person-ally related party is the only one whose rights are violated, though many others may suffer profound offense at the bare knowledge.[156]

The relationship is crucial and explains the deep wounds inflicted on many relatives by some of the organ retention practices recently revealed. As Campbell and Willis remark 'For the lay person disrespectful treat-ment of the body of a loved one represents a personal attack'.[157] Feinberg maintains that profound offence warrants the intervention of the criminal law even when 'the moralistic case is severed from their argument',[158] and would also form the basis for the availability of a civil action for relatives who have suffered as a consequence.[159] Relatives are themselves poten-tially wronged by such conduct as a product of the illegitimacy of such actions themselves or as a consequence of the denial of their decision-making functions on behalf of the deceased, as well as where the decea-sed's own wishes are thwarted or rejected. No 'wrongful offence' can, however, arise where the relative's objection was at odds with the wishes of the deceased. There is no right here that is overridden.

### Children and parental rights

Where children are sufficiently mature to possess donation decision-making capacity, they should be treated analogously to adults in this context. In England and Wales, so-called '*Gillick* competent' minors are able to decide to donate or refuse to donate organs or tissues for trans-plantation or research or various other purposes after their death as before their death.[160] A person with parental responsibility may consent or

---

[156] Feinberg, *Offense*, p. 69. It has been argued that such a notion may be incorporated anyhow within the 'harm' principle, by virtue of the indirect psychological harm caused; see A. Simester and A. von Hirsch, 'Rethinking the offense principle' (2002) 8 *Legal Theory* 269 at 283.

[157] A. Campbell and M. Willis, 'They stole my baby's soul: Narratives of embodiment and loss' (2005) 31 *Medical Humanities* 101 at 101. Medical training may explicitly seek to inculcate a 'convenient' Cartesian psychology, to distance the individual from the physical being, to allow practices such as anatomical dissection to be routinely carried out. These authors, however, note that this conception contributed to the failures of communication at Bristol and Alder Hey, etc.

[158] Feinberg, *Offense*, p. 69.

[159] However, such actions are difficult to successfully maintain across most jurisdictions, often due to the difficulty in establishing the existence of psychiatric harm.

[160] *Gillick* v. *West Norfolk Health Authority* [1986] AC 112 (HL). Minors are those under eighteen. This is implicit rather than explicit in the Human Tissue Act 2004, however, although such a position was frequently alluded to in the debates on the Bill; see, e.g., Lord Warner, House of Lords Hansard Debates, col. GC50 11 October 2004. See also M. Brazier and S. Fovargue, 'A brief guide to the Human Tissue Act 2004' (2006) 1 *Clinical Ethics* 26 at 26.

refuse to consent where the minor lacked decision-making capability.[161] There are no age thresholds specified.[162] By contrast in Scotland, there are provisions in the Human Tissue (Scotland) Act 2006 permitting children over twelve years of age to give an 'authorisation' (as it is coined there in preference to consent) for such ends, and for persons with parental rights and responsibilities to be permitted to give an authorisation in respect of children under twelve years of age and as regards children over twelve years of age who had not previously made their own authorisation.[163] In the US, the Uniform Anatomical Gift Act 2006 states that adults aged eighteen years or over may make anatomical gifts, as can minors who are either emancipated or entitled by virtue of their age to apply for a driver's licence under relevant state law.[164]

With regard to children, especially younger children, without capacity to make their own decisions, the Report of the Scottish Independent Review Group on Retention of Organs stated 'It is absolutely clear to us, as it was to the inquiries held in England, that parents must have overriding authority in respect of consent to hospital post-mortem examinations in respect of young children', adding 'It must be equally clear that they have exactly the same authority in respect of the removal and retention of organs and major pieces of tissue'.[165] The Review Group considered that the right to consent could not be based upon the duty to protect the best interests of their deceased children, as it regarded such a concept as 'inherently inappropriate' and without clear application to deceased individuals.[166] Its views about parental entitlement after death were founded on 'an analysis of the family unit and in particular to the obligations and powers which flow from the notion of parenting itself'.[167] It concluded by stating 'Recognising the intimate bond between parent and child, and the privacy of the family unit, allows us to reinforce the priority of parental decision-making for their young children even after death'.[168]

The Report alludes to both Page's view of parental rights stemming from the nature of parenthood as a special value, and independent simply from the function of caring and protecting their children *per se*, and to Schoeman's ideas of 'connectedness': 'We share ourselves with those with whom we are intimate.'[169] Wilkinson is critical of both views. He rejects

---

[161] Section 2, Human Tissue Act 2004.
[162] See D. Price and A. Garwood-Gowers, 'Transplantation using minors: Are children other people's medicine?' (1995) 1(1) *Contemporary Issues in Law* 1.
[163] Sections 9 and 10.     [164] Section 4, Uniform Anatomical Gift Act (UAGA) 2006.
[165] See Final Report of the Scottish Independent Review Group on Retention of Organs, 2000, at section 1, para. 11 and section 53.
[166] *Ibid.*, section 1, at para. 12.     [167] *Ibid.*, section 1, at para. 15.
[168] *Ibid.*, section 1, at para. 16.     [169] *Ibid.*

the notion that such decision-making powers may rest on the 'personal' interests of the parents themselves or that such a role may be linked to the protection of the interests of such children themselves, as they no longer have any interests persisting after death, at least where the children are too young during their lives to have any conception of death and posthumous organ/tissue donation.[170] He also dismisses the idea that parents have property rights over the dead bodies of their children, and argues that it is dubious to assert an interest in parenthood which extends to control over dead bodies as there is no further role in shaping such children's lives nor any intimacy or connectedness with the dead.[171] He maintains that the only direct reason for obtaining the consent of parents is to avoid distressing them. But once more this merely grounds a power of veto rather than a broader entitlement to consent/authorise.

Whilst it is indeed the case that many young children have no surviving autonomy interests of their own, it would seem to be too dismissive to reject the proxy decision-making role of parents surviving the deaths of their children. The vigour with which the parents at Bristol and Alder Hey in particular reacted to the neglect of their views, and to secrecy and to deceit, testifies to their perceptions of their role – indeed, duties, – in this regard. It is their relationship to the child which is societally viewed as conferring decision-making powers, and which includes decisions relating to the use and proper disposal of the child's remains.[172] They stand in the child's 'decision-making shoes' in almost all cultures and societies. Brazier has identified various, overlapping, interests that parents may have in their dead child.[173] Arguably such interests may found a *prima facie* human right to respect for one's private or family life under Article 8 of the European Convention on Human Rights. This allows for the protection of the family unit through respect for the views of parents as guardians of the family's values, as well as protection for the parents' interests as parents. This would seem to provide for parents to make donation decisions *for* their deceased children.

### Concluding remarks

The autonomy of the tissue source has been systematically undervalued in this context, including after death. Whilst an increased pervasiveness of

---

[170] See also D. Knowles, 'Parents' consent to the post-mortem removal and retention of organs' (2001) 18(3) *Journal of Applied Philosophy* 215.

[171] T. Wilkinson, 'Parental consent and the use of dead children's bodies' [2001] 11(4) *Kennedy Institute of Ethics Journal* 337 at 344–6.

[172] It would appear that parents have such a duty in virtually all Western jurisdictions.

[173] M. Brazier, 'Organ retention and return: Problems of consent' (2003) 29 *Journal of Medical Ethics* 30 at 31.

consent requirements has partially rectified this in certain jurisdictions, especially in the context of research upon the living, there remains an inherent vagueness and ambiguity as to the interests which consent seeks to protect and a tension between the decision-making powers of relatives and their deceased kin. It is crucial that the source of authority for donation is located in the tissue source and that the law protects the interests of donors and their right of control of such material.

# 3    Eliciting wishes

As Healy states 'The key question of consent in organ procurement is essentially one about the source and degree of authority over the dead: *Who*, in principle, controls the decision to procure?'[1] In this chapter we are primarily considering deceased donors, in so far as it is unambiguously the entitlement of competent living patients rather than others to generally determine the use of their body parts. I seek to address this question of 'whose wishes count', to explore the relative weight to be afforded to the wishes of the various actors, and how these should be prioritised and balanced in the event of differences. This necessarily reflects the interests identified in chapter 2, transplanted into a concrete, practical context. Although very much of the material below emanates from the transplantation sphere, it is equally generalisable to the research context.

### Who is the donor?

The 'donor' is typically equated to the 'primary decisionmaker'. For instance, Healy states 'In practice, though, the decision to donate is made by the deceased person's family or next of kin. *They are the real donors*' (my emphasis).[2] This last comment is grounded in the customary practice in the US,[3] which also finds reflection in the UK, Australasia and most other parts of the world with explicit consent systems, and even in some presumed consent jurisdictions. Nonetheless, an alternative view is evolving. The 2006 version of the US Uniform Anatomical Gift

---

[1] K. Healy, 'The political economy of presumed consent', 2005, at http://repositories.cdlib. org/uclasoc/trcsa/31 at 12.

[2] K. Healy, *Last Best Gifts* (University of Chicago Press, 2006), p. 37 [Healy, *Last Best Gifts*]. See also J. Childress, 'The body as property: Some philosophical reflections' (1992) 24(5) *Transplantation Proceedings* 2143 at 2143.

[3] See United States Task Force on Organ Transplantation, *Organ Transplantation: Issues and Recommendations* (Washington, DC: Department of Health, Education, and Welfare, 1986) at 31.

Act (UAGA), for instance, states that the donor 'means an individual whose body or part is the subject of an anatomical gift'.[4] The 'gift' is that of the person from whose body such material is taken and used.[5] This is no mere semantic quibble. It goes to the very heart of the issues surrounding organ and tissue donation for therapy and research. The authority for donation should therefore derive *from* the deceased. This perception is increasingly guiding practice. The Institute of Medicine (IOM) Report asserted

These findings suggest that the United States may be in the midst of a paradigm shift from relying on the next of kin to make donation decisions for deceased individuals to using donor consent documentation, whenever available, as the official mechanism of consent for organ donation.[6]

There is, at least at a policy level, a similar shift in emphasis in the UK, reflected in the guidance (in particular the Codes of Practice) accompanying the Human Tissue Act 2004 and the Human Tissue (Scotland) Act 2006. Such emphasis is especially strident in Scotland, where it is intended to be reinforced through the use of the concept of 'authorisation'. It can however also be noted elsewhere, e.g. in Germany, Australia, etc.[7] Michielsen has gone so far as to say that compliance with the wishes of the deceased is theoretically the basis of all transplant laws.[8] The donation decision is, initially at least, the decision of the donor to make. If the priority is to implement the wishes of deceased persons, the objective should be to increase the available and reliable evidence of such wishes, preferably to the point where all such wishes are 'known'.[9] There is a trend toward the establishment of registries around the world (quite a speedy process in the US states) which, by virtue of the fact that the wishes of the deceased (to donate) are now specifically recorded,

---

[4] Uniform Anatomical Gift Act 2006, section 1(7).
[5] Even as regards minors and adults who have never possessed decision-making capacity such persons should be seen as 'donors' and not merely 'sources'.
[6] Institute of Medicine Report, *Organ Donation: Opportunities for Action* (Washington, DC: National Academies Press, 2006) at 175 [Institute of Medicine, *Organ Donation*]. First-person (donor) state registries are being swiftly established to facilitate this policy shift. See state list at www.unos.org.
[7] See, e.g., National Health and Medical Research Council, *Organ and Tissue Donation After Death, for Transplantation*, Australian Government, 2007 at 5.
[8] P. Michielsen, 'Informed or presumed consent legislative models', in J. Chapman, M. Deierhoi and C. Wight (eds.), *Organ and Tissue Donation for Transplantation* (London: Arnold, 1997) 344 at 345 [Michielsen, 'Informed or presumed consent'].
[9] See G. Pennings, 'Ethics of organ retrieval', in Y. Englert (ed.), *Organ and Tissue Transplantation in the European Union* (Dordrecht: Martinus Nijhoff, 1995) 166 at 167 [Pennings, 'Ethics'].

directly raise the pivotal issue.[10] Are they simply a background to relatives' decision-making or do they 'generate' such a decision in their own right?

Despite the pervasive historical practice of deferring to relatives, there is considerable evidence that people regard their decisions to donate as being ones which should be unable to be overridden by relatives after death.[11] A survey conducted in 1993 in the US revealed that only 14 per cent of respondents believed that the organ donation decision should be left to relatives after a person's death.[12] Indeed, laws habitually stipulate that donation may legitimately proceed upon the consent of the deceased alone. This is the policy laid down in the Human Tissue Act 2004, in all the US states (which have implemented one or other versions of the UAGAs), in the Human Tissue (Scotland) Act 2006 and in almost all other laws. Notwithstanding, even in many explicit consent systems, relatives are routinely permitted in practice to veto a decision by the deceased to donate.

It is sometimes suggested that in a presumed consent system donation is the 'norm', by virtue of the will of the deceased being inferred from passivity, by contrast with explicit consent systems where it is not. Yet, there is a contemporary policy aspiration to advance the perception that organ donation is the usual consequence of the death of *any* potentially suitable donor. The Organ Donation Taskforce (ODT) recently stated that all parts of the NHS must embrace organ donation as a usual rather than unusual event.[13] The IOM Report noted that even under current explicit consent laws it is possible to frame the communication with families in terms of an expectation, or 'norm', of donation.[14] Organ Procurement Organisation (OPO) policies in the US have traditionally varied significantly in the extent to which families are persuaded to accept donation when this is the known wish of the deceased,[15] although recent policies adopt a more 'positive' style. This has been described as the

---

[10] There are now sixteen registries in Europe, thirty-eight in the US, three in Canada and one in Australia; see H. Gabel, 'Organ donor registers' (2006) 11(2) *Current Opinion in Organ Transplantation* 187.

[11] In one survey, 92 per cent; see A. Spital, 'Mandated choice: The preferred solution to the organ shortage?' (1992) 152 *Archives of Internal Medicine* 2421 at 2423 [Spital, 'Mandated choice: The preferred solution']; R. Harris, J. Jasper, B. Lee and K. Miller, 'Consenting to donate organs: Whose wishes carry the most weight?' (1991) 21 *Journal of Applied Psychology* 3; S. Corlett, 'Public attitudes toward human organ donation' (1985) 17 (suppl. 3) *Transplantation Proceedings* 103.

[12] A. Spital, 'Mandated choice: A plan to increase public commitment to organ donation' (1995) 273(6) *Journal of the American Medical Association* 504 at 505 [Spital, 'Mandated choice: A plan to increase public commitment'].

[13] *Organs for Transplants: A Report from the Organ Donation Taskforce*, Department of Health, 2008, paras. 1.23–1.24.

[14] Institute of Medicine Report, *Organ Donation* at 217.    [15] Healy, *Last Best Gifts*, p. 63.

'presumptive approach' and guides families through open-ended questions presenting organ donation as an expected outcome.[16] Nonetheless, it is recognised that undue pressure and coercion should be avoided. It has been alleged that some recent strategies cross this line. Truog maintains that organ procurement co-ordinators fail to convey their 'dual role' as both grief counsellors and procurers, and use language which is often misleading or even manipulative, thus undermining the notion of informed consent to donation.[17] Clearly there are crucial subtleties here associated with the communication process. But as a general point it may be questioned whether any kind of 'presumption' is appropriate at all where there is no evidence that the deceased wished to donate.

### Recording views

It has been invariably left to individuals in all jurisdictions to decide if, and how, they would like to record their wishes either to donate materials for transplantation or research; or not to do so, where this is an available option.[18] This has been described as the 'voluntary system'. The invariable consequence has been that the large majority of individuals have not directly recorded their wishes regarding donation at the time of their death. This is the case in both explicit and presumed consent systems. In the UK, the NHS Organ Donation Register has been, in view of its relative infancy, fairly successful in recording the wishes of 27 per cent of the population to donate for transplantation. Notwithstanding, this represents only a modest percentage of the population as a whole. The most successful nation is the Netherlands, where the percentage of Dutch citizens of full age included in the register is about 45 per cent, although in the US an even higher percentage of individuals have apparently indicated their desire to donate via their driving licence or organ donor card.[19] In most nations some form of official donor card is also in circulation, which may additionally convey the wishes of some citizens who wish to donate but have not recorded such wishes on an available register.

---

[16] S. Zink and S. Wertlieb, 'A study of the presumptive approach to consent for organ donation: A new solution to an old problem' (2006) 26 *Critical Care Nurse* 129. See also G. Siegel and R. Bonnie, 'Closing the organ gap: A reciprocity-based social contract approach' (2006) 34(2) *Journal of Law, Medicine and Ethics* 415.

[17] R. Truog, 'Consent for organ donation – balancing conflicting ethical obligations' (2008) 358 *New England Journal of Medicine* 1209 at 1210.

[18] Although for a short period in Texas and Virginia recording of wishes was required when applying for driving licences.

[19] According to the Gallup Organization poll of 2,000 citizens, 53 per cent; see *2005 National Survey of Organ and Tissue Donation Attitudes*.

Just as most explicit consent jurisdictions have registers catering only for requests to donate, many presumed consent jurisdictions record only objections to donation, not positive wishes to donate. It is desirable that all systems enable individuals to register both positive wishes as well as objections, ideally for both therapy and research purposes. A handful of jurisdictions have such a dual register.[20] Thus, whilst Pennings states 'In an opting-out policy, a person who is willing to serve as a donor can take no positive action to confirm this wish. The same is true for a non-donor in an opting-in policy',[21] this is not universally true. Individuals in Belgium are able to record a positive wish to donate despite it being a presumed consent system, and the converse possibility exists in the Netherlands, an explicit consent system.[22] Nonetheless, the wishes of most individuals are still not directly known in any system. Of course many individuals will have informed their family as to their wishes whether they have 'registered' their wishes as well, or not. But the evidence suggests that no more than half of individuals, in Europe and North America at least, have raised this subject with relatives prior to their death.[23] The upshot is that the wishes of 'donors' are not reliably known through any formal mechanism in a very substantial percentage of cases, nor are they likely to be in the foreseeable future. This has generated support for the notion of mandated choice and enhanced respect for donor self-determination. As Saunders asserts 'Even if the number of organs retrieved were to be the same, it offers the possibility of realizing the wishes of the donor – who really would be a donor, one who gives, and not just the supplier of organs'.[24]

[20] For instance, Belgium, the Netherlands, Portugal, Sweden, and Australia.

[21] Pennings, 'Ethics' at 167. Although Pennings uses the terminology of 'opting out' in this context, I choose the general expression 'presumed consent', see chapter 5.

[22] Whilst no registers of objectors exist in the US, section 7 of the 2006 version of the Uniform Anatomical Gift Act stipulates that an individual is entitled to *refuse* to make an anatomical gift either signed in a record or in their will or in the presence of at least two witnesses during the individual's terminal illness or injury.

[23] A European Commission survey revealed that across the Member States only 41 per cent of individuals had raised the subject of donation with their relatives; see Special Eurobarometer Report, *Europeans and Organ Donation*, European Commission, May 2007 44–5 [Special Eurobarometer Report]. Spital's survey of adults in the US found that only 38 per cent of respondents had discussed their wishes regarding organ donation with an immediate family member; see Spital, 'Mandated choice: A plan to increase public commitment' at 505.

[24] Professor John Saunders, Written Evidence to the National Assembly for Wales, at www. assemblywales.org/bus-home/bus-committees-third1/bus-, para. 42.

## Mandated choice

Mandated choice is the most direct approach to donation decision-making. Whilst one could wait for a sufficient critical mass of citizens to record or directly communicate their wishes in accordance with current practices, it appears that it may be some considerable while before official voluntary recording will incorporate the wishes of even a majority of the populace, let alone the large majority.[25] As a consequence, measures to *require* individuals to make advance decisions are increasingly being put on the table. Although largely theoretical in the main, such policies have been tried and abandoned in both Texas and Virginia, and are to be implemented in 2013 in New Jersey. Whilst some individuals will not record their wishes even if compelled to do so, and some will not be 'reached' even by official methods of recording (such as a Census) anyhow,[26] such a policy will nevertheless be likely to record the wishes of deceased persons to a much greater extent than is presently the case.

Mandated choice is often criticised for forcing choices on individuals who may not have even formed an opinion on the matter at that stage. To what extent it is ethically appropriate to place pressure on individuals to decide is unclear, whatever the cultural and societal hue of the jurisdiction concerned. Katz has described it as a 'negligible intrusion' when weighed against the potential benefits to society,[27] whereas others regard it as a significant state incursion into the private sphere. Many argue that we are entitled *not to make choices* (to decide not to choose) and that if the state were to force one to commit on this issue it would be overreaching itself. However, a mandated choice is not the same as a forced choice. The absence of an explicit choice currently amounts to a positive decision of some form by default in any event. To the extent that one is already making a choice through one's inertia, it is not forcing any new state of affairs upon another person, nor is any *particular* choice being foisted upon individuals.[28] Thus, the potency of this (coercion) argument will depend upon how such a system is set up and what choices are offered. The structure of any mandated choice is pivotal to its ethical acceptability and public palatability.

---

[25] Although one would anticipate a gradual slowing of registration, in fact in the UK registration rates have steadily and consistently risen, with nearly 1 million further donors registering in the twelve months to 31 March 2008.

[26] For example, the homeless and those with literacy and communication issues.

[27] B. Katz, 'Increasing the supply of human organs for transplantation: A proposal for a system of mandated choice' (1984) 18 (Summer) *Beverley Hills Bar Journal* 152 [Katz, 'Increasing the supply'].

[28] See also G. den Hartogh, *Farewell to Non-commitment: Decision Systems for Organ Donation from an Ethical Viewpoint*, Monitoring Report Ethics and Health, Centre for Ethics and Health, The Hague, 2008 at 32 [Den Hartogh, *Farewell to Non-commitment*].

In presumed consent jurisdictions the default is presently a decision to permit organ and tissue donation (subject perhaps to a relative's veto) whilst in explicit consent jurisdictions it is a decision to delegate the decision to the family. As Herz states

Indeed, during every moment of legally competent adulthood, every American is making the choice to posthumously (1) donate organs, or (2) not donate organs, or (3) let family and physicians determine whether to donate his or her organs.[29]

Thus, to provide a choice which includes the option of 'not deciding at all' is, whilst appealing, not one currently available. At the very least one is deciding implicitly to delegate the decision after death. Such an option would also be likely to result in only a relatively modest percentage of individuals deciding positively either way (largely because of a reluctance to consider one's own demise),[30] which would be unsatisfactory because we would still be left not knowing what most people wanted. Thus, it is more compelling to offer the above threefold menu, the latter being the status quo in most explicit consent systems in any case, where no decision has been made. In jurisdictions such as the UK, the Netherlands and Germany, where individuals are entitled to nominate a *specific* individual for this purpose, perhaps sidestepping the relative(s) otherwise prioritised under the applicable legislative scheme, such an option should be additionally available. Some have seen the need to accompany mandated choice with a strong message about the desirability of organ donation, or even the need to accompany any non-donation decision with cogent reasons, in order to persuade donors to decide to donate.[31] This would, however, appear to introduce a coercive element into the issue of *what choice is made*. It is the quality not the slant of the information which is the most critical aspect.

What is especially intriguing is that mandated choice, whilst not universally popular (the British Medical Association rejected it summarily in the UK),[32] is not generally perceived as a *radical* option despite its marginalisation of relatives.[33] A survey in the US in the 1990s revealed 90 per cent support for a programme of mandated choice,[34] and the

---

[29] S. Herz, 'Two steps to three choices: A new approach to mandated choice' (1999) 8 *Cambridge Quarterly of Healthcare Ethics* 340 at 343 [Herz, 'Two steps'].

[30] Where this option was offered in Virginia, 24 per cent declared themselves undecided.

[31] P. Chouhan and H. Draper, 'Modified mandated choice for organ procurement' (2003) 29 *Journal of Medical Ethics* 157.

[32] British Medical Association, Organ Donation in the 21st Century: Time for a Consolidated Approach, BMA, 2000 at 10.

[33] The Institute of Medicine Report, however, appreciated that evading families' wishes could be the most controversial aspect of such schemes. Institute of Medicine, *Organ Donation* at 180.

[34] Spital, 'Mandated choice: The preferred solution' at 2421.

Council on Ethical and Judicial Affairs of the American Medical Association (AMA) has expressed a preference for mandated choice over presumed consent.[35] The IOM Report commented 'Under a fully implemented mandated-choice model that is within the framework of UAGA, individual decisions would be known and honored'.[36] Indeed, proposers of mandated choice often explicitly declare it to be *designed* to transfer control back to the individual and away from the family.[37] Notwithstanding the intention, this would be the effect, a feature which would dramatically alter the face of organ donation in almost every society. Pennings observes 'This policy would limit the involvement of the next-of-kin to those occasions in which the potential donor is not considered competent, e.g. children and mentally incompetent persons'.[38]

Klassen and Klassen argue that families should have a decision-making role even if the deceased individual's wishes are explicitly known.[39] They allude to the comfort that relatives often receive from donation. But we are not here dealing with individuals without the ability to make decisions for themselves, only individuals with decision-making capacity.[40] Whilst one *could* have a mandated choice scheme but nonetheless leave the decision ultimately for the relatives to make, expressing a positive or negative wish as regards donation appears to counteract the normal operating (ethical) presumption that it is a decision properly left for the family to make.

---

[35] Council on Ethical and Judicial Affairs, American Medical Association, 'Strategies for cadaveric organ procurement: Mandated choice and presumed consent' (1994) 272 *Journal of the American Medical Association* 809. It described the former as an 'ethically appropriate strategy' and the latter as raising 'serious ethical concerns', at 812. This is interesting to the extent that, by contrast with weak presumed consent systems, relatives would have *no* say in the disposition of the deceased's organs unless expressly given delegated authority.

[36] Institute of Medicine, *Organ Donation* at 177. It added 'Decisions would be binding, although opportunities to change the decision would be readily available' at 178–9.

[37] See, e.g., R. Veatch, 'Routine inquiry about organ donation – an alternative to presumed consent' 325(17) *New England Journal of Medicine* 1246 at 1248; Katz, 'Increasing the supply'; A. Spital, 'The shortage of organs for transplantation: Where do we go from here?' (1991) 325 *New England Journal of Medicine* 1243; Den Hartogh, *Farewell to Non-commitment* at 34.

[38] Pennings, 'Ethics' at 169.

[39] A. Klassen and D. Klassen, 'Who are the donors in organ donation? The family's perspective in mandated choice' (1996) 125 *Annals of Internal Medicine* 70 at 71 [Klassen and Klassen, 'Who are the donors']. Research conducted in the US in the 1990s found that only 43.2 per cent of families agreed with mandated choice; see L. Siminoff and M. Mercer, 'Public policy, public opinion, and consent for organ donation' (2001) 10 *Cambridge Quarterly of Healthcare Ethics* 377 at 380.

[40] As I have advocated, Spital suggests granting individuals a choice giving their families a power of veto. See Spital, 'Mandated choice for organ donation: Time to give it a try' (1996) 125 *Annals of Internal Medicine* 66 at 68 [Spital, 'Mandated choice for organ donation: Time to give it a try'].

Where such wishes are reliably known there is no need for 'proxy' decisions to be made. As has been asserted, 'the compulsory choice system
appears attractive, primarily because it does full justice to the right to self-
determination'.[41] Thus, mandated choice *should* serve to effect a choice
which clinicians are required to implement, logistical and clinical factors
aside, and not just provide an advisory view for relatives.

Many critics of mandated choice seem more exercised by what they see
as undue pressure to choose rather than the actual effect of the choice.
Such proposals have generally taken the form of an approach by way of
applications for drivers' licences or income tax returns. The former model
was adopted in Texas and Virginia and is to be applied in New Jersey in
2013. To what degree sanctions should be imposed for failing to respond
to the question is debatable. Spital suggests that an individual should not
be entitled to a driver's licence or acceptance of a tax return unless the
question is answered.[42] To be too authoritarian and punitive, though,
could be interpreted by the public as being too heavy-handed and might
prove counterproductive.[43] The process has an educational element as
well as serving to directly increase evidence regarding donor wishes. In
some societies, compulsion to participate in social 'events' or 'decisions' is
more common than in others – for example, the requirement to vote in
Australia.

Thus, whether individuals should *have* to make such a choice (possibly
accompanied by sanctions for refusal) or alternatively be offered regular
and easy *opportunities* to do so, is a contentious one. Mandated choice
could be diluted so as to merely mandate the need for citizens to be *asked*
about organ donation at some specific point or occasion in their lives, or at
regular intervals. This would merely work as a support for the existing
voluntary scheme. In the Netherlands registration forms are sent to all
citizens on their eighteenth birthday, setting out a choice of responses;
either 'yes', 'no', 'leave decisions to the next-of-kin' or 'leave it to a
specified person'.[44] Initially 36 per cent of the population (4.5 million)
registered a choice,[45] rising now to 45 per cent. Whilst modestly

---

[41] Den Hartogh, *Farewell to Non-commitment* at 31.
[42] Spital, 'Mandated choice for organ donation: Time to give it a try' at 68.
[43] Den Hartogh has observed that the more coercive the sanction the more likelihood of a
    backlash and induced resistance; see Den Hartogh, *Farewell to Non-commitment* at 73.
[44] See Department of Health, Welfare and Sport, *The Organ Donation Act*, International
    Publication Series No. 3, The Hague, 2000: 55 per cent said 'yes', 35 per cent 'no', 10
    per cent left it to the next of kin in general and fewer than 1 per cent of individuals left it to
    a specified person.
[45] A. van Netten, 'Donor registration campaign: Ministry of Public Health involves personal
    request to 12.2 million Dutch citizens 18+ years' (2000) 32 *Transplantation Proceedings*
    123.

successful, this highlights how much further there is to go in recording the wishes of the large majority of the population.

A telephone survey of 1,002 US citizens in 1993 found that if a system of mandated choice were established, 63 per cent would sign up to donate, 24 per cent would not and 13 per cent were unsure.[46] Klassen and Klassen, however, argue that eliminating a role for the family under such a system has the potential to backfire in terms of donation rates.[47] Moreover, on account of the weak link between behavioural research and actual behaviour, and because survey respondents are speculating in relation to situations with which they have no experiential basis, such figures cannot be relied upon. The two states that have previously adopted mandated choice programmes reported relatively low numbers of pro-donation registrants.[48] However, it appears that in Texas individuals, when they applied for their driving licences, were not only given the simple choice of deciding to donate or not to donate, but those who did not decide at all were defaulted to the 'no' category (resulting in 80 per cent of individuals becoming non-donors). Nevertheless, there is a proper concern that, forced to choose, especially in a situation where they have had little or no prior notice or information of the decision, forced choices will turn into negative choices with the family generally excluded from the decision-making process. Dhar and Simonson have shown that the options selected in a forced-choice task tend to be those that seem safer; that are easier to justify; and that help alleviate decision conflict, discomfort and potential regret associated with being forced to make a choice, despite the lack of a clear preference.[49]

Like the AMA Committee Report before it, the IOM Report believed that mandated choice could be implemented in an ethically appropriate manner, although a broad-based and multi-dimensional educational campaign was essential; something apparently lacking in Texas.[50] The IOM, however, recommended that mandated choice not be implemented in the US at present, on account of the possibility of this leading to a reduction in the number of organs becoming available, although consideration should be given to setting up a pilot. As den Hartogh noted, the

---

[46] Spital, 'Mandated choice: A plan to increase public commitment' at 504.

[47] Klassen and Klassen, 'Who are the donors'. It was observed that the 63 per cent who say they would donate under such a scheme is only negligibly different from the approximately 50 per cent consent rates generally found under existing schemes.

[48] *Ibid.*, at 71. Only 31 per cent of individuals registered as donors in Virginia, whilst 45 per cent registered as non-donors.

[49] R. Dhar and I. Simonson, 'The effect of forced choice on choice' (2003) 11 *Journal of Marketing Research* 146.

[50] Institute of Medicine, *Organ Donation* at 180.

reason for non-implementation to date is simple, 'the fear that the system will have a counterproductive effect'.[51]

## Deceased's wishes

In recent years we have witnessed increasing weight being given to the wishes of deceased persons, even in explicit consent systems. Nevertheless, official policy and practice still tend to part company with regard to the respect afforded to the views of deceased persons and their relatives.

Almost all legislation categorically states that organs and tissues may be removed from a deceased person for transplantation and/or research where the deceased person has consented to it (and this has not been withdrawn) and that no organs/tissues may be removed where the deceased objected to it. However, there is no legal symmetry between consent and a refusal of consent. As Wilkinson notes there is an important distinction here between negative and positive (claim) rights.[52] Although the consent of the deceased is sufficient justification for removal and use (and any storage connected thereto), the removal and use of body parts is not *mandated* as a function of the positive liberty to consent. In other words, there is no positive right to donate even though there is a duty not to act counter to the deceased's objections; what is permitted is not required.[53] There may be many reasons, clinical or otherwise, why health professionals might decide not to remove or use human material despite the existence of such consent. The most compelling and probable non-clinical one is the objection of a relative. Deference to such objections is pervasive, even in nations practising strong presumed consent.[54] Their decisions have invariably remained pivotal even following the advent of donor cards and local or national donor registries. Wilkinson has referred to the 'double veto' that exists here; that refusals by either the deceased *or* family are able to override the positive wish of the other to donate, but

---

[51] Den Hartogh, *Farewell to Non-commitment* at 32.

[52] T. Wilkinson, 'Individual and family consent to organ and tissue donation: Is the current position coherent?' (2005) 31 *Journal of Medical Ethics* 587 [Wilkinson, 'Individual and family consent']. This situation pertains in practice in the UK, New Zealand, the US and very many other jurisdictions.

[53] *Ibid.*, at 589. This distinction is not necessarily to be found rooted in the right to bodily integrity, however.

[54] It is reported that in Poland the views of relatives are always respected; see W. Rowinski, Z. Wlodarczyk and J. Walaszewski, 'Legal and ethical aspects of organ transplantation in Poland: Past, present, and future problems' (2003) 35 *Transplantation Proceedings* 1189 at 1190. This is also frequently the situation in Austria.

points out that arguments for giving one party a veto in fact tend to undercut giving the other a similar veto.[55]

The Potential Donor Audit (PDA) conducted in the UK revealed that where the deceased had included his/her name on the Organ Donor Register this was the most likely factor to influence relatives' decisions to agree to donate.[56] There is nonetheless evidence that even in explicit consent systems relatives do sometimes override the expressed wish of the deceased to donate. Whilst this seemingly 'unfortunate' scenario has been routinely dismissed as being so rare as to be able to ignored, more recent data suggests that it is considerably less uncommon than had previously been thought.[57] Although objections from the deceased are invariably respected (the PDA showed that the fact that the patient had stated a wish not to become a donor was the main reason for relatives refusing to give consent; 16 per cent of all refusals), it should be noted that in many explicit consent jurisdictions there are no mechanisms for directly recording objections and the family are the virtually exclusive vehicle for conveying them.

The reasons for the deference accorded to relatives appear to reside in concerns regarding potential distress and the possible public relations backlash from failing to implement their wishes, despite compliance with the law, with the result that still fewer organs are subsequently donated. The aftershocks of events at Alder Hey, Bristol, etc., may perhaps be still felt in the UK. Donation rates apparently declined in France in the immediate aftermath of an incident in 1992 involving corneas taken from a nineteen-year-old killed in a road accident. Whilst the 'consent' of the parents did not extend to the deceased's eyes, the applicable law did not in fact require the consent of relatives at all.[58]

---

[55] Wilkinson, 'Individual and family consent' at 588.

[56] K. Barber, S. Falvey, C. Hamilton, D. Collett and C. Rudge, 'Potential for organ donation in the United Kingdom: Audit of intensive care records' (2006) 332 *British Medical Journal* 1124 [Barber et al., 'Potential for organ donation'].

[57] An English study of twenty-six families who declined to allow organ donation from a deceased relative found that twelve families were positive about donation and in nine instances knew that the deceased person wished to be a donor; see M. Sque, T. Long, S. Payne and D. Allardyce, 'Why relatives do not donate organs for transplants: "Sacrifice" or "gift of life"?' (2008) 61(2) *Journal of Advanced Nursing* 134 at 139. It was also noted in Parliament that eleven donors on the Organ Donor Register had not become donors; see Dr Harris, House of Commons Standing Committee G Debates, col. 95, 29 January 2004.

[58] G. Nowenstein, 'Organ procurement rates: Does presumed consent legislation really make a difference?' [2004] 1 *Law, Social Justice and Global Development Journal*, at http://elj.warwick.ac.uk/global/04-1/nowenstein.html. Rates recovered in the latter part of the 1990s.

*Life policies*

I shall now examine the official policies themselves. We are here considering only cases where the deceased had consented/gifted/ authorised the removal of the requisite body parts for the relevant purposes. It has already been noted that neither in policy nor in practice are organs or tissues removed where there is evidence that the deceased objected.

To emphasise that the 'gift' made by the deceased (donor) was *sufficient* in itself to permit organ and tissue donation, the 1987 version of the UAGA in the US included a specific provision which stated that 'An anatomical gift that is not revoked by the donor before death is irrevocable and does not require the consent or concurrence of any person after the donor's death'.[59] Despite the language of 'irrevocability' it remained the practice of some OPOs to respect the objections of relatives. The 2006 UAGA revision now asserts even more forcibly that a donor's autonomous decision is to be honoured and implemented, and states that others are 'barred' from making, amending, or revoking an anatomical gift made by the donor. It would henceforward be *unlawful* for an OPO to act upon an attempted revocation of a gift by surviving family members.[60] In Kluge's terminology, the deceased's decision to donate has been converted from a 'full' consent to a 'binding' consent, i.e. not merely sufficient but irrebuttable.[61] This last provision in particular underpins the assertion in the IOM that the US is undergoing a 'paradigm shift' in favour of using donor consent documentation, whenever available, as the official mechanism of consent for organ donation.[62] The 2001 amendments in Denmark similarly require that the stated wish of the deceased person to donate must be accepted by the next-of-kin, and the necessity for relatives to respect the deceased's consent to donate was also affirmed in the Netherlands in 2006.[63]

---

[59] Section 2(h).
[60] Section 8(a), Uniform Anatomical Gift Act 2006. See also S. Kurtz, C. Strong and D. Gerasimow, 'The 2006 revised Uniform Anatomical Gift Act – A law to save lives' [2007] *Health Law Analysis* 44 at 45. The commentary states that the provision is designed to *take away from families* the power to amend or nullify such a gift.
[61] E.-H. Kluge, 'Organ donation and retrieval: Whose body is it anyway?', in H. Kuhse and P. Singer (eds.), *Bioethics: An Anthology* (London: Blackwell, 2006) 483 at 485. However, this nevertheless authorises but does not *mandate* organ removal and use.
[62] Institute of Medicine, *Organ Donation* at 175.
[63] See H. Gabel, 'Donor registries throughout Europe and their influence on organ donation' (2003) 35 *Transplantation Proceedings* 997 at 997. In Denmark, Law No. 432 of 29 May 2001 amends Law No. 402 of 13 June 1990. In the Netherlands, see Law of 23 June 2006. See also Den Hartogh, *Farewell to Non-commitment* at 65.

The language in the UAGA is generally stronger in affirming this position than contemporary explicit consent legislation elsewhere.[64] Nonetheless, the same essential policy is enshrined in the Human Tissue Act 2004, the Human Tissue (Scotland) Act 2006, the 1997 Law in Germany and in many other laws – to afford primacy to the decisions of the deceased person. This is generally reinforced in supporting guidance such as the Human Tissue Authority (HTA) Codes of Practice relating to the 2004 Act.[65] The Notes on the Human Tissue Act issued by the HTA state that 'The new Human Tissue Act makes the wishes of the deceased paramount ... This new permission in the HT Act gives added weight to the wishes of the 13.4 m people on the NHS Organ Donor Register, donor card carriers and others who have agreed to donate.'[66] The wording of the previous 1961 Act is slightly strengthened in the 2004 Act, which states that where the deceased has made a decision to either consent or refuse to consent to organ/tissue donation, it is the deceased's decision (alone) which, *de jure*, governs. However, despite this, there is nothing in the Act which disenfranchises relatives from vetoing any such decision *de facto*, even though it is perfectly lawful to remove such material for transplantation or research in such circumstances.

The Scottish legislation was heavily influenced by the Report of the Independent Review Group on Retention of Organs at Post-Mortem, which stated that as regards the retention and use of organs and tissues for research 'Where a competent adult has left written instructions on this matter, these wishes should be respected, irrespective of the views of surviving relatives'.[67] Whilst the 2006 Act on its face does not preclude relatives from 'overriding' a decision (an authorisation) to donate made by the deceased person, the Scottish Executive has clearly stated that the new concept of authorisation for organ donation is 'an expression which is intended to convey that people have the right to express, during their

---

[64] Although the Estonian Law of 30 January 2002 states that relatives may not veto a deceased person's explicit will to donate; section 11. Whilst it is a presumed consent law, the Law of 13 June 1986 in Belgium also states that where an explicit consent is given by a (pre)deceased person this cannot be overruled by a relative's veto.

[65] Para. 39 of the Code of Practice on the Donation of Organs, Tissues and Cells for Transplantation, states that if the deceased had not recorded his or her wish then approaches should be made to relatives to ascertain what the wishes of the deceased would have been; Human Tissue Authority, Department of Health, July 2006. See also Code of Practice on Consent, Human Tissue Authority, Department of Health, July 2006.

[66] Human Tissue Authority Briefing Notes on the Human Tissue Act 2004, 30 August 2006.

[67] Report of the Independent Review Group on Retention of Organs at Post-Mortem, 2000, Summary of Recommendations, para. 27, and section 2, paras. 42 and 58. It stressed this position, even stating that this was the intended policy under the previous Human Tissue Act 1961, although that latter statute was regarded as poorly phrased.

lifetime, their wishes about what should happen to their bodies after death, in the expectation that those wishes will be respected'.[68]

In Germany, the donor's fundamental rights are an emanation from the State's Basic Law (the German Federal Constitution) which creates an obligation to respect the dignity of each individual. Such rights of self-determination do not terminate with the death of the individual but extend beyond death to the treatment of the corpse.[69] This means that it is the deceased's wishes that are determinative as regards the removal and use of parts of the individual's cadaver.

Generally, under all such statutes operating in explicit consent systems, where the deceased made no decision prior to death a relative or relatives is/are permitted to consent to such activity instead. However, under the 2004 Act this is not permissible with respect to use for either public display or anatomical examination.[70] The question arises why relatives have no discretion in relation (only) to these latter uses, which seemingly must be answered on the basis of the degree of intrusion, destruction and (*prima facie*) loss of dignity involved. The greater the degree of invasion and destruction the greater the imperative for there to be a *personal* decision of the deceased to such ends. Research conducted in Sweden by Sanner comparing attitudes to organ donation, post-mortem examination (autopsy) and anatomical examination showed that the latter was indeed perceived as the most extreme procedure and that rates of acceptance reflected this. She states that 'This means that if a more extreme procedure is accepted, all of the less extreme procedures are also accepted'.[71] It appears that this holds as regards attitudes to the use of *one's own* cadaver as well as that of a relative. Nonetheless, one would argue that it is the right to remove and use *per se* which necessitates the authority of the tissue source, not the degree of intrusion upon the lifeless remains.

---

[68] Scottish Executive, Human Tissue (Scotland) Act 2006: A Guide to its Implications for NHSScotland. HDL (2006) 46, Edinburgh: Scottish Executive, para. 8; see www.sehd.scot.nhs.uk/mels/HDL2006_46.pdf. See also www.hta.gov.uk/_db/_documents/Information_about_HT_(Scotland)_Act.pdf. See J. Payne, Organ Donation, SPICe briefing, 29 February 2008, Scottish Parliament at 5 [Payne, SPICe briefing].

[69] In addition, Article 4(1) and (2) of the Basic Law grants the individual the right to adduce his own faith or Weltanschauung in deciding what is to be done with his body after death. See German National Ethics Council Report, *Increasing the Number of Organ Donations: A Pressing Issue for Transplant Medicine in Germany*, Opinion, Berlin, 2007 at 38.

[70] Section 3(3)–(4).

[71] M. Sanner, 'A comparison of public attitudes toward autopsy, organ donation, and anatomical dissection: A Swedish survey' (1994) 271 *Journal of the American Medical Association* 284. Almost everyone who accepted anatomical dissection also accepted organ donation and autopsy, and everyone who accepted organ donation also accepted autopsy.

### Nominated representatives

In a smattering of jurisdictions, individuals are enabled, during their lifetime, to nominate a person or persons to make decisions relating to donation after their death. This is generally limited to adults. Under the Human Tissue Act 2004 these are termed 'nominated representatives'. These are true 'proxies'. Similar provisions exist under the laws in the Netherlands and Germany.[72] In Scotland, there is no such provision with respect to transplants, although a person may nominate a person (a 'nominee') to decide whether to authorise the removal, retention and use of organs at post-mortem to be used for audit, education, training, or research.[73] It has been suggested that such a concept may act as a mechanism allowing one to circumvent decision-making after death by a relative whom one does not wish to entrust with it.[74] This is a little crude, though. Just because one knows a relative one does not trust with the decision does not necessarily mean that one knows another who one does!

### Relatives

Relatives have a variety of distinct roles in the context of organ and tissue donation, which may vary according to whether there is an explicit or presumed consent scheme in effect; assuming of course that the legal scheme is implemented in practice.[75] Strictly speaking in presumed consent systems they have no role as individuals entitled to *consent* to organ donation, as there is 'direct' evidence of the deceased's own wish to donate based on the failure to object, which is sufficient authorisation in and of itself. In weak presumed consent systems, relatives may, however, express *objections* on behalf of the deceased (based on their own knowledge of the deceased's views), or on their own behalf, or both.

In rare instances in explicit consent jurisdictions, the law mandates that the decision made by the family should be the decision which it is anticipated that the deceased would have made.[76] Whether of course any eventual decision did truly reflect the known or expected wishes of the deceased is an unknown quantity. In Scotland, whilst this is not made patent on the face of the legislation, the same policy was clearly intended.

---

[72] German Law of 5 November 1997; Dutch Law of 24 May 1996.
[73] Sections 29 and 30, Human Tissue (Scotland) Act 2006.
[74] See, e.g., R. Winterton MP, House of Commons Hansard Debates, Standing Committee G, col. 206, 5 February 2004.
[75] See generally C. Naylor, 'The role of the family in cadaveric organ procurement' (1989) 65 *Indiana Law Journal* 167.
[76] E.g. in Germany, see Law of 5 November 1997, section 4(1).

A Briefing Paper produced by the Scottish Parliament explicitly affirmed this, stating 'In giving their authorisation, the Act stipulates that the relative should be doing so on the basis of what they believe the deceased's wishes would have been'.[77] This is also the policy stance of the Council of Europe.[78] Pennings notes that the (proxy) power of consent of relatives is generally founded on their greater ability to infer what the deceased would have wanted to occur, and rooted in the principle of substituted judgement. It is not meant to respect the autonomy of the proxy him/her self.[79] As asserted in chapter 2, the interests of the relatives themselves do not provide the foundation for general dispositional powers over the corpse. Veatch alludes to the original policy underpinning the uniform laws in the US as contrasted with the practice in the 1980s and early 1990s

Familial consent, as originally incorporated into the Uniform Anatomical Gift Act, was clearly meant to be a backup in those cases where the autonomous expressed will of the individual could not be determined. Although the language was not available, families were presumably being expected to make a substituted judgment as a second best alternative to individual self-determination ... Now, however, post-mortem familial request is becoming the centerpiece of procurement policy. What was clearly a second-best, decision-making mechanism has become the dominant one.[80]

The aim of the statutory hierarchy of relatives is ostensibly to identify the closest person to the deceased in life, as he/she is the most likely to be knowledgeable as regards the deceased's wishes.[81] Thus the goal of determining the wishes of the deceased provides a proper basis for the hierarchical ranking of relatives according to their usual closeness of relationship to the deceased person. Preferably, this would be flexible enough to cater for specific atypical circumstances.[82] In fact, under the German Law a person is qualified to be a 'next of kin' for these purposes only if he/she has had personal contact with the deceased during the two years preceding the death.[83] There is the potential for problems to arise where a higher-ranked relative refuses to consent but a lower-ranked

---

[77] Payne, SPICe briefing at 6.
[78] Explanatory Report to the Council of Europe's Additional Protocol to the Convention on Human Rights and Biomedicine Concerning Transplantation of Organs and Tissues of Human Origin, para. 102.
[79] Pennings, 'Ethics' at 169.
[80] R. Veatch, 'The newly dead: Mortal remains or organ bank?', in R. Veatch (ed.), *Death, Dying and the Biological Revolution* (New Haven, CT: Yale University Press, 1989) 197 at 215.
[81] Payne, SPICe briefing at 6.
[82] K. Liddell and A. Hall, 'Beyond Bristol and Alder Hey: The future regulation of human tissue' (2005) 13 *Medical Law Review* 170 at 192.
[83] Section 4, Law of 5 November 1997.

relative is allegedly aware of the positive wish of the deceased to donate. Nothwithstanding such knowledge, removal is not formally permissible in such circumstances, at least within the terms of the Human Tissue Act 2004 and the Human Tissue (Scotland) Act 2006. It would be necessary to persuade the higher-ranked relative to withhold or withdraw the refusal and instead consent, or allow another relative to consent in his/her stead. In some nations it is in any case a decision of the majority of the relatives rather than any particular relative or class of relative, or a hybrid model, e.g. in Chile.[84]

Indeed, the most influential factor in relatives' decisions appears to be knowledge of the wishes of the deceased.[85] In reviewing the empirical data in the UK and the US, Sque, Payne and Clark state that

> Primarily the most deep-seated and pervasive reason for agreeing or declining donation was knowledge of the deceased's wishes, particularly if their wishes had been discussed with the family, or the family believed they would have agreed or declined donation. Families also shared a number of concerns which included not understanding death certified by neurological criteria, not wanting surgery to the body, fearing that the body would be disfigured, and feeling the deceased had suffered enough.[86]

These observations reflect the findings of the PDA in the UK, which also found that other reasons for relatives refusing to give consent included relatives being divided over the decision, relatives thinking that the patient had suffered enough and relatives not wanting surgery on the body.[87] Sanner notes the general difficulties attendant upon the illusion of lingering life. She states 'Still, people seem generally not able to imagine a difference between the living and the dead body'.[88] This results in

---

[84] See Section 10 Law No. 19451 of 29 March 1996.

[85] A poll in the US in the 1990s found that 93 per cent of respondents stated they would honour the wishes of the deceased person if such wishes were known; see Gallup Organization, *Highlights of Public Attitudes toward Organ Donation* (Princeton, NJ: Gallup, 1993). See also J. Martinez *et al.*, 'Organ donation and family decision-making within the Spanish donation system' (2001) 53 *Social Science and Medicine* 405.

[86] M. Sque, S. Payne and J. Clark, 'Gift of life or sacrifice? Key discourses for understanding decision-making by families of organ donors', in M. Sque and S. Payne (eds.), *Organ and Tissue Donation: An Evidence Base for Practice* (Maidenhead: Open University Press, 2007) 40 at 41 [Sque *et al.*, 'Gift of Life']. See also T. Long, 'Supporting families' decision-making about organ donation', *ibid.*, 82 at 95. Other reasons that families themselves express for refusing donation include dissatisfaction with the care provided to the deceased and/or the family; religious, personal and cultural beliefs; lack of trust in the health care services; and beliefs that health professionals will not strive to save a person's life if they are aware that they have agreed to be an organ donor at 95–6.

[87] Barber *et al.*, 'Potential for organ donation'. See also a study carried out by the UK Transplant Co-ordinators in 1995; see UK Transplant Co-ordinators Association, Report of a two-year study into the reasons for relatives' refusal of organ donation, London, 1995.

[88] M. Sanner, 'People's attitudes and reactions to organ donation' (2006) 11(2) *Mortality* 133 at 140.

procedures on a corpse being perceived as analogous to those conducted
on a living body. These conceptual difficulties enhance the enormity of
the decision/sacrifice and generate tension for relatives in particular.
Whilst surveys reveal that relatives are unaware of the deceased's wishes
in the majority of instances across most jurisdictions,[89] they are nevertheless invariably afforded the pivotal role as the conduit for the wishes of
the deceased.

### The gift of life?

In this section I wish to consider the nature of organ and tissue donation.
As Ben-David notes, the idea of organ donation amounting to gift-giving
analogous to the giving of a present 'has become part of the accepted
sociological explanation for the phenomenon of organ transplantation'.[90]
Whilst the gift concept may have become accepted wisdom, it is contin-
ually subject to attack from those who perceive it to be either a smoke-
screen for oppression and coercion or a hindrance to higher rates of
transplantation, or both. Siminoff and Chillag allege that the donor is
often the 'gift object' as opposed to the 'gift giver', and that the concept is
'used' by healthcare professionals to manipulate patient behaviour; a form
of social control.[91] They observe that whilst the metaphor may have
increased public awareness it has not translated into adequate donation
rates, despite the hope and expectation.[92] Gerrand has suggested that the
rationale behind the adoption of the metaphor of 'gift-giving' was the
desire to frame organ and tissue donation as an act motivated by the will
to help the needy, i.e. a voluntary act motivated by altruism.[93] However,
gifting should not be conflated with altruism. Gifts are accompanied by a
whole array of different motivations but are no less 'gifts' for that.[94] We do

---

[89]  Special Eurobarometer Report, *Europeans and Organ Donation*, European Commission,
      May 2007.
[90]  O. Ben-David, *Organ Donation and Transplantation: Body Organs as an Exchangeable Socio-
      Cultural Resource* (Westport, CT: Praeger, 2005), p. 49 [Ben-David, *Organ Donation and
      Transplantation*].
[91]  L. Siminoff and K. Chillag, 'The fallacy of the "gift of life"' (1999) 29(6) *Hastings Center
      Report* 34 at 35. The notion of the tyranny of the gift in this context was first raised by Fox
      and Swazey, who stated that it was so extraordinary that it is inherently unreciprocal, and
      argued that it diverts attention from other ethical issues such as selection criteria, re-
      transplantation and quality of life after transplant. See R. Fox and J. Swazey, *The Courage
      to Fail* (University of Chicago Press, 1974) [Fox and Swazey, *The Courage to Fail*].
[92]  *Ibid.*, at 35. They allege that the recipient is burdened by the overwhelming debt owed to
      the donor, the donor's family and healthcare professionals at 37.
[93]  N. Gerrand, 'The notion of gift-giving and organ donation' (1994) 8(2) *Bioethics* 127. She
      suggests that the notion of charity is more apt here.
[94]  Den Hartogh, *Farewell to Non-commitment* at 36.

not typically reject gifts made non-altruistically even though we would prefer that they were given for 'better' reasons.[95] However, the connection to altruism is often simply intended to indicate an absence of any expectation of reward, i.e. commercial dealing.

It has already been noted that there is a growing weight of research suggesting that for families the nature of the donation decision with respect to their deceased relative is more akin to a 'sacrifice' rather than a true 'gift'.[96] However, whilst there is no necessary tension between the notion of the 'gift' and of 'sacrifice', either conceptually or pragmatically – indeed Gillett uses the language of 'sacrificial gifting'[97] – the extent to which a *relative* may 'gift' the organs or tissues of a loved one who had not donated such materials him/her self during life is dubious in the absence of an explicit delegation of such a matter.[98] The real 'sacrifice' here is that of the donor. To the extent that families make decisions they do so on behalf of that other. Kamm comments

> If the relative's body does not belong to his family, taking his organ is not, strictly, taking something from them. This, therefore, cannot be their *sacrifice*. If they suffer, it is as a side effect of our taking what is not theirs in order to help others ... To repeat, the concern of relatives does not give them a right to control the bodily remains of their relative; so, in using his body, we do not make them sacrifice by taking what is theirs, and their suffering is not a sacrifice we impose for the sake of another.[99]

None of this is of course to minimise the actual suffering experienced by families of recently deceased loved ones or the frequent trauma and onerousness of such decision-making.

Much of the conceptualisation of the meaning of 'gifts' can be traced to the work of the anthropologist Marcel Mauss.[100] He maintained that gifts inherently create both a debt and an expectation of reciprocity. It has been said that there is an obligation to give, an obligation to receive and an obligation to repay.[101] Fox and Swazey have remarked that

---

[95] In so far as ethics typically focuses upon *actions* rather than *persons*, it is not normally necessary that morally permissible actions meet motivational constraints.

[96] M. Sque, S. Payne and A. Clark, 'Gift of life or sacrifice? Key discourses for understanding decision-making by families of organ donors' (2006) 11(2) *Mortality* 117.

[97] G. Gillett, 'Ethics and images in organ transplantation', in P. Trzepacz and A. Dimatini (eds.), *The Transplant Patient: Biological, Psychiatric and Ethical Issues in Organ Transplantation* (Cambridge University Press, 2000) 239 at 252.

[98] Den Hartogh, *Farewell to Non-commitment* at 38.

[99] F. Kamm, *Morality, Mortality. Volume 1* (Oxford University Press, 1993), p. 217.

[100] See M. Mauss, *The Gift: Forms and Functions of Exchange in Archaic Societies* (Glencoe, IL: Free Press, 1954).

[101] C. Vernale and S. Packard, 'Organ donation as gift exchange' (1990) 22(4) *Image Journal of Nursing Scholarship* 239 at 240.

As Marcel Mauss could have foretold, what recipients believe they owe to donors and the sense of obligation they feel about repaying 'their' donors weigh heavily on them. These views reflect the notion of gift as 'exchange'. This psychological and moral burden is especially onerous because the gift the recipient has received from the donor is so extraordinary that it is inherently unreciprocal. It has no physical or symbolic equivalent. The inalienability – uniqueness – of the item is in itself a hallmark of gift. A donated organ bearing the identity of the donor is paradigmatically unique. As a consequence, the giver, the receiver, and their families may find themselves locked into a creditor–debtor vice that binds them to one another in a mutually fettering way.[102]

Thus, the debt should be both acknowledged and be capable of being repaid. Ben-David, speaking of deceased donation, observes 'in this particular case, there is none of that reciprocity that appears to be a condition of gift giving ... Hence, the suggestion that organ donation fits the theoretical framework of gift giving is problematic.'[103] Gerrand, Martin and Meslin[104] and others all agree that this, formalised, conception of the gift is not apt to the contemporary (deceased) donation context, generates confusion and may be counterproductive. Titmuss likewise found that the voluntary blood donation system based on giving to strangers was free of any obligations to reciprocate.[105]

Thus, whilst the sociological/anthropological notion of gifts has some resonance in the context of living donation and related recipients (see chapter 7), it seemingly bears limited relevance to the typical deceased donation scenario, where there is no continuing relationship between the donor of the organ and the recipient. Donation would appear to be 'to society' in general terms, driven by an analogous notion of social solidarity advocated by Titmuss with respect to blood.[106] Martin and Meslin nevertheless maintain that the lack of potential reciprocity generates dissonance in relation to organs and constrains levels of donation, in so far as one cannot expect a person to make a 'gift' of such magnitude in an entirely detached and impersonal context.[107] But this is a non-proven empirical

---

[102] Fox and Swazey, *The Courage to Fail*, p. 40.
[103] Ben-David, *Organ Donation and Transplantation*, p. 56. See also Sque *et al.*, 'Gift of life' at 44.
[104] D. Martin and E. Meslin, 'The give and take of organ procurement' (1994) 19 *Journal of Medicine and Philosophy* 61 [Martin and Meslin, 'The give and take'].
[105] R. Titmuss, *The Gift Relationship: From Human Blood to Social Policy* (New York: New Press, 1997) [Titmuss, *The Gift Relationship*]. It has been suggested that this renders his view of gift-giving as being tokenistic, a view I reject.
[106] In so far as the gift implies a relationship between individuals, deceased donation is based more on community-oriented sentiments than individualistic ones; see Den Hartogh, *Farewell to Non-commitment* at 62. Perhaps akin to blood donation, see Titmuss, *The Gift Relationship*.
[107] Martin and Meslin, 'The give and take' at 71.

assertion and ignores the 'relational' aspect of formalised gifting which is almost entirely lacking here. Even with respect to donor families, anonymity and confidentiality are generally preserved and the recipient will usually remain unaware of the provenance of the body part(s). Therefore any notion of reciprocation is largely meaningless, and such enforced 'distance' may even serve to lessen any necessity for reciprocity in the first place. Whilst families of deceased persons and their recipients sometimes seek further contact after the event, this appears to be a highly individual and non-pervasive matter.[108]

---

[108] Nevertheless, even where distance is maintained between recipients and donor families (a policy more evident in Europe than in the US), there is evidence that many donor families wish to receive information regarding the recipient and that recipients wish to have on-going contact with donor families and to express their thanks. This suggests that 'the gift' does continue to exercise a 'pull', although it is not apparently significantly burdensome to either families or recipients. See M. Sque, 'Bereavement, decision-making and the family in organ donation', in A.-M. Farrell, M. Quigley and D. Price (eds.), *Organ Shortage: Ethics, Law and Pragmatism* (Cambridge University Press, forthcoming 2010), and Healy, *Last Best Gifts*, pp. 33–4. See also S. Holtkamp, *Wrapped in Mourning: The Gift of Life and the Organ Donor Family Trauma* (New York: Brunner–Routledge, 2002).

# 4    Consent to donation

Consent is generally seen as the central ethical and legal justification for the removal and use of tissues and organs for the purposes considered here. (Appropriate) consent was variously described as the 'cornerstone' and the 'golden thread' of the Human Tissue Act 2004,[1] intended to reflect the change wrought by that Act contrasted with the previous law which alluded to a 'lack of objection'. The same may be said of the legislation passed in Scotland in 2006, albeit that that statute uses the term 'authorisation' as opposed to consent. Other jurisdictions have analogous provisions with respect to both transplantation and research. With respect to deceased persons, the US Uniform Anatomical Gift Acts (UAGAs) seek to encapsulate the same concept (of explicit permission) in the notion of an 'anatomical gift'. However, not only are there exceptions, or 'holes', in the existing consent requirements, but historically consent has been anything but the norm for the retention and use of *surplus* tissue from living persons or, following post-mortem examination, *for research*.[2] There are, moreover, major challenges in determining what consent means, or should mean, and what conditions need to be fulfilled for a consent to be valid in these contexts. It conceals a plethora of linguistic, philosophical and juristic complexities and difficulties.[3] Its function and role is itself often misunderstood or opaque.[4] 'Consent' nevertheless serves to highlight that body materials are not generally available either to society as a whole or to specific individuals to use, even for accepted purposes, and

---

[1] Dr Ladyman, Under-Secretary of State for Health, House of Commons Standing Committee G, col. 66, 27 January 2004. It has also been described as the fundamental principle of the Human Tissue Act 2008 recently enacted in New Zealand.

[2] Tissue removed in excess of what is required for such a clinical purpose will not, however, be 'surplus'.

[3] See M. Brazier, 'Organ retention and return: Problems of consent' (2003) 29 *Journal of Medical Ethics* 30. See also P. Westen, *The Logic of Consent* (Aldershot: Ashgate, 2004), p.vii [Westen, *The Logic of Consent*].

[4] Beyleveld and Brownsword observe that 'there is a great deal to understand about the idea of consent'. See D. Beyleveld and R. Brownsword, *Consent in the Law* (Oxford: Hart Publishing, 2008), p. 333 [Beyleveld and Brownsword, *Consent in the Law*].

that permission is required to this end. They may not just be 'taken'. Consent signals that individuals have a 'right to control' their bodily materials in these contexts.

Consent has a potentially transformative effect upon the legal and moral rights and duties, and relationship, between the relevant parties. Hurd states 'when we give consent, we create rights for others'.[5] In the current context it will render legitimate acts which would otherwise be wrongs and potentially subject to remedies and sanctions. This draws attention to the necessary conditions of its validity. We should consider how consent is properly tokened or *signalled*, how *informed* the choice to agree to the activity concerned needs to be, and what the *scope* of a consent is. We shall entertain the first matter here and reserve consideration of the remaining two matters for a later chapter.[6] There are common matters here affecting both transplantation and research, although the latter two issues impact peculiarly upon research.

## Fallacies

From a standard liberal perspective no 'wrong' can be done to a person who possesses decision-making capacity and who consents to the use of their body or body parts for a particular end. On a rights-based philosophy, the principal function of consent is to signal some concession in relation to the benefit covered by the right, the giving of consent being the procedural justification for what would otherwise be a violation of the right in question.[7] This is potentially compatible with both interest-based and will-based rights perspectives.[8] Whilst the action may constitute a 'harm', at worst it amounts to a non-wrongful harm, as a consequence of which no censure can attach. The (private) wrongfulness of action therefore turns upon the failure to respect the decision-making autonomy of the tissue source. It chimes with a view of respect for the dignity of persons, where dignity is viewed in terms of empowerment.[9] Beyleveld and Brownsword state that 'If a regime systematically rejects the relevance of consent where a private wrong is alleged, it cannot be founded on respect

---

[5] H. Hurd, 'The moral magic of consent' (1996) 2 *Legal Theory* 121 at 121 [Hurd, 'The moral magic']. Strictly speaking it would seem that consent serves to create an immunity rather than any claim right.

[6] See chapter 6, Informed consent.

[7] Beyleveld and Brownsword, *Consent in the Law*, p. 238.

[8] J. Feinberg, *The Moral Limits of the Criminal Law*, Vol. I, *Harm to Others* (Oxford University Press, 1984). Feinberg promotes an interest-based perspective.

[9] D. Beyleveld and R. Brownsword, *Dignity in Bioethics and Biolaw* (Oxford University Press, 2002), chapter 1.

for human rights and the autonomy of agents'.[10] Utilitarian rationales, by contrast, do not accord priority to rights *per se*; they ascribe only instrumental significance to both rights and consent.

Foot observes that harms to others require justification over and above mere consent to their doing.[11] Consent is not an entire legal explanation for the legitimacy of harms inflicted by third parties on willing individuals.[12] Beyleveld and Brownsword allude to the *fallacy of sufficiency* in this context – i.e. that there is no wrong where consent is given to the act which constitutes the *prima facie* wrong.[13] Whilst there is no *private* wrong as between these parties – at least under a rights-based scheme – there may still be a *public* wrong committed; thus compelling reasons may be required even where consent has been given.[14] Thus, whilst exclusively liberal thinking may seemingly part company with public policy expressed in laws,[15] such perspectives are reconcilable on the basis that where a person consents to a harm no wrong can be done *to her* by its infliction, but that there remains the possibility that there are private harms caused to others, or overriding harms to society.[16] There are differences between the civil and the criminal law with respect to the function and sufficiency of consent.[17] Thus, looked at in the round, consent cannot validate general *practices* or *policies* in their own right. Laws everywhere appear to reflect an amalgam of liberal and dignitarian perspectives; an expansive view of respect for persons.[18]

The Nuffield Council on Bioethics Working Party Report, *Human Tissue: Ethical and Legal Issues*, asserted that the central ethical principle

---

[10] Beyleveld and Brownsword, *Consent in the Law*, p. 235. They proceed on the basis of a Gewirthian view that rights are necessary for humans to function as moral agents, demonstrating autonomy in the application of choice.

[11] P. Foot, 'Euthanasia' (1977) 6 *Philosophy and Public Affairs* 85.

[12] For instance, in many jurisdictions, including the UK, whilst attempted suicide has been decriminalised, assisting suicide remains a crime; see Suicide Act 1961.

[13] Indeed, as Smith states 'In other words, consenting to an action does not make it right *per se*; it means that the authorising agent has allowed the particular action'; see S. Smith, (2008) 16(1) *Medical Law Review* 160 at 161, book review.

[14] There may also be private wrongs to non-consenting third parties, e.g. xenotransplantation, where third parties may be placed at risk through potential disease transmission.

[15] See L. Katz, 'Choice, consent, and cycling: The hidden limitations of consent' (2006) 104 *Michigan Law Review* 1.

[16] Such jurisprudential reasoning can be seen, for instance, in *R (on the application of Pretty)* v. *DPP* [2002] 1 All ER 1 (HL) and *Washington* v. *Glucksberg* 117 S Ct. 2258 (1997) in the context of assisted suicide and *R* v. *Brown* [1994] AC 212 *vis-à-vis* offences against the person.

[17] Beyleveld and Brownsword, *Consent in the Law*, chapters 8 and 9.

[18] Kant viewed acts of self-mutilation as wrongs, based on the breach of a duty to self. However, the notion of duties to self has always been controversial; see S. Kagan, *Normative Ethics* (Boulder, CO: Westview Press, 1998), pp. 145–52.

with regard to human lives and the human body is *respect*. It interpreted this to mean that some uses of human tissue are indubitably illegitimate, and that avoidance and limitation of injury is the basic requirement for any type of ethically acceptable use.[19] What amounts to a public wrong can therefore be gleaned from, amongst other things, the purpose for which the acts were performed and the degree of harm involved, with there being a correlation between them.[20] It may, for instance, be acceptable for a living person to donate a part of a liver for transplantation, but not for research. Whilst it might appear that it is consent that is of overriding importance in determining the legitimacy of varying medical uses of the human body, one must appreciate that the legislation in this context is inherently *permissive*. Statutes such as the Human Tissue Act 2004 and analogous provisions elsewhere only enable consent to be given to certain specific, stipulated and pre-ordained purposes.[21] In effect, the legislation has already 'screened out' potentially acceptable forms of activity which would be justified by the, additional, provision of consent.[22]

Removal and use may sometimes be justified even in the absence of consent. It is a misperception that the only justification which may be advanced to a *prima facie* wrong is consent. Whilst consent may provide a potential *procedural* justification so as to negate any potential wrong between the parties, there may be other alternative *substantive* justifications available in some instances based on overriding rights, e.g. self-defence.[23] Such a substantive public interest rationale may be seen to apply in relation to specific forms of research. There is a provision in the 2004 Act allowing material from living or deceased persons to be exceptionally used for research in the public interest by the High Court in circumstances set out by the Secretary of State in regulations. This limited 'concession' was enacted to cater for extreme circumstances where the safety of society as a whole was threatened by a novel, unknown and/or extremely serious sudden outbreak of disease, a virus, or bioterrorism,

---

[19] Nuffield Council on Bioethics Working Party Report, *Human Tissue: Ethical and Legal Issues*, 1995, Nuffield Council, London, 1995, at paras. 6.4–6.16 [Nuffield Council, *Human Tissue*].

[20] For instance, whilst maim has traditionally been regarded as a crime in Anglo-American jurisprudence, being a serious harm inflicted without good cause, extremely serious 'injury' may be legitimately inflicted in a surgical context in pursuit of the clinical interests of a patient.

[21] The 2004 and 2006 Acts create criminal offences for, *inter alia*, non-consented to/ unauthorised activities, but no civil remedies are explicitly generated.

[22] See D. Price, 'Property, harm and the corpse', in B. Brooks-Gordon, F. Ebtehaj, J. Herring, M. Johnson and M. Richards (eds.), *Death Rites and Rights* (Oxford: Hart Publishing, 2007) 199 at 200–10.

[23] See Beyleveld and Brownsword, *Consent in the Law*.

where it might not be possible to obtain the consent of the living/deceased person or any surviving relative.[24] Whilst the High Court 'deems' consent in these situations, the justification is to be found in the collective interest, as opposed to any notion of 'consent'. Likewise, the Act states that consent is not required for the use of surplus material from the living for audit, quality assurance, public health monitoring, or education and training, purposes.[25] It was stated during the Parliamentary debates that use of tissue for public health monitoring and health-related training and education are considered to be necessary for the 'public weal'.[26] In some contexts, consent is illegitimately relied upon as the underpinning justificatory rationale when in reality the justification is properly to be found elsewhere. An example can be found in both the 2004 and 2006 Acts allowing preservation measures to be applied to corpses to temporarily preserve organs (e.g. by cooling) for potential transplantation, whilst efforts are made to secure consent. It has often been suggested that this provision is based on the presumed consent of the now deceased person, but this is not convincing apart from in a presumed consent system where the deceased had not objected.[27] This is a matter regarding which most individuals have no knowledge at all prior to their deaths. It is clearly justified on the basis of the public interest in generating an opportunity for consent to be given to an activity deemed to be advantageous to society, not consent.

Although consent is not the only justificatory feature of ethically acceptable action using human tissue, it is generally a *necessary* element of it, at least as regards individuals with decision-making capacity.[28] Certain commentators have, however, warned against a growing *fixation with consent*, the detaching or uncoupling of consent from its moorings. Brownsword, for instance, remarks

According to the standard version of modern history, we have learned the hard way that informed consent matters. This being so, it would be unfortunate indeed if, as a result of a fixation with consent, we became unclear as to why it matters – and it

---

[24] Section 7(4). Such a case was described by the Minister as 'truly exceptional' and 'rare and unusual' during the Parliamentary debates. The example was given of the Ebola virus. No such regulations have yet been made.

[25] Section 1(9) and Schedule 1, Part 2, Human Tissue Act 2004. There are also provisions in both Acts enabling research to be carried out with existing holdings, i.e. previously archived tissue.

[26] See Dr Ladyman, House of Commons Hansard Debates, Standing Committee G, col. 73, 27 January 2004.

[27] Compare M. Sangster, '"Cooling corpses": section 43 of the Human Tissue Act 2004 and organ donation' (2007) 2 *Clinical Ethics* 23 and D. Bell, 'Emergency medicine, organ donation and the Human Tissue Act' (2006) 23 *Emergency Medicine Journal* 824.

[28] This was the Nuffield Council's view; see Nuffield Council, *Human Tissue*, at para. 6.17.

would be nothing short of tragic if we reverted to thinking that human rights on which consent is parasitic scarcely matter at all.[29]

There is a tendency toward perceiving consent as a 'free-standing ethic or justificatory standard', the view that there is a wrong merely on account of an absence of consent *per se*. Morally speaking, consent may make things right but its absence does not in and of itself make things wrong. We have already noted that consent in this connection is linked to a right of control and is not merely one aspect of a utilitarian balancing act. Beyleveld and Brownsword note that, from a rights-centred perspective, it is to commit the fallacy of necessity to suppose that any kind of justification is called for in the absence of a *prima facie* violation of an agent's rights.[30] The question therefore is what wrong is committed if consent is not obtained prior to the carrying out of the activity concerned. This is necessarily linked to what interests the requirement is intended to serve and protect. If there were no interests demanding protection there would be no need to require consent to safeguard them, and even the routine taking of human material would be permissible, without more. These interests were analysed in chapter 2. They are the interests of the tissue source.

## Types of consent

It is typically maintained that consent may either be *explicit, implicit,* or *tacit*. Explicit consent is an expressed consent, consisting of some overt communication of agreement. In much medical practice, however, consent is frequently implicit, conveyed by other actions, e.g. where when one rolls up one's sleeve to enable a blood sample to be taken. Arguably implicit consent is the basis for the absence of a requirement for consent in relation to surplus tissue from the living for clinical audit, quality assurance and performance assessment in the 2004 Act. Speaking for the Government during the passage of the Human Tissue Bill through Parliament with respect to the exception to the need for consent for clinical audit, quality control and on-the-job training, Rosie Winterton MP stated 'Where tissue is taken from living patients, some purposes are so bound up with general diagnostic and clinical care that the consent the patient gives to the procedure itself can be regarded as consent to those other purposes'.[31] In some, limited, circumstances, consent

---

[29] R. Brownsword, 'The cult of consent: Fixation and fallacy' (2004) 15(2) *King's College Law Journal* 223 at 251.

[30] Beyleveld and Brownsword, *Consent in the Law*, p. 239.

[31] R. Winterton MP, House of Commons Hansard Debates, col. 990, 15 January 2004. See also Australian Law Reform Commission, *Essentially Yours: The Protection of Human Genetic Information in Australia*, ALRC Report 96, Sydney, 2003, at para. 19.23. In the

may instead be tacit. Childress has described tacit consent as a 'consent that is expressed silently or passively by omissions or by failures to indicate or signify dissent'.[32] Finally, legal consent may be *imputed*, although to some this rests on a fiction and cannot be considered a true 'consent'. Beauchamp and Childress are sceptical regarding the latter, stating 'Consent should refer to an individual's actual choices, not to presumptions about the choices the individual would or should make'.[33]

The Human Tissue Act 2004 states that 'appropriate consent' must be obtained for storage and use of tissue for either research or transplantation.[34] In respect of tissue from deceased persons such consent also legitimates the removal of tissue from the corpse itself (as regards living persons, the removal of tissue is governed by the common law). It has typically been claimed or assumed that the 2004 Act is an explicit consent system, and the same applies to the system of authorisation under the Human Tissue (Scotland) Act 2006. However, the 2004 statute does not define what 'appropriate consent' is, only *whose* consent this is in any particular instance; although, of course, such legislation operates against the backdrop of the general law. As McHale states 'One issue which remains to be determined following the Human Tissue Act coming into force is what, precisely, is meant by consent'.[35] The Act merely alludes to the person having made a 'decision' to consent to the activity or not to consent to the activity.[36] This would not be problematic if consent had a clear core agreed meaning. But it does not. Exceptionally, section 3 of the 2004 Act creates requirements as regards an activity involving storage for use, or use, for the purpose of either public display or anatomical examination, where a signed and attested signature to a consent expressed in written form by the deceased is required.[37] In so far as no form of consent is stipulated in any other scenario it might perhaps be perceived that, contrariwise, consent need *not* necessarily otherwise be explicit.[38]

---

same way, the retention of tissue blocks and slides is viewed by the Human Tissue (Scotland) Act 2006 as a vital aspect of the performance of the autopsy itself. Performance assessment may include evaluations of *in-vitro* diagnostic devices.

[32] J. Childress, *Practical Reasoning in Bioethics* (Bloomington, IN: Indiana University Press, 1977), p. 277.

[33] T. Beauchamp and J. Childress, *Principles of Biomedical Ethics*, 6th edn. (Oxford University Press, 2008), p. 107.

[34] The provisions are contained in section 2 as regards children and section 3 as regards adults.

[35] J. McHale, '"Appropriate consent" and the use of human material for research purposes: The competent adult' (2006) 1 *Clinical Ethics* 195 at 196.

[36] Section 3(6)(a). Consent may therefore be given orally in England, Wales and Northern Ireland without any particular formalities, so that relatives would ordinarily be the ones to communicate such a decision.

[37] Section 3(3)–(5).

[38] There frequently are form requirements attached to a legally valid consent in this sphere, though. Section 6(2), Human Tissue (Scotland) Act 2006 stipulates that an authorisation

However, the debates on the passage of the Human Tissue Bill, coupled with the recommendations of the inquiry reports which led to the legislation itself, all envisaged consent as being explicit in all instances for the purpose of the statute.[39] Indeed, the Human Tissue Authority (HTA) Code of Practice on Consent states that 'The giving of consent is a positive act', implying a definite communicative gesture.[40] Indeed, whether even the concept of a 'decision' could be conceptually disengaged from the positive communication of a choice or wish is unclear. It is frequently alleged that presumed consent is no consent because there is no evidence of any 'decision' having actually been made at all.

## The ontology of consent

Legal consent generally encompasses a *factual* consent of some kind, either internal (subjective) or external (objective). Factual consent refers either to a *mental state of acquiescence* or to the *expression* of such a mental state, i.e. a psychological phenomenon or something one does.[41] There may be a fracture between these two notions, in so far as a mental state of acquiescence may exist despite not having been expressed at all, or an expression of agreement may not in fact reflect the individual's underlying (non-consensual) mental state. Indeed, many parents involved in the organ retention episodes supposedly 'consented' expressly to their child's 'tissues' being used for research, when their expectation was that 'tissue' was considerably more limited in scope than it was ultimately taken by the professionals to be, i.e. their understanding and expectations differed from what was expressed on the face of things.

It is sometimes asserted that there is a distinction between consent itself and *evidence* of such consent, whether by way of a consent form or otherwise. The Department of Health Reference Guide to Consent states 'The validity of consent does not depend on the form in which it is given. Written consent merely serves as evidence of consent: if the elements of

made by a person prior to their death must either be in writing or be made orally. The 2006 Uniform Anatomical Gift Act similarly states that an anatomical gift made by a donor must be made either in writing, in a will, or by authorising a statement or symbol on a driving licence or identification card, or in any form of communication (addressed to at least two adult witnesses) during a terminal illness or injury; see section 5(a)(3).

[39] The Government stated that it anticipated 'Explicit consent to be the fundamental principle underpinning the lawful removal, storage and use of bodies, body parts, organs and tissue'; see 'Proposals for new legislation on human organs and tissue', Department of Health, 2003 at 2.

[40] Human Tissue Authority Code of Practice, Consent, July 2006, HTA, para. 17

[41] Westen enquires what it is that negates criminal responsibility: 'Is it a subjective experience on S's part of choosing conduct for herself? Or is it an objective act on S's part of communicating her choice? Or both? Or neither?' See Westen, *The Logic of Consent*, p. 139.

voluntariness, appropriate information and capacity have not been satisfied, a signature on a form will not make the consent valid'.[42] In the House of Lords in *Sidaway* v. *Governors of the Royal Bethlem Hospital*, Lord Diplock stated 'Consent to battery is a state of mind personal to the victim of the battery'.[43] Grubb has similarly observed that 'A valid legal consent is given even where the patient does not demonstrate his agreement providing that *the state of mind* was, in fact, that he agreed. In other words, an unexpressed *actual* consent in law is a valid consent.'[44] This would tend toward the view that consent is a mental state of acquiescence rather than an expression of such a state, despite the more pervasive 'lay' view that consent is something that a person 'does'.[45] However, as we have seen, a move towards consent as being *expressive* can be witnessed in the 2004 and 2006 Acts in the UK.

### Displaying an attitude

Whether consent *should* be seen as either subjective or objective is a matter of policy rather than philosophical enquiry.[46] It depends upon the policy objectives which the law seeks to achieve in the particular context. There are a variety of legislative approaches to consent around the globe in other contexts, with some jurisdictions defining consent as a subjective mental state ('attitudinal') and others as an objective expression of an acquiescing state of mind ('expressive').

From a moral perspective, Hurd and Alexander assert that consent is a mental state and an 'exercise of the will'.[47] There should be some definite mental acquiescence in altering the rights and status of the other party. Wertheimer, however, regards consent as expressive. He states 'It is of the utmost moral relevance to the evaluation of A's behaviour whether A *has reason to think* that B wants him to proceed'.[48] He adds

---

[42] Department of Health, Reference Guide to Consent for Examination or Treatment, 2001, Department of Health, at para. 11. Moreover, the Code of Practice on Consent states 'However, giving consent should not be seen as a single act – the signing of a consent form. Rather, it should be seen as part of a continuing process', Human Tissue Authority Code of Practice, Consent, HTA, July 2006, para. 68.

[43] *Sidaway v. Governors of the Royal Bethlem Hospital* [1985] 1 All ER 643 at 658.

[44] A. Grubb, 'Consent to treatment: The competent patient', in I. Kennedy and A. Grubb (eds.), *Principles of Medical Law* (Oxford University Press, 1998) 109 at 125 [Kennedy and Grubb, *Principles of Medical Law*].

[45] Health professionals frequently speak of 'consenting the patient' and patients of 'giving consent'.

[46] Westen, *The Logic of Consent*, pp. 140–1.

[47] See Hurd, 'The moral magic' at 121 and L. Alexander, 'The moral magic of consent II' (1996) 1 *Legal Theory* 165.

[48] A. Wertheimer, *Consent to Sexual Relations* (Cambridge University Press, 2003), p. 147 [Wertheimer, *Consent to Sexual Relations*].

B's consent is morally transformative because it changes A's reasons for action. If we ask what could change A's reasons for action, the answer must be that B performs some token of consent. It is hard to see how B's mental state – by itself – can do the job.[49]

Feinberg likewise supports the expressive view of consent. He states

*Acts* of consent are especially important when our attention centers on the criminal liability of the actor (A) in two-party cases, and the exculpatory effect of his reasons for action. He does not have any direct insight into B's mental states, so the question of his responsibility must be settled by reference to the presence or absence of explicit authorization by B, not what B's secret desires or hopes might have been.[50]

Feinberg argues that mere psychological willingness or passive acquiescence is not sufficient authorisation to *transfer responsibility* for actions.[51] Whilst Beyleveld and Brownsword allege that acting within the scope of the actor's will is the paramount concern, they state that 'Such a one-sided model, however, fails to protect the interests of agent B who, in good faith, believes that he or she is the recipient of a consent signalled by agent A'.[52] Their view is that, where consent is ostensibly signalled but does not reflect the individual's true subjective will, the actions of the recipient should nevertheless be protected on the basis of the principle of reasonable expectation.[53] They therefore imply that where a person signals their consent, this objectively *constitutes* their consent. There is a tension between protecting the rights of 'consentors' on the one hand and those persons who act on the basis of such (supposed) consent on the other. If the law leans too heavily in one direction it will tend to overprotect one party and underprotect the other.[54]

Even Hurd accepts that there may be good prudential reasons in law to require some overt behaviour manifesting such consent before permitting a legal defence, i.e. an unexpressed acquiescence may not be *normative* or

---

[49] *Ibid.*, p. 146.
[50] See J. Feinberg, *Harm to Self* (Oxford University Press, 1986), p. 173 [Feinberg, *Harm to Self*].
[51] Archard advances a similar opinion. He states 'Consent is an act rather than a state of mind. Consent is something I do rather than I think or feel … The view of consent as something that is done rather than as a state of mind is normally expressed by the statement that consent should be understood in "performative" and not "psychological" terms'. See D. Archard, *Sexual Consent* (Boulder, CO: Westview Press, 1998), p. 4.
[52] Beyleveld and Brownsword, *Consent in the Law*, p. 189.    [53] *Ibid.*, p. 348.
[54] Beyleveld and Brownsword state that 'When we discussed the signalling requirement …, we suggested that legal regimes should be guided by a principle of fidelity (to the consenting agent's will) and by a principle of reasonable transactional expectation (to protect the interests of the recipient). If we ignore the former, we under-protect the consenting agent, but if we ignore the latter, we over-protect the same agent'; *ibid.*, p. 343.

*prescriptive.*[55] Thus, it does not follow that if consent was regarded in essence as a matter of subjective acquiescence the law would regard there as being no justification for acting where there was a lack of consensus in fact. Grubb states

[W]here the patient conducts himself such that it is reasonable to *imply* that he consented to the treatment or procedure, the law merely prohibits the patient because of his conduct from denying that he consented even though, in fact, he did not.[56]

He maintains that this is better understood as a species of estoppel than as a form of 'consent'.[57] Consequently, whether such expression *constitutes* the consent or is an additional requirement attaching to a valid consent may lack practical significance and amount to a mere matter of semantics in most situations. The law is principally concerned with the *adequacy* of consent in any particular context, as opposed to the *meaning* of consent. What is required either way is something which entitles a person to assume that the legal relationship between them has changed and justifies their action, i.e. is transformative. Westen, however, observes that where consent is based on objective expression, punishment is being predicated upon the harms that the actor believes or ought to assume he is inflicting upon the other party, whereas where it is based on a subjective mental state it is predicated on whether that other party actually suffers the harm(s) the offence was designed to prevent.[58] He states

Jurisdictions that define prescriptive consent as an objective expression on S's part are choosing to predicate an actor's punishment for offenses of non-consent solely upon the harms that he believes or ought to assume he is inflicting upon S, and not upon whether he succeeds in actually inflicting them. In turn, jurisdictions that define prescriptive consent as a subjective mental state on S's part are choosing to predicate an actor's punishment for offenses of non-consent in part on whether S actually suffers the harms that the offenses are designed to prevent.[59]

To conflate 'consent' and an 'expression of consent' *per se* is not merely of symbolic significance, though,[60] it raises other challenges. Hurd, who

---

[55]  Hurd, 'Moral magic' at 122.

[56]  A. Grubb, 'Consent to treatment', in Kennedy and Grubb, *Principles of Medical Law* at 125.

[57]  If this were nonetheless to be conceived as a 'consent', it would be a fictionalised (imputed) consent.

[58]  Westen, *The Logic of Consent*, p. 73. Dressler emphasises that the absence of consent is an element of the *actus reus* of rape; see J. Dressler, 'Some cautionary reflections on rape law reform' (1998) 46 *Cleveland State Law Review* 409 at 424. This would not, however, preclude the use of the law of attempts in the criminal law in certain situations.

[59]  *Ibid.*, p. 141. He observes that if a 'victim' chooses an act of sexual intercourse, she does not suffer the primary harm of rape.

[60]  Herring maintains that because the deceased might not even have objected to the nonconsensual removal of material, and thus not be harmed, the offence in section 5 of the

subscribes to the view of consent as an act of will, states that 'One consents to an act subject to certain beliefs about it. False beliefs that cause one to misdescribe another's act may thus vitiate one's consent to that act. Put differently, in cases in which false beliefs result in such a misdescription, there may be consent to *an* act, but there may be no consent to *the* act.'[61] The salutary lessons of Alder Hey highlight the critical need for proper and adequate accompanying information preceding and underpinning every 'consensual' act to ensure that such decisions truly effect the individual's will.

## An appropriate consent?

The Human Tissue Act 2004 generates offences relating to the absence of 'appropriate' consent, ostensibly premised on consent as an expression of agreement.[62] Where the person *did* subjectively agree to the actions of the third party, even though this was not accurately communicated by him, conviction of the third party would punish him even in the absence of any harm caused. However, the third party would have no proper reason to assume he was entitled to act in the first place. Where consent *was* expressed but did not accurately convey the wishes and expectations of the 'consentor', no offence would be committed despite the fact that no subjective consensus existed. Harm may be caused but no blame attaches to the actor. Thus, the notion that consent is expressive provides protection for the actor to the extent that no liability can ensue where the actions are consistent with the overt communications of the 'consentor'.

It may seem as though consent is being regarded as a matter of form rather than substance. But the need for expression can be seen as providing reliable evidence that a 'decision' was in fact made and that agreement really exists, i.e. cogent evidence of the agent's will.[63] As Simons observes, 'The very act of communicating, which requires some self-consciousness

---

2004 Act cannot be directed solely to the interests of the deceased at all; see J. Herring, 'Crimes against the dead', in B. Brooks-Gordon, F. Ebtehaj, J. Herring, M. Johnson and M. Richards (eds.), *Death Rites and Rights* (Oxford: Hart Publishing, 2007) 219 at 236.

[61] Hurd, 'The moral magic' at 127.

[62] Sections 5(1) and 8(2), 2004 Act also state that no liability arises where the professional concerned 'reasonably believed' that appropriate consent had been given, even though it had not. The 2006 Act has an analogous provision. On the surface, this might appear to reflect a view of consent as a mental state; that where consent was seemingly expressed but in fact did not exist, a defence of reasonable (factual) mistake was available. However, this defence was apparently intended principally to cater for situations where a researcher is wrongly informed by another that consent had been obtained for the activity.

[63] S. McLean, 'Consent and the Law: Review of the current provisions in the Human Fertilisation and Embryology Act 1990 for UK Health Ministers', Consultation Document, 1997 at 2.5. See also Beyleveld and Brownsword, *Consent in the Law*, p. 187.

and some effort to articulate feelings, at least renders it more likely that the underlying state of mind communicated is more stable'.[64] If no expression was required, only ambiguous evidence exists that any decision was ever reached, even in terms of a subjective state of mind. Wertheimer similarly states that 'In opting for a performative account of consent, I readily grant that tokens of consent are morally significant precisely because they are reliable indications of desires, intentions, choices, and the like'.[65]

### The sounds of silence

In this section I will consider what moral and legal effect is, and should be, drawn from the silence or passivity of the deceased person.

#### Explicit consent

An explicit consent system is one where only such a consent will suffice to permit removal and use of organs and tissues for transplantation or research after death. This might nevertheless be the consent of the deceased, the consent of relatives (or a prioritised relative), or of a nominated representative (proxy).

Interestingly, in explicit consent systems the absence of an expressed wish to donate during life is not taken as presumed evidence of a wish *not* to donate. To that extent, straightforward analogies with living persons break down. Thus, whilst Gill states that under an explicit consent regime 'if there is no evidence that an individual either wanted or did not want to donate her organs after her death, she is currently treated as though she did not want to donate',[66] this is not strictly correct. Silence does not carry such an inference or otherwise there would be evidence of an objection, which would preclude a relative from giving consent instead in almost all jurisdictions. Silence seemingly amounts to no more than a mere failure to consent.[67] However, the typical explicit consent system has been best described as a 'no-objection-to-delegation' system.[68] This would appear

---

[64] K. Simons, 'The conceptual structure of consent in criminal law' (2006) 9 *Buffalo Criminal Law Review* 577 at 599.

[65] Wertheimer, *Consent to Sexual Relations*, p. 147.

[66] M. Gill, 'Presumed consent, autonomy, and organ donation' (2004) 29(1) *Journal of Medicine and Philosophy* 37 at 37.

[67] Mehlman states 'Currently in the United States, a person is presumed to be *un*willing to donate his or her organs at death unless the person, or the family gives permission. In other words, ours is a system of "presumed nonconsent"'; see M. Mehlman, 'Presumed consent to organ donation: A reevaluation' (1991) 1 *Health Matrix* 31 at 31.

[68] G. den Hartogh, *Farewell to Non-commitment: Decision Systems for Organ Donation from an Ethical Viewpoint*, Monitoring Report Ethics and Health, Centre for Ethics and Health, The Hague, 2008 at 11.

to be the appropriate presumption as this is the *default position* in the absence of any decision being made by the deceased. One can therefore assert that the official stance in such instances is that there is an operative presumption that relatives are entitled to make a decision to donate unless the deceased had pre-emptively taken the matter out of their jurisdiction by making an explicit decision regarding donation before death.

Statutes themselves generally contain no specific statement of what inference should be drawn from the silence of the deceased in such contexts. Interestingly though, the Human Tissue (Scotland) Act 2006 does make certain assertions in this regard. It states that whilst a nearest relative may not give an authorisation for transplantation where he or she has 'actual knowledge' that the deceased was unwilling that his body be so used, the mere fact that no authorisation was given is not to be regarded as such unwillingness.[69] 'Actual knowledge' implies direct oral communication with a relative or the family generally, or some form of written direction.

With respect to nearest-relative authorisation, the 2006 Act further states that where the deceased issued an authorisation for the use of tissue for the purpose of transplantation alone, this does not preclude the nearest relative from giving an authorisation after death for the use of such tissue for research, education or training, or audit, unless the relative has actual knowledge that the adult was unwilling for any part of the body, or the part in question, to be used for such a purpose.[70] Where the deceased has given an authorisation for a certain body part to be used for transplantation, the relative may also give an authorisation for the use of *other* body parts for a different purpose, such as research, unless he/she has actual knowledge that the deceased person was unwilling for the other parts in question to be used for *transplantation*.[71] However, there are some intriguing 'improper inferences' referred to. Not only does the relevant sub-section state that where the deceased's authorisation extends only to the use of certain parts for transplantation this is not to be considered as an unwillingness that such parts be used for other (e.g. research) purposes, but neither should this give rise to an inference of actual knowledge that the deceased did not wish other parts to be used for transplantation; which would preclude a relative giving an authorisation for the use of other parts for purposes such as research.[72] The first of these inferences seems entirely understandable in so far as there is no reason why the thought or decision-making process involved should necessarily have extended beyond the transplant sphere, e.g. entering one's name on the NHS Organ Donor Register. However,

---

[69] Section 7(4)(a) and (5)(a).     [70] Section 7(2) and 7(4)(b).
[71] Section 7(4)(c).     [72] Section 7(5)(b) and (c).

with regard to the latter inference, this would seem to be open to the objection that it *is* usually reasonable to assume from a declared wish that a certain part or parts be used for transplantation that there is an unwillingness that other parts be used for that purpose. This is a presumption which is merited in the circumstances from the failure to authorise *per se*. It is well known that a minority of individuals are perfectly happy for their organs and tissues to be used for transplantation in general, but to have reservations as regards the donation of certain tissues, e.g. corneas.[73]

The Scottish legislation apparently shares such a stance with the latest (2006) version of the UAGA. Section 8(e) states that, in the absence of an express, contrary indication by the donor or other person authorised to make an anatomical gift, an anatomical gift of a part is neither a refusal to give another part nor a limitation on the making of an anatomical gift of another part at a later time by the donor or another person. The difficulty resides in the reference to a 'contrary indication'. However, the provision apparently has its origins in local issues relating to the wording of donor cards issued by specific organisations, which ostensibly limited donation to only one organ.[74] Much depends upon the wording of such forms, but a specific donation of certain parts would normally tend to infer at least a reluctance to donate other body parts. The same issue would perhaps apply where, assuming this was permissible, a deceased person had donated organs to a specific person or class of persons. If the relatives could then donate organs or tissues to persons other than those specified, this would seem to run entirely counter to the wishes of the deceased, which would surely be inappropriate.

As has been noted, all laws state that relatives are not permitted to decide to donate organs where the deceased did not wish such donation to take place. The question then arises as to *what evidence suffices* to establish such an objection? In terms of mechanisms for communicating objections, where there is a register upon which such objections may be recorded, this is the key medium. But many jurisdictions with explicit consent regimes still do not have an opt out register, e.g. the UK, and in the US and Canada. We should turn to the wording of the relevant statutes first, though. Starting with the Human Tissue Act 2004, the statute states that the 'appropriate consent' is only that of a (qualifying) relative where there was no decision of the deceased's to consent to the activity, or a decision of his not to consent to the activity in question, in

---

[73] See B. Kent and R. Owens, 'Conflicting attitudes to corneal and organ donation: A study of nurses' attitudes to organ donation' (1995) 32(5) *International Journal of Nursing Studies* 484.

[74] See section 2j of the 1987 Uniform Anatomical Gift Act and associated Commentary.

force immediately before he died.[75] No guidance is, however, provided as to what constitutes a 'decision' for these purposes. Clearly if the deceased included his name on the organ donor register or had signed a donor card, this would constitute a 'decision', as would inclusion on an opt out register where one existed. The deceased may sign a written document attesting to the wish not to donate, as is formally recognised in certain US state laws based on the UAGA,[76] but such statements are seemingly rarely used there or elsewhere. Thus, as regards objections in particular the normal mode of communication is via relatives. These would invariably have been communicated verbally.

But what constitutes an (oral) 'decision' made in the company of relatives? Obviously a definite expressed wish would suffice, but what about reservations expressed casually and informally, e.g. during a TV programme? These would surely be some of the most likely scenarios. The 2004 Act is unclear here. The intention may instead have been to allow relatives to make the decision in such circumstances, but 'informed by' the remarks of the deceased, rather than disenfranchising them from doing more than communicating the deceased's remarks/views. But if such views were clearly expressed perhaps these would suffice to consti-tute a 'decision' in themselves. Indeed, in Scotland the 2006 Act refers alternatively to 'actual knowledge of the deceased's unwillingness'. This appears to be a looser standard and perhaps more reflective of the typical situation. It would, however, disempower relatives from personal 'decision-making' in a significantly greater percentage of instances.

### Tacit consent

Although Garwood-Gowers states that 'There is no such thing as "pre-sumed consent" in philosophical or legal terms; consent is either implicit or explicit or it doesn't exist at all',[77] the notion of tacit consent does have moral and legal validity in some contexts. The Data Protection Act 1998, for instance, allows for different types of information provision and con-sent regimes for 'sensitive' and 'non-sensitive' personal data, and seem-ingly provides for lack of objection rather than a positive expression of

---

[75] Section 3(6). This does not apply to public display or anatomical examination, see section 3(4).

[76] See, e.g., section 7, 2006 Uniform Anatomical Gift Act.

[77] A. Garwood-Gowers, 'Extraction and use of body materials for transplantation and research purposes: The impact of the Human Rights Act 1998', in A. Garwood-Gowers, J. Tingle and T. Lewis (eds.), *Healthcare Law: The Impact of the Human Rights Act 1998* (London: Cavendish Publishing, 2001) 295 at 310.

assent with regard to the latter.[78] The distinction between 'explicit' and 'implicit' (by which is ostensibly meant 'tacit' consent) was also adopted in a proposal for an instrument on the use of archived human biological materials in biomedical research drawn up by the Council of Europe in 2002, where 'Implicit consent' was defined as 'consent that is assumed in the absence of objection after provision of information',[79] i.e. from silence.[80]

*Prima facie*, therefore, silence/passivity *might* conceivably be capable of amounting to a tacit consent in law for the removal and use of tissue for transplantation or research. However, we have already seen that a lack of any overt positive decision may generate substantial ambiguity as to the individual's state of mind. Beyleveld and Brownsword argue

> In the case of signalling, this invites an orientation towards the agent's subjective state of mind; it underlines the need for a personal, distinct and unequivocal indication of consent on the part of the authorising agent; and it suggests that the standard vehicle for signalling consent should be by way of 'opting in' rather than 'opting out'.[81]

However, whilst many laws in this sphere tend toward an explicit consent model, silence might perhaps be seen as an *expressive* factual consent, i.e. a *form of expression*. Simmons argues that calling consent tacit merely points to the special mode of its expression and states 'But tacit consent is nonetheless given or expressed'.[82] He supports the performative, expressive notion of consent and concurs with Westen that all expressions are socially constructed and are to be interpreted according to the persons' interpretive community.[83]

---

[78] Schedules 2 and 3, Data Protection Act 1998. It would also seem to be envisaged by the EU Directive upon which it is based; see Directive 95/46/EC on the Protection of Individuals with Regard to the Processing of Personal Data and on the Free Movement of such Data.

[79] Council of Europe, *Draft Instrument on the Use of Archived Human Biological Materials in Biomedical Research*, Council of Europe, 2002, articles 2 and 16.

[80] Indeed, even the orthodoxy that silence is no acceptance of an offer in the law of contract is less certain than generally assumed. Furmston states 'It may be going too far, however, to say that silence can never be unequivocal evidence of consent'; see M. Furmston, *Cheshire, Fifoot and Furmston's Law of Contract*, Fifteenth edn., (Oxford University Press, 2007), p. 62. The United States Restatement on Contracts specifically provides for certain circumstances or pre-conditions for such agreements; see American Restatement on Contracts, 2nd edn., 1981, section 69.

[81] Beyleveld and Brownsword, *Consent in the Law*, p. 188.

[82] A. John Simmons, *Moral Principles and Political Obligations* (Princeton, NJ: Princeton University Press, 1979), p. 80 [Simmons, *Moral Principles*] and A. John Simmons, 'Tacit consent and political obligation' (1976) 5(3) *Philosophy and Public Affairs* 274.

[83] Westen, *The Logic of Consent*, p. 68.

But silence could only constitute an expression of agreement under certain societal conditions. Consent should not be inferred from silence unless there is good reason to believe that this was reflective of actual acquiescence. Simmons lays down various general pre-conditions to a legitimate and effective tacit consent.[84] These are convincing requirements, albeit that some are more pertinent to the present context than others. If individuals were directly approached and a proper public information programme were in place, a failure to object might arguably be adequate evidence that the person consented to it.

Whilst we are not investigating consent as an ontological concept *per se*, the typical perception of a normative legal consent has a factual basis. The very idea that consent is 'presumed' suggests to many that it is simply concocted, to serve the interests of others. Nonetheless, even *imputed* consent, an alternative legal construction, may potentially have credibility and is considered in chapter 5. Imputed consent is far from anathema to legal systems around the world. Indeed, there is arguably a form of imputed consent to be seen in the concept of substituted judgement which applies to medical treatment in various jurisdictions, rooted in the assumed wishes and values of individuals without decision-making capacity. Feinberg asserts that whilst evidence of the person's wishes does not amount to consent, it may in some circumstances be the best guide as to whether the person would have consented, and will have the same effect as consent. It can be a 'consent surrogate'.[85] Such imputed consent is 'implied in law'.

### Consent from relatives

The formal policy trend toward explicit consent in the UK is highly significant insofar as such 'explicit consent' will typically be that of relatives, rather than the deceased adult; albeit that this has historically been the *practice* in the context of transplantation in any case. Practices have been more variable in the context of medical research. Evidence relates that many parents or relatives were not previously made aware of the normal post-mortem process or practice of removal and retention at all in many instances.

Whether we consider a relative's consent as a *true* consent depends upon the role of the relatives in this connection. If such relatives are simply communicating the deceased's *decision* on his or her behalf, then relatives

---

[84] Simmons, *Moral Principles*, pp. 80–1.
[85] Feinberg, *Harm to Self*, p. 187. Westen describes this as 'hypothetical consent'; see *The Logic of Consent*, p. 284.

are merely acting as agents of the deceased person in this regard. Of course, relatives might even have been explicitly appointed by deceased persons as *proxies* acting for them following their decease. But not only is the appointment of nominated representatives a comparative rarity at the present point in time, but only a few laws formally cater for such a possibility, e.g. UK, the Netherlands, Germany.[86]

In explicit consent systems, laws give relatives the power to consent even where the deceased had not made any donation decision, and their discretion is not typically constrained in any way. Apparently only in Germany must decisions be formally based as a matter of law on what the deceased would apparently have wanted.[87] In general, then, decisions may be based on the supposed wishes of the deceased, those of other relatives, or on their *own* wishes and beliefs. This suggests that a *personal* decision is being made and that relatives' (own) consent *is* an appropriate use of terminology here. But it has already been seen (see chapter 2) that the powers of relatives are entirely *derivative* from the deceased person him/herself. The Explanatory Report to the Council of Europe's Additional (Transplantation) Protocol states 'Unless national law otherwise provides, such authorisation should not depend on the preferences of the close relatives themselves for or against organ and tissue donation. Close relatives should be asked only about the deceased person's expressed or presumed wishes. It is the expressed views of the potential donor which are paramount in deciding whether organs and tissues may be retrieved.'[88]

But if the relatives are intended to be a conduit for the deceased's views, this is dubious as a form of consent where evidence as to the wishes of the deceased person is either unreliable or entirely lacking. Whilst a *substituted judgement* made on behalf of the deceased is a best guesstimate of their wishes it is not a 'factual consent' – whatever the language of the statute concerned – without reliable evidence that this reflects the will of the deceased person. Beyleveld and Brownsword are scathing about the misleading and improper use of the concept and terminology of consent in the law and assert that substituted judgement requires as a minimum that

---

[86] See section 4, 2004 Act. The 2006 Act in Scotland only creates such a possibility in the context of post-mortem examination and the removal and subsequent retention and use of organs; see sections 29 and 30. See also Netherlands Law of 24 May 1996, section 11(4); German Law of 5 November 1997, section 4.

[87] German Law of 5 November 1997, section 4(1), although the Law of 30 January 2002 in Estonia may also be read in this way.

[88] Council of Europe, Explanatory Report to the Additional Protocol to the Convention on Human Rights and Biomedicine Concerning Transplantation of Organs and Tissues of Human Origin, para. 102.

there is evidence that it is more than likely that the other person would have consented to it.[89] At best in other circumstances it is an *imputed* – fictionalised – consent.

Laws frequently prescribe a ranking order as regards relatives who may consent to donation.[90] For instance, under the Human Tissue Act 2004 a hierarchical list of persons in a 'qualifying relationship' is provided,[91] under the US UAGAs classes of persons are listed in the statute,[92] under the Human Tissue (Scotland) Act 2006 the 'nearest relative' is established according to a ranking list, and under various statutes in the states and territories of Australia the ('senior available') next of kin is typically determined in accordance with a prescribed hierarchy.[93] A listing also appears in the German Transplant Law of 1997.[94] There are less frequently ranking orders for relatives under presumed consent schemes. However, in some of the Australian states and territories the (same) 'senior available next of kin' ranking also applies in respect of 'objections' from relatives, where the deceased had not objected to donation.[95]

There are subtle nuances between legislative schemes, although all stipulate that a person in a lower ranking may not consent to donation where someone higher on the list is available at the time to make the decision.[96] In the UK, both the 2004 and 2006 Acts state that consent may be given by one member of the same class of relatives, even though another member or other members of that same class have objections thereto;[97] although this is not to mandate that such a consent must be acted upon. By contrast, in the US the 2006 version of the UAGA states

---

[89] Beyleveld and Brownsword, *Consent in the Law*, pp. 117 and 124.
[90] In particular, such rankings may not reflect the reality of typical decision-making or authority within families from different ethnic and cultural backgrounds.
[91] Listed in section 27(4).
[92] See section 3, 1968 and 1987 Acts and section 6, 2006 Act.
[93] This is typically, in respect of adults, spouses followed by offspring, parents and siblings; see, e.g., section 4, Transplantation and Anatomy Act 1979 (Queensland); section 3, Human Tissue and Transplant Act 1982 (Western Australia). These provisions apply as regards transplantation, or the use of tissue for medical or scientific purposes.
[94] See section 4(1), German Law of 5 November 1997.
[95] See, e.g., sections 4 and 18, Human Tissue Transplant Act 1979 (Northern Territory); section 5, Transplantation and Anatomy Act 1983 (South Australia). But where the deceased is not lying in a hospital, senior next of kin, in the prescribed order, are permitted to authorise (consent) removal and use for such purposes. See also Lithuania Law No. VIII-1484 of 21 December 1999 as amended by Law No. VIII-1985 of 10 October 2000. By contrast, in the UK up until 2006 under the Human Tissue Act 1961, *any* relative could object.
[96] Generally relatives may be ignored where they cannot be contacted within the requisite time or if they do not wish to make, or cannot make, a decision. See, e.g., section 27(8), Human Tissue Act 2004 and section 50(6) Human Tissue (Scotland) Act 2006.
[97] Section 27(7) Human Tissue Act 2004; section 50(5), Human Tissue (Scotland) Act 2006.

that one member of a class may make a valid gift, but that if another member of the same class objects, a gift may only be made by a *majority* of the members of that class who are reasonably available.[98] This position was canvassed in the consultation leading up to the Human Tissue Act 2004, but was not ultimately adopted.

Moreover, in some explicit consent jurisdictions it is not merely relatives who can consent or make an anatomical gift where the deceased did not decide for him/herself in this regard. The 2006 UAGA, for instance, adds at the end of the list 'any other person having the authority to dispose of the decedent's body'.[99] The latter envisages a coroner or medical examiner, or even a hospital administrator or government official.[100] It obviates the need for an explicit consent to donation from either the deceased or a surviving relative, and would permit donation even where there are no surviving relatives. However, the commentary on the provision notes that this would rarely if ever apply to *organ* donation in view of the probable time lapse involved, although it might perhaps relate to the decedent's eyes or other tissues. The (ethical) source of such a power is unclear and would drive a wedge between organ and tissue donations.

### Authorisation

The language of consent has come to dominate the contemporary transplant and research policy scenes. The Human Tissue Act 2004 elevates it to its centrepiece and the notion was the central concept emphasised within the organ and tissue retention inquiry reports. However, in Scotland the notion of authorisation has been preferred, driven by the recommendations of the Scottish Review Group on Retention of Organs at Post-Mortem.[101] Whilst wanting to maintain a consistent approach across the UK, the Scottish Parliament, to whom matters are devolved, adopted the terminology of authorisation in the Human Tissue (Scotland) Act 2006. This was applied across the board to decisions made with respect to deceased adults as well as children.

---

[98] Uniform Anatomical Gift Act 2006, section 9(b). See also S. Kurtz, C. Strong and D. Gerasimow, 'The 2006 revised Uniform Anatomical Gift Act – a law to save lives' [2007] *Health Law Analysis* 44 at 46 [Kurtz *et al.*, 'The 2006 revised']. Under the Uniform Anatomical Gift Act 1987, it was stated that a gift could not be made where it was known that another member of the person's *same* class had an objection, section 3(3). See also Section 10 of the Chilean Law No. 19451 of 29 March 1996.

[99] Section 9(a). Adult grandchildren are also included for the first time. The 2004 Act includes long-standing friends on the list of 'qualifying relatives'.

[100] Kurtz *et al.*, 'The 2006 revised' at 44.

[101] Scottish Review Group on Retention of Organs at Post-Mortem: Final Report, 2000.

The views of the Scottish Review Group were themselves partially a function of the general context in which the retention controversies arose, the retention and use of tissue from *children* after post-mortem examination. It was observed that the notion of consent is somewhat incongruous in the context of children who are now deceased, as the authority granted to parents to consent is delimited by the concept of 'the best interests of the child' which has no clear application to deceased individuals. It was described as 'inherently inappropriate'.[102] It took the view that the term 'authorisation' strengthened the role of the parents in decision-making as regards how their children should be dealt with and clarifies the scope of their legally valid decision-making powers. The Report additionally considered that the notion of authorisation was most appropriate to meet the needs of those parents who do not wish to receive information about post-mortem examination and/or the subsequent removal and retention of organs and tissues, but who do not object to them. It stated 'Whereas, in law, a valid consent is generally expected to follow the provision of information, authorisation is not constrained by this requirement'.[103]

However, more broadly, the notion of authorisation was regarded as stressing the pre-eminence of the wishes of deceased adults in relation to donation. It was considered that this was one of the failings of the 1961 Act. As regards the practice of asking relatives to agree to the use of the dead body, rather than simply asking about the wishes of the deceased person, it remarked that this was 'understandable' but 'fails spectacularly to respect the competently expressed wishes of the person now deceased'.[104] The Report stated 'We reiterate our view that it is for the deceased during his or her lifetime to direct, if they so wish, what is to be done with their body after death'.[105] To what extent the language of 'authorisation' emphasises this as compared with 'consent' may be a matter of semantic inference, though, rather than any formal difference in the terminology employed. It was certainly anticipated that the adoption of the terminology of authorisation would render the Scottish legal position distinctive. However, neither in practice nor in theory have parental powers been constrained by any notion of 'best interests' – whatever that might mean in this context – as regards donation of organs or tissues from deceased offspring. This is to apply the concept out of its intended context, where risk and harm are situation-specific. Thus, the effect of this change as regards children is likely to be more symbolic than real. As regards adults, such an alternative conception *per se* will also probably be insubstantial. In reality, clinicians are likely to continue to

---

[102] *Ibid.*, section 1, para. 12.     [103] *Ibid.*, section 1, para. 17.
[104] *Ibid.*, section 1, para. 40.     [105] *Ibid.*, section 2, para. 58.

frequently if not invariably defer to the negative wishes of relatives on both sides of the border, whatever the wording of the law, in the absence of an accompanying cultural shift. In any event, the guidance issued as regards the remainder of the UK by the HTA itself stresses the primacy of the wishes of the deceased. Of course, there is room for practice to diverge in Scotland, but that is essentially a matter of will rather than by dint of the differing language used. To achieve radical change a considerably more mandatory form of wording is probably necessary, such as that in the 2006 UAGA.

# 5    Presumed consent

Presumed consent is a central and perennial topic of transplantation debates in particular, and is viewed by many as a panacea for an insufficient supply of organs and tissues.[1] Yet there are few topics in this sphere as divisive and productive of so much controversy and confusion. Indeed, its very character as a donation policy is something of an enigma. For my purposes here, I take 'presumed consent' to refer broadly to consent to be found in the failure to communicate an objection.[2] As a matter of law, such regimes may be either hard (strong) or soft (weak). In the former, removal and use is permissible unless the deceased objected during his/her lifetime. For instance, in Austria, organs may be removed from a deceased person unless the physician is possessed of information that the individual refused consent to donation prior to death.[3] Poland has a similar law.[4] In weak systems, a relative (or relatives) reasonably contactable after death must also be offered an opportunity to veto donation by way of an objection. These form the majority.

In the UK presumed consent has very recently moved – surprisingly in view of its rejection in the debates leading to the Human Tissue Act 2004 – to the top of the political agenda, with the Government-established Organ Donation Taskforce (ODT) being requested to take it on board.[5] It was also a major topic included in the US Institute of Medicine (IOM)

---

[1] The alternative terms 'contracting out' and 'opting out' are sometimes used. However, I reserve them for separate use here.

[2] Some commentators exclude tacit consent from this definition. However, I take a broad approach so as to avoid fine distinctions and wrap up a wide range of usages.

[3] Austrian Federal Law of 1 June 1982, section 62a. See also section 9, Costa Rican Law No. 7409 of 12 May 1994.

[4] Law of 1 July 2005.

[5] See *The Times*, 20 September 2007. The initial catalyst was the explicit endorsement of presumed consent in the Annual Report of the Chief Medical Officer 2006: Organ Transplants: The Waiting Game 27–33. The Kidney Transplant Bill (HL Bill 11) introduced by Baroness Finlay which would have allowed one kidney to be removed in the absence of evidence of a decision to refuse to donate, received a Second Reading in

Report, *Organ Donation: Opportunities for Action*, in 2006.[6] The ODT and the IOM both considered that presumed consent should not be introduced in their respective jurisdictions at the present time.[7] By contrast, the German National Ethics Council recently recommended that presumed consent be introduced in Germany,[8] and the Indian Government is planning to introduce a presumed consent law (initially for corneas only).[9] Policies have been much influenced by geographical location and social, juridical and cultural background and milieu, with the majority of European nations adopting presumed consent but relatively few others.[10] However, even where a presumed consent is embedded in law, this is no guarantee that it is rigorously practised by all or even most professionals on the ground.

Whilst presumed consent has achieved most publicity and notoriety in the context of transplantation it is also applicable to the use of tissue for research, and even more generally. The formal legal position contained in the previous Human Tissue Act 1961, which was at the epicentre of the organ retention controversies in the UK,[11] was presumed consent for research as well as transplantation, and certain US states have specifically enacted laws supposedly applying presumed consent to medical research.[12] Whilst presumed consent in this context generally refers to donation by deceased persons, in the context of research it also has potential practical application to the living. This dimension is considered in chapter 6.

the House of Lords but lapsed at the end of the 2007–8 Parliamentary session. Ironically, the Human Tissue Act 1961, which was at the heart of the organ and tissue research/retention scandals in the UK, was on its face a presumed consent law.

[6] Institute of Medicine Report, *Organ Donation: Opportunities for Action* (Washington, DC: National Academies Press, 2006) [Institute of Medicine, *Organ Donation*].

[7] Organ Donation Taskforce, *The Potential Impact of an Opt Out System for Organ Donation in the UK*, Department of Health, 2008 at 34 [ODT, *The Potential Impact*]. It recommended a review in five years' time. A Committee of Welsh Assembly Ministers also rejected presumed consent in 2008; see http://news.bbc.co.uk/1/hi/wales/7531859.stm.

[8] German National Ethics Council Opinion, *Increasing the Number of Organ Donations: A Pressing Issue for Transplant Medicine in Germany* (Berlin: German National Ethics Council, 2007) [German National Ethics Council].

[9] 'Organ transplant law may soon make way for presumed consent', MSN News 2008, at http://news.in.msn.com/national/article.aspx?cp-documentid=1282316.

[10] Singapore being a notable exception especially within Asia, see Human Organ Transplant Acts 1987 and 2004. In South America, there is a legal patchwork, with countries such as Argentina having a presumed consent law, and others such as Venezuela, Peru and Chile having explicit consent laws. Some nations have moved between presumed and explicit consent systems, most notably Denmark, Sweden and Brazil.

[11] See D. Price, 'From Cosmos and Damien to van Velzen: The human tissue saga continues' (2003) 11 *Medical Law Review* 1.

[12] E.g. a Minnesota law provided that hospitals were permitted to remove the brains of deceased persons who suffered from Alzheimer's disease in order to discover a cure unless the coroner was aware of any objections; see Minn. Stat. Ann. Section 145.131 (West, 1989).

This chapter seeks to examine the philosophical and jurisprudential essence of 'presumed consent', the pre-conditions to its ethical and legal acceptability, and factors bearing on its suitability for adoption as public policy in any specific region. In so doing, it is necessary to compare explicit and presumed consent models. It must be recognised that neither system currently operates ideally, and thus we are effectively searching for the *preferable* system of the two; or perhaps the least of the two evils. There is an inherent tendency in many regions to view explicit consent as the optimal scheme subject only to its capability to deliver adequate rates of donation to meet demand, and to gloss over the implicit flaws in its operation and premises inherent in its design.[13] Explicit consent generally seeks to accommodate the interests of all affected parties on the donation side, often in the process fudging the proper entitlements and responsibilities of each.

At the heart of the debate is whether a 'presumed' consent is any sort of real consent at all, or merely a misnomer. Saunders remarks that 'Presumed consent is no consent' and is an affront to the moral principle that is the foundation of consent itself.[14] On this view, such a policy can only be justified by reference to the supposedly greater volume of resulting organs and tissues, resting upon a beneficence or communitarian rather than autonomy rationale. For instance, McClachlan states

> To say that it can reasonably be presumed that we consent to donate our organs if we do not specifically say that we do not consent is absurd. It is a deceitful piece of sophistry. There might be a good utilitarian case for having an opt-out rather than an opt-in system of organ donation. However, this would mean that there is a case for using our organs even in the absence of our consent. If consent matters in this area, then only the explicit consent of the people concerned can justify the using of their organs after their deaths. If consent does not matter and the use of their organs can be justified without it, then consent does not matter. We should not appeal to the bogus notion of presumed consent.[15]

If presumed consent is properly to be seen as a form of 'real', factual, consent then it would need to be a *tacit* consent.[16] Alternatively, consent

---

[13] See P. Fevrier and S. Gay, 'Informed consent versus presumed consent: the role of the family in organ donations' (2004), at http://ssrn.com/abstract=572241.

[14] Professor John Saunders, Written Evidence to the National Assembly for Wales, at www. assemblywales.org/bus-home/bus-committees-third1/bus-, paras. 13–14 [Saunders, Written Evidence].

[15] H. McLachlan, 'Presumed consent is no consent at all', at www.bmj.com/cgi/eltters/336/7638/230#189028.

[16] By 'real' here is meant a consent which incorporates elements of either factual attitudinal or expressive consent, in Westen's parlance; see P. Westen, *The Logic of Consent* (Aldershot: Ashgate, 2004), Introduction [Westen, *The Logic of Consent*]. See further chapter 4 in this volume.

would need to be *imputed* based on convincing reasons for assuming that elements of a factual consent existed in the circumstances. The latter, 'legally constructed', consent smacks to many of no more than *inventing* consent. For instance, Ruth Richardson has opined

In the present day, from time to time, suggestions are raised ..., that we should extend the law covering organ transplantation in line with a policy referred to as presumed consent. This is one of the many misnomers with which the language of transplantation is peppered. Here, lip service is paid to the *need* for consent, but in practice its existence is irrelevant, because it is *assumed* to exist. Presumed consent is public-relations-speak for the denial of a need even to seek consent.[17]

This view, in its turn, generates the perception that organs or tissues are not donated, but are instead 'taken' by the State for the benefit of others, potentially jeopardising public trust. Goodwin opines that 'Indeed, presumed consent undermines the very "gift of life" concept. Ultimately, the extractions in these instances are not "gifts", but rather "takings" that would otherwise require due process from the state.'[18]

### Rationale(s) for presumed consent

The central arguments for, and alleged advantages of, presumed consent are that it will:
1. Give greater effect to the wishes of now deceased persons
2. Remove a considerable burden from the shoulders of bereaved relatives (other than the parents of young children)
3. Result in a higher volume of organs and tissues being obtained.

As regards the first rationale, we should distinguish between actual formulated *decisions* and the known or anticipated *wishes* of the individual. Whilst the former may be regarded as an orthodox, tacit, consent, the latter could only give rise to an imputed, non-factual, consent.

The second item can only be justified if it is ethically *appropriate* to lift this alleged 'burden' from relatives, which has already been the subject of analysis in chapters 2 and 3. Cohen avers 'We ask the wrong persons, at the worst possible times, questions they should never have been asked'.[19] However, if the decision *is* properly one for relatives to make, they should be assisted in making such a difficult decision rather than being sidelined

---

[17] R. Richardson, *Death, Dissection and the Destitute*, 2nd edn. (London: Phoenix Press, 2001), p. 421.

[18] M. Goodwin, *Black Markets: The Supply and Demand of Body Parts* (Cambridge University Press, 2006), p. 123 [Goodwin, *Black Markets*].

[19] C. Cohen, 'The case for presumed consent to transplant human organs after death' (1992) 24(5) *Transplantation Proceedings* 2168 at 2169.

or constrained in their powers. This cannot truly be a 'rationale' for such a system in any event. It is merely an (alleged) incidental advantage of giving effect to the first-mentioned rationale.[20]

The IOM Report asserted 'The primary argument in favour of presumed consent is that it would increase the availability of transplantable organs and that such an increase could save lives and enhance the quality of the lives of transplant recipients. If a presumed-consent policy did not have a strong prospect of increasing the number of available organs, there would be no reason to adopt it.'[21] But whilst this may reflect the primary (political) impetus and catalyst for change, it ought not necessarily to be viewed as *the* exclusive rationale for its adoption. It might be right to introduce presumed consent in some situations even where donation rates would *not* necessarily rise. Chris Rudge, the UK 'Transplant Tsar', remarked 'And the question to ask is not whether presumed consent is a better way of getting organs for transplant, but whether it is a better way of getting consent'.[22] In any event, whilst presumed consent might generally tend to enhance donation rates, this end-product is the consequence of a whole variety of interrelated factors (resource, organisational, logistical, geographical, institutional, religious, cultural, economic, demographic, etc.) without direct legal influence. Thus, I maintain that enhanced donation rates are presently neither a 'necessary' nor a 'sufficient' reason for the introduction of presumed consent, although self-evidently they would be a crucial advantage.

Indeed, it is instructive to envisage the ideal system and then to work backwards. If the *true* wishes of *all* individuals were definitely and accurately known prior to their deaths, and we never needed to infer or guess a deceased person's wishes as regards donation, it is submitted that this would be the preferred system, *regardless* of whether this generated more or less organs. It would simply be the *right* system, both ethically and legally, by virtue of the respect afforded to the self-determination of the

---

[20] As den Hartogh observes with respect to the Dutch Government's 'policy' of reducing the number of family refusals, if the next of kin have as much right to refuse as to consent, reducing the number of refusals cannot be a policy aim; see G. den Hartogh, *Farewell to Non-commitment: Decision Systems for Organ Donation from an Ethical Viewpoint*, Monitoring Report Ethics and Health, Centre for Ethics and Health, The Hague, 2008 at 12 [Den Hartogh, *Farewell to Non-commitment*]. It is sometimes said that relatives must inevitably be involved because of the need to take a social history of the donor in order to minimise potential problems from communicable diseases, etc. This is a *separate* conversation, however. No matter how easily such conversations become conflated, this does not automatically confer authority to make donation decisions.

[21] Institute of Medicine, *Organ Donation*, at 12.

[22] 'Giving organs must be seen as being in the donor's best interests, says new transplant director', *The Times*, 4 August 2008.

individual. We should not lightly override the wishes of individuals even where existing lives are at stake.[23] To adopt such a policy would signal a utilitarian or communitarian philosophy, i.e. removal entirely as a form of moral requirement or entitlement of others, which is yet to prove ethically compelling in most contemporary societies. The wishes of deceased persons are paramount to a suitably ethical donation model. For these reasons the schemes under consideration in this chapter will be described as 'presumed consent', with the expression 'opting out' being used to describe an at least partly communitarian (conscription)-based model.

### Give or take?

Even under regimes of routine taking, without any requirement for consent at all, there may nonetheless be a possibility of opting out. Dickens, Fluss and King, for instance, remark 'Presumed consent legislation treats cadaveric materials as a public asset, but permits individuals who object to their own or deceased family members' materials being removed to prohibit recovery'.[24] Whilst sometimes referred to as presumed consent schemes, as in the above quotation, they are essentially divorced from any notion of individual rights entitlements, even though some leeway is given to those with objections, by analogy with, e.g. conscientious objection to military service.[25] Thus, despite their rationales being substantially at variance, there may nonetheless be a resemblance between schemes based on procedural and substantive justifications. Beyleveld and Brownsword state that 'When the distinction is so qualified, there might be some blurring of the line between what, for justificatory purposes, is to be characterised as non-consensual (i.e. obligatory but subject to allowances) and what as consensual'.[26] The underlying justificatory basis of a system may not be transparent.[27] For instance, whilst the UK currently

---

[23] See S. McGuinness and M. Brazier, 'Respecting the living means respecting the dead too' (2008) 28(2) *Oxford Journal of Legal Studies* 297 [McGuinness and Brazier, 'Respecting the living'].

[24] B. Dickens, S. Fluss and A. King, 'Legislation on organ and tissue donation', in J. Chapman, M. Deierhoi and C. Wight (eds.), *Organ and Tissue Donation for Transplantation* (London: Arnold, 1997), p. 101 [Dickens *et al.*, 'Legislation']. See also E.-H. Kluge, 'Improving organ retrieval rates: Various proposals and their ethical validity' (2000) 8 *Health Care Analysis* 279 at 286.

[25] Providing a right to opt out might be seen as a means of maintaining the trust of those with forceful opinions against donation.

[26] D. Beyleveld and R Brownsword, *Consent in the Law* (Oxford: Hart Publishing, 2008), p. 203 [Beyleveld and Brownsword, *Consent in the Law*].

[27] Veatch and Pitt argue that the lack of any explicitness as regards consent in some of the presumed legislation in Europe highlights the lack of a consent rationale behind such policies; see R. Veatch, 'The myth of presumed consent', in R. Veatch, *Transplantation*

implements an opting out policy for HIV testing of patients attending genitourinary clinics and for pregnant women attending antenatal care, it is unclear whether a consent basis was intended or not.[28] The tendency of *substantive* justificatory schemes is, however, toward limited information and opportunities for legitimate objections to be recorded; leading to potential arbitrariness and inequality.[29]

Many schemes are and have been patently (authoritarian) communitarian or utilitarian in policy orientation, whatever label – presumed consent or otherwise – is applied to them, i.e. these laws were never intended to operate as (presumed) *consent* laws in the true sense. Historically, this has been most typically a feature of anatomical dissection laws. In the UK, such regimes can be seen to date back to the Anatomy Act 1832 where, in Richardson's words, 'the destitute were to be dissected in the name of medical progress'.[30] Many other nations had similar experiences.[31] More recently, they have been associated with policies and practices pertaining to the retention and use of organs and tissue for research following post-mortem examination, such as the autopsy laws of some former socialist states, e.g. Hungary.[32] This legacy taints many commentators' views regarding presumed consent and continues to dog open-minded debate even today.

The organ and tissue retention scandals at various locations in the UK (and abroad) reveal a similar picture, although principally as a function of practice rather than policy. It was the failure to approach and adequately inform relatives that was the principal grievance (as well as the failure

---

*Ethics* (Washington, DC: Georgetown University Press, 2000) 167 at 168 [Veatch, *Transplantation Ethics*]. However, it does not to my mind seem to be crucial whether a law states its alleged rationale on its face.

[28] See NHS, *Reducing Mother to Baby Transmission of HIV*, Health Service Circular 199/183, at www.dh.gov.uk/assetRoot/04/01/21/28/04012128.pdf. See also P. du Zulueta and M. Boulton, 'Routine antenatal HIV testing: The responses and perceptions of pregnant women and the viability of informed consent. A qualitative study' (2008) 33 *Journal of Medical Ethics* 329.

[29] This type of approach would seem to be reflected in the original draft advice issued by the HTA in respect of existing holdings or anonymised surplus tissue to be used for ethics-approved research, that objections should be respected where communicated, even though no consent is required for their use in the first place; see, e.g., Human Tissue Authority draft Code of Practice, Removal/Collection, Retention and Disposal of Human Organs and Tissue, 2005, para. 43.

[30] R. Richardson, 'Human dissection and organ donation: A historical and social background' (2006) 11(2) *Mortality* 151 at 161. The unclaimed poor and inmates of work-houses became available for the use of medical science.

[31] Laws elsewhere were modelled on the 1832 Act, as in many states in the US; see D. Sipes, 'Does it matter whether there is public policy for presumed consent in organ transplantation?' (1991) 12 *Whittier Law Review* 505.

[32] See B. Blassauer, 'Autopsy', in H. Ten Have and J. Welie (eds.), *Ownership of the Human Body* (Dordrecht: Kluwer Academic Publishers, 1998) 19.

sometimes to heed the wishes that were solicited) – which in fact the law itself implicitly necessitated – rather than the fact that only 'objections' were sought by law as opposed to positive consent. The Alder Hey Report relating to the organ and tissue retention practices at the Royal Liverpool Children's Hospital revealed both ignorance of the provisions of the law (then the Human Tissue Act 1961) as well as reluctance to adhere to its dictates.[33] Indeed, in so far as practices in the transplantation and post-mortem examination contexts deviated sharply in the UK despite being governed by the same provisions of the same statute, one can observe the *irrelevance* of the law to practice at this time.[34] The absence of independent mechanisms for deceased persons to pre-posthumously record their objections, combined with a lack of prior knowledge of such likely practices, and the failure to properly consult with relatives, meant that the voice of deceased persons (or the parents of deceased children) were simply not heard at all in very many instances. As Saunders has remarked 'When individuals or their families are not told that they can object or how to object to organ donation, "presumed consent" becomes in effect a strategy for avoiding "consent" entirely'.[35]

Some of the more recent state medical examiner laws in the US are perhaps an analogous example in the sphere of transplantation. Goodwin regards such laws, permitting the removal of corneas and/or pituitary glands in the absence of a known objection from the deceased or relatives, as policies based only on 'taking'; although she dubs them 'presumed consent' laws.[36] As the IOM Report stated

These cornea retrieval statutes do not presume consent; rather, they authorize routine removal subject to the objection of the family. There appears to be little or no effort to educate the public about these laws, and there is no evidence of widespread public understanding that these routine-removal laws exist and will be applied under certain circumstances.[37]

---

[33] The Royal Liverpool Children's Inquiry Report, Stationery Office, 2001 at 361 and 365, at www.rlcinquiry.org.uk/download/index/htm [Royal Liverpool Inquiry].

[34] In the context of transplantation, consent had always been sought from relatives. Only by the turn of the millennium was consent routinely sought for the retention of material removed at post-mortem for research.

[35] Saunders, Written Evidence, para. 18.

[36] Goodwin, *Black Markets*, p. 123. In the mid-1990s, various US states passed 'presumed consent' laws, many of them based on the provisions of the 1987 Uniform Anatomical Gift Act (which applied only to therapy and transplantation), although mostly applicable only to either corneas or pituitary glands; see E. Jaffe, 'She's got Bette Davis's eyes: Assessing the non-consensual removal of cadaver organs under the takings and due process clauses' (1990) 90 *Columbia Law Review* 528 at 535–7; and T. O'Carroll, 'Over my dead body: Recognizing property rights in corpses' (1996) 29 *Journal of Health and Hospital Law* 238 [O'Carroll, 'Over my dead body'].

[37] Institute of Medicine, *Organ Donation* at 207.

Indeed, the application of such laws has not infrequently been subject to successful constitutional challenge.[38] But one cannot justifiably generalise from one specific context or experience to another.

Thus, whether a legal scheme *operates* as one founded on 'presumed consent' is partially a function of the infrastructural and educational features accompanying it, rather than legal aspiration *per se*. As Akveld and de Charro have commented 'Preference for a certain system does not necessarily follow from the concept of respecting the rights of self determination. The extent to which self determination is respected and done justice to does not depend on the system as such, it depends more on the organisation of the system and on the way in which assistance functions within a given system.'[39] It is my assertion, however, that presumed consent is *capable* of functioning in an entirely ethical and transparent fashion.

Presumed consent is nonetheless regularly perceived to be *conceptually* synonymous with 'routine taking'. The IOM Report observed that 'Presumed-consent and routine-removal policies are commonly confused or deliberately conflated'.[40] A blurring thus occurs as between consensual and non-consensual removal policies and systems. Moreover, 'presumed consent' is regularly presented as a simple antonym to 'explicit consent',[41] implying either that removal occurs with 'no consent at all' or alternatively that consent is immaterial in the face of 'the taking by the State'. The *contrast* is consequently based in many instances on illicit premises. A related mistaken juxtaposition is the contrast of 'presumed consent' with 'informed consent', to which I shall return in chapter 6.[42] In such a paradigm, it is ordinarily seen as *state* acquisition of organs, perhaps

---

[38] See Comments, 'Forced organ donation: The presumed consent to organ donation laws of the various states and the United States constitution' (1998–9) 9 *Albany Law Journal of Science and Technology* 349 [Comments].

[39] J. Akveld and F. de Charro, 'Organ donation and regulation', in F. de Charro, D. Hessing and J. Akveld (eds.), *Systems of Donor Recruitment* (Dordrecht: Kluwer, 1992) 113 at 116.

[40] Institute of Medicine, *Organ Donation* at 205. One can see this, for instance, in President's Council on Bioethics, 'Organ Transplantation: Ethical Dilemmas and Policy Choices', 2006/7, Background Paper, available at www.bioethics.gov/background/org_transplant. html. Jacobs has stated 'Another label for presumed consent is, in fact, "routine salvaging"'; see M.-A. Jacobs, 'Another look at the presumed-versus-informed consent dichotomy in postmortem organ procurement' (2006) 20(6) *Bioethics* 293 at 294.

[41] See D. Price, *Legal and Ethical Aspects of Organ Transplantation* (Cambridge University Press, 2000), chapter 2. By implying that explicit consent, and only explicit consent, truly *is* consent.

[42] The Institute of Medicine Report preferred the expression 'informed choice' here, remarking that although the concepts were grounded in the same ethical principles, this was a decision concerning the disposition of the body after death as opposed to the survival or quality of life of a living person; see Institute of Medicine, *Organ Donation* at 176.

even state/collective *ownership* of organs, and sometimes analogised with national or other community service.[43] The UK shadow health secretary recently remarked in this context, 'The state does not own our bodies or have a right to take organs after death'.[44]

The IOM Report, however, rejected the view that these policies are conceptually akin. It commented 'Routine removal is broadly communitarian, whereas presumed consent – like expressed consent – is largely individualistic, even though it may include a role for the family'.[45] It condemned the use of the label 'presumed consent' by proponents of routine removal.[46] It is noteworthy that these remarks emanate from an American source where presumed consent is regularly accused of being at odds with the values espoused and endorsed within that individualistic, libertarian, society. The German National Ethics Council likewise explicitly recognised the libertarian values embedded within German society, yet nonetheless expressed support for presumed consent. It asserted

In this connection, the justification for organ removal under the opt-out system lies not in a solidarity-based obligation to donate, but – provided that an adequate basis for presumption is created by appropriate measures – in the presumed consent of the potential donor.[47]

Thus, presumed consent is compatible with libertarianism despite being also supportive of the value of community.[48]

### PC models

The IOM Report set out three potential models for presumed consent:
1. A tacit, silent consent
2. Based on a general theory of human values or on the basis of what reasonable, altruistic people should and would do, or
3. Based on what people would have decided if they could have been asked.

---

[43] See, e.g., L. Fentiman, 'Organ donation as national service: A proposed federal organ donation law' (1993) 27 *Suffolk University Law Review* 1593 at 1598.

[44] A. Lansley, 'Everyone "should donate organs"', at http://news.bbc.co.uk/1/hi/health/6902519.stm.

[45] Institute of Medicine, *Organ Donation* at 206.

[46] Ibid., at 208.

[47] German National Ethics Council at 47. It added 'In particular, however, the opt-out system should not be underlain by an obligation to render assistance, possibly enforceable even against the wishes of the person concerned, but instead by presumed consent to this assistance' at 42.

[48] See R. Dworkin, 'Community and rights', in G. Dworkin (ed.), *Morality, Harm, and the Law* (Boulder, CO: Westview Press, 1994) 36.

These models all revolve, to one degree or other, around the wishes of the deceased individual, either actual, assumed, or hypothetical. Official policies frequently assert that it is the wishes of the deceased that are crucial. Indeed even most relatives state that giving effect to the wishes of the deceased is their main function or role.[49] The first model is an actual, factual, consent whilst the other two are 'constructed' forms of consent. The second model will not be considered further here, though. It is not cogent to argue that an *objective* model of donation should be adopted, divorced from any form of *individual* wishes, even anticipated subjective preferences. The first model is founded on the notion that consent can be properly found expressed in the silence of the deceased person in the specific context and circumstances.

The final model is grounded in convincing evidence as to what the person *would have wished* to occur. Usually this is said to be found in the results of public opinion polls which – in most Western regions – typically show that the majority of people are inclined to donate their organs after their deaths. It is therefore an empirical and generalised proposition. Veatch, however, objects that such polls show that approximately half of all individuals would refuse to donate, leading to an inference of donation being incorrect about half of the time; far too large to support a presumption of consent.[50] But in some instances it may nonetheless best give effect to the wishes of deceased persons in the round, to the extent that these can be properly ascertained. Such a judgement might be bolstered by supplementary inferential evidence at an individual interactional level. On this view, although the principal focus of most of the debate surrounding presumed consent has been upon whether 'consent' can be considered to have been given for donation, it should have instead been upon the extent to which the wishes of deceased persons are respected generally, i.e. *for or against* donation.[51]

---

[49] See M. Sque, 'Bereavement, decision-making and the family in organ donation', in A-M. Farrell, M. Quigley and D. Price (eds.), *Organ Shortage: Ethics, Law and Pragmatism* (Cambridge University Press, forthcoming 2010).

[50] R. Veatch, 'Implied, presumed and waived consent: The relative moral wrongs of under- and over-informing' (2007) 7(12) *Bioethics* 39 at 40. See also Veatch, *Transplantation Ethics*, p. 170.

[51] This dichotomy is at the heart of differing views as to whether Article 17 of the Council of Europe's Additional Protocol, which requires consent or authorisation to be obtained, permits removal on the basis of a 'presumed' consent. Compare H. Nys, 'European biolaw in the making: The example of the rules governing the removal of organs from deceased persons in the EU Member States', in C. Gastmans, K. Dierickz, H. Nys and P. Schotsmans (eds.), *New Pathways for European Bioethics* (Antwerp: Intersentia, 2007) 161 [Nys, 'European biolaw'] who argues not, with E. Teargarden, 'Human trafficking:

It is submitted that all systems should aspire to make available and to implement the wishes of all persons who are the potential sources of body materials, whether living or now deceased, subject only to matters of logistics, resources, medical unsuitability, or the like.

### The locus of consent

There is no denying that, theoretically at least, informed explicit consent *is* the best system for donation if one is seeking to ensure that proper consent is provided for the donation of tissues or organs for transplantation or research, e.g. by adding one's name to the relevant organ donor register or signing an organ donor card. It must be conceded to be inevitable in some instances of presumed consent that body parts will be taken and used for transplantation or other purposes from persons who did not want this to happen (i.e. false positives), or at least had not decided that this should happen. However, observers routinely gloss over the *a priori* issue of *whose* (explicit) consent it is. It must be appreciated that in most explicit consent systems, including those in the UK, North America, Australasia and most parts of Asia, it is the *relatives* that constitute the gateway to organ dona-tion, i.e. it is *not* a pre-requisite for the deceased person to have consented to donation. It is the relatives who make the ultimate decision. The views of the deceased person, if known, merely become a factor in the relatives' decision-making, which is why positive potential organ donors are exhorted, in addition to entering their name on the relevant register (if there is one) and signing an organ donor card, to inform pivotal relatives of their wishes.[52] Thus, in such jurisdictions the focus upon 'consent' tends to shift the debate *away* from the deceased individuals themselves across the board.

Indeed, if *either* the deceased *or* relatives may provide consent, is the scheme underpinned by two separate ethical bases rather than one? If the former, are these in fact at odds with one another? Comparatively little debate has been generated on this subject, yet it lies at the heart of the matter. It has been submitted previously that relatives principally have a derivative role, emanating from the rights of the deceased. The Final Report of the Scottish Review Group on Retention of Organs at Post-Mortem stated 'What is absolutely clear is that relatives of an adult have no automatic legal rights to make decisions on his or her *[the deceased's]*

Legal issues in presumed consent laws' (2005) 30 *North Carolina Journal of International Law and Commercial Regulation* 685 at 722. The Council of Europe's previous Resolution R (78) 29 expressly included presumed consent within its compass.

[52] This is the advice promoted in the UK, the US, Australia, etc.

behalf' [my addition].[53] Beyleveld and Brownsword opine that ideal-type consent involves individuals personally and unequivocally signalling their consent.[54] If such consent should be given instead by an 'other person', this should be the 'alter ego' of the individual. It is hard to see, though, how any such agency, even implied rather than express, can be gleaned from silence under an explicit consent model, apart from where it is permitted to appoint nominated representatives to make the decision. But whilst they do not have personal rights of decision-making nor are they true agents, relatives may be entitled to make decisions based on a substituted judgement as to what the deceased would have wished.

### Defaults: presumed dissent?

It has been remarked that 'Recent insights into the way in which people make decisions indicates that the choice of defaults is of enormous importance',[55] an observation with undoubted applicability to donation decisions. Johnson and Goldstein state

Most public policy choices have a no-action default, that is, a condition that is imposed when an individual fails to make a decision. In the case of organ donation, European countries have one of two default policies. In presumed-consent states, people are organ donors unless they register not to be, and in explicit-consent countries, nobody is an organ donor without registering to be one.[56]

This is not strictly accurate, as we have seen. Whilst a failure to object in a presumed consent system triggers a presumed willingness to donate, a failure to opt in in an explicit consent system does *not* generate an opposite, presumed *objection*. Informally, such silence may reflect passive willingness, unwillingness, apathy, indifference, or a determination to leave it to family members to decide. One can make no generalised assumption in this regard. Formally, though, it is a decision to leave the matter to relatives after death, in so far as in explicit consent systems relatives may, usually in a hierarchical order, themselves consent to donation after the death.[57]

We may, however, query *why*, if a failure to object under a presumed consent model is capable of being evidence of a decision to donate, the

---

[53] Scottish Review Group on Retention of Organs at Post-Mortem: Final Report, 2000, section 1, para. 41.

[54] Beyleveld and Brownsword, *Consent in the Law*, p. 197.

[55] Den Hartogh, *Farewell to Non-commitment* at 15.

[56] E. Johnson and E. Goldstein, 'Do defaults save lives?' (2003) 302 (5649) *Science* 1338 at 1338 [Johnson and Goldstein, 'Do defaults save lives?'].

[57] 'Qualifying relatives', as they are labelled under the Human Tissue Act 2004.

failure to consent to donation during life is not viewed in explicit consent systems as a decision *not* to donate i.e. a presumed dissent? Although it is indubitably the case that some people who do not make a definite decision to donate whilst alive are nonetheless still willing to donate (based on the same opinion poll evidence which suggests that the majority of individuals are willing to donate their organs/tissues after death, see p. 142), this does not explain why relatives are permitted to consent to donate on the deceased's behalf even where they have *no* evidence that this is what the deceased would have wanted. This appears to be chiefly based on pragmatism. Indeed, it seems to be largely *by dint of the fact* that relatively few individuals have explicitly declared their willingness to become organ or tissue donors prior to their death that the *absence* of such an explicit decision to donate by the deceased person is *not* seen as a reason to conclusively decline organ or tissue removal.[58] If we were to insist upon 'first-person' explicit consent in all cases, the volume of organs and tissues for transplants or research would slump dramatically, i.e. the status quo serves to ensure that the possibility of donation still exists even where the wishes of the deceased were not manifest.[59] However, in the absence of a utilitarian rationale this is not compelling without relatives having their own *personal* right to donate. If the obtaining of more organs were a sufficient procurement rationale *per se* then there would be no necessity for a consensual taking whatever. In so far as explicit consent jurisdictions allow relatives to make the decision in all cases whether they are aware of the deceased's actual or probable wishes or not, they are illegitimately overreaching their proper role. To what degree such a decision is in fact 'guesswork' is examined below.

### Related questions

The role of relatives has therefore typically been as *default* 'decisionmakers'.[60] Den Hartogh observes that 'The fact that next of kin are granted the right to decide in so many countries, sometimes contrary to the statutory regulations, is not based on an adequate moral justification but on the sole fact of their presence on the scene and the special

---

[58] The IOM Report noted that if 30 per cent of individuals were to opt out under presumed consent, that is 30 per cent of instances where families would be 'blocked' from donating; Institute of Medicine Report, *Organ Donation* at 215.

[59] F. Kamm, *Morality, Mortality. Volume I* (Oxford University Press, 1993), p. 202 [Kamm, *Morality, Mortality*].

[60] In the context of post-mortem examinations and the retention and use of tissue for research, relatives have always been treated as the relevant decision-makers.

consideration for their circumstance required at that moment'.[61] But such pragmatism cannot ethically ground *personal* decision-making powers. Where relatives are permitted to object in their own right under a *presumed* consent system, on the other hand, this is a concession to potential severe distress as opposed to a recognition of a broader 'decisionmaking' role.

There may be some who do indeed consider that relatives possess their own discrete decision-making authority in relation to deceased individuals, and who cannot therefore comfortably accommodate presumed consent at all. However, the stance adopted here, giving primacy to the wishes of deceased persons is, as has been seen, that taken recently by most political institutions and regulatory agencies in the UK, North America and in Europe as a whole. The Human Tissue Act 2004 treats the wishes of the deceased as the pre-eminent factor,[62] as does the Human Tissue (Scotland) Act 2006.[63] The US IOM dubbed this an apparent 'paradigm shift'.[64]

### Species of consent

To the extent that laws expressly require or are implicitly founded upon the notion of *explicit* consent, presumed consent would apparently fall outwith such schemes. Although the Human Tissue Act 2004 does not require consent to be in any particular form in this context, it was patently the legislative intent; the notion of 'absence of objection' was the central mischief at which the statute was aimed. Silence is seemingly regarded as *an absence of consent* in this context, with the Human Tissue Authority (HTA) stressing that consent amounts to a positive act.[65] Even a clear tacit consent would consequently not suffice. However, these are jurisprudential, jurisdiction-specific, issues divorced from the general question whether silence could ever properly be perceived to be a valid 'consent' to donation. I will leave until later the question whether, assuming that we are dealing with consent in each instance, an 'explicit' consent has any particular moral or legal force which gives it *primacy* over a tacit/presumed consent.

---

[61] Den Hartogh, *Farewell to Non-commitment* at 67.
[62] Human Tissue Authority Briefing, Notes on the Human Tissue Act, 2006.
[63] Scottish Executive, Human Tissue (Scotland) Act 2006: A Guide to its Implications for NHSScotland. HDL (2006) 46, Edinburgh: Scottish Executive.
[64] Institute of Medicine, *Organ Donation* at 175. See also National Health and Medical Research Council, *Organ and Tissue Donation After Death, for Transplantation*, Australian Government, 2007 at 5.
[65] Human Tissue Authority Code of Practice, Consent, HTA, July 2006, para. 17.

We saw in chapter 4 that consent is considerably less monolithic in law than is generally supposed. It has, however, been queried why, as we do not rely upon presumed consent with regard to medical procedures performed upon the living, we should do so as regards the dead. Roseanna Cunningham remarked in the Scottish Parliament 'It turns consent on its head. Consent should be a positive decision. We expect that to be the case in all our human endeavours, from criminal law right down to the tiny print that requires us to opt out of junk mail if we do not want to receive it.'[66] But the analogies are not convincing. In general, a competent person's failure to consent during life is, by default, a decision to refuse consent. We do not offer an alternative decision-maker in the event of a consent not being given. The dead cannot be considered to be synonymous with living people with decision-making incapacity, in addition to which we do not allow others to routinely make decisions on behalf of such living adults apart from with respect to their present and future welfare. Yet, relatives are permitted to give consent to donation after an individual's demise in explicit consent jurisdictions even where the deceased has no present well-being or welfare to preserve.

Whether consent is viewed as *subjective or expressive* (see chapter 4), a tacit consent is *capable* of being conceived – ethically and legally – as a proper consent in the context of organ or tissue donation. Presumed consent may be seen as an expressive form of tacit consent in itself, or alternatively a failure to object might be evidence that the person subjectively acquiesced (consented) to such conduct which the person would be estopped from denying.[67] However, for such an argument to hold and for such silence to have prescriptive force, there would need to be an adequate threshold of qualifying conditions which were satisfied. In addition to the need for any relevant choice to be a product of competence to assess one's interests, knowledge of the circumstances and freedom from pressure,[68] Childress has stipulated similar pre-conditions to those set out by Simmons (see chapter 4) in this context.[69] Thus, it is at least necessary that (a) individuals are aware of the issue being posed and the significance of opting out or remaining silent, (b) that there are easily accessible means

---

[66] Roseanna Cunningham, Debate on Motion S3M-483 (George Foulkes), Col.5546, 24 January 2008.

[67] Some statutes have a good faith immunity in this context, including state legislation in the US.

[68] Westen, *The Logic of Consent*, pp. 177–245.

[69] J. Childress, *Practical Reasoning in Bioethics* (Bloomington, IL.: Indiana University Press, 1997), p. 227. A. John Simmons, *Moral Principles and Political Obligations*, (Princeton, NJ: Princeton University Press, 1979) pp. 80–1 His main theme is that mere residence is insufficient to amount to a consent to political rule and a social contract, in a Lockean regard.

of recording objections, (c) a reasonable period of time is provided in which such a decision can be made, and (d) there are no significant detrimental consequences of dissenting. The last criterion might, for instance, be relevant if knowledge of individuals' dissensions were made widely available, exposing them to potential public shame. It can be clearly seen that prior widespread public education and publication of the process is essential, reinforced periodically.

### Tacit consent

Veatch, Pitt, Harris and Erin, amongst others, all view presumed consent as an artifice, alleging that the manifested evidence is too equivocal to constitute a clear and reliable signal that it is the agent's will to donate.[70] Beyleveld and Brownsword also state that the 'standard vehicle' for signalling consent should be by way of opting *in*, and that silence is simply too unreliable to act upon.[71] Whilst one would agree that the primary task should be to divine and act upon the subjective will of the individual, the latter claim is arguably too inflexible and insufficiently context-specific. The net effect of a general requirement for voluntary, personal explicitly signalled consent would be that only individuals who had positively agreed to donate prior to their death would become donors, which would frequently fail to do justice to the autonomous will of deceased individuals as a whole.

However, as we have seen, the *context* is critical for interpreting the proper inference to be drawn from inactivity. Whilst some presumed consent systems arguably appear to satisfy such threshold requirements, others are transparently lacking. In some instances there are no convenient registries in existence or these are not routinely searched at the point of death in any event. Goodwin comments in relation to the US

But how does a dead person opt out of cornea takings? The opt-out provision is misleading. Living persons are unaware of how exactly to opt out. The fact that there isn't a national or state registry, except in Iowa, where one can opt out of tissue donation, is a significant barrier. States that passed presumed consent laws failed to take secondary measures to give full meaning to an individual or her family's choice to decline extraction. Their failure to do so unquestionably contributes to legal and social backlash against presumed consent policies.[72]

---

[70] See, e.g., C. Erin and J. Harris, 'Presumed consent or contracting out' (1999) 25 *Journal of Medical Ethics* 365; R. Veatch and J. Pitt, 'The myth of presumed consent', in R. Veatch, *Transplantation Ethics* (Washington, DC: Georgetown University Press, 2000), pp. 167–74.

[71] Beyleveld and Brownsword, *Consent in the Law*, p. 187.

[72] See Goodwin, *Black Markets*, p. 122.

Thus, even though the underlying rationale is individualistic as opposed to communitarian, a system may nonetheless *operate* as a routine removal system. However, much hinges upon infrastructure and context. As a Report in the Netherlands stated 'In some circumstances, not objecting may be construed as *tacit* consent: if the law or common practice has good reason to interpret silence in this way, if the person involved is aware of this and if he can lodge an objection in a simple manner at any time he likes. In such cases, tacit consent is true and full consent.'[73] The question is therefore whether a presumed consent system can truly aspire to such a level of evidential cogency.

One crucial issue is the extent to which people are directly 'reached' by the requisite information and opportunity to record their wish. The above Dutch Report argues that the Active Donor Registration System there which contacts every individual on their eighteenth birthday asking them to record their wish to donate, refusal to donate, or decision to leave it to the family to decide, accompanied by full information regarding donation, would satisfy such infrastructural pre-requisites to ground a satisfactory tacit consent system, albeit that at present it instead underpins the opt in policy under Dutch law.[74] Non-responders would be informed that they would be registered as non-objectors and contacted to confirm this and to inform them that they were able to contact the relevant agency to change such status at any time.[75] This is similar to the proposed scheme proffered by the German National Ethics Council for adoption, involving all individuals being contacted and called upon to formally declare their decision, having been informed that organ removal is permissible unless they have registered an objection.[76] There will of course nevertheless be a small minority of people whom it will still not be possible to reach by such a strategy, but arguably at the present time even fewer people are aware of the position in explicit consent systems where they are taken to be delegating the decision to relatives, whether they appreciate this or not. The approaches taken by the Dutch and German Reports are arguably a justifiable basis for an inference of a tacit consent if accompanied by satisfactory information, episodically reinforced. However, many systems would be unable to achieve such a level of individual directness and informedness, and in such cases presumed consent based on tacit consent is not convincing. As Simmons emphasises, although tacit consent may

---

[73] Den Hartogh, *Farewell to Non-commitment* at 12. Like Nys (p. 140 below), he does not, however, equate this to 'presumed' consent.
[74] Ibid.    [75] Ibid., at 22.
[76] German National Ethics Council at 49. The Council, however, recommended that relatives should be able to refuse consent in that event.

constitute a 'sign of consent', *majority* consent should not suffice as actual consent, which must be based in every instance upon evidence of individuals' 'intentionality'.[77]

## Imputed consent

The second, alternative, presumed consent model views consent as *imputed* based on existing evidence of the deceased's anticipated wishes.[78] On this rationale, the passivity of the deceased is regarded as the most compelling evidence of the person's wishes in the round. Nys, however, describes presumed consent as 'fictive' and remarks that 'when someone has not refused removal during his/her life, this cannot be considered the result of a decision not to decide and to give implicit consent. We simply do not know whether one wanted to consent or not. Often the term presumed "consent" is used to label this system but this is misleading.'[79] Garwood-Gowers similarly accuses that whilst it is acceptable to rely on the *clear* wishes of pre-posthumous individuals, presumed consent will result in inappropriate reliance upon evidence as to what individuals *may or may not* have wanted.[80] This forms the essence of the objection of many commentators. But whilst presumed consent may misrepresent the views of some persons, as an argument against presumed consent as a whole it would be decisive only if we removed organs solely from those now deceased individuals who had themselves previously given an explicit consent. In fact, as we have seen, the decision is invariably one for the family in general, who may be in possession of even weaker evidence of the deceased's wish to donate than under a presumed consent regime with an opt out registry. It might simply be a guess. 'Errors' ('false positives') are not the exclusive preserve of presumed consent systems. Viewed in terms of the actual wishes of the deceased person, there will be 'error' in any system where a person is regarded as a potential donor even though they did not wish to donate or where a person who wished to donate does not become a potential donor. We are subtly shifting here from a rationale based on sufficiency of evidence of a decision to donate, toward how best to capture the wishes of deceased persons as a whole, whether for or against donation. A less legalistic approach may be seen to emerge, focusing holistically upon

---

[77] Simmons, *Moral Principles*, p. 77.
[78] Simmons analogously asserts that consent may be 'implied' by certain acts which, although not amounting to consent, are 'closely related' to genuine consent; ibid., pp. 88–9. However, he argues that such a concept is not underpinned by the principle of consent itself but by some alternative ethical foundation, e.g. justice.
[79] Nys, 'European biolaw' at 165. He does not doubt tacit (implicit) consent, however, only 'presumed' consent.
[80] A. Garwood-Gowers, Book Review, (2007) 15(3) *Medical Law Review* 410 at 412.

the autonomous wishes of such persons in general; not simply as a search for 'consent' as a legal justification for an otherwise wrongful act.

Most explicit consent systems fail to set out the legitimate basis for relatives' decisions. Just as in some weak presumed consent systems relatives are simply asked (theoretically) for knowledge regarding any unrecorded objections harboured by the deceased, relatives in explicit consent systems ought seemingly to offer only evidence of known wishes of the deceased communicated during the individual's lifetime. However, even in the latter context the decision of a relative may constitute either transmission of an oral 'decision' ((non-)consent) by the deceased or alternatively a 'divining' of the deceased's preferences i.e. acting as a conduit for that person's anticipated/presumed *wishes*.[81] But in the latter scenarios such a system has shifted, from the perspective of the deceased, from one based on prior *decisions* made by such individuals, to one founded on their assumed *wishes*. This is more transparent as regards objections. It is invariably the case that no consent may be given by relatives where there is knowledge that the deceased objected to donation. Most legislation, however, merely refers, as is the case under the 2006 Act in Scotland, to knowledge of the person's 'unwillingness', without specifying any need for this to have been expressed by way of a, formal, 'decision' – i.e. knowledge of negative *wishes* alone suffices to veto donation.[82] Even more directly, the Uniform Human Tissue Donation Act 1990 in Canada states that a listed relative may consent to the removal of tissue from a deceased person provided that he/she has no reason to believe that the deceased *would have objected* to this.[83]

It is frequently maintained that presumed consent relies upon the dubious and collective evidence of willingness to donate derived from public opinion surveys. Opinion surveys are indeed questionable guides to real levels of willingness to donate. Firstly, such surveys often ask about support for organ donation in general rather than an individual's own disposition to donate.[84] Secondly, even where this is not the case,

---

[81] In some jurisdictions an oral decision suffices for consent or authorisation. This is expressly provided for in section 6 (2)(a)(ii) Human Tissue (Scotland) Act 2006, and during a terminal illness/injury under section 5 (a)(3) of the Uniform Anatomical Gift Act 2006. It is also permitted by inference under the Human Tissue Act 2004, which refers merely to a 'decision', without further qualification.

[82] By contrast, the Human Tissue Act 2004 refers to a *decision* 'of his not to consent to', section 3 (6)(a).

[83] Section 4(5).

[84] For example, in the US a survey conducted in 2005 found that 95 per cent of the US public support organ donation see The Gallup Organization, 2005 National Survey of Organ and Tissue Donation Attitudes and Behavior, at www.organdonor.gov. In the UK, a survey in 2003 revealed that nine out of ten people surveyed supported organ donation; see UK Transplant Press Release No. 44/03.

behavioural research suggests that people are more likely to respond positively when the issue remains a seemingly distant and hypothetical one. Thirdly, there may be a desire to conform to perceptions of proper citizenship. They are nonetheless valuable generalised evidence. However, such polls reveal varying statistics and are time- and jurisdiction-specific. Whilst the Euopean Commission's Eurobarometer Report in 2006 showed that 56 per cent of Europeans were willing to donate (of course not all others were unwilling, many were undecided), there were wide jurisdictional variations – 63 per cent of UK citizens were willing to donate,[85] as well as 69 per cent of citizens in three other explicit consent jurisdictions: Denmark, Germany and the Netherlands.[86] In terms of presumed consent jurisdictions the variation was considerably more marked, with only 29 per cent in Latvia, 33 per cent in Austria, but 73 per cent in Finland and 71 per cent in Belgium. Public opinion polls nonetheless reveal that in the preponderance of European states the majority of the populace *are* in agreement with donating their organs for transplantation after death. The above analysis, however, operates at a macro rather than a micro level, in terms of overall populations rather than individuals. But to what extent can the different systems be seen to result in 'error', as measured against deceased's wishes, *in individual cases*? There are some logical and intuitive reasons to consider that error rates are often higher at present under explicit consent systems, although again nothing conclusive can be demonstrated.

### Best wishes

English and Sommerville observe that

the real choice for society is not between explicit consent and presumed consent. Rather, it is a choice between lack of objection of the relatives and the presumed consent of the individual ... we may ask which of these options is more likely to

---

[85] This is consistent with other UK surveys, e.g. a YouGov survey in October 2007 showing that 62 per cent of respondents were willing to posthumously donate organs; see www.bma.org.uk/ap.nsf/AttachmentsByTitle/XLSorgandonation07/$FILE/organdonation07.xls; and an independent MORI survey in 2007 which found 59 per cent of individuals certain or likely to donate their body, organs, or tissues for medical research, education or transplants; see Human Tissue Authority Stakeholder Evaluation, General Public Qualitative and Quantitative Research, June 2007 at 41.

[86] Special Eurobarometer Report, *Europeans and Organ Donation*, European Commission, May 2007 at 7–8 [Special Eurobarometer Report]. Citizens in Northern Europe were most likely to declare their willingness to donate (Sweden = 81 per cent; Finland & Belgium = 73 per cent) whilst citizens in Eastern Europe were least likely to do so. A Forsa survey in 2003 found that two-thirds of German citizens were willing to donate their organs after death; see German National Ethics Council at 17.

reflect the deceased's wishes. Arguably, if it were common for families to discuss tissue and organ donation, it would be clearly the former since relatives would convey those conversations. Generally, however, this does not happen.[87]

We should therefore ask how these different systems/models 'match up' in terms of their reflection of the true wishes of donors. The Eurobarometer Survey revealed that across the Member States as a whole only 41 per cent of individuals had even raised the subject of donation with their relatives.[88] Other evidence supports the notion that fewer than 50 per cent of relatives in the UK know the deceased's wishes at their death.[89] Similarly in the US.[90] Registers generally record only the wishes of a minority of individuals.[91] In the face of substantial uncertainty about the deceased's wishes, relatives are nonetheless entitled, even obliged, to make a decision.[92] In explicit consent systems (allegedly) unethical removals, viewed from the perspective of the wishes of the deceased, will therefore consistently occur, in particular where relevant relatives are unaware of the individual's wishes or act upon their own views. The superiority of the explicit consent model is nonetheless typically *premised* on the notion that unwilling removal and use renders a donation system ethically defective. Thus, whilst relatives have a role to play with respect to the wishes of the deceased, the ability to 'consent' under explicit consent schemes ordinarily cannot be properly viewed as any legitimate form of 'proxy consent'. As Beyleveld and Brownsword

---

[87] V. English and A. Sommerville, 'Presumed consent for transplantation: A dead issue after Alder Hey?' (2003) 29 *Journal of Medical Ethics* 147 at 149 [English and Sommerville, 'Presumed consent'].

[88] Special Eurobarometer Report at 44–5. Figures ranged from 75 per cent in the Netherlands to 24 per cent in Austria and 16 per cent in Romania.

[89] A figure of 43 per cent was revealed by the Eurobarometer survey, *ibid*. A BBC survey in 2007 found that 51 per cent of individuals had not discussed their donation wishes with their loved ones; see http://news.bbc.co.uk/1/health/4165656.stm. A poll of 1009 Scottish adults in 2004 revealed that just under half of respondents willing to donate organs had informed their family of their wishes; see G. Haddow, '"Because you're worth it?" The taking and selling of transplantable organs' (2006) 32 *Journal of Medical Ethics* 324 at 325 [Haddow, 'Because you're worth it'].

[90] A survey in the 1990s found that only 38 per cent of individuals had discussed their wishes with their family; see A. Spital, 'Mandated choice: A plan to increase public commitment to organ donation' (1995) 273(6) *Journal of the American Medical Association* 504.

[91] 27 per cent of the UK population (15 million) had placed their names on the NHS Organ Donor Register as of March 2009. The highest rate of registration is in the Netherlands, presently around 45 per cent of the population.

[92] Studies in Germany have shown that as many as 90 per cent of individuals had not conveyed their wishes to relatives; see C. Wesslau, K. Grosse, R. Kruger, O. Kucik, F. Nitschke, D. Norba, A. Manecke, F. Polster and D. Gabel, 'How large is the organ donor potential in Germany? Results of an analysis of data collected on deceased with primary and secondary brain damage in intensive care unit from 2002 to 2005' (2007) 20 *Transplant International* 147.

state, to base a 'consent' on a substituted judgement where there is convincing evidence as to the person's wishes is one thing. To guess is another.[93]

### Error

In an explicit consent system relatives can make 'decisions' either to donate *or* not to donate, and there are therefore two potential sources of error. There is abundant evidence, though, that in explicit consent systems where the deceased person declared a willingness to donate (e.g. by placing the name on the organ donor register) relatives will very typically, although not invariably, agree to donation.[94] They will also generally agree to donation where they are in possession of alternative evidence of the deceased's willingness to donate.[95] However, as noted above, deceased persons fail to discuss such matters with relatives in most instances, regularly leaving relatives either to *second guess* the deceased's wishes or make such a decision for themselves. In the face of uncertainty regarding the deceased's wishes, relatives very frequently refuse to consent to donation. Despite the fact that we can plausibly infer that most individuals in the UK are inclined to donate, the Potential Donor Audit (PDA) revealed rates of relative refusal of organs in 2005–6 around 40 per cent, as high as 70 per cent in some regions and amongst some groups.[96] In the Netherlands, in the 55 per cent of instances where the deceased had not registered a positive wish to donate, more than two-thirds of relatives refused to consent.[97] By contrast, rates of refusal are much lower in soft presumed consent jurisdictions such as Belgium (approximately 10 per cent).[98] Sue Sutherland, previous Chief Executive of UK Transplant, has

---

[93] Beyleveld and Brownsword, *Consent in the Law*, p. 117.

[94] Relatives approve donation in the UK in 90 per cent of instances where the individual had placed his/her name on the Organ Donor Register; see ODT, *The Potential Impact* at 14.9.

[95] See also M. Sque, S. Payne and J. Clark, 'Gift of life or sacrifice? Key discourses for understanding decision-making by families of organ donors', in M. Sque and S. Payne (eds.), *Organ and Tissue Donation: An Evidence Base for Practice* (Maidenhead: Open University Press, 2007) 40 at 41 [Sque, Payne and Clark, 'Gift of life?'].

[96] The Eurobarometer Survey showed *projected* refusal rates ranging from 26 per cent (Sweden) to 68 per cent (Romania); see Special Eurobarometer Report at 12. The UK figure was 37 per cent. The latest PDA figures, for the financial years 2006–8, continue to show overall refusal rates of around 40 per cent, see (2008) 68 *NHS Blood and Transplant Bulletin* 11.

[97] Den Hartogh, *Farewell to Non-commitment* at 73. Similarly high rates of refusal have been traditionally seen in the US, at around 50 per cent; see H. Nathan, 'Organ donation in the United States' (2003) 3(Suppl. 4) *American Journal of Transplantation* 29 at 31.

[98] The figure is somewhat higher in France, at around 30 per cent.

remarked that 'A key reason why relatives feel unable to agree to donation is that they do not know what their loved one would have wished. We know however that family members rarely object if they know their relative wanted something positive to come from their death.'[99] Such refusal rates are not surprising. Quite apart from their perceived role in ensuring or facilitating the respectful preservation and disposal of the corpse, and coping with their own grieving, it is in any event a difficult decision, a 'sacrifice' as some have termed it.[100] There is a need for staff to display a high capacity for empathy, consistent with the relatives' sense of bereavement.[101] In a substantial proportion of these cases the deceased might have been entirely content for donation to have ensued, and thus 'error' (false negatives) will have occurred in a significant volume of scenarios.

In presumed consent systems, by contrast, those who wish to donate are more likely to have their wishes fulfilled as they have no need to do anything positive to signal their agreement and it is unlikely such wishes will be overridden by relatives where he/she did not formally object. The German National Ethics Council stated 'One reason why a larger number of organ donations is achieved even under the extended opt-out system is no doubt that the relatives are not required to take any specific action as a condition for the permissibility of organ removal. In a situation that is in any case extremely traumatic for them, they are in effect able simply to let matters take their course with regard to the removal of organs.'[102] Michielsen has observed that generally the number of refusals is inversely correlated with the degree of responsibility given to the family as regards the decision to donate.[103] He has remarked that 'From the emotional point of view, there is a fundamental difference between having to take the responsibility for permitting organ removal and not making use of the right to oppose removal'.[104] Moreover, it is plausible that relatives will at times refuse to consent partially on account of the failure of the deceased to 'opt in' whilst alive, generating the (often dubious) perception that he or she was *not* a willing donor.[105]

---

[99] UK Transplant News Release, Tuesday 25 March 2003, at www.uktransplant.org.uk/ukt/newsroom/news_releases/article.jsp?releaseId=47.

[100] See Sque, Payne and Clark, 'Gift of life?' and Haddow, 'Because you're worth it'.

[101] German National Ethics Council at 21.    [102] *Ibid.*, at 28.

[103] P. Michielsen, 'Informed or presumed consent legislative models', in J. Chapman, M. Deierhoi and C. Wight (eds.), *Organ and Tissue Donation for Transplantation* (London: Arnold, 1997) 344 at 354 [Michielsen, 'Informed or presumed consent'].

[104] P. Michielsen, 'Organ shortage – what to do?' (1992) 24(6) *Transplantation Proceedings* 2391 at 2392.

[105] The German National Ethics Council Report assumed that some relatives would be swayed by this consideration at 23.

Conversely, in explicit consent systems relatives may 'inadvertently' agree to donation, unaware of the deceased's (latent) objections. Indeed, there is often (although not invariably) no mechanism in explicit consent jurisdictions for recording objections *apart* from informing relatives, to *ensure* that organs are not used where the deceased was unwilling.[106] This is a substantial failing.[107] Yet, presumed consent regimes typically have just such a register. The greater reliability of an opt out register in ensuring non-donation where there are real objections is very plausible. Whilst one could carry written notification of a refusal to donate on one's person so that it might be found on the body at death, this is an uncertain strategy and generates practical difficulties, even assuming there is any obligation to conduct a search for such material. Nonetheless, such cases can be expected to be relatively uncommon in view of the difficulty close relatives experience in making such a decision at all, tending to high refusal rates.

The absence of any direct evidence apart from communication with relatives in a high percentage of cases casts doubt on the decision-making of relatives generally, from the perspective of seeking conformity with the deceased's wishes. And in societies where the evidence suggests that most individuals are willing to donate organs for transplant after their deaths, and where individuals' wishes are generally not directly known, rates of 'error' are possibly even greater in *explicit* consent systems. Explicit consent is only 'ideal' where the wishes of the majority of now deceased persons have been reliably and directly recorded, or at a minimum have been conveyed to relatives with decision-making power at the time of death. Only then is 'guesswork' reduced to acceptable proportions. Under presumed consent, there is always, arguably, some direct evidence of the deceased's wishes, and thus the donation 'decision' is more likely to be congruent with such wishes.[108] However, where, as appears perhaps to be the case in Latvia and Austria (based on the evidence of the Eurobarometer survey (see p. 142)), the evidence suggests that most people *do not* wish to donate, a presumed (imputed) consent policy is *not* appropriate.

---

[106] Some nations enable individuals to record willingness to donate as well as objections to donation on official registers, e.g. Sweden, Denmark and the Netherlands.

[107] See also P. Quay, 'Utilizing the bodies of the dead' (1984) 28 *Saint Louis University Law Journal* 889 at 891.

[108] In explicit consent systems a failure to explicitly donate is arguably less cogent evidence of a decision not to donate, in the light of the evidence that many people who have not 'signed up' nevertheless are willing donors.

*Erring on the safe side*

Whilst decisions to refuse donation will often occur in explicit consent systems even where the deceased would have been a willing donor, it is commonly maintained that, compared to the decision to allow some individuals to become donors under a presumed consent system where there is no evidence of a willingness to donate (and may be even an *un* willingness to do so), this is the lesser of the evils, i.e. faced with error, non-donation is better than donation.[109] From the perspective of deceased persons, this is not convincing. The 'neglected wish' to donate in explicit consent contexts is no less a wrong to deceased persons, although this is rarely recognised or appreciated.[110] Without the potential for harm to well-being by the removal of organs or tissue, the autonomous *wishes* of the deceased are the crucial ethical and legal element *per se*. Implementation of a wish to donate may be equally as likely to show respect for persons and their autonomous wishes as a wish not to donate. A humanitarian desire to assist others is not to be dismissed lightly. It is reflective of selfhood and may be driven as much by religious or moral beliefs and values as a decision to refuse to allow removal. Most religions explicitly exhort their followers to help others, especially where the lives of others may be saved. This is often an overriding responsibility. There is no 'safe side' here, and certainly not from the point of view of potential recipients. Either wish is entitled to respect and implementation (subject to necessary constraints). In any event, as we have seen, even if one subscribes to this view one cannot necessarily be sure that more unwilling deceased persons will become donors under a presumed than an explicit consent system.

*Framing effects*

It is sometimes argued that whatever system one puts in place relatives will decide in any event, i.e. presumed consent operates *in practice* in the same way as an explicit consent system anyhow. However, although this phenomenon does indeed occur – as it did previously in the transplant context

---

[109] The German National Ethics Council Report listed the following as possible reasons why a deceased person might fail to register an objection: (1) inertia, (2) acceptance of the 'norm', (3) deferral of a 'non-immediate' decision, (4) too much trouble, (5) lack of awareness of ability to opt out at 27.

[110] See D. Price, 'Property, harm and the corpse' in B. Brooks-Gordon, F. Ebtehaj, J. Herring, M. Johnson and M. Richards (eds.), *Death and Death Rites* (Oxford: Hart Publishing, 2007) 199. Of course, the choice is not between having or not having an intact corpse, but between having an intact corpse prior to destruction, by cremation or burial, and not having one.

in both the UK and France, for instance – this does not necessarily mean that the systems will operate in an identical fashion.[111] Even where the approach is the same, relatives make their decision in a context where the deceased had, for one reason or other, not availed him/herself of the opportunity to object, thus raising the inference that he or she was a willing donor. The policy adopted therefore forms a backdrop to the 'on-the-ground' dialogue between health professionals and relatives and *may* frame wholly different forms of interaction. As has been stated 'In such cases, conversations are based on an assumption of donation'.[112] The US IOM similarly remarked that 'The next-of-kin can be approached quite differently when the deceased's silence is presumed to indicate a decision to donate rather than when it is presumed to indicate a decision not to donate'.[113] Comparatively few objections are offered in such contexts, certainly fewer than where relatives are requested to consent to donation in explicit consent systems. In Spain, even though the presumed consent law is not practised, refusal rates (approximately 20 per cent) are still on the low side compared to most explicit consent jurisdictions. The default indicates the usual decision, the status quo, and research suggests that individuals depart from this only if there is a good reason to do so.[114] This effect may therefore be seen whether or not a presumed consent default position is rigorously enforced in practice.[115]

## Onus

Under presumed consent the onus is upon the deceased to 'opt out', or at least to inform relatives of this view, and this is also a bone of contention. But one should not be led into thinking that there is no onus upon objectors in explicit consent systems. As Dickens states '[An explicit consent regime] also requires people who do not want their organs to be removed after death on consent of their family members to demonstrate their refusal in a way that reasonably anticipates the usually unforeseeable

---

[111] See K. Healy, 'Precious commodities: The supply and demand of body parts: Do presumed-consent laws raise organ procurement rates?' (2006) 55 *De Paul Law Review* 1017 at 1026–31 [Healy, 'Precious commodities'].

[112] Den Hartogh, *Farewell to Non-commitment* at 15. It is noted that in Spain families are approached with the aim of obtaining consent by one means or another at 78 and 80.

[113] Institute of Medicine, *Organ Donation* at 217.

[114] See Den Hartogh, *Farewell to Non-commitment* at 74.

[115] Some research suggests that the 'default position in law' is itself an influential factor upon donation rates; see Johnson and Goldstein, 'Do defaults save lives?' and sources discussed in the text below. See also Den Hartogh, *Farewell to Non-commitment* at 78. This is the position in France, for instance.

circumstances of their death'.[116] It is also argued that it imposes the costs of switching onto the apparent majority, i.e. those wishing to donate in an explicit consent system must take steps to communicate their decision.[117]

### Family

It may be argued that further information should be required to verify or confirm the absence of any objection apart from the failure to register/ record an objection during life. In this respect, relatives may be seen as having a pivotal role. This is the case with respect to either tacit or imputed consent. Even in some explicit consent regimes, relatives are asked to confirm that there is no evidence that would cast doubt on a deceased person's explicit consent to donate, i.e. whether it had been 'withdrawn'. Those closest to the deceased should be approached for possible further information regarding the existence of an objection, including informa- tion as to whether the deceased person had, during life, been capable of making such a decision at all, or at least in the period leading up to death. In the absence of available relatives there may be insufficient evidence upon which to proceed. This suggests that a presumed consent system ought to be 'soft/weak' rather than 'hard/strong' from an ethical stand- point, quite apart from any human rights issues arising from the right to respect for personal and family life under Article 8 of the European Convention on Human Rights.[118] Relatives are only marginalised under 'strong' presumed consent systems, where donation is authorised solely by way of the absence of objection by the now deceased, and even then that it is often the theory rather than the reality.

In weak systems, relatives' objections may be based only on known objections held by the deceased or alternatively be based on relatives' own objections. In France, the 1994 Law stated that organ removal is permis- sible if there are no recorded objections by the deceased, but that if there is no direct knowledge of the wishes of the deceased, the physician must

---

[116] Dickens et al., 'Legislation' at 101–2. Although such a necessity was held not to infringe the person's fundamental rights in the German, opt-in, context; see BVerfG [Federal Constitutional Court] (First Chamber of the First Senate) NJW 1999: 3403.

[117] Johnson and Goldstein, 'Do defaults save lives?'. However, the default is here to allow discretion for relatives to decide in such contexts, not to disallow donation entirely.

[118] The alternative epithets 'hard' and 'soft' are also used. This is a mere terminological difference rather than one with any substantive import. Arguably, where a person lacking competence had appointed a person with a (lasting) power of attorney, they should be entitled to be consulted as regards knowledge of the deceased's wishes. However, as the British Medical Association (BMA) has argued, persons lacking capacity should also be entitled to perform altruistic acts and therefore should not be 'presumed objectors'.

endeavour to obtain the testimony of the family,[119] making it clear as had been the case under the previous law that the relatives were only being approached for information about the *deceased's* wishes.[120] In Finland, by contrast, the law states that 'Organs and tissues of a deceased person may be removed unless there is reason to assume that the person would have objected while still alive, or that a near relative or other close person would object'.[121] This law also gives scope for expression of relatives' own objections.

Whether relatives should be able to object in their own right, as opposed to merely being able to object on the basis of evidence as to the deceased's own wishes, is debatable. The British Medical Association (BMA) would concede the right of relatives to object on their own behalf, but only in cases where donation would be productive of severe distress.[122] This might perhaps be a legitimate basis for a veto, but requires further debate. A personal right to object may perhaps even be necessary in order to satisfy the right to respect for private and family life under Article 8 of the European Convention on Human Rights. It might seem inappropriate, though, to allow relatives' own personal objections to be actuated where the deceased *tacitly* consented to donate, although it might possibly be politic to sometimes concede such an entitlement even then. Gevers *et al.* assert 'Apart from the fact that relatives may be in the best position to express the presumed will of the deceased, they are emotionally deeply involved. Their feelings deserve respect and it is hard to see how health care staff could put aside their eventual resistance against organ removal.'[123] Of course, even if this was not permissible, there is no way of preventing the supposed expressions of wishes of the deceased being infused by personal wishes and beliefs. It might seem anomalous that relatives would be officially entitled to object under a presumed consent system where the deceased did not object, but not to override a deceased person's explicit consent. Whilst some laws do in fact reflect such a differential stance, e.g. in

---

[119] Although many clinicians nonetheless continued to ask for consent from families for donation; see G. Nowenstein, 'Organ procurement rates: Does presumed consent legislation really make a difference?' (2004) 1 *Law, Social Justice and Global Development Journal,* at http://elj.warwick.ac.uk/global/04-1/nowenstein.html [Nowenstein, 'Organ procurement rates'].

[120] Article L. 671–7, Law No. 94–654 of 29 July 1994. See now articles L 1232–1 to L 1232–6 of the Code of Public Health as amended by Law No. 2004–800 of 6 August 2004.

[121] Law No. 101 of 2 February 2001, section 9.

[122] British Medical Association, 'Organ donation – presumed consent for organ donation', January 2008, at www.bma.org.uk/ap.nsf/Content/OrganDonationPresumedConsent. Such a provision is not, however, to be typically found in existing legislation.

[123] S. Gevers, A. Janssen and R. Friele, 'Consent systems for post mortem organ donation in Europe' [2004] 11 *European Journal of Health Law* 175 at 177 [Gevers, 'Consent systems'].

Belgium,[124] such a distinction is less compelling under a system premised on tacit rather than imputed consent, where there is direct evidence of the deceased having made a donation 'decision', i.e. factually consented.

Thus, at minimum a presumed consent model requires a mechanism for educating and informing individuals and allowing them to record objections before their deaths, as well as for proper engagement to be made with relatives after that person's death. In *In re Organ Retention Group Litigation*, Gage J stated 'There may be little conceptual difference between consent and non-objection, but the latter in my view implies a more passive approach than a requirement for consent'.[125] But if relatives are not approached at all and informed about relevant matters, how can they 'object' on behalf of the deceased (or maybe themselves) in any meaningful way? As the Alder Hey Report observed, how can there be no reason to believe that there was any objection to retention and/or use for research when professionals declined to approach relatives in the first place?[126] Relatives would need to be informed the person had died, that he/she had not registered an objection prior to death and that it was intended, subject to their objection (either offered on their own initiative or after having been directly solicited), to use the organs or tissues for transplantation and/or research.[127] It is not sufficient to wholly leave the onus upon relatives to communicate any known objections without direct contact.[128] Indeed, in the US,[129] many of the medical examiner laws have been found to breach constitutional requirements of procedural due process on this basis.[130] Moreover, there should be no coercion which

---

[124] Although Belgium is a presumed consent jurisdiction, the law specifically states that the explicitly stated wish of a person to donate after death suffices for donation and that this cannot be vetoed after death; see Law of 13 June 1986, section 10 (4).

[125] *In re Organ Retention Group Litigation* [2005] QB 506 at [127].

[126] See Royal Liverpool Inquiry at 362–3.

[127] It has been suggested that in the US relatives must be told that they have a constitutional right to refuse donation; see *Newman* v. *Sathyavaglswaran* 287 F 3d 786 (US Ct. App, 9th Cir. 2002). Whether relatives possessing such knowledge should be obliged to volunteer objections on their own initiative would appear to be a moot point. It is the practice in Belgium to leave it to relatives to raise objections on their own initiative. See Evan Harris MP, House of Commons Hansard Debates on the Human Tissue Bill, col. 1032, 15 January 2004.

[128] The law in Belgium does not require that relatives be approached regarding objections, although this is the invariable practice.

[129] Fourteen states had such provisions in relation to *all* organs and tissues, although not actually practised in such jurisdictions apart from in respect of corneas and pituitary glands. See K. Keller, 'The bed of life: A discussion of organ donation, its legal and scientific history, and a recommended "opt-out" solution to organ scarcity' (2002–2003) 32 *Stetson Law Review* 855 at 886; and O'Carroll, 'Over my dead body'.

[130] See, e.g., *Brotherton* v. *Cleveland* 923 F 2d 477 (6th Cir. 1991). The Ohio statute in that case permitted the removal of corneas without any enquiries being made as to the intent

might deter relatives from offering up such objections, and an easy means of communicating objections should be in place, after sufficient time to consider the matter has been provided consistent with the potential use of the tissue for the requisite purpose.

I am not of course here considering the position of parents and their now deceased children. Minors lacking decisionmaking capacity are not proper candidates for presumed consent in any event. The BMA is correct in asserting that the consent of the parents must be obtained in all instances to enable such material to be used for transplantation, and this applies equally to tissues removed, retained and used for research. Thus, the manifestly improper conduct described in the Alder Hey and Bristol Inquiry reports was rightly castigated where the objections of parents were either unsolicited or ignored. Minors without capacity cannot properly 'decide' not to opt out. Minors are excluded under the laws of France and Belgium, for instance, although in the latter parents may object for the minor during minority.[131] In relation to minors, parental responsibility confers primary decision-making authority in its own right.

## Commitment

One outstanding issue is the degree of *commitment* that should be manifest in any valid 'consent/authorisation'. We must ask whether an attitude short of a positive desire to donate should be adequate as the basis for donation. Westen notes that both unconditional endorsement and conditional preference will invariably suffice as the basis for (factual) consent, but that whether indifference should or does suffice is a matter of policy.[132] Thus, indifference will suffice for some binding decisions.

English and Sommerville observe that very many individuals, possibly the majority of the populace, are happy to become donors but not suffi-ciently highly motivated to take positive steps to record this wish on the

of the deceased or relatives, i.e. where the coroner was unaware of any objections, without more. See also *Whaley* v. *County of Tuscola* 58 F 3d 1111 (6th Cir. 1995). It has been argued that consistently with its previous jurisprudence the Supreme Court itself would be likely also to declare similar state provisions unconstitutional for lack of a mandated sufficient due process; see Comments. This has by no means been the invariable outcome in the State courts, however. See, e.g., *State* v. *Powell* 497 So 2d 1188 (Fla. 1986) (Florida Supreme Court upheld the constitutionality of a presumed consent cornea donation law); *Georgia Lions Eye Bank Inc.* v. *Lavant* 335 SE 2d 127 (Ga. 1985) and *Tillman* v. *Detroit Receiving Hospital* 360 NW 2d 275 (Mich. Ct. App. 1984).
[131] Belgium Law of 13 June 1986, section 10(2). Of course, what amounts to 'minority' for these purposes will vary as between jurisdictions.
[132] Westen, *The Logic of Consent*, pp. 28–30. He suggests that it is less appropriate for crucial personal decisions.

register or by completing and signing a donor card.[133] This seems extremely plausible. Yet, under an explicit consent model relatives may give consent on behalf of deceased individuals who possessed a decidedly neutral, ambivalent, or even reluctant view toward donation. Similarly in a presumed consent system. Whilst those who desire to donate are more likely to have their wishes implemented, 'willingness' to donate as inferred from silence may also wrap up those who are ambivalent, indifferent or 'not unwilling', and even slightly unwilling. The flip side to English and Sommerville's point is that in presumed consent systems, in so far as the individual concerned has to take actual physical steps to opt out, although objectors are rather more likely to have their views respected by dint of the existence of a register, it is likely that only those who have *substantial* objections will opt out. Those with conscientious objections based on religious or moral beliefs or suchlike are likely to make such an effort, whereas those with lesser objections might not. Those with mild objections may be equally as likely to have their views subjugated under either system.

Overall, what are we to make of this? It seems that the price of ensuring that the supposed (favourable) views of the majority of individuals and those with strong objections are respected in certain contexts is that a substantial percentage of donors under presumed consent may not have strong favourable views regarding donation; they may even be indifferent or slightly unwilling. On the converse side, under explicit consent, whilst those who are very favourable towards donation will generally become donors, those with more modest inclinations towards donation will less often become donors, and it is more conceivable that some of those with substantial objections may be overlooked. One way to obviate the latter problem though is to have a 'two-way' register, which exists in some nations, allowing the registration of objections as well as wishes to donate.[134] Indeed, *whatever* type of consent regime is in place, there ought to be a permanent registry in existence able to reliably record either consents *or* objections to donation, to ensure that the wishes of the deceased determine the fate of such individual's body parts. This is essential to further the posthumous autonomy of that individual. The Scottish Council on Human Bioethics has remarked regarding the recent legislation implemented in Scotland (although this applies to the UK as a whole) that 'The absence of fail-safe mechanisms to allow people to

---

[133] English and Sommerville, 'Presumed consent' at 149.

[134] These generally exist in presumed rather than explicit consent jurisdictions, for instance Sweden, Italy and Belgium. However, Denmark, Australia and the Netherlands also have such frameworks.

record their wishes, be they positive or negative, in the Act is a cause of concern'.[135]

Perhaps differing perceptions here stem from a conceptual divergence as regards the basis for organ removal and use. Is this one based on a necessity for a positive request/offer to donate, or instead one where we can be clear that the person did not substantially object to it? If donation may be based on weakish tendencies either way, or indifference or apathy, then we should perhaps be attempting to ensure that donation does not occur where any substantial objections exist and otherwise allow the practice to take place, as opposed to seeking clear requests to donate. To expect every deceased donation to be accompanied by a strong favourable motivation may be to expect too much.

### Donation rates: the 'aching gap'

Few reliable and comprehensive empirical surveys have been conducted examining the independent effect of presumed consent on donation rates either within specific jurisdictions or across jurisdictions. Commentators' and researchers' views and deductions differ markedly but are frequently based on inaccuracies of legal interpretation or a failure to take on board differences between laws and practice.[136] Michielsen rightly notes that 'To evaluate the impact of a presumed consent law in a given country it is essential to first examine the way and the extent to which its essential premises are applied'.[137] These remarks apply to all systems.[138] Moreover, cross-country comparisons are also frequently founded upon simplistic comparisons of donation rates and legal system types, neglecting to take account of confounding differentials and influences.[139] There have, however, been four major studies which accounted for a multiplicity of variables and contained regression analyses. These all suggest that

---

[135] House of Lords European Union Committee, *Increasing the Supply of Donor Organs within the European Union*, Volume 1: 17th Report of Session 2007–08, HL Paper 123–1, para. 296 [House of Lords].

[136] For instance, one study classified the UK as being a presumed consent jurisdiction when this merely existed in form not substance; see R. Coppen, R. Friele, R. Marquet and S. Gevers, 'Opting-out systems: No guarantee for higher donation rates' (2005) 18(11) *Transplant International* 1275. Similarly, whilst Spain has the highest donation rate in Europe and has a presumed consent law, this is not directly implemented in practice, leading to varying interpretations in the literature.

[137] Michielsen, 'Informed or presumed consent' at 352.

[138] A useful overview is contained in Gevers, 'Consent systems'.

[139] E.g. the conclusion that presumed consent laws have no correlation with higher donation rates, but having failed to exclude countries with very low transplantation rates in general; see, e.g., W. Land and B. Cohen, 'Postmortem and living organ donation in Europe' (1992) 24 *Transplantation Proceedings* 2165.

presumed consent does generally lead to higher donation rates. Gimbel *et al.*'s study was based on twenty-eight European nations and found that all four independent variables tested had an impact on donation rates in the countries studied, i.e. presumed consent laws, number of transplant centres per million population (p.m.p.), percentage of the population enrolled in tertiary education, and percentage of the population that was Roman Catholic. They concluded that presumed consent had had a significant impact on deceased donors p.m.p. in Europe.[140] Unlike the other studies considered below, this was based on *practice* rather than the genus of the law itself. Johnson and Goldstein have remarked, based on their own experiments and data analysis, that 'Our data and those of Gimbel *et al.* suggest changes in defaults could increase donations in the United States of additional thousands of donors a year'.[141]

Neto *et al.* studied thirty-four countries (including some Latin American countries and nations with low deceased donor rates) over a five-year period, accounting for seven variables including the existence of a presumed consent law. The latter factor was found to be associated with an increased donation rate of between 21 and 26 per cent.[142] Healy examined seventeen OECD countries over a twelve-year period controlling for four variables in addition to the existence of a presumed consent law. The latter was found to be associated with an increase on average of 2.7 donors p.m.p., but unlike the other studies this was not found to be statistically significant.[143] Another survey conducted by Abadie and Day concluded, having taken into account other potential determinants of donation rates (GDP per capita, health expenditure, religious beliefs, and number of road traffic and cerebrovascular deaths) in twenty-two Western nations, that presumed consent countries have on average approximately 25–30 per cent higher donation rates than explicit consent countries.[144] Moreover, they argue that defaults in legislation may affect donation decisions by families *even if* they are not enforced in practice.

---

[140] R. Gimbel, M. Strosberg, S. Lehrman, E. Gefenas and F. Taft, 'Presumed consent and other predictors of cadaveric organ donation in Europe' (2003) 13(1) *Progress in Transplantation* 17.

[141] Johnson and Goldstein, 'Do defaults save lives?' at 1339.

[142] G. Neto, A. Campelo and E. De Silva, 'The impact of presumed consent law on organ donation: An empirical analysis from quantile regression for longtitudinal data' at eScholarship Repository, 2007, at http://repositories.cdlib.org/bple/alacde/050107-2.

[143] Healy, 'Precious commodities'. However, when Italy and Spain (the outliers) were removed from the analysis the effect was more positive, although still not 'strongly significant', at 1036.

[144] A. Abadie and S. Gay, 'The impact of presumed consent legislation on cadaveric organ donation: A cross-country study' (2006) 25(4) *Journal of Health Economics* 599.

Whilst the Organ Donation Taskforce Report in the UK found 'no convincing evidence that it would deliver significant increases in the number of donated organs',[145] presumed consent does seemingly *tend* toward maximisation of donation rates in general, as the above studies show.[146] It is nonetheless extraordinarily difficult if not impossible to isolate the effect of any one specific variable, such as a change in the organ donation regime, in relation to organ donor rates. Presumed consent is unlikely to be a panacea for the shortage of organs, even if it might tend to higher donation rates.[147] It is neither sufficient nor necessary. The tendency to higher rates may only be significantly realised in conjunction with the existence of other structural, resource, or psychological factors. Contrariwise, systemic and institutional changes *might* be capable of achieving higher procurement rates independently of the character of the law, as experience using the 'Spanish model' appears to testify. The number of ICU beds, transplant co-ordinators and doctors and nurses and specialised units, etc., the predominant cause of death, and the characteristics of the patients on the waiting list, are all undoubtedly influential factors.[148] Likewise the attitude of professionals and geographical factors. This would seem to be clear from the fact that different regions in the same jurisdiction and implementing the law in the same way have extremely varying rates of donation and transplantation – for instance, in different parts of Germany (twice as high in some centres than others) and in Italy.

---

[145] ODT, *The Potential Impact* at 134.

[146] The York Centre for Reviews and Dissemination, which conducted an analysis of existing data, stated 'The between country comparison studies overall point to presumed consent law being associated with increased organ donation rates (even when other factors are accounted for) though it cannot be inferred from this that the introduction of presumed consent legislation *per se* leads to an increase in donation rates', and 'The before and after studies suggest an increase in donation rates following the introduction of presumed consent legislation, however, it is not possible to rule out the influence of other factors on donation rates'; Appendix I, *A Systematic Review of Presumed Consent Systems for Deceased Organ Donation*, University of York, at 10; ODT, *ibid.*, Appendix I.

[147] It is sometimes noted that even where relatives refuse to agree to donation in a substantial percentage of instances, this still approximates to the percentage of allegedly willing donors in opinion polls; usually 60–70 per cent or so. But the German National Ethics Council observed that this fails to take account of the number of potential donors who are not proceeded with because of early indications of unwillingness from relatives. See German National Ethics Council Opinion at 18.

[148] R. Matesanz, 'Factors influencing the adaptation of the Spanish Model of organ donation' (2003) 16 *Transplant International* 736.

## PC or not PC?

Presumed consent (PC) will not be workable in the face of significant opposition from the public and/or relevant health professionals, or at least might prove to be counterproductive in relation to donation rates. In the 1990s, the King's Fund Institute counselled caution with respect to its introduction in the UK, finding that 'the medical profession, the transplant community and public opinion are split over the ethics of such a law. If such a change provoked an acrimonious public debate it could damage the reputation of, and public confidence in, the transplant technology as a whole.'[149] However, professional support for presumed consent has increased since the 1990s: the British Transplantation Society supports a weak presumed consent model, as does the BMA, the Royal College of Surgeons, the Royal College of Pathologists and the Royal College of Nursing.[150] Patient groups are divided.[151] In the US, the American Medical Association (AMA) is currently opposed to presumed consent in the light of the absence of convincing evidence that it would enhance donation rates.[152]

Public support for presumed consent in the UK would appear to be waxing rather than waning. A YouGov survey of 2,034 adults carried out on behalf of the BMA in 2007 found that 64 per cent thought that the UK should move to a system of presumed consent. This contrasts with a similar survey conducted by the BMA in 2004 which found 60 per cent of individuals in support,[153] and the same result in a BBC survey in 2005 involving a representative sample of 2,067 adults.[154] This is only 'limited and incomplete evidence' of public attitudes, as was pointed out in the evidence submitted to the Taskforce.[155] Attitudes are less positive in the

---

[149] King's Fund Institute, *A Question of Give and Take*, Research Report 18 (London: King's Fund, 1994) at 82 [King's Fund Report].

[150] The Intensive Care Society, however, displayed clear opposition at its May 2008 meeting.

[151] The British Kidney Patients Association, National Kidney Federation, Kidney Wales Foundation and Welsh Kidney Patients Association favour presumed consent, but the Patients Association, Patient Concern, Jeanette Crizzle Trust and BODY, amongst others, are against it.

[152] See AMA, at www.ama-assn.org/ama1/pub/upload/mm/369/;ceja_7a05.pdf. UNOS is currently opposed to such a policy; see www.unos.org/Resources/bioethics,asp?index=2.

[153] A poll of 1,009 adults in Scotland in 2004 showed that the majority supported a soft presumed consent law; see Haddow, 'Because you're worth it?' at 326.

[154] In addition, a BBC Watchdog telephone poll of nearly 52,000 people in 2001 found 78 per cent in favour. This contrasts with an Omnibus survey of 2,000 people for the National Kidney Research Fund which found 57 per cent of respondents in favour, a Department of Health survey in 1999 which found only 28 per cent in favour, and a 2004 survey of the Scottish public which revealed only 37 per cent in favour; see Haddow, 'Because you're worth it?' at 326.

[155] ODT, *The Potential Impact*, Appendix I at 10.

US. Preliminary results from a National Survey of Organ Donation in 2005 revealed that 43.2 per cent of individuals supported presumed consent, compared to 53.6 per cent against, and 30.9 per cent of individuals stated that they would opt out if a presumed consent law were to be enacted.[156] This latter statistic was partly responsible for the IOM suggesting in 2006 that the time had not yet come for presumed consent in the US.[157]

An extensive preceding educational campaign and the appearance of fairness in the system are essential pre-requisites to public support and the existence of a workable system. Lack of faith in officials, healthcare professionals and the government leading to scepticism and mistrust could perhaps lead to even lower donation rates. In Brazil a lack of trust in 'the system' led to a backlash and the public en masse deciding to opt out, which contributed to the rapid demise of the presumed consent law.[158] There may be a particular problem within some sections or groups within society.[159] In 1994 the King's Fund Report suggested that certain sections of society, orthodox Jews and Muslims perhaps, should be afforded the opportunity to be excluded from any presumed consent law which might be enacted in the UK.[160] Muslims were in fact excluded en bloc from the presumed consent law enacted in Singapore in 1987.[161] However, separate treatment of different minority groups might tend to be divisive rather than simply being respectful of diversity. The ODT, in fact, found the majority of faith groups consulted opposed to the introduction of presumed consent in the UK,[162] despite all the major religions of the world generally being 'officially' in favour of organ donation after death in general.[163] Perceptions of inequality may be

---

[156] Institute of Medicine, *Organ Donation* at 215. See also L. Siminoff and M. Mercer, 'Public policy, public opinion, and consent for organ donation' (2001) 10 *Cambridge Quarterly of Healthcare Ethics* 377 [Siminoff and Mercer, 'Public policy'].

[157] Institute of Medicine, *Organ Donation*, at 225. An earlier US study of 600 family members found that only 22.5 per cent supported a move to a presumed consent law; see Siminoff and Mercer, 'Public policy' at 381.

[158] See E. Bailey, 'Should the State have rights to your organs? Dissecting Brazil's mandatory organ donation law' (1998–9) 30 *University of Miami Inter-American Law Review* 707 and C. Csillag, 'Brazil abolishes "presumed consent" in organ donation' (1998) 352 *The Lancet* 1367. Apparently there had been no significant public information campaign preceding the introduction of the law.

[159] Wright has emphasised that trust in the healthcare system is vital and that presumed consent could especially alienate particular groups; see L. Wright, 'Is presumed consent the answer to organ shortages?' (2007) 334 *British Medical Journal* 1089.

[160] King's Fund Report at 63. In 1995 the Muslim Law (Shariah) Council UK issued a directive supporting organ donation and transplantation.

[161] Although the law is apparently due to be reformed to apply presumed consent to all residents.

[162] ODT, *The Potential Impact* at 30.

[163] Certain Native American Indians and Aborigines, amongst others, hold negative views toward donation.

particularly damaging. There is already a perception prevailing in many societies that certain classes of individuals are disadvantaged in terms of access to organs for transplantation.[164] Such perceptions may even be generated by the scheme in itself. As Goodwin shows, the US state presumed consent cornea removal laws applied only in the context of medical examiners, yet a disproportionate class of one type of individuals came within their purview, predominantly poor black citizens. Particular attention should be paid to vulnerable groups, such as those on the margins of society, and individuals who, due to some form of mental incapacity, are unable to choose whether to become organ donors or not. Distrust may, however, be discrete to one sphere of activity. Whilst mistrust of the professionals ran deep in the UK in the late 1990s in the context of post-mortem retention practices, this would not appear to have extended significantly to the transplantation arena.

### Research

How much of the above analysis applies with respect to the retention and use of tissue from deceased persons for research? Firstly, there is not the same desperate shortage of material for such purposes as there is with respect to organs for transplantation, nor are individual lives immediately compromised in terms of length or quality by any such shortage.[165] Secondly, it is important to be aware that the absence of explicit consent to such retention and use following post-mortem examinations was at the heart of some of the recent controversies, even if it was not the necessary cause of it. Thirdly, individuals are generally even less aware during their lives of the possibility of tissue from their corpse being able to be used to these ends. Wicclair asserts that because research on deceased persons is so varied and unknowable, and so much less visible to the public, presuming agreement is more doubtful.[166] In the light of this, and the lack of any donation registry, relatives would typically be best placed to decide what the deceased would have wished to have taken place in such circumstances. A decision should be obtained from qualifying relatives based on a substituted judgement evaluation. Thus, there is a less compelling

---

[164] For example in Australia Aborigines are transplanted at a lesser rate than other sections of the population; see National Health and Medical Research Council, *Organ and Tissue Donation After Death*, Australian Government, 2007 at 9. Goodwin, *Black Markets*, p. 118.

[165] Although investigation of tissues at autopsy may sometimes reveal important and unique data relating to certain disease states and conditions, especially paediatric autopsies.

[166] M. Wicclair, 'Ethics and research with deceased patients' (2008)17 *Cambridge Quarterly of Healthcare Ethics* 87 at 93.

case for presumed consent in the immediate term in this context.[167] Of course, with regard to young children explicit parental consent would be mandatory in any case.[168]

But would it be inconsistent in policy terms for explicit consent to be necessary for research but not transplantation purposes? The HTA stated its belief that presumed consent for organ transplantation might undermine current provisions for fully informed consent in the 2004 Act,[169] and the Retained Organs Commission stated that it found it difficult to see how different principles could apply to different uses of post-mortem body parts.[170] In so far as relatives see transplantation as more immediately and directly 'therapeutic' than research, it is not indefensible for different models to be operating, though. As the Law Reform Commission of Canada stated

[E]ven if in some instances there are clear benefits that would justify a policy of presuming consent for use by medical science of the dead body, the benefits from medical education and research are significantly less immediate and tangible. Presumed consent to organ and tissue transplantation might be legitimized, for example, because procurement has the immediate, likely and identifiable benefit of saving lives or healing.[171]

But could a presumed consent system for organ and tissue donation for transplantation *co-exist* harmoniously and unproblematically with an explicit consent system for donation for research and/or other purposes? This would mean that if after death the deceased had not recorded an objection to donation for transplantation it would be permissible to remove and use the relevant body parts subject only, and depending on the nature of the presumed consent system in force, to a relative objecting thereto after death. On the other hand a relative would have to give explicit consent/authorisation for the use for research where the deceased had made no decision prior to death. This might appear anomalous. However, different laws have applied as between organ and tissue *transplantation* in the US for some while, e.g. *vis-à-vis* various state cornea removal laws. It

---

[167] This is the view of the Chief Medical Officer, Sir Liam Donaldson (expressed to the House of Lords Select Committee on the European Union), who sparked the recent initiative relating to presumed consent in the context of transplantation.

[168] Although very many of the organ retention controversies have related to parents of young children, this was rarely exclusively so apart from at Bristol Royal Infirmary. Indeed, the Isaacs Inquiry Report related wholly to a spousal scenario.

[169] Human Tissue Authority News release, 'Statement on Chief Medical Officer's announcement', 24 July 2007.

[170] Retained Organs Commission, *Remembering the Past, Looking to the Future*, NHS, 2004, para. 5.29.

[171] Law Reform Commission of Canada, *Procurement and Transfer of Human Tissues and Organs*, Working Paper 66, 1992 at 115.

might nevertheless appear to be difficult for such decision-making processes to practically co-exist, and without conflation occurring, i.e. to keep such processes 'separate'. In practice, though, different personnel, processes and timings would frequently be involved. Just as tissue procurement for transplantation often occurs after a post-mortem examination has been undertaken, as opposed to the ordinary organ procurement process around the time of death, the same may be said as regards the procurement of certain tissues from deceased persons for research.

## A PC world?

It would presently appear to be precipitate for most Western societies to embrace a 'donation' system not founded upon some form of consent.[172] Some individual authority for donation is required to recognise the interests an individual has in their person even after death, and in order to truly make a 'gift' to others.[173] Consent is a basic ideological and political commitment in all societies with developed organ transplant systems, and this is incompatible with routine taking. In order for the properly protectable interests of deceased persons extending beyond death to be overridden in the interests of others there would need at a minimum to be shown to be a demonstrable, overwhelming and immediate need that could not be met by other less drastic means.

It is submitted here that such a consent may sometimes equally be presumed as opposed to explicit. However, for any such policy to be appropriately and ethically and legitimately implemented, it is mandatory for there to be a proper and adequate information programme and a suitable supporting infrastructure. In the absence of such pre-conditions any 'consent' in this connection is mere rhetoric and illusory; 'opting out' may better capture the essence of such a scheme. Such a policy is *at the expense of* individual autonomy and founded instead on a communitarian *raison d'être*. If what is intended is indeed the routine taking of organs or tissues, it is not appropriate to dub this (presumed, or any other type of) 'consent' at all.

Presumed consent systems are typically more 'oriented' around the wishes of deceased persons themselves, and are preferable in that specific respect. In evidence to the House of Lords Select Committee, the Scottish

---

[172] This is mandated in these very terms in the Additional Protocol on the Transplantation of Organs and Tissues of Human Origin, Council of Europe, 2002, Article 17. The term 'authorisation' is employed analogously in some jurisdictions to stress the need for explicit permission to proceed, e.g. in Scotland.

[173] See McGuinness and Brazier, 'Respecting the living' at 297.

Council on Human Bioethics asserted that it should only be possible to remove organs from a deceased person if this person had given their prior informed consent to the procedure. They considered that it should not be possible for relatives to authorise the retrieval of organs for transplantation in an explicit consent system where the deceased had left no wishes in this regard.[174] But in the light of the failure of most individuals to communicate any indication of their wishes prior to their deaths, this would have a critical impact on donation rates in all jurisdictions. It would also fail to promote individuals' true wills in a high proportion of instances, i.e. by virtue of the influence of inertia, etc. As a consequence, explicit consent systems afford decision-making prerogative to relatives. It has been observed regarding the Netherlands that the legislator avoided an absolute consent system because it would ostensibly result in too few organs being donated. That is the reason why next of kin were afforded the opportunity to donate in the event that the deceased had not made any decision.[175] Such systems are normally ambivalent, however, with regard to the significance of a deceased's wishes, thus threatening to have a damaging impact upon personal autonomy generally. Kluge states

These protocols also have serious ethical implications for the ethics of informed consent. What the transplant societies are in effect saying with their guidelines is that the informed donor consent will not be considered binding if the donor is no longer capable of enforcing his or her wishes. Such an attitude sends the message that organ donation really doesn't mean anything: that the wishes of others really carry the day.[176]

The *delegation* default under an explicit consent regime also encourages laziness or evasiveness in donor decision-making prior to death. Oz *et al.* have suggested that public education campaigns may lack effectiveness because the onus of decisionmaking in explicit consent systems is not upon the deceased. They state

Perhaps one explanation for why improving public awareness alone has failed to make a significant impact is that its effectiveness hinges on the public seeing personal relevance in the matter. Making this issue personal for them will not happen if we continue to leave the decision to others (the next of kin). Organ donation would become a very personal and relevant issue under a system of either presumed consent or mandated choice, and perhaps education then would play a real role.[177]

---

[174] See House of Lords, para. 285. The Council is concerned about the potential for serious mistakes where relatives make decisions ignorant of the deceased's wishes.

[175] Den Hartogh, *Farewell to Non-commitment* at 25.

[176] E.-H. Kluge, 'Organ donation and retrieval: Whose body is it anyway?', in H. Kuhse and P. Singer (eds.), *Bioethics: An Anthology* (London: Blackwell, 2006) 483 at 485.

[177] M. Oz *et al.*, 'How to improve organ donation: Results of the ISHLT/FACT poll' (2003) 22 *Journal of Heart and Lung Transplantation* 389 at 395.

What we are left with is a fudge, and one which does not err towards enhanced volumes of donors either. As den Hartogh (describing the existing explicit consent system in the Netherlands) asserts

It is difficult to find a sound justification of the present non-absolute consent system. Although this is an attempt to compensate for the limited yield from an absolute consent system, it departs from the essential characteristic of a consent system, i.e. that the default lies in refusal. The default is shifting to delegating the decision to the next of kin, and none of the moral principles we have discussed have given us good reason to do exactly this.[178]

This messy 'compromise' serves to hinder the donation enterprise and transplantation as a whole. What is required is a bold commitment to one (consent) strategy or other.

However, if a presumed consent system is permissible or even perhaps preferable, we must enquire what *type* of presumed consent system should be established. Is this one grounded in the *factual*, tacit consent of the (deceased) individual, or an *imputed* consent grounded in the best interpretation of the anticipated wishes of deceased persons?

Presumed consent may potentially consist of a tacit consent rooted in passivity. The IOM Report in the US opined that

Presumed consent as tacit, silent consent can be ethically valid in social practices that involve extensive and effective public education in order to ensure public understanding and that make widely available clear, easy, non-onerous, and reliable ways for individuals to register their refusal.[179]

However, this arguably necessitates a direct approach being made to individuals and the adequate recording of objections, coupled with an on-going sufficiency of information regarding the system. The proposal for the active donor registration system (ADR) in the Netherlands, whereby all individuals are directly contacted but where the default for non-responders would be non-objection (i.e. tacit consent), is an example of a scheme which would seemingly be adequate to ground such a consent.[180] The choice of the default is supported by the needs of end-stage organ failure patients requiring transplantable organs. As den Hartogh states 'Since non-registration under the ADR system may be considered

---

[178] Den Hartogh, *Farewell to Non-commitment* at 54.
[179] Institute of Medicine, *Organ Donation* at 226–7.
[180] Information and advertising campaigns may fail to 'reach' some individuals, especially perhaps those, such as the homeless or travellers, on the fringes of society, or those with language or communication deficits. But such identifiable individuals are already vulnerable to becoming potential donors under every system, whatever their views. Thus, whatever infrastructure is put in place to faithfully reflect the wishes of a person prior to their death there will be some doubt about reliability.

as tacit yet true and full consent, the right to self-determination is not impaired in any way whatever'.[181] He regards the role of relatives as superfluous under such a system, although it may be argued that there is useful function, possibly even an imperative, in having contact with relatives at the time of death to ascertain any potential change of heart or impediment to decision-making capacity or capability.

Many systems will fail to satisfy such essential pre-requisites. In that event, many deny that there is a sufficient basis to underpin an adequate 'consent' to donation based on the individual right of choice or self-determination of the 'donor'.[182] Certainly in such instances, a failure to object is typically less compelling evidence of a willingness to donate than where a wish to donate has been expressly communicated by one means or other.[183] Nonetheless, it would appear that presumed consent regimes better reflect most individuals' true wishes in *some* contemporary societies presently, or at least reflect such wishes to no lesser extent than under an explicit consent system. One might therefore endorse a notion of 'consent' as legally *imputed*. This is a perfectly proper policy option. A system founded on this latter rationale ostensibly requires a more central role for relatives in supplementing knowledge regarding the deceased's will and wishes. Although relatives may have, in view of their personal knowledge of the individual, the best notion of what the person *would have decided* had they addressed their mind to it, even under an explicit consent model we are now moving away from an actual to a hypothetical, or imputed, consent. The relative's role has transmuted from a communication medium to a decision-making function based on substituted judgement as to the deceased's likely wishes. The similarities between such systems can be seen in the following remarks of Beyleveld and Brownsword, who state 'We have just said that consents by opt-out are a fiction; agents are, conveniently, deemed to will to participate. The parallels with the fiction of consent in a substituted judgement are obvious.'[184]

Very much depends, though, upon the existing available inferential evidence as to what the wishes of deceased persons are in the particular society. Further, it is critical to be sensitive to public and professional perceptions and the prevailing cultural and societal milieu. Presumed consent would appear suitable only in societies where shared or collective decision-making is not

---

[181] Den Hartogh, *Farewell to Non-commitment* at 71.
[182] E.g. Den Hartogh and Nys.
[183] That this is more compelling evidence of the person's wish to donate can be seen in the Belgian Law, which permits a relative to veto a presumed consent, but not an explicit recorded consent. See Law of 13 June 1986, section 10 (4).
[184] Beyleveld and Brownsword, *Consent in the Law*, p. 345.

the norm, although it is unnecessary that the society be viewed as oriented toward communitarianism. Whilst it related to the living rather than the dead, the failure of the Australian corporation, Autogen, to appreciate that in Tonga the historical and socio-cultural context required a *group* rather than an individually based consent policy, was a salutary lesson and was at the heart of the failure of the intended genetic database there.[185]

Presumed consent does not, however, always match up with the popular conventional view of a paradigmatic consent, especially where consent cannot be truly regarded as encapsulating any real 'factual' (i.e. tacit) consent. Imputed consent and the idea of 'presuming' consent to exist where none in reality (factually) exists is regarded by many as an unacceptable fiction. It is this mismatch that generates allegations of totalitarianism and state intrusion upon the bodies of the dead. An alternative option especially in the latter context might perhaps be to adopt different terminology to capture and describe the individual authority for donation (i.e. based on best evidence of deceased persons' wishes across the board), but this is itself problematic. There is apparently a public expectation of 'consent' for donation. The incongruity between terminology and popular perception could potentially have deleterious effects on clinicians' relationships with patients and families and levels of donation. Indeed, the ODT concluded that presumed consent has the potential to erode the trust between clinicians and families at a distressing time.[186] Perceptions are more crucial than reality here. Coupled with the baggage of past failings, a lack of a shared understanding of the character of presumed consent and significant misconceptions – and perhaps a lack of trust in professionals, governments, or both – the present climate will often militate against its current introduction no matter how beneficial or justified it may apparently be. Not only will loss of faith in the system undermine its credibility, but it could do damage to even the existing levels of donation within the society.[187] This was a particular concern of both the ODT and the IOM.[188]

---

[185] See R. Nwabueze, *Biotechnology and the Challenge of Property: Property Rights in Dead Bodies, Body Parts and Genetic Information* (Aldershot: Ashgate, 2007), p. 167, although accusations that the people of Tonga were exploited seem misplaced. Individual consent from volunteers was sought for samples to be taken and full information provided; see L. Skene, '"Sale" of DNA of people of Tonga' (2001) (March/April) *Genetics Law Monitor* 7.

[186] ODT, *The Potential Impact* at 17.

[187] Although this is more convincing where relatives are not given a veto at all, i.e. in strong presumed consent systems. In addition to Brazil, donor rates also declined in the immediate aftermath of the inception of the presumed consent law in Latvia, although they increased fairly dramatically thereafter.

[188] The IOM was also especially concerned that the large percentage of the population would opt out if a presumed consent policy was introduced, still further reducing the available pool of organs; Institute of Medicine, *Organ Donation* at 215.

The ODT recommended that the time was not ripe for presumed consent, a view endorsed by the House of Lords Select Committee on the European Union. The latter recommended that any future shift in this direction needed to be preceded by moves to strengthen the organisation of organ donation services and public awareness.[189] The US-IOM Report likewise stated

> The committee believes that it would be premature to attempt to enact presumed-consent policies at this time. Although the committee is supportive of the principles of a presumed-consent approach (namely that under certain clear and well-defined circumstances, in the absence of an individual's expressed decision, one may presume his or her consent rather than refusal to donate), the first step is to build sufficient social support before introducing presumed consent in the United States.[190]

Such social support and public acceptability is essential. It may need to be built up in anticipation. Although once more pertaining to living persons, the opting out policy employed in relation to the Icelandic health sector genetic database resulted in a major ethical controversy despite apparent widespread public support, seemingly as a function of the absence of significant public information or engagement activity.[191]

Nonetheless, over the short term presumed consent is a valuable policy to pursue in some jurisdictions, pending the pervasive collection of substantial and reliable evidence of individuals' wishes after their deaths. In the *truly* ideal system, one would have reliable knowledge of the real wishes of all deceased persons, *whether for or against donation*. In such circumstances, an explicit consent system is the proper option. Where the explicit wishes of most individuals are *not* directly known, the issue is how we handle such uncertainty.[192] The options are to either attempt to drastically eliminate such doubt or to handle such doubt in the most appropriate way. The first strategy, based on eliciting explicit wishes, might have to be based around some system of mandated choice, which

---

[189] House of Lords, paras. 312–313.

[190] Institute of Medicine, *Organ Donation* at 225–7. The UNOS Ethics Committee has likewise previously argued that whilst not ethically unacceptable *per se*, the conditions would not be right for the foreseeable future for introducing presumed consent in the United States; see UNOS, 'An Evaluation of the Ethics of Presumed Consent and a Proposal Based on Required Response', 1993, at www.unos.org/Resources/bioethics. asp?index=2. See also Report of the Council on Ethical and Judicial Affairs, Presumed Consent for Organ Donation, American Medical Association, CJEA Report 7 – A-05, 2005.

[191] See G. Laurie, 'Evidence of support for biobanking practices' (2008) 337 *British Medical Journal* at 338.

[192] See M. Radin, *Contested Commodities* (Cambridge MA: Harvard University Press, 1996), pp. 123–30.

has so far found limited favour. One can only expect rates of voluntary requests to donate (e.g. via registers) to increase gradually, so that a significant timescale is implicated before the wishes of the large majority of the populace become officially 'known'. Moreover, it is not realistic to expect that in the short term individuals will share their views with relevant relatives to a much greater extent than at present (the Eurobarometer Survey suggests that this tendency is in fact generally declining). Alternatively, to best handle continued substantial doubt it would seem to be appropriate to start instead with a presumption which best reflects the views of the majority; as far as we can tell.

# 6    Informed consent

The taking, storage and use of human material for research has emerged as a major legal and bioethical sphere of contention.[1] Gostin has remarked that 'the legal and ethical issues about the use of stored tissue are probably the most profound, complex, and troubling of any ethical issue we have in science today'.[2] Historically, consent was not routinely sought for the storage and use of human tissue for research.[3] This was principally a function of the fact that most tissue used for research was not removed originally for such (secondary) purposes, but instead as part of a diagnostic or therapeutic procedure. In 1994 the Health Council of the Netherlands Report, *Proper Use of Human Tissue*, stated 'It is not usual to seek consent to the storage of tissue, other than in the case of material primarily intended for use in research … The general rule that emerges is that patients and donors are not aware that material taken from them is stored.'[4] Similarly with regard to the US, Clayton states 'In the past, it appears that investigators sometimes used these resources with relatively little oversight, and without the consent of the individuals from whom

---

[1] It is estimated that 20 million new specimens are collected in the US each year; see L. Andrews, 'Harnessing the benefits of biobanks' (2005)(Spring) *Journal of Law, Medicine and Ethics* 22 at 23 [Andrews, 'Harnessing the benefits']. 282 million specimens were already in storage in the US in 1999; see National Bioethics Advisory Commission Report, *Research Involving Human Biological Materials: Ethical Issues and Policy Guidance*, Rockville MD, NBAC, 1999 at viii [NBAC Report].

[2] L. Gostin, quoted in E. Strauss, 'The tissue issue: Losing oneself to science' (1997) 152 *Science News* 190, September 20.

[3] Dekkers and Ten Have state that such practices were so widespread they could be described as 'normal'; see W. Dekkers and H. Ten Have, 'Biomedical research with human body "parts"', in H. Ten Have and J. Welie (eds.), *Ownership of the Human Body* (Dordrecht: Kluwer Academic Publishers, 1998) 49 at 52.

[4] Health Council of the Netherlands Report, *Proper Use of Human Tissue*, 1994, The Hague, No. 1994/01E, para. 6.1.3 [Health Council, *Proper Use*]. As regards post-mortem tissue, Professor Green, giving evidence to the Bristol Royal Infirmary Inquiry, stated that it was not until the mid-1980s that pathologists in the UK gave serious consideration to the issue of consent and that such tissue was viewed as the property of the pathologist/institution; see Bristol Royal Infirmary Inquiry Interim Report 2001, at www.bristol-inquiry.org.uk/interim_report/index.htm at 56.

these materials and information were obtained'.[5] Indeed, this appears to have been the case with respect to the use of surplus clinical material for *any* purpose, including tissue transplantation, not just research. Anderson and Bottenfield note that femoral heads removed during hip replacement surgery have been routinely banked (in the US and elsewhere) and that patients were often not informed that their tissue might be used for another patient, i.e. as part of a bone transplant.[6] Such remarks are equally pertinent with regard to tissue taken from the dead at post-mortem examination. As Rosie Winterton, speaking for the Government, stated during the passage of the Human Tissue Bill, 'It had become routine for tissue taken post mortem to be kept for archives, research and education, but without proper discussion with those close to the deceased'.[7] This led to the Inquiries conducted at the Royal Liverpool Children's Hospital (Alder Hey) and Bristol Royal Infirmary, etc.[8] In its Final Report, the Retained Organs Commission noted that there had often been a paternalistic desire to, as the relevant clinicians saw it, spare grieving relatives further suffering, or simple ignorance of the clinicians obtaining consent.[9] Whilst such practices were especially pervasive within Europe and North America,[10] they are a global phenomenon. Traditionally prevalent practices have, however, recently been exposed to the media and public spotlight and found wanting from a contemporary perspective.

Informed consent was stated to be the 'underlying principle' of the Human Tissue Act 2004.[11] Whilst there are those who argue that the protection of individual rights has inappropriately come to dominate

---

[5] E. Clayton, 'Informed consent and biobanks' (2005)(Spring) *Journal of Law, Medicine and Ethics* 15 at 15 [Clayton, 'Informed consent']. See also R. Weir and R. Olick, *The Stored Tissue Issue* (Oxford University Press, 2004), p. viii [Weir and Olick, *Stored Tissue*].

[6] M. Anderson and S. Bottenfield, 'Tissue Banking – Past, Present, and Future', in S. Youngner, M. Anderson and R. Schapiro (eds.), *Transplanting Human Tissue: Ethics, Policy, and Practice* (Oxford University Press, 2004) 14 at 16.

[7] R. Winterton MP, House of Commons Hansard Debates, col. 985, 15 January 2004.

[8] See www.bristol-inquiry.org.uk/interim_report/index.htm and www.rlcinquiry.org.uk/ download/index.htm See also HM Inspector of Anatomy, Investigation of events that followed the death of Cyril Mark Isaacs, May 2003, at www.doh.gov.uk/cmo/ isaccsreport/.

[9] Retained Organs Commission, *Remembering the Past, Looking to the Future*, NHS, 2004 [ROC, *Remembering the Past*]. In the UK, such clinicians were not usually pathologists.

[10] See also the *Final Report of the Independent Review Group on Retention of Organs at Post-Mortem in Scotland*, 2000 [Final Report], the Northern Ireland Organ Retention Report, Belfast, 2001 and the Madden Report on Post Mortem Practices and Procedures (2006), at www.dohc.ie/publications/pdf/madden.pdf. Note also the Strontium 90 studies conducted in the UK between the 1950s and 1970s on (thigh) bone samples without consent. See further D. Nelkin and L. Andrews, 'Do the dead have interests? Policy issues for research after life' (1998) 24(2 & 3) *American Journal of Law and Medicine* 261 at 273–4.

[11] R. Winterton MP, House of Commons Hansard Debates, col. 987, 15 January 2004.

the ethical and legal landscape, consent is nonetheless the key present concern.[12] But informed consent presents its own significant and particular challenges in relation to surplus tissue, and indeed secondary use in general. Moreover tissue banks and biobanks store tissue for research purposes which cannot be always clearly defined or anticipated at the outset. The German National Ethics Council noted that the scientific potential of biobank samples and data can often only be fully exploited if their use is not confined to individual research projects specifiable in advance.[13]

In the UK, the Wellcome Trust and the Medical Research Council (MRC) commissioned research on public attitudes to human biological samples as part of their public consultation process preliminary to the creation of UK Biobank.[14] Their Report stated 'While few people outside the medical profession and interest groups know much about the use of human biological samples, there appears to be broad acceptance of their use in medical research generally, *provided* this takes place with the informed consent of donors or their representatives (usually relatives)' (my emphasis).[15] Research in the US also shows that the public generally consider consent necessary even for the use of surplus tissue for research.[16] However, many of the studies around the world are modest in scale and results apparently vary as between patients and volunteers.[17]

---

[12] See G. Williams, 'Bioethics and large-scale biobanking: Individualistic ethics and collective projects' (2005) 1(2) *Genomics, Society and Policy* 50 and J. Kaye, 'Abandoning informed consent', in R. Tutton and O. Corrigan (eds.), *Genetic Databases: Socio-Ethical Issues in the Collection and Use of DNA* (Oxford: Routledge, 2004) 117.

[13] German National Ethics Council Opinion, *Biobanks for Research*, Berlin, 2004 at 12 [German National Ethics Council].

[14] Report, *Qualitative Research to Explore Public Perceptions of Human Biological Samples*, 2000, Wellcome Trust and Medical Research Council [Wellcome, *Qualitative Research*]. The use of samples in genetics research was less readily accepted, although the greater the understanding the more positive the view. Attitudes to pharmaceutical companies were ambivalent.

[15] *Ibid.*, at 15. Patients and relatives of patients tended to be even more positive towards medical research than the public at large.

[16] A study of 273 Ashkenazi Jews found that the majority regarded written consent as necessary for the re-use of stored samples, whether initially collected in a clinical or a research setting; see M. Schwartz *et al.*, 'Consent to the use of stored DNA for genetics research: A survey of attitudes in the Jewish population' (2001) 98 *American Journal of Genetics* 336 [Schwartz, 'Consent to the use of stored DNA']. A study by Weir and Olick found that 69 per cent of respondents felt that consent should be necessary if it was intended to conduct research on their tissue samples; see Weir and Olick, *Stored Tissue*, p. 27.

[17] Weir and Olick's study involved only ninety-three outpatients. A questionnaire study of healthy volunteers in a dental practice in England found that 18 per cent of respondents would not give consent to the use of their samples for research, and only 65 per cent would give consent for research into genetic disorders; 42 per cent would want to be informed if their tissues were going to be stored after donation and 35 per cent stated that they would want to be consulted if their tissues were to be used for further research. However, only

The post-mortem retention of material for research has proved more controversial. Nevertheless, despite the recent scandals, the public is generally supportive of research using tissues following post-mortems.[18] Moreover, the large majority of the relatives embroiled in the organ retention disputes of the 1990s declared themselves willing to consent to donation had they been properly approached.[19] Indeed, one frequent complaint relating to the practices at Alder Hey in particular was that such material was routinely stockpiled *without* there being any foreseeable or realistic prospect of it being used for any future significant research.

Despite the contrary ostensibly prevailing view, the National Bioethics Advisory Commission (NBAC) in the US stated in 1999 that 'Fundamentally, the interests of subjects and those of researchers are not in conflict'.[20] In so far as the public in most nations are seemingly sympathetic to the goals of medical research and content to donate their own tissue, whether living or dead, as well as that of their loved ones after their death, such remarks are compelling. Nonetheless, the need to maximise tissue availability and the interests of expediency have often led to the relaxation, or distortion, or devaluing, of important ethical principles.

### Regulation

There is legislation in many jurisdictions covering the removal of tissue from deceased persons for research purposes, which may also apply to research on the whole cadaver.[21] The 2004 and 2006 Human Tissue Acts in the UK govern removal for research as well as transplantation, as do the Uniform Anatomical Gifts Acts (UAGAs) in the US, and various laws elsewhere. These UAGAs have been implemented in all US states in one form or another. Organ and tissue retention and use for research following post-mortem examination is also governed by state law, although only a

100 questionnaires were completed. See M. Goodson and B. Vernon, 'A study of public opinion on the use of tissue samples from living subjects for clinical research' (2004) 57 *Journal of Clinical Pathology* 135.

[18] See Retained Organs Commission, *Qualitative Research to Explore Public Perceptions Regarding Retention of Organs and Tissue for Medical Practice, Teaching and Research*, Research Report, London, 2002.

[19] See also Retained Organs Commission, *Remembering the Past* at 9.

[20] NBAC Report at ii.

[21] The Human Tissue Act 2004 regulates the use of the whole cadaver for research, but only 'research in connection with disorders, or the functioning of the human body'; see Schedule 1 Part 1, Human Tissue Act 2004. There may be even greater sensibilities raised in relation to 'whole-body' research. See generally M. Wicclair, 'Ethics and research with deceased patients' (2008)17 *Cambridge Quarterly of Healthcare Ethics* 87. The latter may provide the opportunity for testing medical devices, experimental medications, etc. See generally W. Gaylin, 'Harvesting the dead' (1974) 249 *Harpers* 23.

minority of states have specific laws, leaving the issue principally within the province of the common law.[22] The storage and use of human tissue for research is also governed in Scotland by the Human Tissue (Scotland) Act 2006 and in the rest of the UK by the Human Tissue Act 2004.[23] However, the Scottish legislation applies only to tissue taken from deceased not living persons, whereas the 2004 Act applies to both.[24] Detailed informed consent requirements attaching to the initial *removal* of tissue from the living in the first place are a function of the general law in any event. Issues relating to storage (consent and licensing) tend to affect only tissues rather than whole organs, for both transplantation and research. By contrast with organs, many tissues may be stored for a very considerable while and remain fit for purpose. In the US, specific laws are generally absent relating to the storage and use of materials from the living, but federal regulations in the form of the Common Rule (45 CFR 46) apply to all federally conducted or federally supported research involving (only) living human subjects.[25] The twin pillars of the Rule are Institutional Review Board (IRB) approval and informed consent.

There are two separate issues arising for consideration in this chapter. Firstly, whether any form of basic consent is, morally or legally, required for the removal, storage and use of tissue, for therapy or research and, secondly, if so, what degree and specificity of information is required to underpin any valid consent. Many of these matters have particular relevance to research as opposed to transplantation, in so far as they relate to *further* use.

### Basic consent

Traditionally there was no pretence of obtaining consent for the use of surplus tissue from either living or deceased persons for research. In some instances, laws even clearly permitted this. In many Australian states and

---

[22] M. Klaiman, 'Whose brain is it anyway?' (2005) 26 *Journal of Legal Medicine* 475.

[23] Research ethics committee approval is also required in relation to 'NHS' research.

[24] In Scotland, the removal and use of tissue from the living is governed entirely by the general law. It was nevertheless the intention that the law should, as far as possible, be consistent across the UK in these regards. See Human Tissue (Scotland) Bill: Policy Memorandum, SP Bill 42-PM, Scottish Parliament, 2005, at para. 24. Statutory regulations do detail some of the information required to be communicated to prospective *transplant* donors; see Human Organ and Tissue Live Transplants (Scotland) Regulations 2006 SSI 2006 No. 390. reg. 2(5).

[25] Weir and Olick, *Stored Tissue*, p. 130. United States Department of Health and Human Services, Code of Federal Regulations, Title 46: Protection of Human Subjects, 2005 [Code of Federal Regulations]. Not only do several states have laws requiring that researchers comply with the Common Rule whether federal funds are used or not, but most health institutions comply with them across the board in any event.

territories, consent for hospital post-mortem examination was explicitly stated to be sufficient to permit the retention and use of body parts for transplantation or research,[26] and fourteen US states (as well as Washington, DC) have legislation allowing body parts removed at post-mortem examination to be retained and used for research without the need for consent.[27] However, in most contexts the law remained unclear and such a practice simply grew organically, perhaps endorsed in professional guidance. In 1996 the guidance of the Royal College of Physicians in England was that 'The anonymous use for research ... of tissues removed at ... autopsy is a traditional and ethically acceptable practice that does not need consent'.[28]

In the UK, the Report of the Nuffield Council on Bioethics Working Party recommended in the 1990s that when a patient consents to medical treatment involving the removal of tissue, this should be taken to *include* consent to the subsequent disposal or storage of the tissue, and also to any *further* acceptable use, provided that this was regulated by appropriate ethical, legal and professional standards.[29] Both the Nuffield Council Report and the decision of the California Supreme Court in *Moore* v. *Regents of the University of California* (see chapter 8) were explicitly linked to public policy and utilitarian concerns relating to the supply of material for research purposes. The legal rationale relied upon by the Nuffield Council was abandonment,[30] although emphasis was placed on 'other safeguards'. Indeed, Gevers and Olsthoorn-Heim remark that 'The emphasis in the report is less on the role of patients' consent as a mechanism for control, and more on procedures used to organise and regulate the removal, storage and further use of human tissue'.[31] They contrast

---

[26] E.g. section 28, Transplantation and Anatomy Act 1983 (South Australia).

[27] See D. Sperling, *Posthumous Interests: Legal and Ethical Perspectives* (Cambridge University Press, 2008), p. 99.

[28] Royal College of Physicians, *Guidelines on the Practice of Ethics Committees in Research Involving Human Subjects*, Royal College of Physicians, 1996. See J. Bennett, 'The organ retention furore' (2001) 1(3) *Clinical Medicine* 167 at 168.

[29] Nuffield Council on Bioethics Working Party Report, *Human Tissue: Ethical and Legal Issues*, Nuffield Council on Bioethics, 1995, paras. 9.14 and 13.12. See Weir and Olick, *Stored Tissue*, p. 59, for a list of attitudes of professional bodies in the US. The Dutch Health Council, however, considered there was a need for 'some form of assent' to such further use; see Health Council, *Proper Use*, at para. 7.1.1.

[30] See R. Smart *et al.*, 'Ownership and uses of human tissue: Does the Nuffield Bioethics Report accord with opinion of surgical inpatients' (1996) 313 *British Medical Journal* 1366.

[31] S. Gevers and E. Olsthoorn-Heim, 'DNA sampling: Dutch and other European approaches to the issues of informed consent and confidentiality', in B. Knoppers (ed.), *Human DNA: Law and Policy: International and Comparative Perspectives* (Dordrecht: Kluwer Law International, 1997) 109 at 117 [Gevers and Olsthoorn-Heim, 'DNA sampling'].

'patient-' and 'procedure'-oriented approaches, placing the Nuffield Report firmly in the latter camp, by contrast with the Dutch Health Council Report, which was regarded as falling within the former category. The latter asserted that it was important for persons to 'have a say in what happens' with tissues removed from their bodies, whether initially removed for treatment or research.[32] Whether procedural protections such as independent committee review can wholly or partially suffice as substitutes for consent requirements is a function of what interests require protection in the first place, discussed below.

## Anonymised samples

There are frequently consent concessions in law as regards the storage and use of 'anonymised' surplus tissue for research, including in the 2004 Act.[33] However, the notion of 'anonymised tissue' is an ambiguous and controversial one, and care with such terminology is essential.[34] Furness states 'Unfortunately, the term "anonymization" has been used imprecisely. Some use it to include secure coding of samples or data, where the "key" to the code is held by a trusted third party so that, if there is ethical and scientific justification, a link can be re-established. In many cases, the benefits of anonymization can be achieved by using such a confidential coding system, so it is important not to confuse the two.'[35]

In fact the 2004 Act does not use the language of anonymisation at all, neither does the federal Common Rule. The former states that consent is not required for research within the Act where it is ethically approved in accordance with regulations made by the Secretary of State and 'it is to be, or is, carried out in circumstances such that the person carrying it out is not in possession, and not likely to come into possession, of information from which the person from whose body the material has come can be identified'.[36] The Human Tissue Authority (HTA) Code of Practice on

---

[32] Health Council, *Proper Use* at 31.

[33] Section 1(9). In the Netherlands, anonymous surplus tissue may be used for research in the absence of an objection, see Gevers and Olsthoorn-Heim, 'DNA sampling' at 112.

[34] Knoppers notes that the term 'anonymous' (referring to samples which never had identifiers) is regularly confused with 'anonymised' (referring to the deliberate removal of identifiers) in this context; see B. Knoppers, 'Biobanking: international norms' (2005) (Spring) *Journal of Law, Medicine and Ethics* 7 at 7 [Knoppers, 'Biobanking'].

[35] P. Furness, 'Research using human tissues – a crisis of supply?' (2001) 195 *Journal of Pathology* 277 at 281.

[36] Section 1(9)(b). Even where it is not legally required, good practice states that individuals should be informed about such potential uses(s), e.g. by a clearly displayed notice; see Medical Research Council, *Human Tissue and Biological Samples for Use in Research – Operational and Ethical Guidelines*, MRC, London, 2001, para. 3.2 [MRC, *Human Tissue and Biological Samples*]. The ethical approval here is Research Ethics Committee approval.

Consent states that tissue may still be 'non-identifying' even though the samples are *not* permanently and irrevocably unlinked to identifying data, and that linking through a third party may be made where necessary.[37] This was confirmed during the Parliamentary debates on the Bill.[38] It is also clear from the HTA Code of Practice that such tissue need only be 'anonymised' at the time of the intended research for such an exemption to be applicable, and that no consent is required for the process of anonymisation itself.[39]

The Common Rule excludes non-personally identifiable information and samples, namely 'research involving the collection or study of existing data, documents, records, pathological specimens, or diagnostic specimens, if these sources are publicly available or if the information is recorded by the investigator in a manner that subjects cannot be identified, directly or through identifiers linked to the subjects'.[40] However, such samples must already be being stored, e.g. in hospital pathology laboratories. All research on new samples requires informed consent. Whilst Clayton comments that this means that 'any linkage' by way of identifiers (whether the 'key' is in the hands of the researcher or a third party) will bring the research within the Rule,[41] the general definition of 'human subjects' refers to research involving 'readily ascertained' identifiable private information,[42] which may seemingly permit significantly more research with accompanying information to fall outside the scope of the Rule. This tension and vagueness relating to the applicability of the Rule generated pressure for additional guidance, which emanated in the form of the NBAC Report, *Research Involving Human Biological Materials: Ethical Issues and Policy Guidance*, in 1999.[43] The NBAC interpretation of the Rule is that research conducted with *unidentified* samples is not regulated by the Rule at all, but that research conducted with *unlinked* samples is regulated but eligible for exemption from IRB review. However, there were four identified categories of 'unlinked' samples which generated considerable complexity and substantial variation in

---

[37] Human Tissue Authority, Code of Practice, Consent, HTA, July 2006, para. 28.

[38] See, e.g., Rosie Winterton MP, House of Commons Hansard Debates, col. 97, 28 June 2004 and Lord Warner, House of Lords Hansard Debates, col. 1081, 25 October 2004. It is non-identifiability in the hands of the researcher that matters. Moreover, where members of the clinical team are involved in conducting the research, links to clinical records may be retained provided that they do not contain information affording direct patient identification.

[39] The process of anonymisation does not amount to the 'processing' of personal data for the purposes of the Data Protection Act 1998, either; see *R* v. *Department of Health, ex parte Source Informatics* [2001] QB 424 (CA).

[40] Code of Federal Regulations, section 46.101.

[41] Clayton, 'Informed consent' at 16.      [42] Section 46.102(f).      [43] NBAC Report.

how IRBs interpreted the guidance. Federal policy in this sphere is now overseen by the Office for Human Research Protections and it published further guidance in 2004 which stipulated that research involving coded private information or specimens (i.e. where the investigators cannot readily ascertain the identity of the individual) is not research involving human subjects.[44] However, if a key to the code exists, the investigators must be prohibited from having access to it. The guidance applies to both existing specimens and specimens to be collected in the future for purposes other than the currently proposed research, and significantly expands the scope of exempted research.

If consent could have been obtained but the samples were anonymised simply in order to remove the need to obtain consent, there would appear to be grounds for objection. Weir and Olick remark that 'this practice is problematic, disingenuous, and occasionally deceptive when, for example, clinician investigators obtain a tissue sample for diagnostic purposes, know that they plan later to anonymise the sample, for research purposes, do not convey that information to the source of the sample, and subsequently remove the identifiers without consent'.[45] They suggest that consent should even be sought for the anonymisation process itself. In the UK, the HTA's Code on Consent expresses an apparent preference for consent as opposed to anonymisation, but this is essentially within the discretion of the researchers and the relevant Research Ethics Committee (REC).[46] Clayton et al., authors of a consensus document, recommend that IRBs weigh the benefits of any research with to-be-anonymised tissues against the difficulty of requiring the investigators to recontact the individual sources for their consent for such anonymisation.[47]

Whilst epidemiological studies to determine the prevalence of a particular genetic mutation may be carried out on samples without any accompanying identifiable information, the value of much research is obtained from the conjunction of the samples and the clinical patient information relating to it. Indeed, the NBAC recommends that IRB exemption may not be granted where the unlinking of samples unnecessarily reduces the value of the research.[48] In the UK, RECs could also decide that research

---

[44] Office for Human Research Protections and Department of Health and Human Services, *Guidance on Research Involving Coded Private Information or Biological Specimens*, 2005.
[45] Weir and Olick, *Stored Tissue*, p. 53.
[46] The Human Tissue Authority Code of Practice, Consent, published in July 2006, states in para. 29 that 'In general, obtaining consent is preferable to developing complex systems for keeping samples unlinked. It represents best practice and has the added benefit of facilitating the process of obtaining ethical approval.'
[47] E. Clayton et al., 'Informed consent for genetic research on stored tissue samples' (1995) 274 *Journal of the American Medical Association* 1786.
[48] NBAC Report at iii.

using unlinked samples was insufficiently meritorious for ethical approval to be granted. There are other advantages of using identifiable samples for both researchers and donors. Anonymisation might impede investigation of unexpected results, prevent individuals from withdrawing their tissues from a study or finding out patient-specific health-related information which emerges from the research which might be of value to them.[49] Whether withholding such information is legitimate is a subject of dispute. UK Biobank appears to eschew such a possibility and individuals ostensibly give up their right to receive such information when they initially consent to be involved.[50] However, others have disputed whether this would relieve UK Biobank of its common law duty to take reasonable care of those to whom it owes a duty.[51] It has been suggested that it urgently review its policy in the context of treatable genetic diseases revealed during research.[52] The German National Ethics Council similarly opined that whilst routine communication would involve inordinate expense and effort, and donors may explicitly concede receiving relevant feedback at the outset, information bearing on the donor's life may need to be communicated regardless.[53]

Of course, it may be perceived that anonymisation is necessary to ensure adequate recruitment to a particular study, although a nationwide telephone survey conducted in the US suggests that the importance participants attach to anonymity may be overstated.[54] The evidence is ambiguous, though. The trusted intermediary model has much to offer here, allowing information to flow in both directions but with personal identifying information being denied to the researchers themselves. It also allows a tissue source to withdraw from the research at a later point in time. One should have a non-waivable right to withdraw consent to the use of a person's sample and data, even despite the signing of clauses in agreements declaring this to be impermissible, although it should not be

---

[49] Even where withdrawal occurs, this does not necessarily mean that the samples need be destroyed.

[50] See UK Biobank Ethics and Governance Framework, at www.ukbiobank.ac.uk/docs/EGF20082.pdf.

[51] C. Johnstone and J. Kaye, 'Does the UK Biobank have a legal obligation to feedback individual findings to participants?' (2004) 12 *Medical Law Review* 239.

[52] *Ibid.*, at 240.    [53] German National Ethics Council at 60.

[54] M. Rothstein, 'Expanding the ethical analysis of biobanks' (2005)(Spring) *Journal of Law, Medicine and Ethics* 89 at 94 [Rothstein, 'Expanding the ethical analysis']. A US telephone survey of 504 individuals in 2002 found that 65.8 per cent of respondents thought that their consent should be required for research on personally identifiable clinically derived samples but only 27.3 per cent for anonymised clinically derived samples; see D. Wendler and E. Emanuel, 'The debate over research on stored biological samples' (2002) 162 *Archives of Internal Medicine* 1457 [Wendler and Emanuel, 'The debate'].

possible to withdraw the results of research already carried out using them.[55]

This 'consent dispensation' in the 2004 Act seemingly emanates from the view that harm to the person could only result where confidentiality and privacy was not maintained. It would appear that this law as a whole is underpinned by the safeguarding of informational privacy interests, tied to potential harm to the tissue source. Of course, there would be an infringement of physical integrity associated with many activities covered by the Act, but this would not be the case with regard to *surplus* tissue taken from living patients. The Opinion of the German National Ethics Council also seemingly equates the interests of donors with respect to samples with their interests with regard to personal data. It averred that 'the personality rights of the former carrier of the bodily substance are unaffected if the substance is used without any individualizing linkage to his person',[56] and considered that unobjectionable research on anonymised substances should be possible even without the consent of the subject,[57] opining 'In this case there is no particular need for donor protection'.[58]

There is, however, a further moral dimension which is being overlooked. The primary moral right of control is broader than simply a right not to be *harmed* in the aforementioned ways. The primary wrong is committed where a person is disenfranchised from exercising their right to control the future use of the tissue *per se*.[59] As Clayton states 'Informed consent is not just about enabling people to decide whether or not to accept certain risks. The process of asking acknowledges the individual whose information and tissue are contained therein.'[60] Informed consent fulfils functions of trust, honouring the involvement of the individual in research undertaken for the public benefit and recognises rights of authority. Indeed, the risks relating to inappropriate disclosure of personal data are already catered for to a large degree by medical confidentiality and data protection laws. In the US, the Health Insurance Portability and Accountability Act applies a Privacy Rule which is applicable to any data that is not 'de-identified'. Whilst *researchers'* key interest is in the

---

[55] This is the view of the German National Ethics Council at 14.
[56] German National Ethics Council at 46.    [57] *Ibid.*, at 49.    [58] *Ibid.*, at 17.
[59] Andrews states 'even if a sample could be anonymized, research on it without consent may still disturb the tissue source. Such research may conflict with the personal preferences or religious beliefs of the tissue source'; see Andrews, 'Harnessing the benefits' at 24.
[60] Clayton, 'Informed consent' at 19. The risks of some forms of human tissue research pertain to population groups as well as individuals. Such risks may exist even if personal identifiers have been stripped away, but where demographic data such as gender, race or ethnicity still attach.

knowledge generated by the donated specimen this is by no means the whole story for donors, who are also concerned with their contribution to certain types of research by way of their own bodily materials.

Whilst RECs are tasked to protect individuals against unethical or controversial forms of research, any broad right 'to control' what types of research a person's tissue may be used for has been relinquished; the public interest has been determined to override any such rights. As Rothstein states 'Research with unidentifiable samples raises the risk that the subject's sample will be used for research of which the sample donor does not approve (e.g. behavioural genetics) or otherwise violates the sample donor's strongly held beliefs (e.g. by failing to return bodily tissues in violation of religious precepts)'.[61] The assumption during the passage of the Human Tissue Bill appears to have been that RECs will be able to 'handle' difficult ethical issues arising from such research studies, either where consent is not initially required at all (non-personally identifiable samples), or as a result of generic consent (see below). Maybe this reflects the Nuffield Council on Bioethics' earlier confidence in procedural safeguards, and the views of the NBAC which regarded consent as an 'adjunct' to IRB review.[62] But what is 'controversial' is not an 'objective' universal characteristic but exists in the mind of the beholder, and in this connection this links back to the specific donor.[63]

## Informed consent

Where consent has been given for one type of use (e.g. transplantation), further consent is required for any different *genus* of use (e.g. research),[64] for instance where tissue intended for transplantation proves to be unsuitable for that purpose. But the tissue may have already been used for one particular research project or type of research, for which consent was given, and is now stored with a view to it being used in a further, different, research project or type of research, for which consent has not been specifically obtained. Thus, where it is intended to subsequently use such tissue for *further* research, there is a question whether the original consent extends to it, either explicitly or by implication, or whether an additional consent would need to be sought. Similar issues arise where it is

---

[61] Rothstein, 'Expanding the ethical analysis' at 90.    [62] NBAC at v.

[63] RECs and IRBs can only apply an 'average' subject's response not the particular values of individuals; see T. Schonfeld, G. Gordon, J. Amoura and J. Brown, 'Money matters' (2007) 7(2) *American Journal of Bioethics* 86 at 87.

[64] As under the 2004 Act, although it may be used for medical diagnosis or treatment or another purpose specified in regulations or for the purpose of decent disposal; see section 8(4). See also the Uniform Anatomical Gift Act 2006.

anticipated that stored surplus tissue removed initially for therapeutic reasons be subsequently used for research. There is the very particular difficulty here, though, that research uses may later reveal themselves, but which could not have been anticipated at the time of the original removal procedure. Indeed, with respect to surplus tissue removed for clinical reasons, including post-mortem examination, one will not necessarily be able to be sure that such tissue, or at least all of such tissue, will be used for research at all.[65] In the context of surplus tissues, there are some particular practical issues also. Balleine opines 'Pre-operative consent is neither practical in the context of busy clinical practice nor considerate of the patient's emotional well-being. Approaching patients post-operatively may be considered by some as intrusive, especially as researchers are frequently not the clinicians responsible for care of the patient.'[66] Nevertheless, Article 22 of the Council of Europe Biomedicine Convention arguably envisages the need for a consent to be given for further use regardless of the purpose of the original removal, although it does not specify the nature of the consent required.[67]

Any consent initially obtained may need to be couched in very broad terms to cater for later contingencies,[68] which generates legal and ethical quandaries. Kapp remarks

Whether linked to present patient treatment or totally separate, a current research project can be described to a prospective tissue donor with enough precision to allow for meaningful informed consent. By contrast, it is difficult, if not impossible, for a participant in a research protocol to give meaningful prospective consent to the use of tissue in a possible future research protocol that cannot currently be described. Common practice has been for IRBs to allow investigators to ask patients receiving treatment to give a generic approval for the current banking of tissue, but only on the condition that use of the tissue in specific research protocols in the future would require an additional consent from the

---

[65] For a critique of the current UK situation relating to human fetal tissue research, see S. Woods and K. Taylor, 'Ethical and governance challenges in human fetal tissue research' (2008) 3 *Clinical Ethics* 14.

[66] Cited in Australian Law Reform Commission, *Essentially Yours: The Protection of Human Genetic Information in Australia*, ALRC Report 96, Sydney, 2003, para. 19.77 [ALRC, *Essentially Yours*].

[67] Article 22 states 'When in the course of an intervention any part of a human body is removed, it may be stored and used for a purpose other than that for which it was removed, only if this is done in conformity with appropriate information and consent procedures'. It has been suggested that tacit consent may suffice in this connection; see Gevers and Olsthoorn-Heim, 'DNA sampling' at 111.

[68] Vague open-ended statements have routinely been included at the end of clinical trials consent documents, discussed by Weir and Olick in relation to the CDC NHANES III Study; see *Stored Tissue*, pp. 6–8.

patient, based on specific information conveyed about the particular genetic study at that later point in time.[69]

The Human Tissue Act 2004 requires 'appropriate consent' be given with respect to the storage and use of material for research and transplantation whether it emanates from a living or a deceased person. However, it does not apply to the *removal* of tissue from the living. In any event, the legislation neglects to define 'appropriate consent', leaving this ordered by common law and via guidance issued by the HTA via Codes of Practice.[70] Weir and Olick state 'The law's approach to informed consent in research is predominantly concerned with two sorts of questions: What information must a physician–investigator disclose to a patient or research participant? And what standard of disclosure should be used to answer this query and to assess whether the physician–investigator has fulfilled the requisite duties of disclosure?'[71] The first issue to address here is 'consent to what'?

### Generic consent

During the passage of the Human Tissue Bill the Government made it clear that in its view the legislation allowed for a 'generic' consent to be given for research purposes, i.e. consent to 'research' *in toto*. In the House of Lords debates, Lord Warner remarked 'Let me state clearly that the Bill does not require consent to be specific to each research project for which tissue might be used. Consent can be broad. Consent to research can be generic and enduring.'[72] Whether this would suffice in law is yet to be tested, although this view is endorsed in the HTA Code of Practice on Consent which states that consent can be either 'general', 'specific', or 'general and specific'.[73] 'General' consent involves consent to the use of tissue for research in general, i.e. without being limited to a specific research project. Alternatively, consent may be given for a specific research project or for research generally but with exceptions, or for research of a certain type only, e.g. research into a specific condition.[74]

There is undoubtedly a tension here, which may undermine the legal and/or ethical validity of a consent. One normally consents to *the* act rather than *an* act, creating the potential for misapprehension. Roscam

---

[69] M. Kapp, 'Ethical and legal issues in research involving human subjects: Do you want a piece of me?' (2006) 59 *Journal of Clinical Pathology* 335 at 336.

[70] Guidance in such Codes is not legally binding in itself, but may affect licensing decisions.

[71] Weir and Olick, *Stored Tissue*, p. 135.

[72] Lord Warner, House of Lords Hansard Debates, vol 664, col. 370, 22 July 2004.

[73] Human Tissue Authority, Code of Practice, Consent, HTA, July 2006, para. 105.

[74] *Ibid.*

Abbing has asserted that 'Informed consent, based on a patient's autonomy over the use of his data and tissue, is of utmost importance in relation to (pharmaco)genetic research ... Blanket unconditional consent for research is not acceptable, since one cannot give consent to what one does not know.'[75] Weir and Olick even cast doubt on a broad consent limited to a specific type or class of research. They state 'This model of general consent fails to fulfil either parts of the rationale for informed consent because it neither encourages choice nor tries to protect patients from psychosocial harm(s)'.[76] McHale notes the possibility of a person later claiming that their Article 8 (European Convention on Human Rights) rights were infringed through being given insufficient information, invalidating any consent given.[77]

The House of Lords Select Committee on Science and Technology Report, however, asserted that generic consent was essential in the context of using tissue samples and other data for research, with appropriate safeguards.[78] The practicalities of future and secondary research use arguably militate against an alternative policy. The Royal College of Pathologists have remarked that 'If tissue samples are to remain useful for future projects, unplanned at the time of sampling, it is logically impossible to obtain consent which is specific to the project in question at the time of sampling. If we do not accept some form of "generic" consent for research use it would be necessary to have to re-contact each tissue donor for renewed consent before each new project.'[79] Research tissue banks and biobanks, in particular, would have enormous difficulties. The German National Ethics Council opined that

To ensure that biobanks, once established, do not quickly lose their value, it must be made possible for donors to consent to the use of their samples and data for undefined research projects to be specified only at some future date. It is occasionally objected that such a broad consent to use does not constitute informed consent ... However, if donors have been informed of the indefinite nature of the

---

[75] H. Roscam Abbing, 'Pharmaco(genetic) research from a human rights perspective' (2001) (March/April) *Genetics Law Monitor* 5 at 6.

[76] Weir and Olick, *Stored Tissue*, p. 252.

[77] J. McHale, '"Appropriate consent" and the use of human material for research purposes: The competent adult' (2006) 1 *Clinical Ethics* 195 at 196 [McHale, '"Appropriate consent"'].

[78] Fourth Report of the Select Committee on Science and Technology, *The Opportunities and Challenges Arising from the Use of Human Genetic Databases*, House of Lords, 2001.

[79] Royal College of Pathologists, *Transitional Guidelines to Facilitate Changes in Procedures for Handling 'Surplus' and Archival Material from Biological Samples*, Royal College of Pathologists, 2001, at para. 14 [RCP, *Transitional Guidelines*]. This view is mirrored in the statements of the College of American Pathologists; see 'Uses of Human Tissue', 1996, pp. 6–7.

actual future applications, they will be aware that they are agreeing to an uncertainty.[80]

Thus, the current stance favours efficiency, pragmatism and reduction of costs. However, very limited generalised information may also be *sufficient* information for many individuals. To that extent limited information may *serve* rather than undermine autonomy, in the same way that limited information about post-mortem examination sometimes does.[81] In any event, O'Neill rightly emphasises that consent is always 'propositional' and 'incompletely described', so that an entirely specific consent is illusory.[82] What is required is only a proper effort to accurately communicate sufficient information to enable a genuine choice to be made. Whilst Andrews argues that general blanket consent to all future research should not be considered sufficient to meet the standards of informed consent,[83] Rothstein is concerned that otherwise such samples would then be anonymised across the board.[84]

It has been suggested that public attitudes support a general policy of generic consent. Wendler argues on the basis of his analysis of thirty published studies relating to this subject (although only to blood samples), that individuals do not wish to make decisions regarding the specifics of research projects anyhow, only to research in generic terms. He states that 'The literature on individuals' views supports one-time general consent as the best approach for this purpose'.[85] Analysis of existing consent for research use has also shown that most research participants authorise the unlimited future use of their samples when given the opportunity to do so.[86] A US study examining 1,670 consent forms found that 87.1 per cent of research participants chose to permit the future use of their tissue for research on any medical condition. The researchers ultimately concluded 'These findings suggest that providing research participants with a simple binary choice to authorize or refuse all future research might allow

---

[80] German National Ethics Council at 52.

[81] See discussion in the Scottish Report of the Independent Review Group relating to the concept of 'authorisation' relating to the retention of tissue following post-mortem examination; Final Report at section 1, para. 17.

[82] O. O'Neill, 'Some limits of informed consent' (2003) 29 *Journal of Medical Ethics* 4.

[83] Andrews, 'Harnessing the benefits' at 28.

[84] Rothstein, 'Expanding the ethical analysis' at 92.

[85] D. Wendler, 'One-time general consent for research on biological samples' (2006) 332 *British Medical Journal* 544 at 544 [Wendler, 'One-time general consent']. In the six studies which examined this issue, 79–95 per cent were willing to provide one-time general consent.

[86] D. Chen *et al.*, 'Research with stored biological samples: What do research participants want?' [2005] 165 *Archives of Internal Medicine* 652 at 652 [Chen *et al.*, 'Research with stored biological samples']. Only 1.2 per cent, given the option, chose to restrict the permitted research to the same medical condition.

individuals to control use of their samples, simplify consent forms, and allow important research to proceed'.[87] Of those given the choice of re-contact or refusing all future research, 90.6 per cent chose re-contact, whereas of those given the choice between re-contact and authorising all future research only 17.2 per cent chose re-contact.[88] This research is supported by a questionnaire study conducted in Sweden, which found that 85.9 per cent of respondents were content to allow ethics committees to make the decisions and that informing donors about the research objectives was rated the lowest of the priorities listed.[89] These conclusions are also endorsed by the findings of one or two other studies.[90] But not only is such research not all unequivocal in one direction, it shows only that the large majority of individuals have no such claims.

One significant drawback of generic consent relates to the absence of detail regarding aspects to which a patient or research subject might have had objections. There is a common practice of obtaining consent to unexplained blanket research by means of consent forms accompanying therapeutic procedures involving tissue removal, including in the context of some clinical trials. Where possible, however, information about likely or possible classes of research ought to be conveyed, to allow caveats and objections to be prospectively raised and recorded. Baroness O'Neill has cogently argued for the opportunity for individuals to exercise a right of control by being able to stipulate types of research about which they have scruples.[91] Although the Government accepted during the Parliamentary debates on the Bill that where there is evidence of a person's objection to the use of their tissue for specific research, this should be respected even though this is not legally required, the question is: what mechanisms might exist to be able to facilitate such a wish?[92]

---

[87] *Ibid.*

[88] Of research participants given the choice of re-contact or authorising or refusing all future research, 26.2 per cent chose re-contact.

[89] K. Hoeyer, B. Olofsson, T. Mjorndal and N. Lynoe, 'The ethics of research using biobanks' (2005) 165 *Archives of Internal Medicine* 97. Only a small percentage of respondents (5.6 per cent) were unhappy with the information they had received despite the low level of awareness that they had even made a donation at all. The authors noted the contrast between this study and an earlier study by Wendler which found that, based on telephone interviews, most respondents would require their consent to be obtained for the use of clinically derived, personally identifiable, samples for research; see Wendler and Emanuel, 'The debate'.

[90] E.g. S. Hamilton, J. Hepper, A. Hanby and J. Hewison, 'Consent gained from patients after breast surgery for the use of surplus tissue for research: An exploration' (2007) 33 *Journal of Medical Ethics* 229.

[91] O. O'Neill, *Autonomy and Trust in Bioethics* (Cambridge University Press, 2004), pp. 159–60.

[92] See, e.g., Rosie Winterton, House of Commons Hansard Debates, col. 105, 28 June 2004; Lord Warner, House of Lords Hansard Debates, col. GC419, 15 September 2004.

Under the Common Rule also a research subject may provide informed consent for future, unspecified research. The NBAC nonetheless counselled researchers and IRBs that general releases for research given in conjunction with a clinical or surgical procedure must not be presumed to cover all types of research over an indefinite period of time, and that consent forms should be developed to include a range of options with regard to future research.[93] There is a strong possibility that an REC in the UK might also refuse to approve a later study relying on generic consent to research *in toto*, viewing the initial consent as not appropriately extending to the new study/use, and require that patients be re-contacted to seek further consent.[94] This would be particularly likely where the further use was in some way potentially controversial, such as certain genetic research. Specificity may even sometimes be seen as necessary by researchers themselves to secure sufficient recruitment to a particular study. Researchers will be tempted by generic, general consent to facilitate maximum future research flexibility. But, in practice, a middle way may well often be taken, confining the potential broad research field in some fashion, e.g. to research in relation to a specific condition or disease.[95] There are consequently interesting issues of research strategy and regulation raised by these matters, albeit that generic consent need not be seen as ethically or legally unacceptable *per se*.

Where blanket consent for research is being sought in respect of surplus tissue the opportunity to subsequently qualify or withdraw such consent should be provided, accompanied by the provision of broad information to reflect upon over time, setting out a mechanism to record specific objections.[96] Alternatively the consent form could have a 'menu' of types of research which might be specifically consented

---

[93] NBAC Report iv–v.

[94] Rothstein notes that in the US IRBs are reluctant to approve blanket consent for most future research, and observes that individuals often wish to restrict the use of their sample to research into a particular (type of) disease. See 'Expanding the ethical analysis' at 92. The Medical Research Council endorses blanket consent for 'research projects approved by research ethics committees', and notes that it is then for RECs to determine the adequacy of such consent in each specific instance; see Medical Research Council, *Human Tissue and Biological Samples for Use in Research: Clarification Following Passage of the Human Tissue Act 2004*, MRC, 2005, para. 4.4.

[95] Research suggests that individuals are generally happier to participate in research if their samples and records are to be used for research on specific diseases; see Wellcome, *Qualitative Research*.

[96] The College of American Pathologists previously recommended that patients consenting to surgery should be asked if they *objected* (rather than consented) to any resected tissue being used for research; see W. Grizzle *et al.*, 'Recommended policies for uses of human tissue in research, education, and quality control. Ad Hoc Committee on Stored Tissue, College of American Pathologists' (1999) 123 *Archives of Pathology and Laboratory Medicine* 296.

or objected to.[97] However, a 'genuine' informed consent given in advance of surgery by a tick on a surgical consent form accompanied by little or no information or explanation is frequently unconvincing. Either way it must be possible to 'qualify' one's consent; to make consent conditional.

Where re-contact and additional consent *is* required, this could be perhaps done by means of a letter stipulating that a failure to respond would be taken to constitute tacit consent to participation, to avoid the practical issues set out below relating to archived tissue.[98]

## Specific uses

Some specific uses may be particularly controversial or contentious. One might assume, for instance, that one's tissues would not be commercially exploitable or used in genetic research. RECs would certainly be a source of some protection *vis-à-vis* such 'controversial' research, but there is the obverse concern that such research might be rejected as a whole where certain specific information had not been communicated to the individual previously.

The HTA Consent Code states, as regards identifiable tissue, that 'Patients should be told if their samples will or could be used for research involving the commercial sector. They should be given appropriate information on the range of activities and researchers which may be involved and whether these include commercial pharmaceutical companies.'[99] A similar view was expressed by the German National Ethics Council.[100] Indeed, Wilkinson has argued that such information is an ineliminable component of a valid consent.[101] UK research in fact suggests that most individuals are indifferent to the involvement of pharmaceutical companies in tissue research. In one study, only 0.06 per cent of patients (of 3,140 participants) were influenced to refuse consent by this factor.[102]

---

[97] There is no reason to believe that this will result in lesser consent rates; see T. Malone *et al.*, 'High rate of consent to bank biologic samples for future research: The Eastern Co-Operative Oncology Group experience' (2002) 94(10) *Journal of the National Cancer Institute* 769.

[98] Chen *et al.* argue that their findings support such a strategy; see Chen *et al.*, 'Research with stored biological samples' at 655.

[99] Human Tissue Authority, Code of Practice, Consent, HTA, July 2006, para. 80.

[100] German National Ethics Council at 57.

[101] S. Wilkinson, 'Biomedical research and the commercial exploitation of human tissue' (2005) 1(1) *Genomics, Society and Policy* 27.

[102] A. Jack and C. Womack, 'Why surgical patients do not donate tissue for commercial research: Review of records' (2003) 327 *British Medical Journal* 262 [Jack and Womack, 'Why surgical patients'].

However, the evidence is not unequivocal.[103] Moreover, knowledge that profits may be made from one's tissue would appear to be an essential component of trust. This may be seen to have been at the heart of the issue in the *Moore* and *Greenberg* cases in the US in particular (see chapter 8).

The HTA Code also asserts that tissue donors should be informed as to any possible implications arising from the proposed research, such as genetic tests.[104] Such an accommodation seems valuable, although this may depend upon precisely what 'genetic' means in this context.[105] Genetics research sometimes generates a further dimension of potential psychological harm from inappropriate information disclosure relating to individuals' medical conditions, genetic pre-dispositions and (alleged) behavioural characteristics, which might have a detrimental effect upon one's social life, employment and insurance prospects. Weir and Olick also note that subjects may have important interests in how research will affect the welfare of others, e.g. their families or social or ethnic group.[106]

### The standard of disclosure

With respect to the living, where the tissue was originally removed for research, such research will be *non-therapeutic*. It is generally accepted, although the common law remains vague in this regard, that this necessitates a greater degree of information disclosure than for therapeutic procedures. The Nuffield Council on Bioethics Working Party Report called for 'special safeguards'. It considered that whereas for therapeutic procedures there are two *levels* of consent, for non-therapeutic procedures there is only one. The first level relates to the nature and purpose of the intervention and the second to the risks involved in the procedure. The

---

[103] Whilst Wendler reports two studies showing that people were only marginally less willing to provide a sample for commercial research, see Wendler, 'One-time general consent', a Swedish study found that about one-third of respondents opining about biobank research would have answered differently on account of this factor; see T. Nilstun and G. Hermeren, 'Human tissue and samples' (2006) 9 *Medicine, Health Care and Philosophy* 81.

[104] Human Tissue Authority, Code of Practice, Consent, HTA, July 2006, para. 77. This essentially reflects the Medical Research Council's advice; see *MRC Guidance on Ethics of Research involving Human Material Derived from the Nervous System*, 2003, para 1.1. In a public attitudes' survey, many members of the public proved uneasy about genetic research; see Wellcome, *Qualitative Research*.

[105] Zimmern stresses that 'genetic information' can be obtained from various sources, but is frequently and confusingly equated with information derived from DNA or chromosomal analysis; see R. Zimmern, 'What is genetic information?' (2001) (March–April) *Genetics Law Monitor* 9 at 10.

[106] Weir and Olick, *Stored Tissue*, p. 142. There is some research suggesting that individuals are more inclined to consent to research using their DNA for disease studies than for studies examining behavioural traits; see Schwartz, 'Consent to the use of stored DNA'.

first is required in order for a valid consent whereas the second is largely governed by what reasonable doctors generally regard as appropriate (at least in the UK).[107] Medical discretion, however, has no role to play as regards non-therapeutic procedures, and thus all relevant information must be provided. The Report stated 'We recommend that those involved in the removal of tissue from donors should ensure that the explanation given to the donor is explicit about the range of potential uses of the tissue and about any risks the donor may incur either in having the tissue removed or as a consequence of its removal'.[108]

The above discussion relates to tissue to be *removed* for research, rather than surplus tissue. But in any event the question nonetheless remains as to what *degree* of information needs to be generally imparted for use for research. One cannot reveal every risk or consequence to a prospective participant; it would simply not be feasible. The HTA Code of Practice on Consent states as regards the storage and use of tissue that 'To give consent, patients (or the person with parental responsibility) must understand the nature and purpose of what is proposed and be able to make a balanced judgement. They should be told of any "material" or "significant" risks inherent in the way the sample will be obtained, how the tissue will be used and any possible implications of its use, e.g. genetic tests.'[109] As McHale observes 'Here the Code of Practice clearly builds upon the approach taken at common law in relation to consent to treatment, where the courts have been moving towards a more patient-centred standard of disclosure of information'.[110] Indeed, in many overseas jurisdictions (e.g. many US states) what information about risks should be disclosed is governed by what the *prudent patient* would have wanted, as opposed to what disclosure reasonable doctors regard as appropriate. In rare instances, it is even founded upon what the particular patient would themselves have wished to be informed about.

A distinction needs to be drawn between the adequacy of a consent required in order for a procedure to be legitimately performed for the purposes of the criminal law and the degree of knowledge required in order for the professional concerned to have fully satisfied the duty of care owed to a consenting party. This issue arose in the context of claims relating to the performance of post-mortem examinations. In *In re Organ Retention Group Litigation*, Gage J stated that, having regard to the previous law under the Human Tissue Act 1961, 'I am quite satisfied that s 2 of the 1961 Act requires no more than a consent to a post-mortem being obtained without

---

[107] Nuffield Council, *Human Tissue*, at para. 7.7.     [108] *Ibid.*, at para. 13.16.
[109] Human Tissue Authority, Code of Practice, Consent, HTA, July 2006, para. 77.
[110] McHale, '"Appropriate consent"' at 196.

further explanation'.[111] However, the HTA Code of Practice on Consent states that the individual concerned must understand the nature and purpose of what is proposed.[112] To give a valid consent generally requires that the person be aware of the nature and purpose of the procedure.[113] The failure to adequately inform parents of the fact that certain body parts might be removed during post-mortem examination and retained in some cases might therefore now compromise the actual validity of the 'appropriate consent' for a (hospital) post-mortem examination itself.[114] In *In re Organ Retention Group Litigation*, the claimants also alleged that the failure to explain the nature of the post-mortem examination in such a way as to elicit objections to the removal and retention of organs amounted to negligence resulting in foreseeable psychiatric injury. Gage J held that there was a duty of care owed to the parents to provide some explanation of the post-mortem procedures of which the removal and retention of organs forms a relevant part, in order to provide a proper opportunity to decide upon whether to object.[115] However, this proved to be a pyrrhic victory for some of the claimants, due to the inordinate difficulty in proving psychiatric injury flowing from the non-disclosure.[116] Thus, in certain cases, whilst basic knowledge would be sufficient for there to be valid consent, more detailed information may be necessary in order for the professional to have satisfied his/her professional duty owed to the patients/relatives of the deceased.

In relation to procedures occurring after death, there may perhaps be a lesser need for detailed initial information to have been communicated to the deceased donor, as there are no risks to physical or psychological health accruing from removal. Potential organ donors generally have no more than a broad understanding of what transplantation entails, leading the UK Organ Donation Taskforce (ODT) to remark 'Amongst clinicians there is a certain amount of concern that the carrying of a donor card, or even registration with the donor register, falls short of what would usually be defined as consent in a medical setting'.[117] To deny the adequacy of

---

[111] *In re Organ Retention Group Litigation* [2005] QB 506 at [127]. However, he did add that 'that does not mean that if a relative asks questions or seeks further information those questions should not be answered nor the information supplied'. In these cases, the material concerned had not, however, been retained for research.

[112] Human Tissue Authority, Code of Practice, Consent, HTA, July 2006, para. 77.

[113] *The Creutzfeldt-Jakob Disease Litigation* (2000) 54 BMLR 1 (QBD).

[114] See Human Tissue Authority, Code of Practice, Post mortem Examination, HTA, July 2006, para. 74.

[115] *In re Organ Retention Group Litigation* [2005] QB 506 at [206].

[116] Similarly in the Irish cases of *Devlin* v. *National Maternity Hospital* [2007] IESC 50 and *O'Connor and Tormey* v. *Lenihan*, unreported, 9 June 2005 (High Court).

[117] *Organs for Transplant: A Report from the Organ Donation Taskforce*, Department of Health, 2008, at para. 4.8. See also D. Evans (letter), 'When "consent" is not consent', at http://jme.bmj.com/cgi/eletters/32/5/283.

knowledge upon which such a decision was made would be to disenfranchise such a 'donor', however, where a broad knowledge and understanding ought to suffice.

### Archived tissue

Tissue samples may have been archived following pathological examination at autopsy or following a therapeutic or diagnostic procedure performed upon a living person, or following newborn screening (e.g. 'Guthrie' cards), or where there is further tissue remaining after it has been initially used for a different scheduled or other research purpose. Such material forms the basis of museum collections, in particular. The availability of such material for later research has proved controversial. For instance, in the 1990s public attention was drawn to the (alleged) legal right to carry out research upon filter paper samples of blood taken from newborn children, e.g. stored in the Danish PKU Register.[118] There has been little or no legal or ethical regulation of the use of such material. Furness and Nicholson state 'Histopathology departments, for example, collect large archives of tissue fragments, initially processed for diagnosis, for the direct benefit of patients. These are stored primarily as part of the medical record, but in the past it has been considered acceptable for thin sections to be removed from such tissue blocks for research and other ethically acceptable purposes.'[119] Such samples may be unidentified or identified.

Prior to the 2004 Act, the MRC and the Department of Health endorsed research using archival samples where it would be 'impractical' or unethical to contact patients and seek consent, although there was no guidance as to when this might be so.[120] In some cases the original 'source' may be untraceable or have died, or it might perhaps 'open up old wounds' to remind some individuals of a time when they were extremely sick. Consent 'concessions' are now commonly to be found in legislative instruments as regards archival tissue.[121] Whilst it was stridently objected that prior to the passing of the 2004 Act explicit consent was frequently insisted upon for the use of archival samples, thus blocking

---

[118] See B. Norgaard-Pedersen, 'Use of stored samples from the Danish PKU Register', in B. Knoppers (ed.), *Human DNA: Law and Policy* (Dordrecht: Kluwer Law International, 1997) 303. Such samples are used for research in Australia after having been de-identified.

[119] P. Furness and M. Nicholson, 'Obtaining explicit consent for the use of archival tissue samples: Practical issues' (2004) 30 *Journal of Medical Ethics* 561 at 561 [Furness and Nicholson, 'Obtaining explicit consent'].

[120] Medical Research Council, *Human tissue and biological samples.*

[121] See Knoppers, 'Biobanking' at 8.

research where this was not feasible,[122] that Act now exempts 'existing holdings' (at the date of implementation) from the need to obtain 'appropriate consent' prior to storage or use of tissue from either living or deceased persons for research or other scheduled purposes (although separate provisions apply to existing anatomical specimens).[123] The 2006 Act in Scotland contains an analogous provision in respect of deceased persons.[124] The statutory exemptions are partially a recognition of the fact that such tissue is a potentially very valuable source for such purposes but that there was, at best, often a lack of clarity as to the requirements of consent at the time of their initial procurement. There are apparently greater sensitivities relating to retained cadaveric material after post-mortem examination here. Across the UK a *de facto* moratorium was in place in the aftermath of the breaking scandals, during which time such tissue could be claimed by relatives.[125] Material archived *after* the date of the implementation of the Acts must however satisfy the stipulated requirements relating to consent/authorisation.[126] The Council of Europe draft instrument on the *Use of Archived Human Biological Materials* would not have waived the need for consent for archived material, but would have permitted such consent to be either explicit or implicit.[127]

### Autopsy versus living tissue

Jack and Womack reviewed records with respect to UK family attitudes to research relating to viral markers using samples taken at (forensic) post-mortems.[128] Two-thirds of families gave telephone consent to blood, lymph node and liver samples being taken. By contrast, a similar study found that 98.8 per cent of 2,000 *living* subjects would agree to the use of their surplus

---

[122] Furness and Nicholson, 'Obtaining explicit consent' at 562. At that time it was reported that many research ethics committees were nevertheless requiring that explicit consent be obtained for the use of archival samples to be used in research projects, with the effect of impeding valuable research work (including two major international projects) and even despite the fact that such individuals would invariably have been only too happy for their tissue to be used without being approached.

[123] Section 9. An 'existing holding' is one where the tissue is already being held for use for a scheduled purpose on the day the 2004 Act came into force, i.e. 1 September 2006.

[124] Section 14, Human Tissue (Scotland) Act 2006.

[125] Prior to the passing of the 2004 and 2006 Acts substantial efforts were made to inform the public of their ability to ask about or request tissue. Some archived specimens, however, were unidentified.

[126] See D. Jones, R. Gear and K. Galvin, 'Stored human tissue: An ethical perspective on the fate of anonymous, archival material' (2003) 29 *Journal of Medical Ethics* 343 at 344.

[127] The instrument would have applied to material stored before *and after* the date of the passing of the instrument.

[128] C. Womack and A. Jack, 'Family attitudes to research using samples taken at coroner's postmortem examinations: Review of records' (2003) 327 *British Medical Journal* 781.

tissue for research,[129] a figure replicated in research relating to biobanking in Sweden.[130] Linked to these studies, Furness and Nicholson state that 'There is evidence from surveys of public opinion that the majority of the public regard most "surplus" therapeutically excised tissue as having little or no emotional value. This clearly differs from the situation in respect of autopsy tissue.'[131] The Royal College of Pathologists also considers there to be an important attitudinal difference between living and autopsy tissue.[132] This difference in public attitude is unremarkable, although perhaps for different reasons than merely based on the distinction between living-derived and deceased-derived tissue *per se*. Attitudes relating to post-mortem tissue are especially difficult because of the fact that it is generally the *families* of the donors who are involved with the giving of consent, as opposed to the donors themselves, and who were often parents of children who had died and who were invariably in the throes of the grieving process itself. There is evidence that individuals are more inclined to agree to the use of their own corpse for therapy and other purposes than those of relatives.[133]

The Inquiries leading up to the passing of the 2004 Act all concerned tissue retained following post-mortem examination and illustrate the great concern that that tissue can generate. It is not surprising that the 2004 Act was heavily driven by this experience. Moreover, it is undoubtedly the case that most people are not concerned at all with what use is made of their surplus tissue removed when alive. But we must be clear that the brouhaha at Alder Hey, etc. was a result of the failure to properly seek or implement consent, not to the ultimate retention and use of such tissue for research. Moreover, the fact that most individuals conceive of surplus material as 'waste' does not imply that all do, or should do.

## Consent and information-giving processes

Context is crucial to the formulation of appropriate policy. Communication issues may be especially problematic in the context of surplus tissue to be used for research, as the consentor (clinician/surgeon) will not typically be

---

[129] Jack and Womack, 'Why surgical patients' at 262.

[130] L. Johnsson, M. Hansson, S. Eriksson and G. Helgesson, 'Patients' refusal to consent to storage and use of samples in Swedish biobanks: Cross sectional study' (2008) 337 *British Medical Journal* 345 [Johnsson *et al.*, 'Patients' refusal'].

[131] Furness and Nicholson, 'Obtaining explicit consent' at 561. The Human Tissue Act 2004 draws a distinction between tissue taken from the living and the dead with regard to surplus tissue to be used for Schedule 1, Part 2 purposes.

[132] See Response of the Royal College of Pathologists to *Human Bodies, Human Choices*, Royal College of Pathologists, 2002, para. 4.

[133] M. Sanner, 'A comparison of public attitudes toward autopsy, organ donation, and anatomical dissection: A Swedish survey' (1994) 271 *Journal of the American Medical Association* 284.

the person (researcher or pathologist) involved in the final activities or have detailed knowledge regarding them, and by dint of the fact that the patient may be undergoing a major, possibly even life-threatening, procedure, the retention and use of tissue may be considered a minor, even trivial, issue – a distraction even – from the perspective of both clinician and patient. At a minimum, even if information is imparted, it may not be properly absorbed and reflected upon, i.e. there may be no emotional or cognitive 'space' to accommodate such matters. This is no less true for some diagnostic procedures, such as biopsies looking for cancerous growths, as for surgical resections and the removal of other diseased tissue. Furness also emphasises the considerable resource implications attaching to reliance upon surgical consent forms.[134]

However, to re-contact patients at a later point to seek explicit consent also has substantial resource implications and may even render some research impractical, in addition to creating an additional burden on (some) ex-patients. Even if the resources and time permit to enable re-contact with patients, and it is appropriate to do so, it may amount to a process of attrition to secure the response of a sufficient volume of potential tissue suppliers for such research to be viable. Furness and Nicholson attempted to determine what the practical difficulties were in attempting to contact individuals for consent at a later point in time. They sent 495 letters. Despite further attempts to contact non-responders, the opinions of 26 per cent of individuals had still not been obtained one year later, thus illustrating the difficulties. Of those 328 people who responded to the initial letter, 96.3 per cent gave consent to the use of surplus biopsy tissue in research and only 3.6 per cent objected.[135] The authors note that even lower rates of objection have been revealed in other UK and international studies.[136] A recent retrospective analysis relating to surplus biological samples in biobanks in Sweden for instance, revealed that consent to storage was refused in only one of 690 cases.[137] The fact that studies show that so few disagree with the use of surplus tissue for research is seen by some as a reason to 'assume' consent, or ignore the necessity for it in the first place, and to trust in RECs or IRBs to

---

[134] P. Furness, 'Consent to using human tissue' (2003) 327 *British Medical Journal* 759 at 760 [Furness, 'Consent']. He noted that there are 3 million tissue specimens per annum in the NHS, even ignoring blood samples.

[135] Furness and Nicholson, 'Obtaining explicit consent'. They note that non-responders display apathy rather than objections.

[136] See Jack and Womack, 'Why surgical patients'. Similar low figures have been obtained abroad even in relation to genetic research; see, e.g., B. Stegmayr and K. Asplund, 'Informed consent for genetic research on blood stored for more than a decade: A population based study' (2002) 325 *British Medical Journal* 634.

[137] Johnsson *et al.*, 'Patients' refusal'.

protect individuals' interests. But the fact that only a small minority of individuals would object is not a reason to ignore their wishes.

To others, the survey data suggests that the onus should be on those who object to do so. Unlike previously, we are here examining presumed consent in the context of tissue removed from *living* persons. Furness and Nicholson state 'If a research project is in a non-controversial area and can be shown to have no risk of adversely affecting the interests of the tissue donors, is it acceptable to use implied consent to permit research use? This move would put the onus on the 1–3% who object; they would have to respond to information provided and register their objections. Is this an unreasonable expectation if it avoids blocking medical research, which is conducted for the good of all, when 97–99% are willing for their tissues to be used in research?'[138] Similarly, based on their research in Sweden, Johnsson *et al.* suggest that a presumed consent policy would be a more proportionate bureaucratic and regulatory response in this context.[139] The Royal College of Pathologists, whilst asserting that the overall policy goal was to achieve the explicit consent of all patients, previously advocated a presumed consent strategy, stating 'To implement these changes rapidly, and to avoid blocking essential work, it will initially be necessary to invite objections to the use of surplus and archival tissue, rather than to seek positive consent from all patients'.[140] It recommended that measures be taken to inform patients of how surplus tissues might be used and the benefits to society, and what safeguards have been put in place, by way of one or more of the following options: (a) an additional section on surgical consent forms, (b) notices on the walls of phlebotomy rooms and GP surgeries, (c) information sheets provided at each contact within the NHS and (d) advertisements in the media or 'mailshots' to homes.[141] This was, however, intended only as a transitional policy.

There are various supporters of presumed consent in this context.[142] Laurie, however, urges caution and the avoidance of any simplistic correlations, noting that a failure to refuse consent or withdraw may be evidence of apathy or ignorance as opposed to support for an opting out approach.[143] This is a highly charged subject. In 1998, Iceland implemented a presumed

---

[138] Furness and Nicholson, 'Obtaining explicit consent' at 564. See also Furness, 'Consent'.
[139] Johnsson *et al.*, 'Patients' refusal'.
[140] RCP, *Transitional Guidelines* at para. 8.     [141] *Ibid.*, at para. 4.
[142] See, e.g., P. Van Diest, 'No consent should be needed for using leftover body material for scientific purposes' (2002) 325 *British Medical Journal* 648, J. Savalescu, 'No consent should be needed for using leftover body material for scientific purposes' (2002) 325 *British Medical Journal* 649.
[143] G. Laurie, 'Evidence of support for biobanking practices' (2008) 337 *British Medical Journal* 337.

consent model for its genetic database which attracted very considerable dispute.[144] Nonetheless, there are presumed consent laws in force in many countries e.g. in Denmark and France, relating to the use of tissue from living persons for research.[145]

As we have seen, where proper information is provided to patients and an easy means of recording objections afforded to all, it may perhaps be appropriate to move away from a requirement for explicit consent. But we must not too easily assume that such conditions have been satisfied and that a *tacit* consent has been given. As regards the Data Protection Act 1998, Pattinson remarks as regards the placing of notices prominently on the walls of GP surgeries or clinics or hospitals informing of potential uses of data 'Is the failure to opt out a sufficient indication, taking into account the vulnerable and distracted position of many of those in hospitals or GP surgeries awaiting medical assistance? Over eagerness to infer or impute consent will render the patient's consent no more than a legal fiction.'[146] This suggests that the *process* of soliciting objections may well fail to meet the appropriate threshold for a tacit consent. Many patients would seemingly remain entirely unaware that such tissue might be stored and used for such purposes in the future at all. There is a need for direct information such as information sheets to be given to all patients in such a context to this end and a straightforward mechanism for recording objections or caveats.[147] Without such pre-requisites there would even arguably be insufficient to ethically and legally ground an *imputed* (presumed) consent based on the persons' anticipated wishes, despite the empirical evidence as to the wishes of the overwhelming majority of the people.

---

[144] Health Sector Database Act 1998. The Act relates to medical data and does not govern the collection and use of tissue samples, which is governed instead by the Act on Biobanks No. 110/2000. Under the latter statute, although explicit consent is required for the storage and use of samples in a non-clinical setting, in a clinical context consent is presumed for samples to be stored and used. See, e.g., 'World Medical Association opposes Iceland gene database' (1999) 318 *British Medical Journal* 1096. Individuals need to specifically opt out in writing to the Director of Public Health. Apparently over 10 per cent of Icelanders have done so.

[145] See letter, 'Human tissue bank regulations' (2006) 24(5) *Nature Biotechnology* 496.

[146] S. Pattinson, *Medical Law and Ethics* (London: Thomson/Sweet & Maxwell, 2006), para. 6.2.4.2, p. 186. Nonetheless, many healthcare facilities rely upon lack of objection as consent to the use of *patient information* for research.

[147] There was a view, explicitly referred to by Government spokespersons during the passage of the Human Tissue Bill, that where there is evidence that a person *did in fact* object to a specific form of research such an objection should be respected even though there is no legal requirement to secure consent, e.g. use of non-identifiable surplus tissue for REC-approved research or research using existing holdings. See, e.g., Rosie Winterton MP, House of Commons Debates, Hansard, col. 105, 28 June 2004. But, to the extent that adequate information is not provided, the 'right' to object is a merely an 'opt out' rather than any form of 'consent'. If only those who are aware are able to object, this generates arbitrariness and discriminatory practices.

# 7 Living donation

Living donation is the backbone of many organ transplantation systems and a vital and substantial supplement to deceased donation in many others. It is being increasingly relied upon in many developed transplant nations, as rapidly rising demand for organ replacement therapy outstrips available supply. As the European Commission stated 'The use of living donors is an increasing alternative given the failure to meet the growing need for organs with cadaver donation'.[1] By virtue of the typically more limited harms normally associated with the removal and use of tissue for transplantation or research, the primary focus here is upon organs for transplant. Not only has there been rapid growth in living donation rates in many parts of the world, but policies have largely come to embrace living donation as a standard therapy. This policy shift can be seen in the new regime in the Human Tissue Act 2004 and the Human Tissue (Scotland) Act 2006, which implicitly confer legitimacy and support by way of comprehensive monitoring. It can also be witnessed at an international level in the statements of the Council of Europe and the World Health Organisation (WHO), seemingly to cater for an ever-increasing reality and predicament. Whilst atypical, in certain jurisdictions, including the US, such procedures are not governed by specific laws and, subject to general guidance (from the United Network for Organ Sharing (UNOS) in the US), are dictated by individual centre policies.[2]

But whilst living organ donation has now become 'mainstream', and regarded as a crucial element of a successful donation strategy in many regions, it has always been controversial.[3] Even today some critics

---

[1] Commission of the European Communities, Impact Assessment: Organ Donation and Transplantation: Policy Actions at EU Level, 2007, Brussels, at 30 [Commission of the European Communities, Impact Assessment].

[2] Since 2006, UNOS has been obliged to develop policies for living organ donors which members must apply; see OPTN/UNOS, Guidance for the Development of Program-Specific Living Kidney Donor Medical Evaluation Protocols, 2006.

[3] See, e.g., W. Glannon, 'Underestimating the risk in living kidney donation' (2008) 34 Journal of Medical Ethics 127 [Glannon, 'Underestimating the risk'] and A. Cronin, 'Allowing autonomous agents freedom' (2008) 34 Journal of Medical Ethics 129.

maintain that it is an illegal practice which contravenes the moral and ethical proscription of non-maleficence, or *primum non nocere*, perhaps implicitly harking back to the early Thomistic notion of *totality*.[4] Scheper-Hughes has also alluded to the 'tyranny of the gift' in this context, alleging that even living related donation is more accurately described as 'poaching' than a voluntary act of giving.[5] Fox and Swayzey had previously observed that 'the psychological and moral burden is especially onerous because the gift the recipient has received from the donor is so extraordinary that it is inherently unreciprocal'.[6] Indeed, the very shortfall of organs available from other sources generates increasing pressure upon living individuals to offer their own bodies for the benefit of others. And all this is without regard to the extent of (parts of) organs that are now transplantable and transplanted, and the expanding sources of such organs.[7]

Even if not perceived as unethical or unlawful, some commentators have serious reservations about the *scale* and *scope* of living organ donation as it is practised in a contemporary context. Ross, amongst others, describes herself as 'deeply disturbed by the trend'.[8] Since the earliest days of transplantation living organ donation has been typically perceived, optimistically as it transpires, as a 'temporary strategy' to deal with end-stage organ failure and the shortage in the deceased organ supply. But whilst many strategies may be contemplated or attempted, living organ donation alone has the capacity to respond speedily, flexibly and

---

[4] See, for example, M. Potts and D. Evans 'Is solid organ donation by living donors ethical? The case of kidney donation', in W. Weimar, M. Bos and J. Busschbach (eds.), *Organ Transplantation: Ethical, Legal, and Psychosocial Aspects* (Lengerich: Pabst Publishing, 2008) 377.

[5] N. Scheper-Hughes, 'The tyranny of the gift: Sacrificial violence in living donor transplants' (2007) 7 *American Journal of Transplantation* 507 at 510 [Scheper-Hughes, 'The tyranny of the gift'].

[6] R. Fox and J. Swazey, *The Courage to Fail* (University of Chicago Press, 1974).

[7] Generally living organ donors must be of legal age; see, e.g., section 8 of the Law of 5 November 1997 in Germany and section 17(2) Human Tissue (Scotland) Act 2006. I do not intend to consider the use of minors as kidney donors here, which was fully dealt with in my previous book; see D. Price, *Legal and Ethical Aspects of Organ Transplantation* (Cambridge University Press, 2000), chapter 8 [Price, *Legal and Ethical Aspects*]. See also the special edition of the *Cambridge Quarterly of Health Care Ethics* (2004) Volume 13(2); and F. Delmonico and W. Harmon, 'The use of a minor as a live kidney donor' (2002) 2 *American Journal of Transplantation* 333 and O. Salvatierra, 'Transplant physicians bear full responsibility for the consequences of kidney donation by a minor' (2002) 2 *American Journal of Transplantation* 297.

[8] L. Ross, 'All donations should not be treated equally: A response to Jeffrey Kahn's commentary' (2002) 30 *Journal of Law, Medicine and Ethics* 448 at 450 [Ross, 'All donations should not be treated equally']. See also B. Hippen, President's Council on Bioethics, Session 4: 'Organ Transplantation and Procurement – Policy Proposals', 22 June 2006, at www.bioethics.gov/transcripts/june06/session4.html.

effectively to any perceived need or crisis. Woodle asserted in 2003 with respect to the US 'At present, living donor transplants represent the only immediate potential means for amelioration of the organ donor shortage'.[9] Organ shortfalls also encourage consideration of unconventional procedures. Recent years have witnessed an unprecedented growth of 'novel' living donor strategies. There has been a major recent reinvigoration of so-called 'altruistic (stranger) donations' of organs (mainly kidneys) in various regions, in addition to which new paired (swap) and pooled/chain exchange protocols involving imaginative linkages designed to overcome incompatibility have sprung up around the world. This unmet 'need' extends also to non-renal organs, such as parts of livers and lungs, with considerably greater risks attaching to their removal. Such creativity and innovation generates its own ethical and legal issues and quandaries, relating to autonomy, consent, non-maleficence, utility, justice and commerce. This chapter focuses on the legitimacy of enhanced reliance upon living donors, the innovative and high-risk procedures in this sphere, and unconventional organ sources.

### A last resort

In 1978 the Council of Europe declared that 'The use of organs from living donors should be restricted and gradually eliminated'.[10] As a statement of aspiration this was explicable, but as a short-to-medium-term goal it was wildly unrealistic, even within Europe. Not only do some nations rely either entirely or heavily upon living organ donors,[11] but in the face of stagnant or declining deceased donation rates living donation is rapidly on the increase today in many parts of Europe, including the UK, and in other parts of the world, e.g., Australia.[12] Living donors now account for 17 per cent of kidney transplant activity in Europe, and 5 per cent of liver transplant activity.[13] In the early days the precise risks of living renal donation were not accurately known, and in particular the long-term effects of reduced renal mass were predicted to be more

[9] E. Woodle, 'A history of living donor transplantation: From twins to trades' (2003) 35 *Transplantation Proceedings* 901 at 902.

[10] Council of Europe, 3rd Conference of European Health Ministers, Paris, 16–17 November, 1987, Part B.

[11] Reliance on living donors has been almost total on the Indian sub-continent and in parts of Asia, Africa and Eastern Europe (e.g. Georgia), and even in Iceland.

[12] In the UK in 2007 living kidney transplants represented 36 per cent of all kidney transplants performed; see Council of Europe Newsletter, International Figures on Organ Donation and Transplantation – 2007, Council of Europe, 2008 at 26. In Australia, nearly 40 per cent of all kidney donations are currently from living donors.

[13] Commission of the European Communities, Impact Assessment at 30.

detrimental than has subsequently proved to be the case. In view of mounting evidence of relatively modest risks, attitudes have relaxed.[14]

Early policy directives were largely phrased in negative and disapproving terms. The WHO's Guiding Principles issued in 1991 stated that 'Organs for transplantation should be removed preferably from the bodies of deceased persons. However, adult living persons may donate organs, but in general such donors should be genetically related to the recipients. Exceptions may be made in the case of transplantation of bone marrow and other acceptable regenerative tissues.'[15] The recently revised guidance issued in 2008, however, is couched in more positive terms and omits any reference to 'preference'.[16] The initial guidance was driven by the particular concern to protect the poor and vulnerable of many constituent nations from organ trading, but a broader view now prevails. Indeed, a higher living donor rate – ordinarily from related donors – may *forestall* attempts to purchase organs abroad. The Council of Europe's recent statements similarly display a more tolerant stance (see p. 200). The EU has stated that co-operation between Member States is important to explore the *promotion* of donation from living donors.[17]

Whilst the risks of living renal donation are fairly modest, they are by no means negligible.[18] Although donor deaths are very rare they do occasionally occur, and living donors are not infrequently listed for kidney transplantation themselves,[19] although it appears the rate is seemingly less than one would expect from any comparable population.[20] As the Report of the Organ Donation Taskforce (ODT) in the UK stated in 2008 'The

---

[14] Nonetheless, the risks are not precisely known, leading to increasing calls for registries to be established to record and monitor risks. See, e.g., L. Ross, M. Siegler and J. Thistlethwaite, 'We need a registry of living kidney donors' (2007) 37(6) *Hastings Center Report* 49. See also Institute of Medicine, *Organ Donation: Opportunities for Action* (Washington, DC, National Academies Press, 2006) at 277.

[15] World Health Organisation, *Guiding Principles on Human Organ Transplantation*, 1991, Guiding Principle 3. In like vein, Council of Europe Resolution (78) 29 on harmonisation of legislation of Member States to removal, grafting and transplantation of human substances stated in Article 4 that 'removal of substances which cannot regenerate must be confined to transplantation between genetically related persons except in exceptional cases where there are good chances of success'.

[16] World Health Organisation Guiding Principles on Human Cell, Tissue and Organ Transplantation, 2008, available at www.who.int/entity/transplantation/TxGP08-en.pdf.

[17] European Commission, *Organ Donation and Transplantation: Policy Actions at EU Level*, Communication to the European Parliament and the Council, COM(2007) 275, Brussels 30.5.2007 at 6 and 9.

[18] Glannon argues that they are consistently underestimated and minimised; see Glannon, 'Underestimating the risk'.

[19] M. Ellison *et al.*, 'Living kidney donors in need of kidneys transplants: A report from the organ procurement and transplantation network' (2002) 74 *Transplantation* 1349.

[20] An increasing number of, equally safe, living donor nephrectomies are performed using laparoscopic rather than open procedures, resulting in shorter hospital stays and a quicker

shortage of deceased donors has resulted in an increased interest in living donation, but it must be noted that living donation of a kidney is associated with a risk of death to the donor of about 1 in 3,000, whilst living liver donation (adult to adult) carries a risk of death to the donor of up to 1 in 100. Nothing demonstrates the critical shortage of deceased donors more clearly than the acceptance – by patients, clinicians and commissioners – of such risks to the life of a fit, healthy, person.'[21] This implicitly asserts the primacy of deceased over living donation.

### Subsidiarity

Taken across the board the results of living kidney donation are generally superior to those achieved from deceased donors. The European Commission accepts that the results in the short to medium term are 'equal to or significantly better'.[22] Certainly living 'pre-emptive' (pre-dialysis) transplantation is the gold standard of renal donation generally. Nevertheless, there is a 'preference' stipulated in many official instruments and some laws for deceased organs to be used. Article 19 of the Council of Europe Biomedicine Convention states that 'Removal of organs or tissue from a living person for transplantation purposes may be carried out solely for the therapeutic benefit of the recipient and where there is no suitable organ or tissue available from a deceased person and no other alternative therapeutic method of comparable effectiveness'. However, it is apparently recognised that this stricture does not apply where a living donor offers *better* prospects for the recipient.[23]

The subsidiarity principle is embedded in the laws of, amongst other states, Belgium, Germany and Hungary, but appears to lack crucial practical significance. Indeed, the very lack of availability of organs from deceased donors is itself the stimulus for the increasing resort to living donors. Waiting times for transplant are lengthening across the board, leading to increased morbidity and mortality.[24] However, there is a

return to work. See F. Dahm *et al.*, 'Open and laparoscopic living donor nephrectomy in Switzerland: A retrospective assessment of clinical outcomes and the motivation to donate' (2006) 21(9) *Nephrology Dialysis Transplantation* 2563.

[21] *Organs for Transplants: A Report from the Organ Donation Taskforce*, Department of Health, 2008 at 4.

[22] Commission of the European Communities, Impact Assessment at 31.

[23] See Council of Europe, Explanatory Notes to the Additional Protocol to the Convention on Human Rights and Biomedicine Concerning Transplantation of Organs and Tissues of Human Origin, ETS No. 186, 2002, paras. 60–1.

[24] The average wait for a deceased donor kidney transplant in the US is five years and in some parts ten years, as a consequence of which the death rate is increasing; see A. Matas, 'Should we pay donors to increase the supply of organs for transplantation? Yes' (2008) 336 *British Medical Journal* 1342 at 1342.

danger of an easy utilitarian attitude to living donors gaining purchase, overlooking the real risks and significant discomforts and inconveniences involved. Perhaps the very normality and prevalence of living organ donation has tended to obscure the continuing dangers. Scheper-Hughes states 'I want to recover the discomfort in dipping too readily into the bodies of living donors. I am suggesting, if not a moratorium, a *slowing down* of the use of living donors, especially young ones.'[25] She urges that living donation be consigned to a back seat as 'an exceptional back-up' to deceased donation. This assertion requires one to question the extent to which reliance is appropriately placed upon living donors and whether other more desirable alternatives are being adequately pursued.[26]

## Live trends

There was still considerable optimism during the late 1980s and early 1990s that deceased organ donation would continue to rise to meet the increasing demand. Moreover, there was the view that good human leukocyte antigen (HLA) tissue matching of deceased donors and prospective recipients, and improved immunosuppression, would eliminate much if not all of the supposed advantage in terms of results from using living donors. Unhappily much of this optimism was misplaced. Even with improved rates of multi-organ retrieval, the numbers of deceased organ donors plateaued in many regions (including the UK and the US) during the 1990s and results from living donors continued to show clear benefits over deceased donation, even from non-genetically related, or only distantly related, individuals. The supply–demand differential continues to grow, even ignoring the now surging rates of new end-stage organ failure occurring today.

In 2001 in the US the number of living kidney donors exceeded the number of deceased donors for the first time, and the same phenomenon occurred in Switzerland in 2002.[27] Very considerable rises in the volume of living donation can be witnessed in many regions in the last decade. In the

---

[25] Scheper-Hughes, 'The tyranny of the gift' at 510.

[26] See the critique of Scheper-Hughes in A. Spital and C. Jacobs, 'The beauty of the gift: The wonder of living organ donation' (2007) 21 *Clinical Transplantation* 435 [Spital and Jacobs, 'The beauty']. They argue that living donation 'demonstrates humanity at its best' at 438.

[27] M. Quante and S. Wiedebusch, 'Overcoming the shortage of transplantable organs: Ethical and psychological aspects' (2006) 136 *Swiss Medical Weekly* 523 at 524. The number of living donors in the US rose by 10 per cent per annum between 1996 and 2001; see H. Nathan *et al.*, 'Organ donation in the United States' (2003) 3(Supp 4) *American Journal of Transplantation* 29 at 34 [Nathan, 'Organ donation in the United States']. In 2007, 19.9 living kidney transplants per million population (p.m.p.) were

UK, living donors now comprise more than 36 per cent of all kidney transplants, the same as in the US,[28] and in the Netherlands it is 43.7 per cent.[29] In the UK, this has been the product of a 'deliberate push' to help boost living donor transplant rates as a whole,[30] partly achieved through increased and dedicated funding.

As circumstances have generated pressure to increase the number of available organs, not only have the indications for deceased donation been 'extended' – some would say 'relaxed' – so living donation has gradually radiated out from blood family, i.e. those with genetic ties, across Europe and North America in particular.[31] It was inevitable that, with very acceptable clinical results, spouses would themselves champion their own cause, but even the use of close friends is now quite commonly regarded as a sufficient 'bond' justifying work-up for potential donation. Increased acceptance of donations by genetically unrelated donors has resulted from witnessing good clinical outcomes, with improved immunosuppression reducing the influence of close HLA matching.[32] Whilst initial caution could be seen in the early policies of the Council of Europe and the WHO (see p. 199),[33] their later policies display a considerably more liberal and flexible approach to relatedness, leaving greater discretion to Member States to determine the nature of permissible relationships.[34] In the UK, the 1989 Human Organ Transplants Act necessitated prior approval of

performed, 36 per cent of all kidney transplants; see Council of Europe Newsletter 2008, *International Figures on Organ Donation and Transplantation 2007*, Council of Europe, 2008 at 27 [Council of Europe Newsletter 2008].

[28] See Council of Europe Newsletter 2008. There were 702 living donors in 2006–7 contrasted with 224 in 1997–8; see NHS Blood and Transplant, *Transplant Activity in the UK 2006–2007*, 2007. The HTA approved 988 living donor kidney transplants in 2007–8.

[29] Council of Europe Newsletter 2008. In 2006, the proportion of living organ donors was considerably higher in some regions, e.g. 64 per cent in Rotterdam. See also G. van Dijk and M. Hilhorst, *Financial Incentives for Organ Donation: An Investigation of the Ethical Issues*, Centre for Ethics and Health, 2007 at 25. In 2005, 43 per cent of Canada's kidney transplants also involved living donors.

[30] 'Living organ donor drive launched', BBC News online, 30 May 2005, at http://news.bbc.co.uk/2/hi/health/4586565.

[31] In the US, there was a tenfold increase in the volume of unrelated donors between 1991 and 2001; see Nathan, 'Organ donation in the United States' at 40. In the US, 35 per cent of kidney donors are now biologically unrelated.

[32] 'A Report of the Amsterdam Forum on the Care of the Living Kidney Donor: Data and Medical Guidelines' (2005) 79 *Transplantation* S53 at S61.

[33] Council of Europe, 3rd Conference of European Health Ministers, Paris 1987, article 8. World Health Organisation Guiding Principles on Human Organ Transplantation, 1991, Guiding Principle 3.

[34] See Committee of Ministers, Resolution CM/RES(2008)6 on Transplantation of Kidneys from Living Donors Who are Not Genetically Related to the Recipient, Council of Europe, 2008. See also World Health Organisation Guiding Principles on Human Cell, Tissue and Organ Transplantation, 2008, which now refer to 'legally or emotionally' as well as 'genetically' related persons.

transplants involving non-genetically related donors. Whilst principally an anti-commercialisation policy it nonetheless served to stifle the development of living donation by strangers in particular.[35] The Human Tissue Act 2004 now applies safeguards and hurdles to *all* living organ donations, albeit with enhanced scrutiny by the Human Tissue Authority (HTA) in cases of higher risk or novel procedures.[36] There are, however, still strict laws governing relationship in some European jurisdictions, e.g. in Portugal (where the donor must be genetically related),[37] and within Central and South America, e.g. Panama, Mexico, etc. There is therefore considerable legal diversity in this sphere.

In addition to a broadening of living donor *sources*, the range of *organs* used for transplantation taken from living donors has expanded significantly, to include living liver, lung, pancreas/islet and small bowel/intestine transplants.[38] Living liver donor transplantation is now an established procedure in many parts of the world, with more than 12,000 procedures having been performed since 1989.[39] The overwhelming preponderance of procedures has been performed in Japan (brain death has been slow to be accepted in many parts of Asia), the US, Canada and Germany, but programmes have latterly started in Russia, France and many other nations.[40] The first adult-to-adult procedures on the NHS were recently performed in the UK, the first involving a son donating 60 per cent of his liver to his father.[41] The risk to the donor is linked to the removal procedure, skills of the operating team, the volume of liver removed and whether a left or right lobe is taken. The mortality risks, admittedly based on incomplete data, are approximately 0.1 per cent for a left-lobe

---

[35] ULTRA did not approve any stranger donations under the 1989 Act, although it apparently had no principled objections; see ULTRA, Annual Report 2002–4, Department of Health at 6.

[36] See Human Tissue Act 2004 (Persons who Lack Capacity to Consent and Transplants) Regulations 2006 SI 2006 No. 1659. Different provisions apply in Scotland, see Human Organ and Tissue Live Transplants (Scotland) Regulations 2006 SSI 2006 No. 390. Whilst the Human Tissue (Scotland) Act 2006 does not contain provisions relating to licensing or the monitoring of living donor transplantation, the HTA carries out such functions on behalf of Scottish Ministers in respect of Scotland also.

[37] Portugal's Law No. 12/93 on Organ Transplantation requires there to be consanguinity up to the third degree.

[38] See S. Amiel and M. Rela, 'Live organ-donation for islet transplantation' (2005) 365 *The Lancet* 1603.

[39] S. Nadalin *et al.*, 'Current trends in live liver donation' (2007) 20 *Transplant International* 312 at 323 [Nadalin, 'Current trends'].

[40] See generally P. Northup and C. Berg, 'Living donor liver transplantation: The historical and cultural basis of policy decisions and ongoing ethical questions' (2005) 72 *Health Policy* 175.

[41] See 'First NHS live liver transplant', at http://news.bbc.co.uk/2/hi/uk_news/england/west_yorkshire/6262328.stm.

donation and 0.4–0.5 per cent for a right-lobe donation.[42] There have been at least twelve right-lobe donor deaths and 3 left-lobe donor deaths around the globe.[43] The estimated risks of significant morbidity are around 35 per cent for right-lobe donation.[44] Adult-to-adult liver transplants are subject to enhanced scrutiny under the 2004 Act, involving approval by a panel of HTA members.[45]

The first living lung lobe donation procedure in the UK was performed at the Harefield Hospital in 1995, but the large majority of such procedures have been performed in the US, principally by the team led by Starnes at Los Angeles. By contrast with living liver donation, living lung donation requires *two* donors to each donate a lobe of lung to the recipient, and unlike livers, lung tissue will not regenerate. Starnes' team has experience of 253 lung lobectomies, which revealed that 20 per cent of donors had one or more post-operative complication.[46] As yet there have been no donor deaths or cases of major or life-threatening complications, although donors will have less reserve lung function for the future and may be hampered during participation in competitive sports.[47] Living lobar lung donation is generally regarded as acceptable in the UK by virtue of the fact that, due to a shortage of deceased organs, 50 per cent of cystic fibrosis sufferers die whilst still awaiting an organ.[48] Similarly, in the US such donation is generally preferred where the patient has a clinically deteriorating condition and is unlikely to survive to receive an organ from a deceased person. But in so far as results are not generally superior to those achieved from deceased donors, and on account of the risks, it is not preferred to deceased donation across the board.[49] Living liver donor transplantation results have also generally been comparable with those achieved using deceased donors. However, deaths on the waiting list for

---

[42] Nadalin, 'Current trends' at 322.

[43] S. Florman and C. Miller, 'Live donor liver transplantation' (2006) 12 *Liver Transplantation* 499 at 502 [Florman and Miller, 'Live donor liver transplantation'].

[44] Nadalin, 'Current trends' at 322.

[45] Resolution of the Committee of Ministers of the Council of Europe on Adult-to-Adult Living Donor Liver Transplantation CM/RES, March 2008 states that States Parties should establish an independent mechanism for approving non-directed living donations in addition to non-genetically related living kidney donations, at para. 5.

[46] M. Bowdish, 'A decade of living lobar lung transplantation: Perioperative complications after 253 donor lobectomies' (2004) 4 *American Journal of Transplantation* 1283.

[47] The mortality rate for those who have had a part of a lung removed (resected) on account of lung cancer is around 1 per cent.

[48] Although not for *severe* cystic fibrosis; see T. Liou, F. Adler, D. Cox and B. Cahill, 'Lung transplantation and survival in children with cystic fibrosis' (2007) 357(21) *New England Journal of Medicine* 2143.

[49] See G. Patterson, 'Living lobar lung transplantation: Is it a necessary option?' (2004) 4 *American Journal of Transplantation* 1213 at 1214.

transplantation are substantial, more than 10 per cent in the US.[50] Once more it is the shortage of organs for transplantation rather than superior results *per se* which principally drives this therapy. By contrast, living kidney donation outcomes are markedly superior to deceased donor transplantation in general, and this in the face of low risks to donors would appear to justify the use of the procedure even where an organ from a deceased donor *is* available.

### Ethical perspectives

Relatively few would endorse the radical libertarian position that a person should be entitled to do with their body as they please, even to the point of death, provided that they do not cause harm to others. The autonomy of the individual is seemingly constrained by duties owed by physicians to society as a whole as well as to their profession in particular. The clinician is a moral agent and requires some justification for what would otherwise constitute a 'harm' to the patient, over and above consent.[51]

It has been asserted that the cardinal principle of medical ethics is that the physician acts always and only for the benefit of the sick. Meilander contends that this is an obligation to be wholly attentive to the well-being of the patient.[52] On this view, living donor transplantation (LDT) appears to be a clear transgression of the medical ethic.[53] Indeed, it is sometimes noted that living donation is itself *designed* to make the well 'sick'. But even if one is obliged to see living donation in these terms, it might still be open to argue that generosity should be capable of carving out an exception to the norm, thus permitting clinicians to engage with it, e.g. by virtue of shared bonds with family and other close loved ones.[54] The above view of the central medical ethic appears to derive from the notion that the pursuit of health is the point of medicine, i.e. it is intrinsically valuable. However, health can also be seen as instrumentally valuable to the achievement of

---

[50] Florman and Miller, 'Live donor liver transplantation' at 499.
[51] Veatch, however, argues that such assessments are only for the potential donor and clinician to decide; R. Veatch, *Transplantation Ethics* (Washington, DC: Georgetown University Press, 2000), chapter 12.
[52] G. Meilander, President's Council on Bioethics, Session 2: 'Living Organ Donation: Outcomes and Ethics', 7 September 2006, at www.bioethics.gov/transcripts/sept06/session2.html. This was also the view expressed by Leon Kass.
[53] See Schaub, President's Council on Bioethics, *ibid*.
[54] Some commentators argue that it is the very nature of such relationships that are the central justification for living organ donation itself; see, e.g., G. den Hartogh, *Farewell to Non-commitment: Decision Systems for Organ Donation from an Ethical Viewpoint*, Monitoring Report Ethics and Health, Centre for Ethics and Health, The Hague, 2008 at 81 [Den Hartogh, *Farewell to Non-commitment*].

various other ends. Moreover, the ethic might in any event be conceived more holistically in terms of 'benefitting' the patient generally.

The notion of *primum non nocere*, or the duty of non-maleficence, may also be seen to act as a constraint upon living donation derived from both general and professional moral norms. However, if applied strictly, even blood or bone marrow donation would be illegitimate, as well as many forms of non-therapeutic research. Once more, the duty may perhaps be seen in terms of *benefit* to the individual. Moreover, we can perhaps argue that it is the individual's own view of benefit which should be predominant.[55] As De Marco has remarked 'The trouble with determining whether benefit is appropriate given risk is that what counts as a high risk in relation to benefit involves subjective evaluation ... Morality is not about taking polls, and there are no objective measures of risk/benefit evaluations.'[56] Pellegrino alleges that it is the duty of beneficence which is the central obligation of clinicians and that the patient's good must be seen more broadly than simply his or her *medical* good.[57] He argues that there are other, higher, levels of good for a person, including the person's subjective view, the good of humans across the board and the spiritual good. The central ethic of the profession dictates a broader approach, which would allow the consensual taking of some organs from living persons for donation subject to some degree of proportionality between risks and benefits.

Some moral intuitions about living organ donation can be traced back to St Thomas Aquinas and the Catholic doctrine of totality, which holds that since parts are ordered for the good of the whole, they may be disposed of if necessary only for the good of the person as a whole.[58] But once more this begs the question of what 'benefit' means for such purposes. Initially it apparently implied an entirely biological orientation, yet contemporary theologians have tended to reinterpret the principle and distinguish between *anatomical* and *functional* bodily integrity; the donation of a kidney may not compromise the latter whereas the removal of a

---

[55] See Schneider, President's Council on Bioethics, Session 2, at www.bioethics.gov/transcripts/sept06/session2.html.

[56] J. De Marco, 'In defense of live kidney donation' (2004) 4(4) *American Journal of Bioethics* 33 at 34.

[57] Pellegrino, at www.bioethics.gov/transcripts/sept06/session2.html. A narrow view would also challenge procedures such as cosmetic surgery, etc.

[58] Pope Pius XII, 'The Moral Limits of Medical Research and Treatment', address given on 14 September 1952, at www.papalencyclicals.net/Pius12/P12PSYCH.HTM, No. 13. More recently, Pope Benedict XVI described organ donation in general as a 'peculiar form of witness to charity', and spoke supportively of living organ donation consistent with the doctrine of totality, i.e. restriction to non-vital organs. See www.uktransplant.org.uk/ukt/newsroom/bulletin/current_bulletin/pope_says_yes.jsp.

cornea would. Biological function rather than bodily integrity *per se* has become the basis for permitting certain forms of donation.[59] Pope John Paul II himself remarked that science challenges individuals 'to love our neighbour in new ways'.[60]

Some view living donation as in contravention of Kant's dictate that one should not use individuals purely as a means to the ends of others. This is contrary to the dignity of the individual. Kant himself stated 'To deprive oneself of an integral part or organ (to maim oneself) – for example, to give away or sell a tooth to be transplanted into another's mouth, or to have oneself castrated in order to get an easier livelihood as a singer, and so forth – are ways of partially murdering oneself'.[61] Kant did not, of course, contemplate living organ donation, although the above quotation may suggest that he would not have allowed such a measure even to save another's life.[62] However, although he required that any such actions be done to discharge one's duties to oneself or others, he allowed for the removal of diseased parts of the body constituting a threat to the whole, i.e. self-preservation, and thus may also have permitted losses which do not wholly destroy the person's integrity as an embodied integrated self, e.g. a kidney (although not a heart or liver), for the benefit of *others*.[63]

The Nuffield Council on Bioethics Working Party Report, *Human Tissue: Ethical and Legal Issues*, suggested that the avoidance and limitation of injury are basic requirements for the ethically acceptable use of human tissue, and that consent *per se* cannot render such actions legitimate.[64] 'Injury' was said to occur where action destroys, damages, or degrades, but must be viewed in context. Procedures which might otherwise be seen as injurious may instead perhaps be viewed as avoiding or limiting injury and so *reflective of* respect for human lives and bodies. The Report asserted that many activities that are not themselves therapeutic nevertheless contribute, either *directly* or *indirectly*, to therapeutic ends, including

---

[59] See M. Cherry, *Kidney for Sale by Owner: Human Organs, Transplantation, and the Market* (Washington, DC: Georgetown University Press, 2005), pp. 118 and 125 [Cherry, *Kidney for Sale by Owner*].

[60] Address to the Society for Organ Sharing, see (1991) 23(5) *Transplantation Proceedings* 17.

[61] I. Kant, 'The Metaphysics of Morals' (1797), in M. Gregor (ed.), *Practical Philosophy* (Cambridge University Press, 1996) 547–8.

[62] He considered that as bodies are part of our selves, to will their own destruction is to use life to produce lifelessness, a contradictory end; see I. Kant, *Lectures on Ethics* (trans. L. Infield) (New York: Harper Row, 1963), pp. 147–8. However, imperfect obligations render such actions permissible even if not mandatory.

[63] See Cherry, *Kidney for Sale by Owner*, p. 136. See also C. Cohen, 'Selling bits and pieces of humans to make babies: *The Gift of the Magi* revisited' (1999) 24(3) *Journal of Medicine and Philosophy* 288 at 293.

[64] Nuffield Council Working Party, *Human Tissue: Ethical and Legal Issues*, Nuffield Council on Bioethics, 1995, paras. 6.4–6.16.

'archiving human tissue, with the understanding that archived tissue might later be used for follow-up treatment of the same patient, for follow-up studies, for medical training, for medical audit purposes, for scientific education or for certain sorts of medical and scientific research'.[65] This recognises the potential legitimacy of *donation* for both transplantation and research.

## The eye of the beholder

Elliott argues that no matter how laudable the 'sacrifice', clinicians as moral agents should not necessarily endorse 'the sacrifice' as this suggests that the recipient's interests are being valued above those of the donor.[66] But this would surely depend upon the extent of the sacrifice. We would not, for instance, presumably reject very minimal sacrifices such as blood donations. Pattinson notes that one of the central issues here relates to whether we owe duties to ourselves,[67] and that virtue theorists may be increasingly uneasy with self-sacrifice proportionately to the degree of risk involved; potentially representing a flaw in one's moral character.[68] But not only is the very notion of duty to selves highly contentious and disputed in itself, but again very much depends upon the degree of risk/harm involved.

Spital considers that the clinician must be convinced that the donor as well as the recipient will benefit from the donation, a view shared by the National Health and Medical Research Council of Australia and the Law Reform Commission of Canada.[69] Whilst the assessment of net benefit (i.e. whether 'the risk is worth it') is apparently, as far as Spital is concerned, for the donor to weigh, and takes into account spiritual and emotional, and not merely clinical, considerations, such an assessment should be taken as bound up in the autonomous decision to donate rather than being an independent evaluation for the clinician

---

[65] *Ibid.*, at para. 6.13.
[66] C. Elliott, 'Constraints and heroes' (1992) 6 *Bioethics* 1 at 9. See also C. Elliott, 'Doing harm: Living organ donors, clinical research and *The Tenth Man*' (1995) 21 *Journal of Medical Ethics* 91.
[67] Whilst Kant considered that we do owe such duties, as our bodies are part of our 'selves', such issues are extremely contentious; see S. Kagan, *Normative Ethics* (Boulder, CO: Westview Press, 1998), pp. 145–52.
[68] S. Pattinson, *Medical Law and Ethics* (London: Thomson/Sweet & Maxwell, 2006), p. 442.
[69] *Organ and Tissue Donation By Living Donors: Guidelines for Ethical Practice for Health Professionals*, National Health and Medical Research Council, 2007, Canberra at 6 [*Organ and Tissue Donation By Living Donors*]; Law Reform Commission of Canada, *Procurement and Transfer of Human Tissues and Organs*, Working Paper 66, Ottawa, LRC, 1992 at 47.

to make.[70] Such a criterion seems unreasonably paternalistic bearing in mind the private and subjective nature of such a determination,[71] assuming the validity of the donor's consent to donate and limits on the degree of permissible risk which a donor may take. Nevertheless, taken as a whole, weighing the anticipated balance of risks and benefits as between the donor and the recipient, there should be an *overall* anticipated net benefit.[72] This equation will of course vary with each case, but non-renal donation offers the greatest benefit as well the risks of the greatest harm, so that the most risky procedures also promise the greatest reward. The latter might appear to be no more than a utilitarian justification, but this would be to ignore the independent moral force of the donor's interests in the fortunes of others in their own right, wrapped up in his/her consent. It has been urged that we should try systematically to meet people's demands and not just what we perceive as their needs in this sphere.[73] However, a greater moral claim to donate may be recognised where a close relationship exists between the parties, e.g. parents, in so far as the inability to donate may frustrate a person's typical and substantial interest in his or her relative's well-being.[74]

## Legal ceilings

By virtue of the inherent risks and lack of intrinsic (clinical) benefit to donors, it is entirely appropriate that the Human Tissue Act 2004 – the first piece of domestic UK legislation to directly address the legality of LDT – states that it is 'illegal unless …',[75] as does the Human Tissue (Scotland) Act 2006. But whilst such legislation provides for the regulation and monitoring of living donations and contains proscriptions on commercial reward, the limits of permissible donation *per se* are governed by the general law. The common law, however, remains vague.

---

[70] A. Spital, 'Donor benefit is the key to justified living organ donation' (2004) 13 *Cambridge Quarterly of Healthcare Ethics* 105.

[71] See F. Kamm, *Morality, Mortality. Volume 1* (Oxford University Press, 1993), p. 226.

[72] Such a balancing exercise can be seen to be mandated under Dutch law; see section 3, Law of 24 May 1996.

[73] M. Rohaninejad and S. Mohammadi, 'Chain exchange transplantation: Could the pool of organs be expanded through donation by transplanted living cases?' (2002) 34 *Transplantation Proceedings* 3045 at 3046.

[74] Ross, 'All donations should not be treated equally' at 448.

[75] Section 33. The 1989 Act was silent as regards the legality of living organ donation *per se*, but in stating that non-genetically related donors could lawfully donate subject to the approval of ULTRA, it clearly *inferred* that genetically related donations meeting common law conditions were lawful.

The Law Commission in its Consultation Paper, *Consent in the Criminal Law*, issued in 1995, stated 'Whatever the true legal analysis, there can be no doubt that, once a valid consent has been forthcoming, English law now treats as "lawful" operative procedures designed to remove regenerative tissue, and also non-regenerative tissue that is not essential for life'.[76] No explicit rationale or supporting argument is provided for this fairly liberal assertion, though. Whilst it appears to reflect current practice, it does not allude to the issue of risk in itself at all. Whilst the removal of regenerative material such as part of a liver may be legitimate, this must surely depend upon the percentage of liver taken and the donor's remaining reserve.[77] In most other jurisdictions, statute law contains a constraint relating to maximum anticipated risk/harm, typically a proscription upon procedures with the potential for serious harm, apart from risks relating to the organ removal itself.[78] Globally speaking, the 'bar' nevertheless appears to be lifting incrementally in terms of acceptable risk. Although societies would not yet accept donation of *both* of 'paired' organs or whole vital organs, the ethical and legal ceiling of living organ donation is uncertain.[79]

A criminal offence may be committed with respect to a living person who has consented to such activity, where bodily harm is caused.[80] Whilst consent may prevent any wrong resulting as between those parties it does not imply that there is no other wrong/harm caused.[81] Bergelson states 'if harm were only violation of rights, then consent, being a waiver of rights, would defeat it. Like a few other scholars, I conclude that we need a broader theory of harm and wrongfulness not limited to the violation of one's rights but encompassing other aspects of people's humanity as well, first and foremost human dignity.'[82] She adds 'by protecting the victim's dignity from most egregious harm, the rule would guard our collective

---

[76] Law Commission, *Consent in the Criminal Law*, Consultation Paper No.139, 1995, HMSO, para. 8.32.

[77] See 'The Ethics Statement of the Vancouver Forum on the Live Lung, Liver, Pancreas, and Intestine Donor' (2006) 81(10) *Transplantation* 1386.

[78] See, e.g., section 8(1)-(2), German Law of 5 November 1997. Article 11 of the Additional Council of Europe Protocol states that the removal must not be carried out if there is a serious risk to the life or health of the donor.

[79] One response is to argue that such choices are not autonomous. However, there is no evidence to support such an assumption. Moreover, protective mechanisms, such as exist *in situ* in the UK and Germany would arguably 'screen out' such cases.

[80] See *R* v. *Brown* [1994] AC 212 (HL).

[81] R. Brownsword, 'The cult of consent: fixation and fallacy' (2004) 15(2) *King's College Law Journal* 223 at 240.

[82] V. Bergelson, 'The right to be hurt. Testing the boundaries of consent', at http://law.bepress.com/rutgersnewarklwps/fp/art37 at 90.

interest in preserving humanity'.[83] This reflects the notion of *public* harm discussed in chapter 4.


### Sacrifice!

Scheper-Hughes alleges that there are 'dimensions of family sacrifice, betrayal and coercion hidden within both forms of living donation, related and commercialized',[84] although this is refuted by most commentators.[85] She remarks upon the burden of the debt owed to the donor, and the fact that the donor may come to 'lord it over' the recipient post-transplant, thus casting doubt upon 'the gift' of organ donation itself. These assertions relate to pre- and post-transplantation pressures, the former generating scepticism as to the validity of any consent given. It is frequently argued that potential related donors are unable in any event to give a legitimate voluntary consent in the light of the suffering of their close relative, such as one of their children, i.e. it is not a free choice.[86] But the notion that in order to be autonomous a consent must be given free from circumstantial pressure is spurious. It would rule out a whole host of everyday 'tragic choices' which we accept without question. Nonetheless, pressure *can* undermine choices. Some allege that even societal or cultural expectations may emasculate what would otherwise be a voluntary choice. The expectation that wives in parts of Asia should do anything necessary to support and help their spouses might perhaps be seen as an instance of such coercive pressure.[87] Indeed, Scheper-Hughes has commented unfavourably upon the gender bias in renal donation generally. But role expectations may be entirely congruous with one's own personal expectations or life plans, internalised without conflict, and thus may not be 'controlling' at all.[88] Sometimes the dichotomy has been drawn between external

---

[83] *Ibid.*, at 6.

[84] Scheper-Hughes, 'The tyranny of the gift' at 509.

[85] See B. Kaplan and R. Williams, 'Organ donation: The gift, the weight and the tyranny of good acts' (2007) 7 *American Journal of Transplantation* 497 at 498 and B. Hippen and J. Taylor, 'In defense of transplantation: A reply to Nancy Scheper-Hughes' (2007) 7 *American Journal of Transplantation* 1695 at 1695–6.

[86] E.g. A. Forsberg, M. Nilsson, M. Krantz and M. Olausson, 'The essence of living parental liver donation – donors' lived experiences of donation to their children' (2004) 8 *Pediatric Transplantation* 372.

[87] See, e.g., M. Mani, 'The argument against the unrelated live donor', in C. Kjellstrand and J. Dossetor (eds.), *Ethical Problems in Dialysis and Transplantation* (Dordrecht: Kluwer, 1992) 163 at 167.

[88] See also M. Morley, 'Increasing the supply of organs for transplantation through paired organ exchanges' (2003) 21 *Yale Law and Policy Review* 221 at 250. There is considerable

and internal pressure.[89] But should the emphasis instead be upon *dissonance*? Some external pressures may be wholly resistible by the specific prospective donor yet some internal conflicts unmanageable. There is a need to screen for what lawyers refer to as undue influence,[90] unconscious internal neurotic conflicts and psychopathology.[91] Ambivalence is also a primary indicator of poor post-donation donor outcomes.[92]

Strathern has observed that 'Gifts between persons can make statements about relationships'.[93] Crombie and Franklin's ethnographic research revealed that genealogical relationships *per se* (other than parents) did not suffice to indicate who would be likely to offer to donate an organ nor when dissonance would be revealed in the donation decision, but nevertheless found that certain relationships are 'pointers' to potential problems, e.g. some siblings, especially those who have their own families through marriage.[94] As regards relationships, the only general rule is that there are no general rules, and each individual relationship is unique. This draws attention to the need for screening, assessment and psychosocial support mechanisms both before and after surgery, rather than blanket prohibitions. A psychosocial as well as medical evaluation is recommended by expert consensus statements, and by most national transplantation societies,[95] comprising two elements: (1) assessment of the psychological

---

evidence that the decision to donate is frequently a shared family decision, sometimes co-ordinated by one pivotal family member. See B. Walton-Moss, L. Boulware, M. Cooper, L. Taylor, K. Dane and M. Nolan, 'Prospective pilot study of living kidney donor decision-making and outcomes' (2007) 21 *Clinical Transplantation* 86. Studies have shown no difference in psychosocial profiles of male and female kidney donors; see M. Achille, J. Soos, M. Fortin, M. Paquet and M. Hebert, 'Differences in psychosocial profiles between men and women living kidney donors' (2007) 21 *Clinical Transplantation* 314.

89  See, e.g., R. Sells, 'Voluntarism of consent in both related and unrelated living organ donation', in W. Land and J. Dossetor (eds.), *Organ Replacement Therapy: Ethics, Justice, Commerce* (Berlin: Springer-Verlag, 1991) 18 at 21.

90  See *Re T (Adult: Refusal of Treatment)* [1993] Fam. 95 (CA).

91  Y. Erim, M. Malago, C. Valentin-Gamazo, W. Senf and C. Broelsch, 'Guidelines for the psychosomatic evaluation of living liver donors: Analysis of donor exclusion' (2003) 35 *Transplantation Proceedings* 909 at 910 [Erim *et al.*, 'Guidelines for the psychosomatic evaluation'].

92  See G. Switzer, M. Dew and R. Twillman, 'Psychosocial issues in living organ donation', in P. Trzepacz and A. Dimatini (eds.), *The Transplant Patient: Biological, Psychiatric and Ethical Issues in Organ Transplantation* (Cambridge University Press, 2000) 42 at 50.

93  M. Strathern, *The Gender of the Gift* (Berkeley, CA: University of California Press, 1998), p. 171.

94  A. Crombie and P. Franklin, 'Family issues implicit in living donation' (2006) 11(2) *Mortality* 196 at 209.

95  See 'Consensus statement on the live organ donor' (2000) 284(22) *Journal of the American Medical Association* 2919 at 2922, where it is recommended that this be carried out by a trained mental health professional, and 'The consensus statement of the Amsterdam Forum on the Care of the Live Kidney Donor' (2004) 78(4) *Transplantation* 491, issued by the Ethics Committee of the Transplantation Society.

stability of the potential donor, and (2) verification of informed and voluntary consent.[96] The vetting of *all* living organ donations – by way of interview by an independent assessor who reports to the HTA – is to be welcomed despite falling short of a full psychosocial evaluation (it is principally testing for evidence of reward, duress, or coercion, difficulties of communication, and decision-making capacity and understanding).[97]

Crombie and Franklin also revealed that some relationships function less than ideally after the event and that some do feel the subsequent burden of being the recipient of a 'gift of life', e.g. a duty to look after themselves to avoid 'wasting' the organ, etc.[98] Although their work highlighted the need for psychosocial support post-donation, the 'dysfunctional' examples revealed by their empirical study are the exception, and do not permeate the more typical types of donation to any significant degree. Despite the concerns, studies show that, with limited exceptions, donors of both kidneys and parts of livers were glad to have donated and experienced no regret, even where the decision itself generated considerable stress at the time.[99]

## Altruistic strangers: a once impenetrable taboo[100]

It is ironic to note that it is the very closeness of the relationship which is the source of concern in the previous section, yet stranger donations generate doubts precisely because of the *absence* of any such relationship. Living individuals who offer to donate organs to strangers have typically been regarded with scepticism and mistrust.[101] As Matas states 'The

---

[96] Erim *et al.*, 'Guidelines for the psychosomatic evaluation'.

[97] Between September 2006 and August 2008, 1,717 Independent Assessor reports were submitted, 1,714 of which had been approved; Independent Assessor bulletin Issue 11, 2008, HTA.

[98] Their UK research revealed post-operative tensions relating to reciprocity and effects on the subsequent relationship in a minority of donor/recipient sibling pairs and in the case of some adolescents receiving from a parent; see P. Franklin and A. Crombie, 'Decisions about living kidney donation: A family and professional perspective', in M. Sque and S. Payne (eds.), *Organ and Tissue Donation: An Evidence Base for Practice* (Maidenhead: Open University Press, 2007) 138 and C. Eggeling, 'Psychosocial consequences of transplantation for the counsellor and the donor' (1999) 4 *British Journal of Renal Medicine* 21. In the US, Simmons *et al.* reported that although feelings of guilt about the inability to reciprocate did occasionally arise, most had no major difficulties with accepting the gift; see R. Simmons, G. Klein and R. Simmons, *Gift of Life: The Effect of Organ Transplantation on Individual, Family and Societal Dynamic* (Chichester: Wiley, 1977).

[99] See, e.g., *Questioning Attitudes to Living Donor Transplantation*, EUROTOLD, 1997 and Spital and Jacobs, 'The beauty' at 436.

[100] As described in R. Gohh, P. Morrissey, P. Madras and A. Monaco, 'Controversies in organ donation: The altruistic living donor' (2001) 16 *Nephrology Dialysis Transplant* 619 at 619.

[101] See M. Evans, 'Organ donations should not be restricted to relatives' (1989) 15 *Journal of Medical Ethics* 17. A survey of US renal centres in 1994 found that only 15 per cent of

mindset that it was wrong for someone to take the risk of donor nephrectomy without knowing the recipient became entrenched'.[102] However, this intuition was founded on little or no reliable empirical data. Indeed, even early evidence suggested that it was a misinformed view.[103] A more recent study carried out in British Columbia using psychopathological and personality tests on unsolicited anonymous kidney donors found that twenty-one of the forty-three participants passed the stringent criteria to be considered potential living anonymous donors.[104] There is therefore empirical evidence to support the view that, far from being a vulnerable population, such individuals are very self-directed and without psychopathology.[105] As Sadler remarked 'Here, then, were a group of very fine human beings'.[106] Maybe, then, because we are not able to aspire to such charitable standards and ideals ourselves, we mistrust those who do?

Indeed, and by contrast with professional attitudes, public opinion has been consistently sympathetic and supportive. A survey of the US public revealed that even in 1988 70 per cent of respondents would support living anonymous donation,[107] and a more recent survey revealed that one in four Americans declared themselves willing to donate a kidney or part of another organ to a stranger.[108] Although many contemporary clinicians consider a more individualised and less dogmatic posture appropriate, some transplant centres are still not prepared to countenance altruistic

centres would even consider using such donors; see A. Spital, 'Unrelated living kidney donors: An update of attitudes and use among U.S. transplant centres' (1994) 57 *Transplantation* 1722.

[102] A. Matas, C. Jacobs, J. Kahn and C. Garvey, 'Nondirected kidney donation at the University of Minnesota', in T. Gutmann, A. Daar, R. Sells and W. Land (eds.), *Ethical, Legal, and Social Issues in Organ Transplantation* (Lengerich: Pabst Publishing, 2004) 195 at 195. Hamburger and Crosnier remarked nearly forty years ago that 'individuals who … [offer] to donate a kidney to a prospective recipient to whom they are not connected by any kind of emotional tie are frequently pathologic by psychiatric criteria'; see J. Hamburger *et al.*, *Renal Transplantation: Theory and Practice* (Baltimore, MD: Williams & Williams, 1972), p. 239.

[103] See, e.g., H. Sadler *et al.*, 'The living, genetically unrelated, kidney donor' (1971) 3 *Seminars in Psychiatry* 86.

[104] A. Henderson, M. Landholt, M. McDonald, W. Barrable, J. Soos, W. Gourlay, C. Allison and D. Landsberg, 'The living anonymous kidney donor: Lunatic or saint?' (2003) 3 *American Journal of Transplantation* 203 [Henderson *et al.*, 'The living anonymous kidney donor'].

[105] M. Jendrisak *et al.*, 'Altruistic living donors: Evaluation for nondirected kidney or liver donation' (2006) 6 *American Journal of Transplantation* 115 [Jendrisak *et al.*, 'Altruistic living donors'].

[106] See A. Spital, 'Increasing the pool of transplantable kidneys through unrelated living donors and living donor paired exchanges' (2005) 18(6) *Seminars in Dialysis* 469 at 470.

[107] A. Spital and M. Spital, 'Living kidney donation: Attitudes outside the transplant center' (1988) 148 *Archives of Internal Medicine* 1077.

[108] National Kidney Foundation Press Release June 22 2000, at www.kidney.org/general/news/strangers.cfm. See also Jendrisak *et al.*, 'Altruistic living donors' at 119.

donation, although it is growing in acceptance.[109] Programmes have recently been developed in North America, the UK, the Netherlands (Rotterdam), New Zealand (Christchurch) and Sweden (Malmö), with no major problems reported thus far. In the UK, the HTA has so far approved twenty-five such procedures.[110]

Legal regimes in some jurisdictions nevertheless remain unaccommodating to such donations by virtue of the absence of any pre-existing genetic or emotional relationship, e.g. France, Germany, Hungary and Portugal.[111] Indeed, in Bavaria a surgeon was prosecuted in 1996 for removing a kidney from another surgeon, one Professor Hoyer, who wished to donate a kidney to a stranger in need.[112] Many laws are simply silent on this issue, though, as in the US, where the matter is left to the discretion of individual centres. In the UK such donations have never been illegal as such, but the relevant regulatory agency, ULTRA, did not approve any prior to its functions being ceded to the HTA consequent to the passing of the Human Tissue Act 2004. Where the parties were not previously known to each other there is a greater prospect of a commercial motivation being involved which, amongst other things, underpinned the policy embedded in the earlier Human Organ Transplants Act 1989.[113] The 2004 Act and the accompanying Codes of Practice, by contrast, anticipate stranger donations and provide for a process of enhanced prospective independent review. Regulations passed under the Act provide that where the donor is not genetically related to, or known to, the intended recipient, the HTA's decision on whether to permit such a procedure must be made by a panel of no fewer than three members of the Authority.[114]

Stranger donations are regularly dubbed 'altruistic donations'. Typical linguistic usage emphasises the other-regarding or 'selfless' nature of

---

[109] M. Crowley-Matoka and G. Switzer, 'Nondirected living donation: A survey of current trends and practices' (2005) 79(5) *Transplantation* 515.

[110] See Human Tissue Authority, at www.hta.gov.uk/contentdisplay.cfm?widcall/= customwidgets.content_view-l@cit_id=634. See also http://news.bbc.co.uk/2/hi/uk_news/ england/cornwall/7144418.stm.

[111] Law No. 94–654 of 29 July 1994, Article L. 671–3 as amended by Law 2004–800 of 6 August 2004; Portugal Law No. 12/93. In India it appears that patients would prefer to purchase an organ from a stranger than have a relative donate an organ to them; see L. Cohen, 'Where it hurts. Indian material for an ethics of organ transplantation' (1999) 128 *Daedalus* 135. The Council of Europe asserts that States may legitimately either permit or prohibit altruistic donation, but if permitting should have an independent mechanism of approval; see Resolution CM/RES(2008)6, 2008.

[112] Although this was prior to the implementation of the legislation passed in November 1997 the legal position in Germany as regards strangers remains unchanged.

[113] See Price, *Legal and Ethical Aspects*, pp. 314–33.

[114] Human Tissue Act 2004 (Persons who Lack Capacity to Consent and Transplants) Regulations 2006 SI 2006 No. 1659, reg. 12(1), (4) and (5).

altruistic acts. Ironically it is the *lack* of obvious personal advantage that is the source of much scepticism here, despite such individuals being the *most altruistic* donors of all. Wright observes 'Some argue that ALD [anonymous living organ donation] provides the donor with little benefit and thus, cannot justify the potential harm to the donor'.[115] It is perhaps odd that in this connection only psychological or ethical egoism are regarded as legitimately able to underpin such decisions. This runs counter to the general rhetoric. In any event we do not typically scrutinise reasons for action extremely closely in this context. Contrariwise, whilst we might generally *prefer* selflessness in the normal related donation context we do not ordinarily reject donation merely on account of selfish motives.[116] These sceptics fail to appreciate that the (psychological) benefit of altruistic donation for the donor is the manifestation of altruism itself.[117] Nonetheless, those observers who argue that it is the special relationship and responsibility between the parties that generally justifies consensual organ donation between living individuals have difficulties with the notion of stranger donation.[118] It is not clear, though, why perceived imperatives to those in need should be wholly circumscribed by genetic or familial relationship.[119]

Some argue that strangers should not be permitted to take the same risks as family members, or at least that stricter criteria should apply.[120] Indeed, the Committee of Ministers of the Council of Europe has recently recommended that adult-to-adult living donor liver transplants be restricted to donors and recipients who have a close personal relationship as required and defined by law.[121] Only a small percentage of centres perform living liver donation between strangers. According to UNOS figures, up to the end of 2006, 402 anonymous living kidney donations in the US had occurred compared with only 23 living anonymous liver

---

[115] L. Wright, abstract, 'Of altruists and egoists: Anonymous living organ donations', Programme, Conference: Organ Transplantation: Ethical, Legal and Psychological Aspects, 1 April 2007, section 38 [Wright, 'Of altruists']

[116] Den Hartogh observes that living donors have extremely mixed motives and rejects the need to find a particular motive for donation on the basis of the intrusiveness of the necessary preceding enquiry; see *Farewell to Non-commitment* at 85. Parents and spouses typically have self-regarding as well as other-regarding concerns bound up in donation decisions.

[117] See Wright, 'Of altruists'.

[118] See, e.g., Den Hartogh, *Farewell to Non-Commitment* at 85. He would allow this only where a situation of urgency exists as regards the availability of organs for transplant.

[119] See Henderson *et al.*, 'The living anonymous kidney donor'.

[120] L. Ross, 'Solid organ donation between strangers' (2002) 30 *Journal of Law, Medicine and Ethics* 440 [Ross, 'Solid organ donation between strangers'].

[121] Resolution of the Committee of Ministers of the Council of Europe on Adult-to-Adult Living Donor Liver Transplantation CM/RES(2008)4, March 2006, para. 4b.

donations.[122] But in so far as many of these same centres carry out living *related* liver transplants the question arises why strangers should not be able to take similar risks. As well as aiming to avoid potential commercial dealings, this view appears to be founded upon the notion that family members have greater moral obligations to loved ones, i.e. they have a *prima facie* moral obligation to donate, and have a greater interest in the fate of their nearest and dearest.[123] However, *all* living organ donation is arguably morally supererogatory rather than obligatory, even between close relatives. There may be a stronger claim to be permitted to donate, but no exclusive liberty to donate.[124]

It is wholly appropriate for stranger donors to be subject to rigorous psychological screening and assessment, though. There is a moral obligation to safeguard donors' psychological as well as physical health by careful work-up. The HTA recommends that early mental health assessment take place to ensure that there is no relevant psychiatric or psychological illness, to establish competence to consent and to explore *suspect* motivations.[125] In the US also, a full psychosocial and psychological evaluation is carried out in all cases of non-directed living donation. By contrast, in both the UK and the US, a *full* evaluation is generally only carried out in *problematic* instances of living related donation, i.e. where there are specific concerns about cognitive deficits or other psychological risk factors.[126] A consensus conference held in the US in 2006 stressed the individual nature of each donation, the uniqueness of the motivational factors for donation and the psychosocial and protective factors related to living anonymous kidney donors.[127] It recommended that prospective donors be rejected where, *inter alia*, they have unrealistic or ulterior

---

[122] Outcomes have generally been good for both donors and recipients, although strict donor selection is advised; see L. Wright, K. Ross, S. Abbey, G. Levy and D. Grant, 'Living anonymous liver donation: Case report and ethical justification' (2007) 7 *American Journal of Transplantation* 1032 [Wright *et al.*, 'Living anonymous liver donation']. Even stranger lung lobe donations have sporadically occurred.

[123] See, e.g., Ross, 'Solid organ donation between strangers'.

[124] J. Kahn, 'Making the most of strangers' altruism' (2002) 30 *Journal of Law, Medicine and Ethics* 446.

[125] See    www.hta.gov.uk/transplantation/organ_donation/altruistic_donation.cfm    and www.uktransplant.org.uk?ukt/about_transplants/organ_allocation/kidney_(renal)living_donation/ altruistro_nondirected_donation.jsp.

[126] A. Matas, C. Jacobs, C. Garvey and D. Roman, 'Nondirected living donors', in R. Gaston and J. Wadstrom (eds.), *Living Donor Kidney Transplantation: Current Practices, Emerging Trends and Evolving Challenges* (London: Taylor & Francis, 2005) 151.

[127] M. Dew, C. Jacobs, S. Jowsey, R. Hanto, C. Miller and F. Delmonico, 'Guidelines for the psychosocial evaluation of living unrelated kidney donors in the United States' (2007) 7 *American Journal of Transplantation* 1. It mandated psychosocial evaluation in every case.

motives, such as individual or societal approval, compensation, atonement, redemption, or media attention.[128]

In the UK and most other locations, allocation is entirely *non-directed* in accordance with pre-determined (usually national) protocols.[129] In the US it is generally accepted that the normal UNOS allocation criteria should govern allocation but that the kidney should go first to the programme's list, rather than a regional or national list.[130] The idea that the local centre should be able to allocate such organs entirely at their own discretion is now regarded as running counter to principles of justice linked to medical need and utility. Provided that anonymity is ensured, non-directedness helps to prevent potential coercion and commercial influence. However, in the US living donors are equally entitled to direct their donation to a *known* stranger recipient. UNOS takes the view that there is no proper role for the state in interfering in privately formed living relationships, whether with a private individual or a celebrity or whomever. Patients make contact with potential donors in a myriad of ways, often using the media or by way of dedicated websites such as *matchingdonors.com*.[131] However, there is considerable disquiet about donations established via the Internet, and the potential for ability to pay and to solicit organs to come to the fore.[132] Such solicitation is opposed by the American Society of Transplant Surgeons and the Australian Government, although supported by the American Medical Association (AMA) where others are not disadvantaged.[133]

[128] Wright *et al.*, 'Living anonymous liver donation'.
[129] In New Zealand they are applicable only to patients waiting in South Island.
[130] UNOS, Allocation of Organs from Non-Directed Living Donors, 2002. UNOS has stated that 'Living non-directed donation is truly a hybrid between cadaveric and living donation and these organs must be viewed as a unique national public resource'.
[131] See generally, C. Robertson, 'Organ advertising: Desperate patients solicit volunteers' (2005) 33 *Journal of Law, Medicine and Ethics* 170.
[132] See 'Internet kidney op gets go ahead', at http://news.bbc.co.uk/2/low/americas/3758392.stm. The Dutch Minister for Health, Welfare and Sport has apparently endorsed such donations but no Dutch transplant centre currently permits them; see Den Hartogh, *Farewell to Non-commitment* at 82.
[133] See American Society of Transplant Surgeons, 'Statement on Solicitation of Donor Organs', January 2005, at www.asts.org/donorsolicitation.cfm; Australian Government, *Organ and Tissue Donation By Living Donors* at 15; Council on Ethical and Judicial Affairs of the American Medical Association, 'Transplantation of Organs from Living Donors', Report 5–A–05. Conditional donation is deemed to be unacceptable by UNOS, however. See generally R. Truog, 'The ethics of organ donation by living donors' (2005) 353(5) *New England Journal of Medicine* 444. Directed stranger donation may conceal implicit group discrimination, but see M. Hilhorst *et al.*, 'Altruistic living kidney donation challenges psychosocial research and policy: A response to previous articles' (2005) 79 *Transplantation* 1470; A. Spital, 'Must kidney donation by living strangers be nondirected?' (2001) 72 *Transplantation* 966; and M. Hilhorst, 'Directed altruistic living organ donation: Partial but not unfair' (2005) 8 *Ethical Theory and Moral Practice* 197.

## Swaps?

Swap, paired, exchange or pooled-type living donation arrangements were first pioneered in 1991 (although the idea of a general 'pool' was suggested by Rapaport as early as 1986).[134] They are designed to meet the problem created where a donor, perhaps a family member or friend, is prepared to donate a kidney to the patient but is unable to do so either because of ABO blood or human leukocyte antigen (HLA) incompatibility, or on account of positive cross-matches, and another pair are in the same predicament, but the donor in one pair *is* a suitable donor for the recipient in the other pair, and vice versa. In South Korea numerous pairs have been linked together in a chain to maximise potential donative ability; – so-called 'swap-around' schemes – [135] and elsewhere as many as six pairings have been simultaneously carried out.[136] There is considerable potential in such programmes which are now springing up all over, for instance in the Netherlands, the US, Switzerland, Canada, Australia, Romania and the UK,[137] although some centres are now able to routinely overcome blood incompatibility obstacles.[138] In the Netherlands, all seven kidney transplant centres created a common national exchange programme in 2004. The UK also has a national programme and the first paired procedures have already taken place;[139] the first pooled transplants are anticipated shortly. Overall fifty such paired/pooled donations are expected to be performed annually. They are underpinned by the infrastructure established under the 2004 Act necessitating enhanced review, involving the requirement for approval by a panel of HTA

[134] F. Rapaport, 'The case for a living emotionally related international kidney donor exchange registry' (1986) 18(Supp 2) *Transplantation Proceedings* 5.

[135] See K. Park and J. Lee, 'Paired-exchange in living donor kidney transplantation', in R. Gaston and J. Wadstrom (eds.), *Living Donor Kidney Transplantation: Current Practices, Emerging Trends and Evolving Challenges* (London: Taylor & Francis, 2005) 143 [Park and Lee, 'Paired-exchange']. See also F. McLellan, 'US surgeons do first "triple swap" kidney transplantation' (2003) 362 *The Lancet* 456.

[136] Six recipients received kidneys from six donors at the Johns Hopkins Hospital in Maryland; see *The Times*, 10 April 2008.

[137] See E. Woodle, R. Boardman, A. Bohnengal and K. Downing, 'Influence of educational programmes on perceived barriers toward living donor kidney exchange programmes' (2005) 37 *Transplantation Proceedings* 602.

[138] There is now the possibility of ABO incompatible living donors being able to donate to an intended recipient as a result of desensitisation, i.e. the removal of isoagglutinin and HLA antibodies, although this is not yet widely available. See Y. Futagawa and P. Terasaki, 'ABO incompatible kidney transplantation – an analysis of UNOS Registry data' (2005) 19 *Clinical Transplantation* 122. Moreover, blood conversion techniques are being developed. See 'Blood conversion breakthrough could be life-saver for thousands', *The Times*, 2 April 2007. It may soon be possible to routinely manufacture blood of different types from stem cells; see *The Times*, 20 August 2008.

[139] See 'Couples swap kidneys in UK first', at http://news.bbc.co.uk/1/hi/health/7025448.stm.

members. Although there are no laws impeding such arrangements in either the UK or the US, some countries have inhibiting laws insisting upon an existing genetic or emotional relationship, e.g. in Portugal, Poland and France,[140] and there are similar limitations across Australia with the exception of Western Australia.[141] In Germany only genetically or emotionally related donors are permitted to donate, although individual cases have been approved by judicial ruling.[142]

It is predicted that in the US 3,500 potential living donors are excluded per annum by virtue of blood type incompatibility or positive cross-match.[143] In the UK, evidence from thirteen centres between 2003 and 2005 found that 46 per cent of potential pairs were ABO blood group incompatible.[144] To achieve maximum effect a certain critical mass is needed. It is reported that in the US no paired donation programme had achieved more than twenty donor/recipient pairings up to 2005, thus limiting the potential benefit of such schemes. Moreover, blood group O type recipients will rarely be able to avail themselves of the benefit of such paired or swap arrangements as they require a blood group O donor, whereas O donors are potentially universal donors for *all* patients with end-stage renal disease. The overwhelming preponderance of living exchanges involve blood group O recipients with incompatible donors. Because of the potential for disadvantaging O blood group recipients, it has been decided in the UK to match only O blood group donors with O blood group recipients.[145]

There are various concerns relating to such exchanges, including ensuring that proper informed consent has been given in view of the additional clinical and ethical complexity of the procedure and as to the

---

[140] French law allows spouses and emotionally related persons to donate, but not altruistic strangers.

[141] See *Organ and Tissue Donation By Living Donors* at 51. One or two donations of this type have already been performed there.

[142] The first crossover transplant was performed in Hamburg and Essen after a favourable ruling by the Federal Social Court; see A. Tuffs, 'Surgeons perform Germany's first crossover kidney transplantation' (2005) 331 *British Medical Journal* 798. This decision bears out Schreiber's comment that 'there are arguments that a close personal link can develop between unmatched pairs of living donors and recipients after the development of a need for transplantation'; see H.-L. Schreiber, 'Present and future legal aspects of living donor transplantation' (2003) 35 *Transplantation Proceedings* 903 at 903.

[143] D. Segev, S. Gentry, J. Malancon and R. Montgomery, 'Characterisation of waiting times in a simulation of kidney paired donation' (2005) 5 *American Journal of Transplantation* 2448.

[144] R. Johnson, J. Blackwell, L. Burnapp, D. Pugh, S. Fuggle and C. Rudge, 'The potential for paired living kidney donation in the UK', at http://uktransplant.org.uk/ukt/statistics/presentations/pdfs/march_06/Paired_donation.pdf.

[145] See UK Transplant, 'Arrangements for paired/pooled living kidney donation', at www.uktransplant.org.uk/ukt/about_transplants/organ_allocation/kidney.

voluntariness of the consent to donate. Ross notes that 'Paired exchanges eliminate many of the medical excuses that traditionally were available to hesitant donors'.[146] Veatch, however, argues that the provision of such excuses is not in any event the responsibility of the transplant team.[147] It is nonetheless important that donors are given maximum opportunity to withdraw, in so far as concerns about ambivalence are heightened in view of the inability to fall back on blood or tissue incompatibility as a reason for not proceeding.[148] Another potential issue arises if the procedures are not performed simultaneously, as otherwise the 'later' donor might then, after the other removal was performed, be tempted to 'back out'. Such concern can be largely met by 'carefully choreographed' (simultaneous) removal arrangements (as the *New York Times* described them),[149] at the same or different centres. Of course, such 'ideal' arrangements cannot always be attained, though. Moreover, there are concerns relating to privacy and confidentiality, especially if the pairs are treated at the same centre. Park notes that 'donor exchange must be managed carefully to avoid interfamilial conflicts'.[150] Under most exchange schemes, anonymity is maintained (as in the Netherlands), or at least operates as the default position. This will assist in avoiding friction between different pairings, especially where transplant outcomes are significantly at odds with each other. For this reason, some clinicians insist upon the same quality of kidney. Indeed, some potential recipients insist that their donor not be significantly older. There is also the possibility that one centre or group of professionals will be markedly superior to the other. Menikoff states 'One can only imagine the legal controversies that will take place as things go wrong, as they surely will in at least some of these transactions'.[151] Ross also notes that there is no data regarding the psychological benefit or regret experienced by direct versus (indirect) exchange donors.[152] However, in so far as the transplantation of one's loved one or friend has

---

[146] L. F. Ross, 'The ethical limits in expanding living donor transplantation' (2006) 16(2) *Kennedy Institute of Ethics Journal* 151 at 152 [Ross, 'The ethical limits'].

[147] R. Veatch, 'Organ exchanges: Fairness to the O-blood group' (2006) 6 *American Journal of Transplantation* 1 at 1 [Veatch, 'Organ exchanges'].

[148] A Dutch study showed that (forty-eight) donors did not experience any additional pressure to donate over and above the ordinary living donor control group; see L. Kranenburg *et al.*, 'The implementation of a kidney exchange program does not induce a need for additional psychosocial support' (2007) 20 *Transplant International* 432.

[149] D. Grady and A. O'Connor, 'The kidney swap: Adventures in saving lives', *New York Times*, 5 October 2004, D1.

[150] Park and Lee, 'Paired-exchange' at 145.

[151] J. Menikoff, 'Organ swapping' (1999) 29(6) *Hastings Center Report* 28 at 30 [Menikoff, 'Organ swapping'].

[152] L. F. Ross *et al.*, 'Ethics of a paired-kidney-exchange program' (1997) 336(24) *New England Journal of Medicine* 1752 at 1753.

been achieved, albeit indirectly, there is no compelling reason to believe that motivation would not be high beforehand, and feelings of regret would be expected to be rare afterwards.

There are other forms of living exchange arrangements which have greater moral and legal implications, though. So-called *unbalanced* exchanges have grown up in modest fashion, involving exchanges where the donor *could* have donated to the intended recipient (i.e. he or she was compatible to do so), but instead agreed to donate to another patient whose own donor was incompatible, allowing that other donor to donate to the original donor's intended recipient. In the absence of such a swap the second recipient would have to rely on receiving an organ via the ordinary deceased donor waitlist and thus obtains a significant benefit by being able to receive an organ immediately from a living donor. Ross comments that 'In this case, however, donor 2 is being asked to be "doubly altruistic" – not only to donate, but now to agree to donate to a stranger rather than to his intended, emotionally-related recipient'.[153] Whether it is permissible for transplant teams to raise the possibility of an unbalanced exchange with a donor who could have donated to his or her intended recipient is a tricky moral dilemma. The donor may feel pressure to agree (because of loyalty to the transplant team asking and the plight of the other patient) and is not being asked because it is of any benefit to the individual, in addition to which the complexity of the information relevant to the decision may arguably compromise the possibility of obtaining genuine informed consent. For these reasons, Ross amongst others maintains that such requests are coercive and that a transplant team cannot ethically invite such 'compatible' donors and recipients to participate in such an arrangement.[154] In the Netherlands this is indeed the prevalent national view. Moreover, with respect to Rapaport's vision, de Klerk *et al.* state 'The highest efficiency can be reached with one large crossover pool including all couples irrespective of blood type or cross-match. In our opinion, it is unrealistic and even unethical to persuade a compatible donor to donate to a large anonymous pool instead of directly to a relative or friend.'[155] But not only is this ostensibly to overstate the pressure placed on potential donors, it also overlooks the possibility of benefit to the donor's originally intended recipient.

If the recipient whose donor was compatible received an equally good donated organ, this would seemingly obviate the necessity for additional

---

[153] Ross, 'The ethical limits' at 158.    [154] *Ibid.*

[155] M. de Klerk, K. Keizer, F. Claas, M. Witvliet, B. Haase-Kromwijk and W. Weimar, 'The Dutch National Living Donor Kidney Exchange Program' (2005) 5 *American Journal of Transplantation* 2302 at 2305.

altruism on the donor's part. Spital regards such an equally advantageous exchange as both speculative and unlikely, thus diminishing the potential value of such a strategy.[156] Veatch, however, responds by saying that such mutual advantage is extremely plausible, with a younger or better matched donor, for instance.[157] Thus, it seems that in at least some instances *both* recipients would be advantaged by such an arrangement. The effect would also likely be that one O blood group patient would be removed from the waiting list. As a consequence Veatch asserts that it is morally inappropriate *not* to offer such an arrangement to suitable candidates. Indeed, he argues that many O donors would be extremely disgruntled if such an opportunity were not made available to them. A study conducted in the Netherlands found that around one-third (31 per cent) of living donor and recipient pairs would be willing to participate in such a scheme.[158]

Another novel type of exchange arrangement is so-called 'list-paired exchange' (LDLE), which has seemingly been practised to date only in the US,[159] although such procedures are currently in contemplation in the Netherlands. Where laws insist upon organ allocation according to medical need, there may be perceived to be a juridical impediment to such schemes, although many laws are silent as regards organ allocation criteria anyhow.[160] As for paired donation, the rationale for such schemes is the possibility of more patients benefiting from transplants. This strategy is potentially very suitable where a swap/paired arrangement cannot be established as the donor/recipient pairs are incompatible as a result of blood or (HLA) tissue type. The prospective living donor's kidney is instead given to the first compatible patient on the national waiting list, after which the donor's intended recipient receives the next suitable deceased donor kidney.

---

[156] A. Spital (letter), 'Veatch's proposal may not work' (2006) 6 *American Journal of Transplantation* 855 [Spital, 'Veatch's proposal'] .

[157] R. Veatch (letter), 'Why organ exchanges serve the interests of O-donors' (2006) 6 *American Journal of Transplantation* 856 [Veatch, 'Why organ exchanges'].

[158] L. Kranenburg *et al.*, 'One donor, two transplants: Willingness to participate in altruistically unbalanced exchange donation' (2006) 19 *Transplant International* 995.

[159] It was initially attempted only in UNOS Region 1.

[160] In the Netherlands, list exchanges are regarded as contravening Dutch law which requires allocation to be made according to medical criteria and waiting time; see Health Council of the Netherlands, Living Donor List Exchange: An addition to the Dutch living kidney donor programme?, The Hague, 2007, No. 2007/11 [Health Council of the Netherlands, Living Donor List Exchange]. See generally D. Price, 'Legal systems for organ distribution in Europe: Justice in allocation', in W. Weimar, M. Bos and J. Busschbach (eds.), *Organ Transplantation: Ethical, Legal, and Psychosocial Aspects* (Lengerich: Pabst Publishing, 2008) 163.

One principal argument against list exchanges is that the patient who will receive the first deceased donor kidney will now be the person who has an incompatible living donor rather than the one at the top of the waiting list. He/she will be prioritised by virtue of the availability of his/her willing living donor, i.e. queue jumping.[161] An additional specific problem also arises with patients with blood group O in the case of ABO-incompatible exchanges, based on blood group equity. Because living donors with blood group O are potentially compatible with *all* patients, most of those seeking a list exchange arrangement are blood group O recipients with a non-O donor. Therefore, this may cause blood group O patients on the waiting list to wait even longer than they otherwise would have done to be transplanted, as the pool of O kidneys available has been depleted even further. UNOS Region 1's experience showed that the twenty-one blood group O patients who would have received a kidney had an allocation priority not been in place were transplanted on average between seventy-six and eighty-three days later than they would otherwise have been. However, twenty-two more (living) donors were able to provide organs to end-stage renal disease patients.[162] A similar experience has been reported in Washington.[163] Such exchanges would be morally permissible, of course, if those who would be potentially disadvantaged by such arrangements were to consent to this additional burden. A study by Ackerman *et al.* revealed that 59 per cent of patients would consent to an additional wait (half of whom knew they were blood group O).[164] But it is generally maintained that such consensus would have to be almost overwhelming to ethically justify such a policy; an extremely unlikely contingency. As a consequence Ross supports ABO-compatible but *not* ABO-incompatible list exchanges.[165]

The usual justification for supporting list-paired schemes despite the potential impact on waiting blood group O patients is that the number of organs, and thus the number of transplants, would be increased. This utilitarian justification, however, conflicts with the normal egalitarian

---

[161] The Health Council in the Netherlands regarded such schemes as breaching both formal and material justice; *ibid.*, see www.gr.nl/samenvatting.php?ID=1521.

[162] P. Morrisey (letter), 'In support of list paired exchange' (2006) 6 *American Journal of Transplantation* 434.

[163] J. Gilbert, L. Brigham, D. Batty and R. Veatch, 'The nondirected living donor program: A model for cooperative donation, recovery and allocation of living donor kidneys' (2005) 5 *American Journal of Transplantation* 167.

[164] P. Ackerman, J. Thistlethwaite and L. Ross, 'Attitudes of minority patients with end-stage renal disease regarding ABO-incompatible list-paired exchanges' (2006) 6 *American Journal of Transplantation* 83. Just less than half of those in support would have endorsed a wait of more than six additional months.

[165] Ross, 'The ethical limits' at 162.

perspectives of appropriate organ distribution. Such arrangements will work to the detriment of the worst off (i.e. those at the top of the list are amongst the sickest and those who have waited the longest), and thus even the Rawlsian concept of the *maximin* would not apply in this context. Ross and Zenios remark that 'Justice as fairness only permits policy changes that benefit those who are worst off',[166] and recommend that such list paired exchanges should not be performed. Does it perhaps depend, though, upon whether the additional 'input' *greatly* exceeds the limited detriment meted out to certain unfortunate individuals? Whilst not exclusively, benefit and efficiency is an accepted emphasis in organ allocation. Indeed, in the US UNOS is obliged to take this factor into account by federal law. Veatch suggests that additional wait times of a month or less could be justified as a trade-off between utility and fairness.[167]

The Health Council of the Netherlands which reported on list exchange schemes for the Ministry of Health in 2007 found significant concerns based on procedural justice i.e. equal treatment, asserting

Living kidney donation does not come under the public distribution of scarce resources. Rather it entails a private agreement concluded within a relationship or, where crossover donation is concerned, within a close circle of people brought together for their mutual advantage. LDLE, on the other hand, involves advantage derived from a private transaction being transferred to the public system for distributing organs. It is this transference that introduces the issue of formal justice.[168]

However, there has always been some inherent inequity as between patients based on whether individuals have a compatible willing donor or not, yet this has not been perceived to undermine the justification for living donation in general. *All* living donations give special advantage to such patients *vis-à-vis* patients listed for transplant. Indeed, Wilkinson argues that there is an overlooked conflict with principles of justice even in cases of interfamilial donation.[169] Thus, the 'transference' referred to by the Health Council is a purely formal matter. Every patient who has a living donor transplant has been 'removed' from the deceased donor

---

[166] L. Ross and S. Zenios, 'Practical and ethical challenges to paired exchange programs' (2004) 4 *American Journal of Transplantation* 1553 at 1553. Even rule utilitarianism cannot be easily reconciled with such exchanges.

[167] Veatch, 'Organ exchanges' at 1.

[168] Health Council of the Netherlands, Living Donor List Exchange. Den Hartogh appears to endorse their reasoning; see *Farewell to Non-commitment* at 83. Such schemes have now been rejected by both the Health Council and the Minister of Health, Welfare and Sport.

[169] T. Wilkinson, 'Living donor organ transplantation', in R. Ashcroft, A. Dawson, H. Draper and J. McMillan (eds.), *Principles of Health Care Ethics*, 2nd edn. (Chichester: John Wiley, 2007) 483 at 488.

waiting list. It is possible that after an incompatible living donor has donated to a suitable candidate at the top of the waiting list, that the donor's intended recipient could die or become unable to receive a transplant before a deceased donor organ became available. This appears to be a risk inherent in such a scheme and a factor a living donor would wish to take into consideration initially.[170]

A less controversial strategy, a kind of hybrid list exchange/unbalanced exchange arrangement, would enable an O blood type living donor to donate to a compatible patient on the waiting list in return for the next suitable organ from a deceased donor being made available to his or her intended recipient. Veatch asserts that provided the recipient gained enough benefit from moving from a living to a deceased donor organ this would be legitimate.[171] Spital, however, suggests that this would only rarely be the case.[172] Veatch is less pessimistic and observes that even a limited number of such transplants could offset any detrimental effect to O donors from list exchange schemes generally.[173] Presumably if this was not the recipient's wish, then his or her donor would be persuaded not to donate to the waiting list anyhow.

Another permutation returns us to the altruistic living donor. Whilst this individual usually donates to the person at the top of the relevant waiting list, this person might instead be prepared to donate to a donor–recipient couple who are incompatible with each other, using them as a catalyst for a cascade-type arrangement, with the final donor donating to the deceased donor waiting list. Such arrangements have taken place in the Netherlands and the US. A six-way paired donation arrangement was recently facilitated in Baltimore by way of an altruistic donor.[174] These so-called 'domino paired' exchanges, involving altruistic non-directed donors, have not to date apparently generated problems of an ethical nature, although the experience is still modest (as of early 2007 only

---

[170]  149 paired and 62 list donations had been performed in the US up until the end of 2006. Predictive modelling has shown that more kidneys are matched through list paired than kidney exchange schemes with smaller populations (100 pairs or less), but that as population size increases more patients stand to be matched through kidney exchange arrangements; see S. Gentry, D. Segev and R. Montgomery, 'A comparison of populations served by kidney paired donation and list paired donation' (2005) 5 *American Journal of Transplantation* 1914. In the UK it is estimated that at least thirty–fifty pairs are necessary to ensure that at least 30 per cent of patients get such a transplant; see Evidence of Keith Rigg to the House of Lords European Union Committee, *Increasing the Supply of Donor Organs within the European Union*, Volume 1: 17th Report of Session 2007–08, HL Paper 123–1, at para. 62.

[171]  Veatch, 'Organ exchanges' at 2.    [172]  Spital, 'Veatch's proposal' at 855.

[173]  Veatch, 'Why organ exchanges' at 856.

[174]  The other five patients already had a willing incompatible friend or relative to donate to them; see *The Times*, 10 April 2008.

sixteen transplants had been performed in the Netherlands using this protocol).[175] This is a strategy with significant potential. It has been estimated that in the US if this strategy had been employed initially instead of straightforward living non-directed donation, rather than the 302 procedures actually performed, 583 transplants would have taken place, up to mid-2005.[176] Indeed, it has been suggested that both list exchange and non-directed altruistic donation be best used to facilitate chain exchanges.[177]

## Barter?

Whilst such exchanges do not constitute mutually binding promises forming a contractual arrangement, some allege that such arrangements amount to 'payment in kind', which is generally impermissible under the direct terms of relevant legislation such as the Human Tissue Act 2004 in the UK and the National Organ Transplants Act 1984 (NOTA) in the US. Section 32 of the 2004 Act incorporates the offence of commercial dealing in human material which is committed, *inter alia*, where a person gives or receives a reward for the supply of, or for an offer to supply, any controlled material, or offers to supply any controlled material for reward.[178] 'Reward' is defined by section 32(11) as meaning 'any description of financial or other material advantage'. The US statute refers analogously in section 301 to 'valuable consideration'.

Richard Epstein stridently asserts that 'The thought that this is not valuable consideration is simply a joke to anybody who's serious about what those words mean'.[179] Taylor describes such schemes as 'barter-based'.[180] Menikoff similarly maintains that kidney swaps involve a '"hidden" type of kidney sale', and states 'Neither of the donors would be willing to give up his or her kidney unless the other does the same, thus establishing that there is a true exchange and not merely two separate and

---

[175] W. Zuidema (abstract), 'Domino paired kidney donation with altruistic donors', Organ Transplantation: Ethical, Legal and Psychological Aspects, Conference, Rotterdam, 1–4 April 2007, S28.

[176] R. Montgomery *et al.*, 'Domino paired kidney donation: A strategy to make best use of live non-directed donation' (2006) 368 *The Lancet* 419.

[177] A. Roth, T. Sonmez, M. Unver, F. Delmonico and S. Saidman, 'Utilizing list exchange and nondirected donation through "chain" paired kidney donations' (2006) 6 *American Journal of Transplantation* 2694.

[178] Section 32(1)–(3).

[179] Session 2, 20 April 2006, President's Council on Bioethics: Organ Transplantation: Potential Policy Recommendations, at www.bioethics.gov/transcripts.april06/session2.html.

[180] J. S. Taylor, *Stakes and Kidneys* (Aldershot: Ashgate, 2005), p. 22.

unrelated "gifts"'.[181] Thus, whilst not formalised, there is clearly an expectation of reciprocity from the alternatively situated donor, a form of quid pro quo which has undoubtedly 'induced' the donor to donate. This is why such removal procedures are usually synchronised, as once one removal has occurred the 'opposite' donor has no obvious motivation to proceed.

In the US, the Living Kidney Organ Donation Clarification Act was passed by both the House of Representatives (H.R. 710) and the Senate (S. 487) in 2007, stipulating for clarification that such arrangements do not amount to the provision of 'valuable consideration' and thus do not contravene NOTA.[182] General Counsel to UNOS has remarked that

> The donation of an organ is properly considered to be a legal gift, rather than a contractual undertaking. By definition, there is no 'consideration' at all in a gift transaction. Like all gifts, organ donations may be made for specific purposes. There is no 'valuable consideration' under NOTA s.301 in any of these living donation arrangements. In fact, there is no 'consideration' present at all. The donor receives none, the recipient receives none and none is transferred to a broker.[183]

But surely *exchanged* 'gifts' may form consideration for each other and even for a contractual arrangement? Moreover, consideration normally need not be given or received directly by the donor for a commercial agreement to be in existence. One can have an entirely valid contractual arrangement whereby goods are provided to another on the basis that that other will confer a benefit in either cash or kind upon a third party.[184] Nonetheless, the wording of both NOTA and the Human Tissue Act 2004 support the inference that the 'consideration' or 'reward' is to be given or received by, and *only* by, the individual (donor) concerned. The UNOS General Counsel asserted that 'The condition can only be "consideration" if the happening of the condition will be a benefit to the person who promises to give an organ', and that '" valuable consideration" is not familial, emotional, psychological or physical benefit to the donor or the recipient, which is part and parcel of living organ donation in general'. Indeed, otherwise one might conceive of all living donations as involving consideration passing to the donor for the act of donation, which could jeopardise *all* living organ donations.

---

[181] Menikoff, 'Organ swapping' at 28.
[182] It also provides for the establishment of a national registry that would facilitate the matching of incompatible pairs.
[183] UNOS Position Statement, Kidney Paired Donations, Kidney List Donations and NOTA s 310, September 18 2006.
[184] Indeed, such terms may even be enforceable by such a third party; see Contracts (Rights of Third Parties) Act 1999.

The 2004 Act refers to financial 'or other material' advantage, suggesting perhaps that 'reward' incorporates 'material' *as well as* financial advantage; and one dictionary meaning of 'material' is 'corporeal', i.e. in kind. However, it is suggested that the statute implies an overall *economic* exchange genus. Similarly with NOTA. Advice from the Office of Legal Counsel at the US Department of Justice is that although such arrangements amount to an 'exchange', they cannot be considered to involve any kind of 'purchase', which is the exclusive type of 'consideration' envisaged by section 301.[185] This is supported by the wording of Article 21 of the Council of Europe Biomedicine Convention, which proscribes only transactions resulting in 'financial gain'. From a lawyer's rather than an economist's perspective, not all items of 'value' have a price, i.e. pecuniary worth. Organs have been deliberately taken out of the realms of trading through legal regulation. Unless one can advance a *de facto* as opposed to a *de jure* perspective here (i.e. in reality organs are traded around the world and thus in fact have a pecuniary value in these jurisdictions), one would seem to be simply begging the question in saying that organs have financial exchange value. Merely because one possesses something that another wants and is prepared to 'swap' for it, does not make it an item capable of barter. Moreover, the rationale or mischief behind the proscriptions upon organ trading do not seemingly apply to such exchange arrangements, as no one is being coerced or exploited and no degradation seemingly occurs.

---

[185] Office of Legal Counsel, US Department of Justice, *Memorandum for Daniel Meron, General Counsel, Department of Health and Human Services*, March 28 2007 at 2.

There is a widespread adverse reaction to the notion of property rights in the human body. These are both intrinsic and instrumental reservations, in that they stem from essentialist views regarding the nature of the person and the proper respect and dignity owed, and consequentialist concerns relating to the effects of objectification of the body. The latter are conceptual and pragmatic. In particular, potential commercial trading in body parts is commonly viewed as an inextricable aspect of recognising property in human biological materials, drawing criticisms of commodification and concerns that such rights located in the tissue source would impede or undermine vital activities in the public interest. But not only are such objections able to be countered, the very unique nature of property-based interests is a persuasive factor *in favour* of a framework of property rights in this context. Indeed, it may be that property rights in *donors* paradoxically serve to *constrain* commercial practices and the unauthorised use of such materials by third parties.[1]

Whilst the law's attitude to property rights in human body parts is at best ambiguous, it should not be supposed that property rights are anathema under existing schema. In fact, paradoxically, property rights have been juridically invoked specifically in order to protect the legitimate interests of possessors and users of biological materials, whether this be as part of the process of forensic investigation, anatomical or post-mortem examination, retention of tissue samples for research, etc. Not only are such rights fairly pervasive as regards third-party users of tissue,[2] they are *crucial* in order to further such activities, although their ambit is currently piecemeal and unreliable; failing to provide sufficient confidence for

---

[1] R. Nwabueze, 'Biotechnology and the new property regime in human bodies and body parts' (2002) 24 *Loyola University of Los Angeles International and Comparative Law Review* 19 at 45 [Nwabueze, 'Biotechnology']. See also B. Dickens, 'Living tissue and organ donors and property law: More on *Moore*' (1992) 8 *Journal of Contemporary Health Law and Problems* 73 at 92.

[2] In *R* v. *Bristol Coroner, Ex parte Kerr* [1974] 1 QB 652, for instance, it was held that coroners have a common law right to possess the body until the conclusion of the inquest.

storers and users.[3] As Magnusson states 'Unless some form of proprietary rights are recognised in cadaveric specimens, museums and medical school specimens could be damaged, stolen, or in fact retained with impunity'.[4] Indeed, almost everyone would endorse property rights of some hue or other in this context. That statutory schemes have adopted consent models to regulate the removal, storage and use of such materials for such ends mitigates but in no way obviates the need for property concepts to be employed, no matter how much legislators and politicians may attempt to will them away.[5] The interests of tissue sources (donors) and professionals are, however, currently in tension, with the latter typically being able to assert proprietary rights over various materials against the former, but not vice versa. The interests of donors are notoriously undervalued by contemporary schemes and policies.

Reference is frequently made to the 'limbo' into which human tissues fall immediately after removal from the body, and how, being the property of no one at that time, they are 'available' to anyone. As Dickenson states 'It is because we are propertyless in our own bodies, according to legal doctrines such as abandonment or res nullius, that we are vulnerable, as something akin to objects, to the "new enclosures"'.[6] Arguments in favour of broad legal recognition of property rights in human biological materials tend to emanate from concerns relating to the lack of a 'remedial framework' available to those whose own, or their deceased relative's, tissues have been improperly taken, destroyed, retained and/or used.[7] Whitty states that 'It is necessary to treat separated human organs and tissues as corporeal moveable property in order to protect or recover possession, to prevent damage and destruction; and to enable donation and deposit'.[8]

---

[3] Nwabueze states 'Furthermore, the uncertainty could affect product developments as well as research. Since inventions containing human tissues and cells may be patented and licensed for commercial use, companies are unlikely to invest heavily in developing, manufacturing, or marketing a product when uncertainty about clear title exists'; see Nwabueze, 'Biotechnology' at 21.

[4] R. Magnusson, 'Proprietary rights in human tissue', in N. Palmer and E. McKendrick (eds.), *Interests in Goods* (London: Lloyds of London Press, 1993) 237 at 248 [Magnusson, 'Proprietary rights'].

[5] See R. Fletcher, M. Fox and J. McCandless, 'Legal embodiment: Analysing the body of healthcare law' (2008) 16(3) *Medical Law Review* 321.

[6] D. Dickenson, *Property in the Body: Feminist Perspectives* (Cambridge University Press, 2007), p. 28 [Dickenson, *Property in the Body*].

[7] Both Nwabueze and Hardcastle are particularly concerned by such a lacuna; see R. Nwabueze, *Biotechnology and the Challenge of Property: Property Rights in Dead Bodies, Body Parts and Genetic Information* (Aldershot: Ashgate, 2007), pp. 38–41 [Nwabueze, *Biotechnology*] and R. Hardcastle, *Law and the Human Body* (Oxford: Hart Publishing, 2007) p. 1 [Hardcastle, *Law and the Human Body*].

[8] N. Whitty, 'Rights of personality, property rights and the human body in Scots law' (2004–5) 9 *Edinburgh Law Review* 194 at 221 [Whitty, 'Rights of personality'].

Whilst the legitimate taking, storage and use is presently underpinned by the legal requirement for the tissue source (or a 'proxy') to give consent, and there are various criminal sanctions relating to the non-consensual taking, retention and use of human tissue (e.g. in the Human Tissue Act 2004 and Human Tissue (Scotland) Act 2006), these do not generate on-going rights of *control*. Consent is a one-off, 'front-end' event substantially designed to facilitate rights of use in relevant professionals.

Nwabueze alludes to the particular kind of wrongs which various remedies reflect, and how non-proprietary remedies often fail to do justice to the interests which the aggrieved party is intending to assert.[9] This is linked to the nature of the property interests one possesses with respect to such materials. In this regard, Beyleveld and Brownsword's 'rule-preclusionary' notion of rights in body parts is especially persuasive.[10] It is my contention that professionals initially acquire such (property) rights *from* the tissue source and should act according to this 'remit'. The professional is the recipient, custodian, or trustee of a gift, a gift given for certain specific purposes. To act outside the terms of this gift raises issues as to the subsequent disposition of such tissue, and appropriate remedies should reflect the nature of the claim being asserted.

Arguably, conceptions of property in any case reflect implicitly both the fundamental character and the philosophical underpinnings of such consent schemes, inherently identifying with property entitlements inhering in the tissue source.[11] To some, the very ability to donate, let alone sell, body parts for transplantation or research, infers that such materials are our own to dispose of: the body having been 'dis-organised'.[12] As Childress has observed, if this is not my kidney, what right do I have to give it away?[13]

One concern is that if property rights are recognised in the tissue source, that third parties such as relatives might be availed of proprietary rights in the corpses of others after their deaths. Brazier has, for instance, stated 'If my relative's body is *mine*, be she child, mother, or sister, I may do with my property as I wish. I may elect to sell her component parts in public

---

[9]  R. Nwabueze, 'Donated organs, property rights and the remedial quagmire' (2008) 16(2) *Medical Law Review* 201 [Nwabueze, 'Donated organs'].

[10]  D. Beyleveld and R. Brownsword, *Dignity in Bioethics and Biolaw* (Oxford University Press, 2001) [Beyleveld and Brownsword, *Dignity*]. See also D. Beyleveld and R. Brownsword, 'My body, my body parts, my property?' (2000) 8 *Health Care Analysis* 87.

[11]  See further D. Price, 'The Human Tissue Act 2004' (2005) 68(5) *Modern Law Review* 798 [Price, 'The Human Tissue Act 2004'].

[12]  C. Campbell, 'Body, self, and the property paradigm' (1992) 22(5) *Hastings Center Report* 34 at 36 [Campbell, 'Body, self'].

[13]  J. Childress, 'Ethical criteria for procuring and distributing organs for transplantation' (1989) 14(1) *Journal of Health Politics, Policy and Law* 87 at 89.

auction. I may donate her for display as a plastinated exhibit.'[14] Whilst such rights could be circumscribed, the overriding anxiety is clear. Brazier, however, observes from her experience that most parents reject the idea of their deceased loved one being perceived as their property, and remarks 'The sense of continuing relationship, of still being parents, sharply distinguishes their child, or their husband, from *their* house or *their* car'.[15] Quite rightly the idea of inherent ownership of another, albeit newly dead, human being is not compelling. It is my contention here that, by contrast with current legal trends, it is the *donor/source* who is, alone, the *owner* of original human material.[16] As the Court of Appeals of California stated in the famous case of *Moore* v. *Regents of the University of California*, discussed below

We have approached this issue with caution. The evolution of civilisation from slavery to freedom, from regarding people as chattels to recognition of the individual dignity of each person, necessitates prudence in attributing the qualities of property to human tissue. There is, however, a dramatic difference between having property rights in one's own body and being the property of another.[17]

On appeal, the majority of the Supreme Court ultimately differed, denying property rights to the plaintiff whilst upholding the rights of the users to develop and patent the resulting cell line, although principally on policy grounds.[18] Broussard J (concurring in part and dissenting in part), however, observed that the majority's analysis cannot rest on the broad proposition that a removed body part is not property, but only on the proposition that a *patient* retains no ownership interest in a removed body part.[19] The Court of Appeal had, however, previously opined that

---

[14] M. Brazier, 'Organ retention and return: Problems of consent' (2003) 29 *Journal of Medical Ethics* 30 at 32.

[15] *Ibid.* In *In the Matter of X* [2002] JRC 202, however, the Jersey Royal Court alluded to an 'interest in the nature of ownership' with regard to a minor mother's interest in her aborted foetus, although describing it as 'not a true property interest'.

[16] This appears to have been recognised in England recently in *Yearworth* v. *North Bristol NHS Trust* [2009] EWCA Civ 37 (CA). This is also the view of Lori Andrews; see L. Andrews; 'My body, my property' (1986) 16(5) *Hastings Center Report* 28. She states that while a person can treat his or her body parts as objects of property 'we must not let other people treat one's body parts as property' at 33.

[17] *Moore* v. *Regents of the University of California* [1988] 249 Cal. Rptr. 494 at 504.

[18] The Australian Law Reform Commission Report remarked that 'if full property rights existed in genetic material, its owner could sell it to the highest bidder. In place of the current system of altruistic donation of samples for research, a situation might develop whereby researchers would have to bid for access to genetic material.' The key word here though is, of course, 'full'. See *Essentially Yours: The Protection of Human Genetic Information in Australia*, ALRC Report 96, Sydney, 2003, para. 20.16 [ALRC, *Essentially Yours*].

[19] *Moore* v. *Regents of the University of California* 51 Cal. 3d 120, 793 P 2d 479, 271 Cal. Rptr. 146 at 154. He noted that there would have been no hesitation to find that an action for conversion would properly lie in favour of the laboratory had the cells in question been taken by a thief.

'Defendants' position that plaintiff cannot own his tissue, but they can, is fraught with irony'.[20]

Mason and Laurie comment on a 'widespread ambivalence about property in human material'.[21] This can be witnessed in various statutory and judicial sources.[22] In the US, the notion of 'quasi-property' evolved in connection with the disposal of the corpse, but would not appear to constitute a full property right, although some US courts have found that relatives have constitutionally protected property rights in the dead body.[23] This 'right' of disposal is, however, more in the nature of a duty,[24] and is a fiction primarily designed to overcome a potential legal obstacle to recovery.[25] In the New York case of *Colavito*, although the state and federal courts generally rejected a property-based cause of action, Sack J in the Second Circuit Court of Appeals denied that there was any common law rule that no action for conversion could be brought in respect of body parts.[26] And in *In Re Organ Retention Group Litigation*, whilst the High Court denied there were generally any property rights in cadaveric

[20] *Moore* v. *Regents of the University of California* [1988] 249 Cal. Rptr. 494 at 507.

[21] J. Mason and G. Laurie, 7th edn., *Mason and McCall Smith's Law and Medical Ethics* (Oxford University Press, 2006), para. 15.4 [Mason and Laurie, *Mason and McCall Smith's Law and Medical Ethics*].

[22] The Human Fertilisation and Embryology Act 1990 and Human Tissue Act 2004 both eschew the language of property in favour of consent; see Mason and Laurie, *Mason and McCall Smith's Law and Medical Ethics*, para. 15.2; G. Dworkin and I. Kennedy, 'Human tissue: Rights in the body and its parts' (1993) 1(3) *Medical Law Review* 291 at 298 [Dworkin and Kennedy, 'Human tissue']; and Price, 'Human Tissue Act 2004'.

[23] E. g. *Whaley* v. *County of Tuscola* 58 F 3d 1111 (6th Cir. 1995); *Brotherton* v. *Cleveland* 923 F 2d 477 (6th Cir. 1990); *Newman* v. *Sathyavaglswaran* 287 F 3d 786 (US Ct. App. 9th Cir. 2002) [*Newman*]; *Mansaw* v. *Midwest Organ Bank* LEXIS 10307 (US Dist. Ct. WD Mo. 1998). In these courts it was found that the claim raised a property interest falling within the Fourteenth Amendment, although in the latter case it was held that the plaintiff's (the father of the deceased child) interest was 'a low right on the constitutional totem pole', at [28]. But see also *Georgia Lions Eye Bank, Inc.* v. *Lavant* 335 SE 2d 127 (Ga. 1985) and *State* v. *Powell* 497 So 2d 1188 (Fla. 1986).

[24] See D. Sperling, *Posthumous Interests: Legal and Ethical Perspectives* (Cambridge University Press, 2008), p. 96. [Sperling, *Posthumous Interests*]. See also Justice Fernandez (dissenting) in *Newman* at 801.

[25] The hurdle is invariably the need to prove psychiatric harm. Prosser stated that 'It seems reasonably obvious that such property is something evolved out of thin air to meet the occasion, and that it is in reality the personal feelings of the survivors which are being protected under a fiction likely to deceive no one but a lawyer'; W. Prosser and D. Keeton, *The Law of Torts*, 2nd edn. (St. Paul, MN: West Publishing, 1955), pp. 43–4. The injury is allegedly emotional rather than proprietary, and such rights do not amount to 'deprivation of property in the real sense'; see Nwabueze, 'Donated organs' at 205. See also D. Price, *Legal and Ethical Aspects of Organ Transplantation* (Cambridge University Press, 2000), chapter 3 [Price, *Legal and Ethical Aspects of Organ Transplantation*].

[26] *Colavito* v. *New York Organ Donor Network Inc.* 438 F 3d 214 at 224 (2nd Cir 2006). See also *Colavito* v. *New York Organ Donor Network Inc.* 356 F Supp. 2d 237 (EDNY 2005); *Colavito* v. *New York Organ Donor Network Inc.* 6 NY 3d 820 (NY CA 2006); *Colavito* v.

tissue, it then refused the right of families to possess the separated tissue of their deceased offspring on the basis of the property rights of the pathologists who had conducted the post-mortems.[27] Whilst in *R v. Kelly* Rose LJ maintained that at some point in the future the law may come to apply property rights broadly to human body parts that 'have a use or significance beyond their mere existence', this is yet to come to fruition.[28] However, there are real hopes and indications that this may shortly come to pass following the decision of the Court of Appeal in *Yearworth v. North Bristol NHS Trust*, where it was stated that 'In this jurisdiction developments in medical science now require a re-analysis of the common law's treatment of and approach to the issue of ownership of parts or products of a living human body'.[29]

Harris contends that the essentials of the institution of property are trespassory rules and the ownership spectrum.[30] By the latter he meant the range of relationships presupposed and protected by trespassory rules which are on a spectrum ranging from 'mere property' to 'full-blooded ownership', the latter implying an open-ended range of privileges and powers. By contrast with many commentators, however,[31] Penner cogently argues that 'transferability' is not the defining characteristic of 'property' rights, and places reliance on 'exclusion' as the central aspect.[32]

*New York Organ Donor Network Inc.* 8 NY 3d 43 (NY CA 2006); *Colavito v. New York Organ Donor Network Inc.* 486 F 3d 78 (2nd Cir. 2007) [*Colavito v. New York Organ Donor Network Inc.*].

[27] *In re Organ Retention Group Litigation* [2005] QB 506. Moreover, Gage J opined that had the parents requested the return of their child's corpse following post-mortem examination they would have been able to maintain an action for conversion had this been denied to them, at [161].

[28] *R v. Kelly* [1999] QB 621.

[29] *Yearworth v. North Bristol NHS Trust* [2009] EWCA Civ 37 at [45].

[30] Harris, 'Who owns my body' (1996) 16 *Oxford Journal of Legal Studies* 55 at 59 [Harris, 'Who owns my body'].

[31] Some commentators divide body rights into personal rights and property rights, with personal rights being body rights that protect interests or choices other than the choice to transfer. See S. Munzer, *A Theory of Property* (Cambridge University Press, 1999), pp. 44–56. See also A. Grubb, '"I, me, mine": Bodies, parts and property' (1998) 3 *Medical Law International* 299 regarding 'dispositional liberties' at 310.

[32] J. Penner, *The Idea of Property* (Oxford University Press, 1997), pp. 113 and 128 [Penner, *The Idea of Property*]. However, he emphasises that alienability does not inevitably imply *market* alienability, i.e. the right to buy and sell and contract in relation to such property. See also T. Merrill, 'Property and the right to exclude' (1998) 77 *Nebraska Law Review* 730. The United States Supreme Court has frequently asserted this view; see, e.g., *Kaiser Aetna v. United States* 444 US 164 at 176 (1979) and *Prune Yard Shopping Center v. Robins* 447 US 74 at 82 (1980).

## Property in the human body

Property refers to rights held by individuals which govern legal relations between persons with respect to the items concerned, rather than to such items themselves.[33] We need, however, to distinguish two separate issues. Firstly, whether human biological materials are *capable* of being 'property', i.e. subject to property rights, at all. Although something *is* property only when it is subject to property rights of individuals, only certain entities are potentially to be seen as the subject of property. Cohen contends that 'all external private property is made of something that was once no one's private property, either in fact or morality'.[34] But whereas land and most other external physical items can already be seen to be items which are capable of being property, this status is not self-evident with respect to parts of the body. Indeed, to some the quintessential example of an item not capable of being property is human biological material. Only if this hurdle can be surmounted can one then entertain the further question *whether* property rights have been created with respect to such materials, how, and in whom they vest.

We shall consider the potentiality of property rights in our own living bodies before considering parts of the human body which have been severed from the whole, and then dead bodies or parts thereof. Self-ownership is a Western political philosophy appealing to a certain version of liberty,[35] which not only asserts that our bodies belong to us *per se*, but provides a premise upon which it can be argued that individuals have a right to the fruits of their labours, i.e. for the existence of property rights in body parts which have been severed from the corpus of (usually) living beings. It is the means to acquiring private ownership of the commons.

## Self-ownership: 'glaringly problematic'[36]

*Self*-ownership is said to be an intuitive and foundational concept to which we all subscribe.[37] For liberal theorists, in particular, there is no tension

---

[33] See generally *Yanner* v. *Eaton* (1999) 201 CLR 351 at [18] (HCA). Whilst Campbell argues that one should not attempt to deduce property rights from the nature of the items concerned, see K. Campbell, 'On the general nature of property rights' (2001) 2 *Theoretical Inquiries in Law* 79 at 81 [Campbell, 'On the general nature'], Dworkin and Kennedy nevertheless note the inevitable circularity involved in the analysis here; see Dworkin and Kennedy, 'Human tissue' at 293.

[34] G. Cohen, *Self-ownership, Freedom, and Equality* (Cambridge University Press, 1995), p. 73 [Cohen, *Self-ownership*].

[35] R. Arneson, 'Lockean self-ownership: Towards a demolition' (1991) 39 *Political Studies* 36 at 36.

[36] G. Calder, 'Ownership rights and the body' (2006) 15 *Cambridge Quarterly of Healthcare Ethics* 89 at 92 [Calder, 'Ownership rights'].

[37] Property, personal identity and embodiment may however range from individualist to collective understandings; see D. Joraleman and P. Cox, 'Body values: The case against

with regard to human biological materials and notions of property. Cohen has remarked 'It is an intelligible presumption that I alone am entitled to decide about the use of this arm, and to benefit from its use, simply because it is my arm'.[38] The idea of self-ownership is pervasive and is typically tied to a strong notion of ownership under which one is entitled to do as one wills with one's property provided that it is not used to harm others,[39] and which is often seen as being at odds with notions of egalitarianism and distributive justice.[40]

The concept of self-ownership is accorded most notoriously to John Locke, allegedly providing the basis for the view that external resources become that person's property as a consequence of the investment of self-ownership in that item through labour. As Harris puts it 'My body is the tree; my actions are the branches; and the product of my labouring activities is the fruit'.[41] Locke famously stated 'Every man has a property in his own person; this nobody has any right to but himself. The labour of his body and the work of his hands we may say are properly his.'[42] However, it has been rightly pointed out that Locke did not in fact subscribe to the traditional notion of self-ownership and considered that the human body was made by and belonged to God, the Creator, not Man, i.e. he never said that individuals have property in their physical bodies themselves.[43] Instead, he saw *labour* as the expression of the agency and status of persons, which *are* owned by the individual. The mixing of labour with items in order to generate private property is therefore not rooted in the Lockean notion of *self*-ownership at all.

Self-ownership theories are in any event insufficient. They offer only a theory of the 'extension' of ownership, tending to *suppose* that ownership of the body can be presumed.[44] Harris has argued that such intuition and

---

compensating for transplant organs' (2003) 33(1) *Hastings Center Report* 27. Giordano, for instance, suggests that where the deceased's wishes are not known, the deceased's body may be regarded as 'belonging' to relatives charged with responsibility for it. She alleges that we experience *some* others (significant others) *as a part of ourselves*; see S. Giordano, 'Is the body a republic?' (2005) 31 *Journal of Medical Ethics* 470.

[38] Cohen, *Self-ownership*, pp. 70–1.

[39] Steiner suggests that self-ownership consists of us having 'full liberal ownership of our bodies'; see H. Steiner, *An Essay on Rights* (Oxford: Blackwell, 1994). But see also M. Quigley, 'Property and the body: Applying Honoré' (2007) 33 *Journal of Medical Ethics* 631, applying the 'bundle of rights' concept here.

[40] Nozick, for instance, rejects the notion of redistributive taxation, drawing an analogy with forced labour. See R. Nozick, *Anarchy, State and Utopia* (Oxford: Basil Blackwell, 1974), p. 174 [Nozick, *Anarchy*]. Indeed, property rights generally are implied rights to inequality.

[41] Harris, 'Who owns my body' at 68.

[42] J. Locke, *The Second Treatise on Civil Government*, 1689.

[43] Dickenson, *Property in the Body*, pp. 38–9.

[44] See S. Coval, J. Smith and S. Coval, 'The foundations of property and property law' (1986) 45 *Cambridge Law Journal* 457 at 465.

language is merely rhetorical and does not imply a property relation to one's body. He maintains that not only would self-ownership of our bodies implicate a discrete and unique notion of ownership not to be found in any other context, but that the idea generally stems from the view that because no one else owns a person's body they themselves must do; what he describes as a 'spectacular non-sequitur'.[45] Moreover, most interests or choices with respect to the body may be equally as effectively protected by personal as well as property rights, and invariably are.[46] Thus, the self-ownership thesis is not compelling. As Harris notes 'The bodily-use freedom principle has whatever normative force it has without benefit of self-ownership notions. Property rhetoric in this context is unnecessary, usually harmless, but always potentially proves too much.'[47]

Self-ownership ostensibly invokes a Cartesian (dualist) idea of the physical body controlled and owned by the (mental) person (the incorporeal mind), although some commentators deny it need have such a connotation.[48] Hacking remarks that humans 'are again becoming Cartesian because we now treat the body as an assemblage of replaceable parts, a veritable machine, exactly what Descartes said it was',[49] thereby obscuring the uniqueness of the parts in question.[50] Regarding bodies as merely storehouses of material for biotechnological systems allegedly 'flattens the significance of our everyday lives'.[51] Rao observes that the property paradigm generates a fragmented relationship between the body and its owner both literally and figuratively, the person 'inside' the body, in contrast with privacy, which creates an indivisible corporeal identity.[52] Kant regarded it

---

[45] J. W. Harris, *Property and Justice* (Oxford University Press, 1996), p. 188.

[46] See S. Munzer, 'Kant and property rights in body parts' (1993) 6(2) *Canadian Journal of Law and Jurisprudence* 319 at 321 [Munzer, 'Kant and property rights'].

[47] Harris, 'Who owns my body' at 65.

[48] E.g. C. Farsides, 'Body ownership', in S. Wheeler and S. McVeigh (eds.), *Law, Health and Medical Regulation* (Aldershot: Dartmouth, 1992) 35 at 37.

[49] I. Hacking, 'The Cartesian body' (2006) 1 *Biosocieties* 13 at 13. See also N. Naffine, 'The legal structure of self-ownership: Or the self-possessed man and the woman possessed' (1998) 25(2) *Journal of Law and Society* 193 at 200–3.

[50] See A. Rubinstein, Staff Discussion paper, 'On the Body and Transplantation: Philosophical and Legal Context', President's Council on Bioethics, 2007. The law has often used the machine as a metaphor for the body, as in the US case of *Hawkins* v. *McGee* 146 Atl. 641 at 643 (NH, 1929); see A. Hyde, *Bodies of Law* (Princeton, NJ: Princeton University Press, 1997), pp. 19–33. See also G. Calabresi, 'An introduction to legal thought: Four approaches to law and to the allocation of body parts' (2003) 55 *Stanford Law Review* 2113; S. Schicktanz, 'Why the way we consider the body matters – reflections on four bioethical perspectives on the human body' (2007) 2 *Philosophy, Ethics, and Humanities in Medicine* 30.

[51] H. Fielding, 'Body measures: Phenomenological considerations of corporeal ethics' (1998) 23(5) *Journal of Medicine and Philosophy* 533 at 535.

[52] R. Rao, 'Property, privacy, and the human body' (2000) 80 *Boston University Law Review* 359.

as self-contradictory that a person could be at the same time both a person and a thing. He stated

> Man cannot dispose over himself, because he is not a thing. He is not his own property that would be a contradiction; for so far as he is a person, he is a subject, who can have ownership of other things ... He is, however, a person, who is not property, so he cannot be a thing such as he might own; for it is impossible, of course, to be at once a thing and a person, a proprietor and a property at the same time.[53]

Calder notes that this is not merely a formal categorical objection but alludes to the deeply bizarre idea that one's body is to be regarded as in any sense an 'object'.[54] The idea of the 'person' as 'embodied' is widely accepted and forms part of legal orthodoxy. If an individual breaks the skin of another, 'bodily harm' has been perpetrated on a legal person.[55] Thus, the intimate and inevitable connection between body and self is evident.[56]

There are two different arguments at play here. Firstly, that bodies are not simply things. Secondly, that we should not *treat* bodies as if they were things. The initial point simply asserts that my body is *me*, rather than being *mine*, the second refers to a normative rather than ontological objection which typically relates to potential commodification. Kluge states that most believe that 'people have such a close association with their bodies that to consider bodies and organs as property is tantamount to considering the people themselves as chattels'.[57] There may also be an associated anxiety that if one can own oneself, what is there to stop such ownership vesting in another and implying legitimate slaveholding? These arguments are sometimes merged or at least employed supplementally. The Law Reform Commission (LRC) of Canada stated

---

[53] I. Kant, *Lectures on Ethics* (Cambridge University Press, 1997), p. 157 [Kant, *Lectures on Ethics*].

[54] Calder, 'Ownership rights' at 93.

[55] In *Director of Public Prosecution* v. *Smith* [2006] 2 All ER 16 at 20h; [2006] EWHC 94 at [18] (Admin), Cresswell J stated 'In my judgment, whether it is alive beneath the surface of the skin or dead tissue above the surface of the skin, the hair is an attribute and part of the human body. It is intrinsic to each individual and to the identity of each individual.' The non-consensual severance of hair constitutes a battery. However, had the hair already been detached from the head it might even be stolen; see *R* v. *Herbert* (1960) 25 *Journal of Criminal Law* 163.

[56] Kant states 'But since the body is the total condition of life, so that we have no other concept of our existence save that mediated by our body, and since the use of our freedom is possible only through the body, we see that the body constitutes a part of our self'; see Kant, *Lectures on Ethics*, p. 144.

[57] E.-H. Kluge, 'Organ donation and retrieval: Whose body is it anyway?', in H. Kuhse and P. Singer (eds.), *Bioethics: An Anthology* (London: Blackwell, 2006) 483 at 483–4.

Why, then, should bodies not be regarded as ordinary property? An important answer may be that notions of bodily property do violence to our concepts of personal autonomy and human dignity. Property is traditionally associated with things, not with the human body. To equate the body with a thing is to dehumanize human existence; in the extreme, it suggests the repulsive notion that human beings may be owned. This answer hinges both on a thing–person dualism, and an inference that human bodily parts are reflective of our notion of self. Both are central to substantive objections to the buying and selling of human tissue.[58]

These perspectives reflect the view of the common law. In *Yearworthv. North Bristol NHS Trust*, Lord Judge CJ observed that 'The common law has always adopted the same principle: a living human body is incapable of being owned'.[59]

But even if one were to reject self-ownership of the body, this would not necessarily imply that individuals could not have property rights in parts of their bodies *removed* or *separated* from the body as a whole. To conflate the body as a whole with the parts of that body is to commit the fallacy of division.[60] We are always more than the sum of our parts; we are not *reducible* to the parts of our bodies.[61] The Kantian self-contradiction argument holds much less force here, as the separation of the relevant material might easily be seen to create an 'object' now divorced from the 'subject' of which it once formed part. Dickenson states 'It becomes much more difficult to insist that the body simply *is* the person when tissues from the body are no longer physically joined to the person, or when the body is a conglomerate of extraneous tissues and my own'.[62] Thus, at the moment that the part of the body is severed from the whole, it seems that the item concerned potentially becomes the subject of property rights, i.e. property.

### Separateness

The notion of 'distance' from a subject has been a common one in philosophical discourse. There should be some perceptible boundary – some separation – from self in order for an item to be a 'thing'. Such 'externality' is central to the position of many commentators, including Radin, Penner and Hardcastle.[63] Radin opines that bodily parts may be too 'personal' to be property, and that we have an intuition that property

---

[58] Law Reform Commission of Canada, *Procurement and Transfer of Human Tissues and Organs*, Working Paper 66, Ottawa, LRC, 1992 at 57 [LRC].
[59] *Yearworth* v. *North Bristol NHS Trust* [2009] EWCA Civ 37 at [30].
[60] Munzer, 'Kant and property rights' at 325.
[61] See Calder, 'Ownership rights' at 96.     [62] Dickenson, *Property in the Body*, p. 5.
[63] Hardcastle, *Law and the Human Body*, p. 127.

necessarily refers to something in the outside world, separate from oneself. She states 'This intuition makes it seem appropriate to call parts of the body property only after they have been removed from the system'.[64] Penner argues that things that are intrinsically connected to individuals are not potentially the subject of property rights.[65] Both Penner and Hardcastle maintain that separation is required to create the necessary 'normative distance' to convert biological materials into 'things' capable of being (subject to) property.[66] Such separateness was judicially remarked upon by Lord Bingham in the House of Lords, who stated 'one cannot possess something which is not separate and distinct from oneself. An unsevered hand or finger is part of oneself ... A person's hand or fingers are not a thing.'[67] Clarkson and Keating have remarked 'When Mrs Bobbit cut off her husband's penis this was an offence of violence which infringed his personal rights [yes ... ouch!] rather than his proprietary rights. It makes no sense to think of this as an offence against property and, even it were, her conduct could hardly be described as dishonest. However, once a limb, organ or sample has been removed from the body and stored in, say, a sperm or blood bank, it possesses all the attributes of personal property.'[68] The conceptual impossibility of separating a particular thing from the person to whom it belongs is the hallmark of personal as opposed to property rights. As Penner notes, one cannot rid oneself of one's body as one can with items of property.[69]

## Detachment: 'defenceless in death'?[70]

Hardcastle appears to adhere to the detachment concept even with regard to corpses, and takes the view that any property rights created form part of the deceased's estate.[71] However, the analogy between living bodies and corpses is not compelling. The concepts of externalisation and normative distance which are so pivotal with regard to the living individual seem much less relevant as regards the deceased. At the point of death, there is automatically 'distance' created between the physical remains and the

---

[64] M. Radin, *Reinterpreting Property* (University of Chicago Press, 1994), p. 41 [Radin, *Reinterpreting Property*].

[65] Penner, *The Idea of Property*, p. 114.  [66] *Ibid.*, p. 129.

[67] *R* v. *Bentham* [2005] UKHL 18 at [8]; [2005] 1 WLR 1057.

[68] C. Clarkson and H. Keating, *Criminal Law: Text and Materials*, 5th edn. (London: Thomson/Sweet & Maxwell, 2003), p. 771.

[69] Penner, *The Idea of Property*, p. 121. A right to personal integrity or a right not to be murdered cannot be separated from the specific individual who is entitled to it. They are *personal* rights.

[70] M. Brazier, 'Retained organs: Ethics and humanity' (2002) 22 *Legal Studies* 550 at 564.

[71] Hardcastle, *Law and the Human Body*, pp. 148 and 150.

once living person, and all others. This is the case whether or not any materials are removed from the corpse. Where the person has ceased to exist, the corpse is then arguably as a whole, by its nature, a thing capable of being the subject of property rights. As Penner states 'Yet a corpse has no necessary attachment to any living human. So it can be as much the subject of a property right as anything else',[72] although he notes that there are policy arguments in favour of *treating* the intact corpse as the 'person' until dismembered, by virtue of its association with the once living person.

If Hardcastle's view were to be accepted this would create potential anomalies with respect to the protection of corpses and parts of corpses and uses for differing medical ends. If the body was willed to a medical school for anatomical examination the corpse would presumably be *res nullius* and without protection, yet parts of the corpse removed for transplantation or research would be potentially subject to property rights and be protected. Detachment seemingly has no function in this context. Thus, Rose LJ's boldness and perspicacity in *R* v. *Kelly* require immediate endorsement here, and the law's acceptance of the capability of the creation of property rights in the tissues of the deceased person as a whole.[73] Although he qualified his remarks by referring to bodies or parts having a 'use beyond their mere existence', in reality this applies to all corpses,[74] and no distinction could or should be properly drawn between bodies or parts having already been willed and designated for a valuable purpose, and those only *potentially* to be used thereafter to such ends.[75] It is *death* not detachment that 'distances' such material and creates object rather than subject.[76]

None of this is, of course, to deny that from the perspective of others, in particular grieving relatives, organs and tissues from the deceased are still identified emotionally, psychologically and spiritually with the formerly living 'person'. They constitute part of the 'essence' of that individual. The spiritual and emotional dimensions of this issue necessitate sensitivity of approach and inclusivity. However, symbolic power and difficulties of

---

[72] Penner, *The Idea of Property*, p. 122.

[73] *R* v *Kelly* [1999] QB 621 at 630–1.

[74] Whilst the contemporary 'value' of human bodily materials is a factor favouring property rights, this is a principally sociological rather than normative phenomenon. See L. Becker, *Property Rights: Philosophical Foundations* (London: Routledge & Kegan Paul, 1977), p. 6 [Becker, *Property Rights*].

[75] Rose LJ referred, for example, to parts *intended* for transplantation.

[76] Although title does not generally vest until the property comes into existence, see Dworkin and Kennedy 'Human tissue' at 302–3, laws have often invoked fictions to deem property to exist in individuals before they have come into existence. The same strategy might be employed as regards the once living.

psychological reorientation cannot preserve 'self' even if the person's identity lives, for others, *in their minds* after physical death has ensued.

## Treating AS property: the sacred and the profane

Kant's non-consequentialist objections to treating the human body as property are based on notions of human freedom, humanity and dignity, and self-respect (although Kant did not directly apply all of these arguments to body parts *per se*), all rooted in notions of what is intrinsically degrading or offensive to dignity. The first-mentioned appears to be an argument from universality: that if one could dispose of one part of one's body one could dispose of all, and thus ultimately the very free will of the individual would be compromised and his inherent nature undermined. This argument is extremely problematic.[77] There is no reason why limits could not be imposed upon the extent of permissible severance/donation. Chadwick maintains that the question here is the extent to which bodily continuity is necessary for personal identity. She considers that the continuity of the brain is the most obvious aspect here, and that we can conceive of the loss of a body part – say, a limb – without necessarily regarding there as having been a sacrifice of anything essential for personal identity.[78]

As regards humanity and dignity, Kant considered that 'In the kingdom of ends everything has either a *price* or a *dignity*'.[79] For him, to the extent that a part is capable of being replaced by an equivalent it has a price, and consequently not a dignity. In so far as material from the human body, such as an organ, is a part of what is essential for an individual's dignity as a rational being it is not able to be treated merely as a means to an end, only an end in itself.[80] Thus, objectification of the body is a mark of indignity. Treating the body as a thing is to regard it as something to be used merely as a means. This is captured in the remark made by Justice

---

[77] Munzer remarks that 'to debase oneself need not involve a loss of one's freedom'; see Munzer, 'Kant and property rights' at 324. He argues that Kant conflates loss of freedom and loss of humanity.

[78] R. Chadwick, 'The market for bodily parts: Kant and duties to oneself', in B. Almond and D. Hill (eds.), *Applied Philosophy: Morals and Metaphysics in Contemporary Debate* (London: Routledge, 1991) 288 at 290 [Chadwick, 'The market for bodily parts']. She opposes the sale of body parts, however, on the basis of a duty to promote the flourishing of human beings.

[79] I. Kant, 'Groundwork of the Metaphysics of Morals' (1785), in M. Gregor (ed.), *Practical Philosophy* (Cambridge University Press, 1996) at 37 . As Munzer observes, see 'Kant and property rights' at 319, Kant's objections to property rights in the body are largely inferred from his remarks concerning the sale of such items.

[80] See, e.g., J. S. Taylor, *Stakes and Kidneys: Why Markets in Human Body Parts are Morally Imperative* (Aldershot: Ashgate, 2005), pp. 154–5 [Taylor, *Stakes and Kidneys*].

Arabian about the nature of the plaintiff's claim in his concurring opinion in *Moore*, 'He urges us to commingle the sacred with the profane. He asks much.'[81]

There are twin evils allegedly comprising the objection from objectification: *instrumentalisation* and *fungibility*.[82] The former needs to be perceived from both a human rights and a dignitarian standpoint. From the former perspective it is not credible to view individuals as treated *merely* as a means to the ends of others where the individual consents to, even requests, the activity or intervention. A vital aspect of being self-determining and choosing one's own ends is to be able to exercise control over one's body, i.e. free from the controlling influences of others. Any property rights advanced here would inhere initially in the tissue source and not others, and consequently notions of being 'used' or 'instrumentalised', and analogies with slavery, ring hollow. They are rights *in* not *over* the tissue source. Indeed, Litman and Robertson remark 'If property is viewed more accurately in terms of control over one's body, these criticisms [regarding commodification of the body] may be inapt. If property confers exclusive control to people over their bodies, then their dignity is enhanced, not diminished.'[83]

From a dignitarian perspective, however, autonomy and consent do not affect the essence of the activity. Kant was of the view that our bodies are parts of our *selves*.[84] Munzer contends that this putative argument again commits the fallacy of division to the extent it implies that because the human body as a whole has dignity that each part of the body must equally possess dignity.[85] Treating parts of the body as objects is not synonymous with treating the *person* as object.[86] In any event, Kant would allow the removal of some parts of the body for certain ends, e.g. the removal of a diseased part by way of amputation, in order to meet basic human needs.[87] Cohen observes

Kant was not sufficiently prescient to consider the possibility of human transplantation, but had he known about it, he would have maintained that gifts of the body whose loss would not wholly destroy their donor's integrity as an embodied self do not deny human dignity... However, gifts of the body that involve

---

[81] *Moore* v. *Regents of the University of California* 271 Cal. Rptr. 146 at 148.

[82] See S. Wilkinson, *Bodies for Sale: Ethics and Exploitation in the Human Body Trade* (Oxford: Routledge, 2003) [Wilkinson, *Bodies for Sale*]. He regards these concepts as linked.

[83] M. Litman and G. Robertson, 'The common law status of genetic material', in B. Knoppers *et al.*(eds.), *Legal Rights and Human Genetic Material* (Toronto: Emond Montgomery Publications, 1996) 51 at 60.

[84] I. Kant, *Lectures on Ethics*, trans. L. Infield (New York: Harper & Row, 1963), pp. 147–8.

[85] Munzer, 'Kant and property rights' at 326.

[86] See Wilkinson, *Bodies for Sale*, p. 53.

[87] Dickenson, *Property in the Body*, p. 7. See also Taylor, *Stakes and Kidneys*, pp. 148–9.

dismemberment and destruction of the integrated bodily self, such as the gift of a heart or liver, would be ethically unacceptable to Kant, for the dignity of human beings would also be dismembered by such gifts.[88]

The argument from self-respect maintains that to treat oneself as an object or thing serves to undermine the respect which individuals should show for themselves based on duties owed to themselves or others. However, Kant recognised duties of imperfect beneficence towards others, and in a society where body parts may be capable of saving the lives of others, it is very plausible that Kant himself would have endorsed the donation of some bodily material for their benefit.[89] As Chadwick remarks 'If one may have a kidney removed in order to preserve one's own life, but not to preserve the life of another, this seems to introduce a partiality which is inimical to Kant's view of ethics'.[90]

### Commercification

Many objections to recognising property rights in body parts relate to the potential for commercial dealings. As we have seen, Kantians argue that to *value* human beings is to deny their human dignity. Moreover, concerns that recognition of property rights in body parts would act as an obstacle to successful research initiatives by facilitating bartering in tissues have loomed large in both policy instruments and judicial decisions.[91] However, it is this author's contention that property rights and market alienability rights in human materials are distinguishable and severable. The former are entirely consistent with explicit restrictions on commercial activity relating to transplantation or research (*res extra commercium*).[92] This is without prejudice to views as to whether commercial dealings in human tissue *are* permissible or otherwise. In both these spheres one should nevertheless be mindful of the fact that there needs to be some justification for converting what would ordinarily be regarded

---

[88] C. Cohen, 'Selling bits and pieces of humans to make babies: *The Gift of the Magi* revisited' (1999) 24(3) *Journal of Medicine and Philosophy* 288 at 293.

[89] He would have even apparently permitted male circumcision; see I. Kant, *Lectures on Ethics*, trans. L. Infield (Indianapolis: Hackett, 1963), p. 116.

[90] Chadwick, 'The market for bodily parts' at 294.

[91] See *Moore* v. *Regents of the University of California* 51 Cal. 3d 120, 793 P 2d 479, 271 Cal. Rptr. 146. This was the view of the majority of the California Supreme Court, although this was disputed by both Broussard and Mosk JJ in their dissenting judgments. Oregon enacted a version of the US Model Genetic Privacy Act, granting ownership rights in genetic samples to the tissue source, but this legislation was repealed in 2001. Property rights were perceived to be a disincentive to research.

[92] It is tempting for those who want to forestall a commercial market in organs to contend that bodies are *not* property. But such a stance makes it difficult to explain how then we can *donate* organs.

as a private transaction into an arrangement with public criminal justice dimensions.[93] There are significant costs to individual freedom from any ban. As Dworkin notes 'Allowing people to sell things is one way of recognising their sphere of control'.[94] Indeed, the California Court of Appeals stated in *Moore* 'If this science has become science for profit, then we fail to see any justification for excluding the patient from participation in those profits'.[95] Further, to deny such alleged equitability may undermine trust in clinicians and detrimentally affect the supply of tissues in the future. Indeed, the very potential for substantial profit to be made (only) by researchers and 'developers' has encouraged the latter to be less than honest with patients or research subjects, as *Moore* itself highlights. Much again may hinge upon the perception of the relationship of body to self. The LRC of Canada noted that for those who regard the body as simply a physical substratum for the self, there seem few intrinsic impediments to tissue sales to further the ends of self since the body has only instrumental value. Conversely, for those who reject such mind–body dualism and equate the body with self, human dignity permeates the entire human body and holds it priceless.[96]

The LRC of Canada itself asserted that the debate here must be refined to recognise that bodily parts may be property that carry the right of alienation, even if they cannot be property that carries a right to capital.[97] As Sack J observed in *Colavito* v. *New York Organ Donor Network Inc.*

To be sure, the [New York Public Health] Act prohibits the 'sales and purchases of organs'. But the fact that the State wishes to prohibit the treatment of functioning human organs as though they were commodities does not necessarily imply that it also intends that no one can acquire a property right in them. It does not follow from a law that forbids the sale of a functioning human kidney, that a third party may with impunity take the organ against the express wishes of a potential donor and potential donee.[98]

Regrettably, property and market alienability rights are often conflated, even in recent statute laws. For instance, section 32 of the Human Tissue Act 2004 asserts that where human, controlled, material *has become*

---

[93] See P. Alldridge, 'The public, the private and the significance of payments', in P. Alldridge and C. Brants (eds.), *Personal Autonomy, the Private Sphere and the Criminal Law* (Oxford: Hart Publishing, 2001) 79.

[94] G. Dworkin, 'Markets and morals: The case for organ sales', in G. Dworkin (ed.), *Morality, Harm, and the Law* (Boulder, CO: Westview Press, 1994) 155 at 156.

[95] *Moore* v. *Regents of the University of California* [1988] 249 Cal. Rptr. 494 at 509 (Cal. Ct. App.). See also T. Murray, 'Who owns the body? On the ethics of using human tissue for commercial purposes' (January–February 1986) *IRB: A Review of Human Subjects Research* 5.

[96] LRC at 59.    [97] *Ibid.*, at 57.

[98] *Colavito* v. *New York Organ Donor Network Inc.* 438 F 3d 214 at 225 (2nd Cir. 2006).

*property*, as a consequence of the application of human skill, there can be no offence of commercial dealing in respect of such materials. In Australia also, there are statutory provisions in some states and territories stipulating that the prohibition upon the sale of human organs in human tissue legislation does not apply if the tissue has been subjected to processing or treatment (the implication being that it has then become 'property').[99] This is also a judicial trait. Justice Arabian in *Moore* argued that to afford property rights to donors would result in human tissues being treated as 'fungible articles of commerce' and a viewing of human material negatively as consistent only with an economic mode of valuation.[100]

Radin similarly rejects the notion that commercial exchange is an inherent aspect of property.[101] She urges that some forms of property may not be traded in the market, by virtue of being a disallowed form of social organisation and allocation, and that some property may be wholly commodified, some incompletely (partially) commodified and some completely non-commodified.[102] She distinguishes *personal* and *fungible* property linked to a view of personhood and its uniqueness.[103] She remarks 'When an item of property is involved with self-constitution in this way, it is no longer wholly "outside" the self, in the world separate from the person; but neither is it wholly "inside" the self, indistinguishable from the attributes of the person. Thus, certain categories of property can bridge the gap or blur the boundary between the self and the world, between what is inside and what is outside, between what is subject and what is object.'[104] She maintains that fungible property, not being attached to self, is held only instrumentally, and thus has a commensurable value which may be assessed analogously to money or as money in itself. Personal property, on the other hand, being connected to self, is not interchangeable and has an *incommensurable* value, being unique and irreplaceable.

---

[99] See, e.g., section 32(2) Human Tissue Act 1983 (New South Wales); section 35(3) Transplantation and Anatomy Act 1983 (South Australia); section 27(2) Human Tissue Act 1985 (Tasmania); Transplantation and Anatomy Ordinance 1978 (Australian Capital Territory); section 44(2) Human Tissue Transplant Act 1979 (Northern Territory). Hardcastle states that this is by way of the application of the work or skill exception; see Hardcastle, *Law and the Human Body*, p. 79.

[100] *Moore* v. *Regents of the University of California* 271 Cal. Rptr. 146 at 148. See also E. Gold, *Body Parts: Property Rights and the Ownership of Human Biological Materials* (Washington, DC: Georgetown University Press, 1996), pp. 35–40 [Gold, *Body Parts*]. Gold argues that property discourse in the courts and other policy contexts invariably carries with it the assumption of marketability, *ibid.*, p. 9.

[101] M. Radin, 'Market-inalienability' (1987) 100(8) *Harvard Law Review* 1849 at 1903.

[102] M. Radin, *Contested Commodities* (Cambridge, MA: Harvard University Press, 1996), p. 20 [Radin, *Contested Commodities*]. See also Walzer's 'spheres of justice' and fourteen types of 'blocked exchanges'; M. Walzer, *Spheres of Justice* (Oxford: Basil Blackwell, 1983).

[103] *Ibid.*, p. 54.     [104] *Ibid.*, p. 57.

The concept of property has never been synonymous with absolute or unlimited rights, either ethically or legally.[105] Magnusson remarks that 'In contrast to European civil law, the common law does not require that the full range of rights generally enjoyed over tangible personal property be present in every case for the right to enjoy proprietory status'.[106] Penner argues that whilst the right to transfer property is an aspect of the right of exclusive use of it, the power to sell or otherwise dispose of it by contract is not, even if in many situations this is an additional legitimate power attaching to it.[107]

### Nine-tenths of the law

Harris asserts that 'Stored bodily parts may be the subject of trespassory rules, together with role-duties imposed on particular officials, without either ownership or quasi-ownership being reserved to any person or institution'.[108] He alleges that the clearest examples of role-generated trespassory rules divorced from the realm of property are the powers of relatives or others charged with the proper disposal of the bodies of the deceased.[109] But although it is argued that the (US) notion of quasi-property 'has no relationship with property in the legal sense',[110] the right to possession is a right to *recovery*, for the purpose of disposal, not a mere right to compensation for damaged feelings.[111] Whilst property and possession are distinct, Magnusson notes that 'Conceptually, however, the ability to enforce possession necessarily introduces the concept of property'.[112] Possession is at the root of title, which is in any event 'relative'.[113] If human body parts are

---

[105] See J. Christman, *The Myth of Property: Toward an Egalitarian Theory of Ownership* (Oxford University Press, 1994), pp. 5 and 18.

[106] Magnusson, 'Proprietary rights' at 246.    [107] See Penner, *The Idea of Property*, p. 153.

[108] Harris, 'Who owns my body' at 76.

[109] Harris would also apply this analysis to gametes and organs to be used for therapeutic purposes. The extent of such 'trespassory rules' is generally very vague, though. It is unclear, for instance, whether body parts governed by such 'rules' may be stolen or recovered by way of a civil action for conversion or the like.

[110] Nwabueze, 'Biotechnology' at 31. See also *Gray* (2000) 117 Australian Criminal Reports 22, in which the Queensland Supreme Court held that a right to possession of the dead body does not confer a right to consent to the removal of body parts, etc.

[111] Thus, Nwabueze's assertion that the injury here is emotional rather than proprietary is not entirely apt; see 'Donated organs' at 205. Damages will not *produce* the body for respectful disposal.

[112] Magnusson, 'Proprietary rights' at 250. There must be a (claim) right to possession, i.e. it is normative rather than factual proposition.

[113] Remedies for conversion require some kind of proprietary right, but demand only that the person either possessed the property or had the best right to possession of it. Restitution or redelivery of the goods may be ordered. Trustees, and both bailees and bailors, may sue for conversion. In negligence, recovery requires ownership or a possessory title; see *Leigh and Sillivan Ltd* v. *Aliakmon Shipping Co Ltd* [1986] AC 785 at 809F.

not capable of being subject to property rights even after detachment from the body, then it would seem that there would be no capacity to protect possession of such items and thus their legitimate use for purposes such as research or transplantation.[114] Nwabueze argues that 'Donated human organs should be regarded as property owned by the intended recipient or the donor and, in the case of anonymous donations, by the hospital in possession. Otherwise, we risk having valuable organs destroyed with impunity to the eternal disgrace of a legal system.'[115] However, at present the law's treatment of human body parts can typically be seen to *limit* the powers and rights of the person from whom the tissue originated.

### Creation of property rights

Assuming that detached living body parts or the corpse (or parts of the corpse) are indeed potentially subject to property rights at the time of detachment or death, the question arises as to how property rights are created in them and in whom they vest. We are principally referring here to *private* property although, as we have seen, there is a view that such rights automatically and immediately vest in the collective, i.e. society, after death, for the benefit of the sick and needy. This has already been considered, and rejected, in chapter 2. Becker maintains that there are four sound lines of justification for the *original acquisition* of private property rights: one from utility, one from liberty and two from labour theory.[116] The assumption here is that such items have not been formerly the subject of property rights, and indeed this is the conventional judicial wisdom in both common law and civil law jurisdictions in respect of corpses (i.e. that the corpse is *nullius in rebus*),[117] as well as parts separated from the living. Dickenson states 'Once tissue is separated from the living body, however, the common law generally assumes either that it has been abandoned by its original "owner", or that it is and was always *res nullius*, no one's thing, belonging to no one when removed'.[118] This was the apparent assumption underpinning the Human Tissue Act 2004.[119]

---

[114] Trespassory rules may consequently not facilitate, at least in the absence of a contract being in effect, continuing control to be exercised either by way of a bailment or a trust.

[115] Nwabueze, 'Donated organs' at 209.     [116] See Becker, *Property Rights*.

[117] This may not represent the law in Scotland, however; see Whitty, 'Rights of personality' and *HM Advocate* v. *Dewar* (1945) SC 5.

[118] Dickenson, *Property in the Body*, p. 3. This is perhaps most plausible with regard to diseased resected tissue such as cancerous tumours.

[119] In the House of Commons, Dr Ladyman for the Government stated 'That exception reflects the current legal position as determined by case law, that there is no property in the human body or its parts, so that they cannot be bought and sold, except where human skill has been applied'; House of Commons Standing Committee G Debates col. 215, 3 February 2004.

The conventional view nevertheless has implications for the conceptualisation of organ and tissue donation. The Nuffield Council on Bioethics Working Party Report, *Human Tissue: Ethical and Legal Issues*, stated *vis-à-vis* the *res nullius* approach that 'It would also mean that a person could not prospectively *donate* "his" tissue, once removed from his body. All he could do would be to *consent* to the removal. If this analysis were adopted, the tissue would be the property of the person who removed it or subsequently came into possession of it. The person from whom it was removed would not, however, have any property claim to it' (my emphasis).[120] There is indeed some weak direct authority in England and Australia for the proposition that property rights in living body samples are created and vest in third parties possessed of such material immediately following removal (blood and tissue samples, respectively), although no substantial analysis was provided and the preliminary determination in the latter context was necessary purely for jurisdictional purposes.[121] There are, however, some recent implications within US case law that property rights vested originally *in the tissue source* at the point of removal, although they were then either abandoned or subsequently transferred to a third party.[122] More significantly, in *Yearworth* v. *North Bristol NHS Trust*,[123] a British appellate court has directly endorsed rights in tissue from the living vested in the source, albeit in the context of a claim for compensation.

Swain and Marusyk classify human materials threefold.[124] Firstly there are materials which form part of the persona and are therefore appropriately viewed as part of the person. Once separated such body parts are *res*

---

[120] Nuffield Council on Bioethics Working Party Report, *Human Tissue: Ethical and Legal Issues*, 1995, Nuffield Council, London at para 9.11. [Nuffield Council, *Human Tissue*].

[121] See *R* v. *Rothery* [1976] RTR 550; *R* v. *Welsh* [1974] RTR 478; and *Roche* v. *Douglas* (2000) 22 WAR 331 (WA SC). In the latter, it was necessary for the samples to be regarded as property in order for a judicial order for paternity testing to be made under the rules of the Court. However, the judge declared his view that it would have 'defied reason' and 'ignored physical reality' not to have held them to be property. There was no need to determine the ownership of the property, though, for such an order to be made. See also *Pecar* v. *National Australia Trustees Ltd* BC9605678, Unreported, Supreme Court of New South Wales, 27 November 1996. Analogously in *Hecht* v. *Superior Court* 20 Cal. Rptr. 2d 275 (Ct. App. 1993), the deceased's sperm was found to be 'property' in order for probate jurisdiction to reside in the court. See also *Cornelio* v. *Stamford Hospital* 717 A 2d 140 (Conn. 1998).

[122] *Greenberg* v. *Miami Children's Hospital Research Institute Inc.* 264 F Supp. 2d 1064 (SD Fla. 2003) at 1075 and *Washington University* v. *Catalona* 437 F Supp. 2d 985 (USDC Ed. Mo. 2006) at 997–8 upheld by *Washington University* v. *Catalona* 490 F 3d 667 (US Ct. App. 8th Cir. 2007).

[123] *Yearworth* v. *North Bristol NHS Trust* [2009] EWCA Civ 37 at [45].

[124] M. Swain and R. Marusyk, 'An alternative to property rights in human tissue' (1990) *Hastings Center Report* 12 [Swain and Marusyk, 'An alternative to property rights'].

*nullius*, not owned by anyone but subject to the potential acquisition of ownership by the first person to take possession of them. However, such tissue could not be owned by anyone whilst potentially to be used in the service of transplantation, but would be classified as *trust res nullius*, a thing owned by nobody but held in trust for a recipient (perhaps the donor himself). The third level would view human tissue as *res communes omnium*, things that by natural law are the common property of all humans. However, private property rights would be capable of being generated once something was produced *from* such tissue, drawing on Locke's labour thesis. They state 'Thus the creation of a new thing through merging that thing with one's labor results in property that that person alone has the right to own'.[125]

### Abandonment

The notion of abandonment was explicitly endorsed in the Nuffield Council on Bioethics Report, which stated that a 'preferable approach' would be for it to be entailed in any consent to treatment that tissue removed in the course of that treatment would be regarded in law as having been abandoned by the person from whom it was removed.[126] A distinction is therefore being made between tissue removed for the specific requisite purpose (e.g. research) and tissue originally removed for therapeutic purposes. Such a concept is frequently attributed to the California Supreme Court in *Moore* v. *Regents of the University of California*.[127] In fact, only the intermediate appellate court considered it directly. Moreover, in that decision Rothman J asserted that abandonment was purposive and that 'A consent to removal of a diseased organ, or the taking of blood or other bodily tissues, does not necessarily imply an intent to abandon such organ, blood or tissue'.[128] In the UK also, in order for all control to be lost it is necessary for there to be an intention to relinquish one's entire interest in the property.[129] The notion that such tissue is for the donor to (initially) 'control' is now pervasive, including in the formulation of the Human Tissue Act 2004. The law generally necessitates explicit consent for permissible (further) use, superseding notions of abandonment. It was stated during the Parliamentary debates on the Bill 'The principles of the Bill are that we all own our bodies, we are

---

[125] *Ibid.*, at 14.    [126] Nuffield Council, *Human Tissue*, paras. 9.14 and 13.26.
[127] *Ibid.*, para. 9.12.
[128] *Moore* v. *Regents of the University of California* [1988] 249 Cal. Rptr. 494 at 509 (Cal. Ct. App.).
[129] See A. Hudson, 'Abandonment', in N. Palmer and E. McKendrick (eds.), *Interests in Goods* (London: Lloyds of London Press, 1993) 423.

entitled to determine how material from our bodies is used, and we should have consented to the use made of that material'.[130]

It may be seen that in any event the whole notion of abandonment proceeds from the implicit assumption that the source initially had property rights in tissues removed from his/her body, which is itself anathema to the views of most judges and policy-makers.[131] Moreover, abandonment is the relinquishment of *all* rights and claims to the world at large. Not only is a conditional 'abandonment' to a particular person instead a 'gift',[132] but one may intend to exercise some continuing interest even in discarded waste products.[133] The Dutch Health Council stated that surrender by the patient should only be assumed 'in the case of material which is destroyed or which is to be used in some way known to the person from whom it was taken'.[134]

## First occupancy

It may appear that property rights vested in third parties are the product of 'first occupancy'. Carter states 'It is generally assumed that being the first person to take an object into one's possession or being the first person to occupy a plot of land establishes property rights in whatever has been possessed or occupied'.[135] The notion would appear to originate from the

---

[130] Dr Ladyman, House of Commons Standing Committee G Debates, col. 65, 27 January 2004.

[131] See generally, J. McHale, 'Waste, ownership and bodily products' (2000) 8 *Health Care Analysis* 123. Matthews maintains that, e.g., in removing and possessing an appendix the clinician is merely acting as the patient's agent anyhow; see P. Matthews, 'Property and the body: History and context', in K. Stern and P. Walsh (eds.), *Property Rights in the Human Body*, Occasional Papers 2, King's College London, 1997 27 at 30.

[132] See R. Hardiman, 'Toward the right of commerciality: Recognizing property rights in the commercial value of human tissue' (1986) 34 *University of California at Los Angeles Law Review* 207 at 243–4 [Hardiman, 'Toward the right of commerciality'].

[133] See *Williams* v. *Phillips* (1957) 41 Cr. App Rep. 5 (DC). It may be invariably anticipated, for instance, that surplus tissues removed for therapy will be disposed of in a dignified manner once pathology testing is complete. It is a matter for determination on the facts of each specific case; see *R* v. *Stillman* [1997] SCR 607 (Supreme Court of Canada). In *Venner* v. *State of Maryland* 30 Md. App. 599, 354 A 2d 483 at 498 (1976) (affirmed 279 Md. 47, 367 A 2d 949 (1976)), the Maryland Court of Appeals stated that 'It is not unknown for a person to assert a continuing right of ownership, dominion, or control, for good reason or no reason, over such things as excrement, fluid waste, secretions, hair, fingernails, toenails, blood and organs or other parts of the body, whether their separation from the body is intentional, accidental, or merely the result of normal bodily functions'.

[134] Report of a Committee of the Health Council of the Netherlands, *Proper Use of Human Tissue*, The Hague, No 1994/01E, para. 3.3.1 [Health Council of the Netherlands].

[135] A. Carter, *Philosophical Foundations of Property Rights* (New York: Harvester Wheatsheaf, 1989), p. 78 [Carter, *Philosophical Foundations*]. He argues that Kant endorsed such a view of ownership rights.

Roman doctrine of *occupatio*, and is recognised in Australia, the US, and England and Wales.[136] The suggestion is that human biological materials may become property by mere reduction into the possession of a third party. *R* v. *Rothery* and *Roche* v. *Douglas*, and the US authorities of *Moore*, *Greenberg* and *Catalona*, are all arguably examples of the application of this concept, although it will be maintained below that the latter authorities do not in fact reflect such reasoning at all. Such a principle may apply also to parts of deceased persons. In *In Re Organ Retention Group Litigation*, Gage J suggested in the High Court – adopting the view expressed in *Clerk and Lindsell on Torts*[137] – that property will vest in the first person to alter the biological materials on the basis of first possession. But alteration is not necessarily consistent either with the first occupation doctrine, which requires only a reduction into possession, or with the work and skill exception considered below.[138]

Analogies have been drawn between biological materials and wild animals.[139] Wild animals are indeed *res nullius* until reduced into possession, after which they may then be the subject of theft or an action for conversion. Yet the situation concerning trespassers illustrates that the relevant property rights accrue to the owner of the land rather than the person in physical possession of the animal(s). In any event, the moral weight of first possession as the basis for creating a *right to possession* (as opposed to a mere liberty to possess) is dubious. Whitty comments that 'It might be thought that an original title of ownership of it could then be acquired by the first person to take possession of it (occupation). That seems logical given the initial premise. Intuitively however it also appears unfair to the source, random in its result, and generally impolitic.'[140] As Becker states, the argument from first occupation does not succeed in generating a *justification* for property rights.[141]

---

[136] See, e.g., *Yanner* v. *Eaton* [1999] HCA 53; (1999) 201 CLR 351 at [25].

[137] A. Tettenborn, 'Wrongful interference with goods', in A. Dugdale (ed.), 19th edn., *Clerk and Lindsell on Torts* (London: Sweet & Maxwell, 2006) 1024. It has also been suggested that *R* v. *Kelly* is best interpreted as a case based on first possession, but this is also unconvincing.

[138] For the same reason it is not compatible with a Lockean labour mixture philosophy, as again mere reduction into one's possession would not suffice to generate ownership by such means. However, Locke apparently required little or no 'labour' at all to generate property rights, seemingly highlighting a weakness with his thesis itself; see Cohen, *Self-ownership*, p. 75.

[139] See, e.g., Nuffield Council, *Human Tissue*, para. 9.11.

[140] Whitty, 'Rights of personality' at 223–4.

[141] I.e. a claim right to possession. See Becker, *Property Rights*, p. 30. The arguments based on Kant and Hegel, etc., allegedly fail to provide moral support.

### The labour theory

I shall now turn to the labour theory, which Carter describes as probably the most intuitively obvious basis for claiming the rightful existence of private property.[142] Becker states 'The root idea of the labor theory is that people are entitled to hold, as property, whatever they produce by their own initiative, intelligence and industry'.[143] The pedigree of such an exception is undoubted. John Locke maintained that when one mixes what one owns, one's labour, with something unowned in the external world, one becomes the owner of the resulting mixture. His theory has come under sustained attack, however. Nozick has enquired 'But why isn't mixing what I own with what I don't own a way of losing what I own rather than a way of gaining what I don't?'[144] Indeed, is one's labour really 'mixed' at all? Further, as Harris observes, 'Labour is a commodity but, outside slave-owning or feudal societies, it is not an entity as to which ownership interests are transferred'.[145] Why does such work generate rights over 'it'?[146] It is merely a means. If a laboratory worker separates blood into separate fractionated products or a surgeon splits a liver donated for transplantation, why should such individuals potentially acquire rights over or 'to' the tissue, even against the tissue source?

It is submitted that the labour mixture thesis supporting property rights in bodily parts is insufficient and generates arbitrary and uncertain results. *Any* 'labouring' on human tissue would seemingly be sufficient in itself to satisfy the Lockean standard, regardless of extent or type, and to that extent the philosophical foundations of the thesis seem shaky, uncertain and unconvincing. Moreover, such private property rights ordinarily attach only to third parties, as opposed to the tissue source. In so far as the common law work and skill exception draws its inspiration from a 'labour mixture' rationale it also fails to assert sufficient justification. It is submitted that such third-party rights in original materials in fact emanate *from* the authority of the tissue source, not from any independently acquired rights of their own. The labour mixture theory of the original formation of private property is premised on the idea of separated human biological materials being *res nullius*. If the body parts are not in fact initially *res nullius*, the theory falls away.

Whilst this doctrine largely serves to protect only the interests of third-party possessors, it could conceivably also provide a basis upon which, in certain circumstances, tissue sources themselves might be enabled to

---

[142] Carter, *Philosophical Foundations*, p. 13.    [143] Becker, *Property Rights*, p. 32.
[144] Nozick, *Anarchy*, pp. 174–5.    [145] Harris, 'Who owns my body' at 72.
[146] Becker has observed that, Locke aside, there has been little serious thinking about how labour can entitle one to anything; see Becker, *Property Rights*, p. 32.

assert property rights over such materials. Dickenson contends that where the tissue source *has* invested her labour in the production of the relevant material, such as in enucleated donated ova (for stem cell technologies) and in stored cord blood harvested during the process of labour, she should be entitled to property rights in it by virtue of her 'productive work'.[147] In like vein, Brownsword has suggested that John Moore might have been viewed as involved in a 'joint labour' venture in relation to the contribution of his spleen for medical research and development.[148] Despite this logic, not only has such 'labour' (literally in some instances!) been applied prior to the separation of the materials from the whole, and thus prior to there being any items capable of being the subject of property rights, but this would tend once more to arbitrariness and exceptionalism in the conferment of property rights upon tissue sources; unless one takes the view that one labours on *all* the parts of one's whole body when living. But then that leads inevitably to the same conclusion as the detachment theory anyhow (see p. 205).

### Work and skill exception

The application of work and skill to physical items is often viewed as a mechanism, arguably *the* mechanism, for the creation of property rights in law in human materials. Laws in various jurisdictions, e.g. England, Wales and Australia, have adopted the work and skill 'exception' as a basis for the generation of property rights in body parts.[149] Whilst this has been invariably applied to the dead, the Californian case of *Moore* also seemingly represents a latent application of the work and skill exception as regards the patented cell line.[150] Section 32 of the Human Tissue Act 2004 now incorporates such an exception into a statutory framework, asserting that 'material which is the subject of property because of an application of human skill' is excepted from the proscriptions relating to commercial dealings in human ('controlled') material for transplantation contained

---

[147] *Ibid.*, p. 68.
[148] R. Brownsword, 'An interest in human dignity as the basis for genomic torts' (2003) 42 *Washburn Law Journal* 413 at 472 [Brownsword, 'An interest in human dignity'].
[149] It is unclear if the exception forms part of the law of Scotland; see Whitty, 'Rights of personality'.
[150] Nwabueze, 'Biotechnology' at 59. In his dissent in the Court of Appeals in *Moore* Associate Justice George stated that 'It was only after defendants expended great effort, time, and skills that – in my opinion – plaintiff's spleen acquired any of the characteristics of property, at which time this diseased organ became transmuted from human waste into patentable blood cell lines', suggesting that the spleen itself was not 'property' created by such means, *Moore* v. *Regents of the University of California* [1988] 249 Cal. Rptr. 494 at 537 (Cal. Ct. App. 1988).

within that section.[151] Amongst other things, this reflects the legislator's view that human materials are not ordinarily subject to property rights.

The origins of the exception are to be found in the Australian case of *Doodeward* v. *Spence*, a case concerning a two-headed, preserved stillborn foetus. Giving the leading judgment in the High Court, Griffith CJ stated that 'when a person has by the lawful exercise of work or skill so dealt with a human body or part of a human body in his lawful possession that it has acquired some attributes distinguishing it from a mere corpse awaiting burial, he acquires a right to retain possession of it'.[152] By contrast, he regarded an unburied corpse awaiting burial as *nullius in rebus*. As Hardcastle observes, the judge did not explain how as a matter of legal principle property rights came to potentially be created by the application of work or skill.[153] However, a labour theory rationale is plausible.[154] It is worth just noting, though, before proceeding, the use of the disjunctive (work 'or' skill) in Griffith CJ's judgment.

This exception has been the subject of adoption and consideration in a number of recent UK decisions. In *Dobson* v. *North Tyneside Health Authority*, the Court of Appeal was concerned with a brain removed at post-mortem examination, not returned with the remainder of the body for burial, and subsequently disposed of. The Court opined that whilst it was the case that there was no property in a corpse, this was otherwise where there was a right to possession for the purpose of disposal of the body or where there had been an application of 'work and skill' to material separated from the body (drawing directly on the principle articulated in *Doodeward*).[155] However, in this instance, the latter was inapplicable in so far as the brain had merely been preserved (fixed in paraffin) and thus there was an insufficient exercise of skill. In *R* v. *Kelly*,[156] the Court of Appeal heard an appeal against conviction of the theft of forty human body parts in the possession of the Royal College of Surgeons. Adopting the conventional view that there was no property in a corpse the court none-theless asserted that *parts* of a corpse are capable of becoming property which might therefore be stolen, where they have acquired different attributes through 'the application of skill'. In this instance, it was found that the dissection, fixing and preservation processes were sufficient to invoke the exception, involving hours if not weeks of skilled work. Finally,

---

[151] Section 32(9). This allegedly reflected the existing common law.
[152] (1908) 6 CLR 406 (HCA) at 414. It is unclear whether the other two judges concurred in such reasoning.
[153] Hardcastle, *Law and the Human Body*, p. 29.
[154] Nwabueze asserts that the work and skill exception appears to be a judicial recognition of John Locke's labour theory of property; 'Biotechnology' at 58.
[155] [1997] 1 WLR 596 (CA).     [156] [1999] QB 621.

in *In Re Organ Retention Group Litigation*,[157] the High Court heard three lead claims by parents who had had children die and body materials retained following forensic or hospital post-mortem examinations. The issue of property rights arose in the context of whether English law recognised a tort of wrongful interference. Gage J accepted the defendants' submissions that property rights to the materials vested in them by virtue of the application of (work or?) skill. It was held that the process of selection, preservation and dissection of the materials was sufficient for this purpose, involving the creation of tissue blocks. The judge stated that to dissect and fix an organ from a child's body requires 'work and a great deal of skill', especially where a very young baby was involved.[158] In *Yearworth* v. *North Bristol NHS Trust*, whilst the judge preferred to ground ownership rights in the men who supplied the sperm, he recognised sufficient 'work and skill' involved in the storage process to invoke the exception. Oddly, though, he seems not to have appreciated that this would have served to have conferred rights on the Unit not the men themselves.[159]

It is immediately apparent that a Lockean rationale cannot properly be regarded as underpinning the existing domestic or Australian jurisprudence. The emphasis in these decisions was as much, if not more, upon the application of skill rather than labour *per se*; indeed in *Dobson* the exception was not triggered *despite* the labour applied to the brain.[160] The statutory exemption from the offences of commercial dealing in the 2004 Act, which allegedly mirrors the existing law, in fact relates *solely* to the application of human skill. Thus, labour involving little or no skill would appear to fall outwith the exemption. Nevertheless, Hardcastle is right to assert that the law amounts to little more than rights founded on 'first possession'. Although mere possession is not theoretically sufficient to invoke the work and skill exception, little more than that may in reality be required in order to activate it.[161]

---

[157] [2005] QB 506.

[158] He stated 'The subsequent production of blocks and slides is also a skilful operation requiring work and expertise of trained scientists'; *ibid.*, at [148].

[159] *Yearworth* v. *North Bristol NHS Trust* [2009] EWCA Civ 37 at [45]. Presumably he might have applied the exception in favour of the men, however, on a different analysis of the 'work and skill'!

[160] It has already been observed that the Lockean labour theory, by contrast, requires almost nothing in the way of labour in order to invoke property rights.

[161] Mason and Laurie remark that if dissection and preservation techniques suffice, then merely to carry out an autopsy or to place a sample in formaldehyde is presumably enough to generate property; see Mason and Laurie, *Mason and McCall Smith's Law and Medical Ethics*, para. 15.27. In *Doodeward*, the mere placing of the foetus in a jar of paraffin was sufficient to invoke the exception, although 'mere preservation' was regarded as insufficient in *Dobson*.

The work and skill exception is arbitrary and lacking in normative force. There is major uncertainty with respect to the nature and type of work or skill that will suffice. 'Mere' labour is apparently not adequate, although the reason why is not patent,[162] although of course, if labour of any type or degree would suffice then individuals would be entitled to acquire property rights based on dubious normative authority. Hardcastle is correct that there is the potential here for artificial and arbitrary distinctions to be generated with respect to different biological materials, based only upon the different degree of processing which has occurred.[163] This possibility was explicitly remarked upon in *Yearworth* v. *North Bristol NHS Trust*.[164]

Legislators and judges cling to the orthodoxy that human material *per se* cannot be the subject of property. But it is patent that parties in legitimate consensual possession of human tissue to fulfil various proper purposes require a right to possess the tissue *regardless of whether work and skill has been applied to it*. If a person were to sabotage an organ donated for transplantation, or to take it for their own ends, destroy a cadaver intended for post-mortem examination, or valuable tissue intended for research, it surely should not be pertinent, from the point of view of the right to recover the material, whether work and skill had been applied to it at that moment in time. What if it had instantly been taken following removal? The more 'use or significance' such materials acquire the greater the likelihood of such scenarios playing themselves out.

### Metamorphosis?

There was a requirement explicitly alluded to by Griffith CJ in *Doodeward* and reiterated in the English decisions, that there must be some change in the nature of the item(s) concerned in order to invoke the exception. In *Doodeward*, the court referred to a differentiation from 'a mere corpse awaiting burial',[165] a statement repeated by Peter Gibson LJ in *Dobson*, whilst in *Kelly* Rose LJ alluded to such parts having consequentially 'acquired different attributes', a view to which Gage J also apparently wedded himself in *In Re Organ Retention Group Litigation*.[166] It was no

---

[162] Hardcastle, *Law and the Human Body*, p. 125. He points out that possession *per se* cannot constitute sufficient work and skill for these purposes.

[163] *Ibid.*, p. 143.

[164] *Yearworth* v. *North Bristol NHS Trust* [2009] EWCA Civ 37 at [45].

[165] It was nonetheless implicitly an extremely material issue in the case; *ibid.*, p. 30. Hardcastle observes that Griffith CJ did not assert in *Doodeward* that this was the exclusive means by which property rights could be created.

[166] *In re Organ Retention Group Litigation* [2005] QB 506. In *Yearworth* v. *North Bristol NHS Trust* [2009] EWCA Civ 37 at [38] it was remarked that for the exception to apply the work 'presumably changed their attributes'.

essential part of Locke's labour mixture thesis, however, that the relevant labour change the nature of the item concerned.

It is not possible to locate the current work or skill exception in the doctrine of specification, which emanates from the Roman law classification of *specificatio*. That doctrine requires that a *nova species* (new thing) be created. Whilst *prima facie* English case law might be perceived to be implicitly adopting the doctrine by way of references to 'acquiring different attributes', Hardcastle is right to describe the current exception in law as a 'misguided application' of the specification doctrine.[167] In some of these decisions, the biological materials have been considered to be subject to property rights as a consequence of the application of work or skill notwithstanding the fact that there has been *a mere change of form* rather than any true creation of a new thing (despite the *supposed* requirement that such a new thing be generated).[168] This remark is particularly apposite to the decision in *In Re Organ Retention Group Litigation*, but is also pertinent to *Kelly* (although in that case greater emphasis was placed on the acquisition of different attributes). In the former, it appears that Gage J may simply have misunderstood the essential nature of the final product.[169] In the latter, the parts were separated and preserved rather than fundamentally altered in character, as was also true in *Doodeward* itself, albeit as regards an entire foetus.[170] Added to this, quite apart from the absence in these decisions of any mention of the specification doctrine, there was no apparent *emphasis* upon the need for the creation of a different type of entity. It was merely tacked on as an (alleged) further requirement/afterthought.

Arguably, this should have been *the* crucial matter, though. Hardcastle asserts that the appropriate principle is to be found based in the doctrine of specification in its unadulterated form.[171] There is therefore a role for the work or skill exception in the context of modified, *distinct* types of derived human biological materials. Quite apart from preserving the purity of legal doctrine, this move would serve to emphasise that whilst a specific framework of property and other rights pertain to unmodified separated human

---

[167] Hardcastle, *Law and the Human Body*, p. 143.
[168] Griffiths CJ in *Doodeward* also referred to the corpse having acquired 'pecuniary value'; see *Doodeward* v. *Spence* (1908) 6 CLR 406 at 415, but this appears to beg the question.
[169] See Hardcastle, *Law and the Human Body*, p. 36.
[170] The foetus was merely preserved in alcohol, which prompted the dissenting judge to opine that no labour or skill had been applied to it to invoke the exception; see *Doodeward* v. *Spence* (1908) 6 CLR 406 per Higgins J at 417. However, preservation of certain materials may 'transform' their nature – as, perhaps, in the instances of embalming or plastination of corpses.
[171] He regards modified biological materials, e.g. created by inserting foreign DNA, to be potential candidates for the application of the doctrine; see Hardcastle, *Law and the Human Body*, pp. 10–11, 170.

biological materials, once such materials have ceased to reflect their original character, property rights may be generated based upon a different philosophical and legal source/rationale. In particular, in relation to third parties, rather than the law generally permitting only possessory and usage rights in relation to human material, full proprietary rights might be exercisable in relation to them. This would in particular include the right to transfer and dispose of such material, and possibly even to trade.

A further means of modifying biological materials so that proprietary rights may vest in third parties is through the doctrine of *accession*. This involves the bringing together of entities so that they merge and lose their original identity. In English law this is sometimes alternatively dubbed 'annexation'. For the doctrine to apply, the two forms of property must merge permanently, with one item becoming subordinate to the other. Whilst there is a paucity of precedent to determine whether natural materials may be subject to the doctrine, in principle there is no reason why not, provided that the original material is subsumed into another item. The doctrine of accession could apply, for instance, to amplified DNA and cell lines.[172]

The 2004 Act states that certain modified forms of human biological materials, such as cell lines, are excluded from the statutory provisions by virtue of being 'created outside the body', implying that they may be seen as property as they are not human materials *per se*.[173] They are distinct, having become a new entity by the work of the human or mechanical hand. In *Moore* v. *Regents of University of California*, the California Supreme Court held that the (patented) cell line was 'factually and legally distinct' from the spleen cells taken from Moore's body, and that he had no property rights in respect of them.[174] They had undergone a transformation to immortalise them (to render them capable of self-replication), etc.[175] Not only did this confer proprietary rights to transfer such materials, it facilitated the creation of patent rights in the

---

[172] *Ibid.*, pp. 165–71. See also Hardiman, 'Toward the right of commerciality' at 253–6.

[173] Cell lines are excluded by section 54(7). The Act would also exclude pluripotent stem cells, as the stem cells themselves, rather than the cells from which they are generated, are 'created outside the body'.

[174] Panelli J in *Moore* v. *Regents of the University of California* 271 Cal. Rptr. 146 at 159. Mosk J dissenting, however, noted that whilst perhaps true this was irrelevant to the validity of Moore's claims, which related to the point in time before the patented modified biogenetic material was created at 178. Moreover, Moore did not challenge the patent itself which was admittedly the product of inventive work.

[175] Thus, as the California Court of Appeals noted, the fact that defendants modified the original materials by virtue of the application of their work and skill did not negate a potential action for conversion, but instead influenced the appropriate measure of damages, if any, which should be awarded; see *Moore* v. *Regents of the University of California* [1988] 249 Cal. Rptr. 494 at 508 (Cal. Ct. App. 1988).

researchers – the labourers – who created them. Only one judicial authority has directly addressed the issue of property rights in cell lines, the US
decision in *US* v. *Arora*, where an action for conversion was brought in
respect of the damage caused by the malicious destruction of new cell
lines. Messitte J found the cell line to be a chattel capable of being
converted, remarking that 'if such a cause of action is not recognized, it
is hard to conceive what civil remedy would ever lie to recover a cell-line
that might be stolen or destroyed'.[176] The judge's observations usefully
allude to the lacuna that would otherwise be generated if property rights in
certain materials were not to be recognised by law, a theme to which I shall
return shortly.

It has been seen that whilst the application of human skill, or work and
skill, *per se* is insufficient in itself to legally or ethically ground property
rights in body parts,[177] property rights can attach to human-derived
materials which have been significantly altered by third parties. What is
crucial is the *novelty* of the product in this connection, emphasising that
such materials are no longer mere 'human materials'. There is less difficulty in conceiving of materials which have been merely *derived* from
original human tissue as fungible property, the connection with self
being further distanced.[178] Gold states 'This distinction between untrans-
formed and transformed states is important since the transformation
process may not only change the component itself but the ways in which
we value it after transformation. Specifically, some of the ways in which we
hold body components to be inherently valuable may not be applicable, or
at least less significantly applicable, to the transformed component.'[179]
He argues that there is a significant moral and legal difference attaching to
body parts no longer recognisable as a body component. But lack of
*recognisability* may be too stringent and might exclude cell lines and
analogous materials. Perhaps instead the core notion attempted to be
captured here is whether there has been a sufficient change in the intrinsic
*character* of the material? Bovenberg states 'While mere processing of
biological material might not be sufficient to confer (limited) property
rights, their artificial culture most likely is. This applies *a fortiori* to cell

---

[176] *US* v. *Arora* 806 F Supp. 1091 at 1099 (Md. DC 1994).
[177] Swain and Marusyk's third classification level of private property in materials derived
from human tissue *res communes omnium*, however, explicitly relies on Locke's labour
theory. See Swain and Marusyk, 'An alternative to property rights' at 14.
[178] It has been noted that the prohibition on gain from human material in the Council of
Europe Biomedicine Convention was not intended to apply to products *derived* from
human tissue; see Report of the Medical Research Council Working Group to Develop
Operational and Ethical Guidelines, *Human Tissue and Biological Samples for Use in
Research*, MRC, 1999, at para. 2.4.4.
[179] Gold, *Body Parts*, p. 13.

cultures and cells from which an immortal cell line has been derived. Such a cell line can hardly be considered to "be" the original cell; the longer the sample is in culture, the less it is like the original specimen.'[180] This appears to emphasise the 'character change' in the materials, entitling the 'transformer' to the benefits of such metamorphosis.[181]

It would be necessary, though, that the original human materials from which such separate items were generated were lawfully in the possession of the relevant third-party researcher. In *Doodeward*, the Australian court referred to the person being in 'lawful possession' of the body. This was explicitly stated in Griffith CJ's judgment and was reiterated in *Dobson* by Peter Gibson LJ.[182] It would not only be illegitimate to retain and use the original materials from which such novel materials were derived without the appropriate consent required by law having been obtained, but this would undermine the third party's claim to proprietary entitlement in the modified biological materials produced from them.

### Value added

Locke in fact offered two distinct reasons for his labour thesis. Firstly, that such rights derive from prior property rights in one's labour (labour mixture). Secondly, that such rights are required, in justice, as a return for the labourer's pains (desert).[183] Cohen argues that it is easy to confuse and conflate the two claims, but that they are very different supporting arguments, remarking 'Nevertheless, in the logic of the labour mixture argument, it is labour itself, and not value-creation, which justifies the claim to private property'.[184] Whilst this may be so for Locke, Becker describes the 'desert' rationale as at the heart of the acquisition of private property rights, based on the idea that morality itself demands that where

---

[180] J. Bovenberg, *Property Rights in Blood, Genes and Data: Naturally Yours?* (Leiden: Martinus Nijhoff, 2006), p. 134 [Bovenberg, *Property Rights*]. Cell cultures involve growing cells under artificial conditions. A primary cell culture can be transformed into an immortal cell line using different processes.

[181] However, Parry notes that the mere application of a technological process is unlikely to generate a different public attitude to 'cloned cells' than to cells in their original state, especially where the ability to profit hinges upon it. See B. Parry, 'The new Human Tissue Bill: Categorization and definitional issues and their implications' (2005) 1(1) *Genomics, Society and Policy* 74 at 83.

[182] *Dobson* v. *North Tyneside Health Authority* [1996] 4 All ER at 479b.

[183] Gewirth also advances a specific labour desert formula in connection with his theory of the acquisition of property rights linked to the Principle of Generic Consistency, by virtue of which each person is the productive agent of the goods that fulfil his agency-needs. He has reservations with respect to body parts, but Brownsword argues that such reservations are misplaced; see Brownsword, 'An interest in human dignity' at 470–2.

[184] Cohen, *Self-ownership*, p. 177. He is supported by Olivecrona also here, see p. 109.

someone has added value to the world they are entitled to the grant of property rights to reflect this.[185] Justice entitles the creator of the new, distinct entity to claim proprietary, market alienability rights to the additional value one has added to an item as a result of one's labouring on it.[186] In its interim statement, *The Use of Human Organs and Tissue*, the Department of Health asserted that it is legitimate 'for those who develop new products that derive from human tissue or cell lines to seek a financial return for the application of their skill and labour'.[187] Utility also supports such entitlements, in so far as individuals might otherwise invest too little in such materials, failing to fully develop, exploit and enhance 'products' for the advantage of themselves and society in general.

This also provides a foundation for the entitlement to patent rights attached to (applications of) bodily materials.[188] A Nuffield Council Report, *The Ethics of DNA Patenting*, states the view that (intellectual) property rights in patents can be justified according to either of two types of conventional views for the justification of property rights generally. Firstly, the notion of natural rights in items with which one has mixed one's labour. Secondly, property rights as a matter of public convention justified by a utilitarian notion of property rights as a system of public rules. The view of the Working Party was that the Lockean labour theory was more convincing in the context of intellectual property than in respect of most other forms of property, and that 'it does seem right that someone who creates something new, for example a novel, sculpture or painting, has rights such as copyright, over that which is created. In a similar way, this approach can be applied in the context of industrial or technological inventions to justify the patent system.'[189] It ultimately supported an amalgam of these justifications for the generation of intellectual property rights. But the Council's conception of the mixing of labour relates not simply to the application of labour *per se* but to the 'creation' of something novel, the very hallmark of patenting. The Nuffield Council on Bioethics

---

[185] Becker, *Property Rights*, p. 35.
[186] Although Nozick makes the point that one's entitlement should extend only to the 'additional value' which one has added to it; see *Anarchy*, p. 175.
[187] *The Use of Human Organs and Tissue: An Interim Statement*, Department of Health, NHS, 2003 at 7.
[188] See Becker, *Property Rights*, pp. 48–56.
[189] Nuffield Council, *The Ethics of DNA Patenting*, 2002, Nuffield Council on Bioethics, para. 2.4. It considered that patents over DNA sequences should in future be an exception, and that patents should not generally be available for gene therapy or research tools. The Australian Law Reform Commission, however, considered that genetic materials and technologies should be assessed according to standard legislative criteria; see *Genes and Ingenuity*, ALRC 99, 2004. Patenting stem cells is particularly contentious; see European Group on Ethics, *Patenting Stem Cells*, at http://europa.eu.int/comm/european_group_ethics.

had itself previously remarked that 'The right of ownership in a patent derives from the act of invention'.[190] This notion appears to also undergird the opinions regarding patents of modified body parts advanced by Swain and Marusyk.[191] Such invention potentially generates new intangible, incorporeal property.

### Initial ownership in the tissue source

The detachment theory of creation of (private) property rights in separated human body parts asserts that property rights come into existence at the point of severance. It has been observed that the fact that the 2004 Act implicitly endorses the view that property rights over human material can be acquired through the application of human skill does not preclude the possibility of their creation by other means, even if it is not possible to buy and sell the original human biological materials themselves.[192] This was expressly recognised by the Court of Appeal in *Yearworth* v. *North Bristol NHS Trust*.[193] Hardcastle argues that it is the natural extension of the protection that the law provides for the human body as a whole that such rights should vest automatically in the tissue source at that time, and that this also represents the policy underpinning the requirement for consent for the storage and use of such materials for requisite (scheduled) purposes under the 2004 Act. Moreover, he argues that otherwise there would be a hiatus in the protection afforded in relation to such materials by law and ensuing arbitrariness in coverage.[194] Likewise Whitty remarks, having rejected the doctrine of first possession, that 'A more realistic and just approach, which is supported by some authorities in the Common Law and modern Civil Law is that a part removed from a person's body (e.g. in the course of an operation) is automatically owned by that person by operation of law'.[195]

---

[190] See Nuffield Council, *Human Tissue*, para. 11.32.
[191] Swain and Marusyk, 'An alternative to property rights' at 15.
[192] S. Pattinson, *Medical Law and Ethics* (London: Thomson/Sweet & Maxwell, 2006), p. 473 [Pattinson, *Medical Law and Ethics*].
[193] *Yearworth* v. *North Bristol NHS Trust* [2009] EWCA Civ 37 at [38].
[194] Hardcastle, *Law and the Human Body*, pp. 147–9.
[195] Whitty, 'Rights of personality' at 224. Initially, the MRC Working Group on Human Tissue and Biological Samples for Use in Research opined that 'it was both more practical and more attractive from a moral and ethical standpoint to adopt the position that, if a tissue sample could be property, the original owner was the individual from whom it was taken', Report of the Medical Research Council Working Group to Develop Operational and Ethical Guidelines, *Human Tissue and Biological Samples for Use in Research*, MRC, 1999, at para. 2.2.1.

Support for such a view can be found in political philosophy and contemporary policy instruments. The Dutch Health Council Report was at ease with the idea of property rights in separated body parts vesting in the source, contending that 'the process of separation makes it the property of the person from whom it has been taken'.[196] This may be considered to be a function of the specific nature of the 'property' under consideration. Cohen remarks 'Hence, one may plausibly say of external things, or, at any rate, of external things in their initial state, of raw land and natural resources (out of which all unraw external things are, be it noted, made), that no person has, at least to begin with, a greater right in them than any other does; whereas the same thought is less compelling when it is applied to human parts and powers'.[197]

Hardcastle maintains that such an approach is also supported by precedent at common law, at least as regards tissue taken from the living.[198] Authority is, however, fairly thin in most jurisdictions, although as mentioned previously it is implicitly supported by the reasoning in some of the US authorities. In *Greenberg* v. *Miami Children's Hospital*, for instance, Moreno J declared that 'the property right in blood and tissue samples ... evaporates once the sample is voluntarily given to a third party', implying that initial property rights vested in the tissue source following removal;[199] similarly, in *Washington University* v. *Catalona*. Although both the Court of Appeals and the District Court held that Washington University was the owner of the biological materials donated, they emphasised that the donation was an *inter vivos* gift involving the relinquishment of all property rights inhering in the tissue donors.[200] It spoke of whether the donors '*retain* an ownership interest' (my emphasis).[201] Indeed, this was picked up on in *Yearworth* v. *North Bristol NHS Trust*, where it was noted that the Court recognised that the tissue had been 'donated', albeit that it was an outright unconditional gift.[202] Thus, it would appear to have been accepted that the property rights of the institutions implicated derived from the donative intent of the tissue providers.[203] This paradigm is gaining

---

[196] Health Council of the Netherlands, para. 3.3.1.       [197] Cohen, *Self-ownership*, p. 71.

[198] Hardcastle, *Law and the Human Body*, p. 87.

[199] *Greenberg* v. *Miami Children's Hospital Research Institute Inc.* 264 F Supp. 2d 1064 (SD Fla. 2003) at 1075.

[200] *Washington University* v. *Catalona* 490 F 3d 667 at 674 (US Ct. App., 8th Cir. 2007) upholding *Washington University* v. *Catalona* 437 F Supp. 2d 985 at 997 (USDC Ed. Mo. 2006).

[201] *Ibid.* Consent forms typically stated that donors gave up 'any property rights that they may have'.

[202] *Yearworth* v. *North Bristol NHS Trust* [2009] EWCA Civ 37 at [48].

[203] Section 104(a) of the model Genetic Privacy Act in the US declared that an individually identifiable DNA sample is the property of the sample source, but this is not currently adopted in any of the states.

ground. In Germany, it has been explicitly decided that body tissue removed from an individual, but not intended to be 'reunited' with that individual, is subject to property rights residing in that person.[204] As the California Court of Appeals stated in *Moore* 'A patient must have the ultimate power to control what becomes of his or her tissues. To hold otherwise would open the door to a massive invasion of human privacy and dignity in the name of medical progress.'[205] And in *Yearworth v. North Bristol NHS Trust*, the Court of Appeal also recently endorsed the same notion, albeit that in that case the tissues were intended for the use of the same individuals who were the sources of the tissue. It is not clear if that was an important element of the decision or not, although there would appear to be no reason of principle why it should have been based on the reasoning of the court.[206] Whilst detachment *per se* was not remarked upon as the occasion for the creation of property rights this would appear to be implicit in the decision.

Radin reinforces the need for some control to be able to be exercised over resources in the outside world for 'personhood' to be able to be attained and developed. This points to a *need* for a person to be able to exercise property rights with respect to body parts, contrary to the views of those who regard such a notion as undermining 'personhood' *per se*.[207] The very intimacy of association between the person and such parts now removed from his/her corpus suggests that property rights may be entirely appropriate following separation and, indeed, by virtue of separation. The implication of such a view is that organ and tissue donation for either transplantation or research involves a gift of property of some kind (exactly which kind is considered on p. 296). As Childress says 'all modes of transfer of human organs from one person to another presuppose some notion of property and property rights. Or at least they presuppose some of the cluster of rights associated with property.'[208]

---

[204] Bundesgerichtshof, Urteil 9 November 1993, Aktenzeichen VI ZR 62/93. Paragraph 823 Bürgerliches Gesetzbuch (the German Civil Code).

[205] *Moore* v. *Regents of the University of California* [1988] 249 Cal. Rptr. 494 at 508 (Cal. Ct. App. 1988).

[206] *Yearworth* v. *North Bristol NHS Trust* [2009] EWCA Civ 37 at [45].

[207] See Radin, *Reinterpreting Property*, p. 35. Radin contends that almost every theory of private property rights can be referred to some notion of personhood. Gewirth notes that one's bodily parts are parts of one's personhood as an actual or prospective agent in a much more intimate and direct way than in the case of external things; see A. Gewirth, *The Community of Rights* (University of Chicago Press, 1996) pp. 187–8. Such views are linked to concepts of agency.

[208] J. Childress, 'My body as property: Some philosophical reflections' (1992) 24(5) *Transplantation Proceedings* 2143 at 2144.

Nonetheless, it has been argued that whilst some of the core bundle of sticks, or rights, are appropriately applied to human materials, others are much less so[209] – in particular, the right to security and liability to execution. The former relates to the power of the state to expropriate private property in the public interest, whether with or without compensation, and the latter to the relinquishment of an interest in property in satisfaction of a judgment debt or on insolvency.[210] But not only are property rights malleable and tailored to the situation and the character of the 'property' concerned, but not all 'sticks' need be applicable for property rights to exist.[211]

### Personal or property rights?

As Dickenson remarks 'the common law posits that something can be either a person or an object – but not both – and that only objects can be regulated by property-holding'.[212] *Property* has become shorthand for recognising individual interests in an entity, whilst *person* is shorthand for recognising interests of the entity itself.[213] The rules governing each are distinctive in their nature as well as in their protection, both intrinsically and in terms of regulating relationships with third parties including the state. It has been argued that where the material concerned is destined to be *replaced* in the same, or possibly another, person, that laws relating to persons should continue to apply to it. Swain and Marusyk assert that 'A categorical distinction must be made regarding tissue that is permanently removed from the body as opposed to tissue that is temporarily removed with the intention of having it subsequently become part of the same

---

[209] These standard incidents of ownership are attributed to Honoré. See A. Honoré, 'Ownership', in A. Guest (ed.), *Oxford Essays in Jurisprudence*, 1st series (Oxford University Press, 1961) 107.

[210] Moreover, there are incidental implications, such as the applicability of the takings clause of the Fifth Amendment of the US Constitution, which Hardcastle alleges has itself generated a reticence relating to property in the US judiciary; see *Law and the Human Body*, p. 42. This should not be taken to apply to *personal* rather than *fungible* property, though, in Radin's terms. See discussion in E. Jaffe, 'She's got Bette Davis's eyes: Assessing the non-consensual removal of cadaver organs under the takings and due process clauses' (1990) 90 *Columbia Law Review* 528 at 556–60 and 571–3. Assessing 'just compensation' is particularly problematic in a sphere where organs have no official financial value. See M. Mehlmann, 'Presumed consent to organ donation: A reevaluation' (1991) 1 *Health Matrix* 31 at 55.

[211] See Bovenberg, *Property Rights*, p. 132. In any event, the right of exclusion is the core component of property.

[212] Dickenson, *Property in the Body*, p. 4.

[213] See J. Berg, 'You say person, I say property: Does it really matter what we call an embryo?' (2004) 4(1) *American Journal of Bioethics* 17.

person'.[214] The German Federal Court has determined that a person has property rights in 'their' separated body parts, *but* that where the parts concerned are destined to be replaced in the person's own body (e.g. autografts, autologous transfusions, etc.), they are not 'things', and to interfere with them constitutes 'bodily injury'.[215] The Court held that the stored sperm formed a 'functional unity' with the person's body despite being physically separate from it, by analogy with stored eggs, i.e. although not re-implanted in the same body it would be illogical for the law to differentiate between them.[216] But quite apart from the fact that it seems counterintuitive to regard the loss of isolated stored material as 'bodily harm', it is not obvious why the genus of rights relating to separated tissues should be capable of altering according merely to intention and 'direction'.[217] The outcome in this case was perhaps driven by the desire to ensure a remedy, but there would typically be no similar need in most contexts. The importance of this 'context' was appreciated by the Court of Appeal in *Yearworth* v. *North Bristol NHS Trust*, which itself rejected the claim for personal injury for destruction of stored sperm, dubbing this a 'fiction' which would encourage the law to 'swim in deep waters'.[218]

A system of property rights imposes constraints upon the actions of individuals and governments.[219] These are distinctive rights in terms of both strength and character. Property affords rights *over* the material rather than merely a right to receive recompense for its loss. Beyleveld and Brownsword argue that it is *necessary* to confer property rights in respect

---

[214] Swain and Marusyk, 'An alternative to property rights' at 13. They seemingly regard this intention as crucial, but it is unclear what protective legal framework would apply to the latter, *ibid.*

[215] Bundesgerichtshof, Urteil 9 November 1993, Aktenzeichen VI ZR 62/93. Paragraph 823 Bürgerliches Gesetzbuch. A remedy was sought under the German Civil Code which provides that damages are payable where someone 'intentionally or by negligence wrongfully injures the life, the body, health, freedom or another law of another person'. See J. Taupitz, 'The use of human bodily substances and personal data for research: The German National Ethics Council's Opinion' (2006) 3 *Journal of International Biotechnology Law* 25.

[216] This approach deems the body in its legal sense as 'the sum of those organs and functions of an organism of a person that a person can use as a means (of achieving his or her chosen ends). See F. Heubel, 'Defining the functional body and its parts: A review of German law', in H. Ten Have, J. Welie and S. Spicker (eds.), *Ownership of the Human Body* (Dordrecht: Kluwer Academic Publishers, 1998) 27 at 35.

[217] According to the Court, the former cease to be legally 'things' where they become, through transplantation, united with another person's body.

[218] *Yearworth* v. *North Bristol NHS Trust* [2009] EWCA Civ 37 at [23]. The county court judge in *Yearworth* v. *North Bristol NHS Trust* (12/3/08, Judge Griggs), had described such a possibility as an 'affront to common sense'. See also J. Mead, (2008) 14 *Clinical Risk* 123.

[219] See E. Paul, F. Miller and J. Paul (eds.), *Property Rights* (Cambridge University Press, 1994), p. vii.

of human body parts, on the basis that, in the absence of any objection to a use or where it held no utility for the owner, there would otherwise be no necessary presumption against use by others where this did not appear to be harmful to that person. They state 'Unless rule-preclusionary control is granted to persons to dictate legitimate uses of their bodies after death or removal, persons will be deprived of their legitimate expectation that their most sacred and private beliefs will not be trampled on after they die or have lost immediate control of the objects eliciting their concern'.[220] Their view is that a withholding of permission may be legitimately founded upon nothing more than one's unwillingness to donate such material and need not be supported by any weighty or compelling reasons at all. Such materials are simply ours to control, no more no less; an entitlement to be 'utterly unreasonable' in denying access to others.[221] Whilst such rights, like most other rights, are *prima facie* (presumptive) rather than absolute claims, and must sometimes yield to other claims, they may not simply be dismissed as part of a utilitarian calculus.[222] As Ronald Dworkin famously asserted, 'rights trump utility'.[223]

Pattinson states that 'ownership (once established) determines where the burden of proof lies when establishing who has legitimate control over an entity'.[224] There is a presumption that such materials are not simply available for society to do as it deems appropriate. This position should hold unless there are strong societal reasons why such rights should be potentially overridden (substantive justifications).[225] Although the 2004 Act might perhaps be seen as necessitating consent only where there is a counterbalancing benefit to be achieved by insisting upon it, it is arguably a stronger entitlement than this. One can conceive of the requirement for consent in terms of overall utility, dignity, or rights.[226] It would appear

---

[220] Beyleveld and Brownsword, *Dignity*, p. 188. This is especially pertinent as regards dead persons, in respect of whom there has been a general view that they are 'beyond harm'.

[221] K. Gray and S. Gray, *Elements of Land Law*, 4th edn. (Oxford University Press, 2005), p. 117.

[222] See Beyleveld and Brownsword, *Dignity*, p. 172; and T. Beauchamp and J. Childress, *Principles of Biomedical Ethics*, 6th edn. (Oxford University Press, 2008), p. 352.

[223] R. Dworkin, *Taking Rights Seriously* (Cambridge, MA: Harvard University Press, 1977), p. xi.

[224] Pattinson, *Medical Law and Ethics*, p. 467. He argues that the rule preclusionary conception of property underlies the Human Fertilisation and Embryology Act 1990 and parts of the Human Tissue Act 2004, see pp. 468 and 473.

[225] It has already been made clear that there may be *substantive*, societal reasons for permitting such activities even in the absence of the procedural justification of consent; see chapter 4.

[226] This despite the exceptions regarding the need for consent in the context of surplus 'anonymised' tissue in REC-approved research, and use of tissue for audit, quality assurance, etc.

that it is invoked in the service of the latter in the context of both the 2004 and 2006 Acts in the UK. The person's 'right to control' the disposition of body parts emanating from their bodies was repeatedly alluded to during the Parliamentary debates on the Human Tissue Bill.[227] This is a clear nod to implicit property rights.

## Remedies

Bjorkman and Hansson argue that the important normative issue is not whether the bodily rights a person possesses are characterised as 'property rights' or not, but what combination of rights a person should have to a particular item of biological material. Whether that bundle qualifies to be dubbed 'property' or 'ownership' is a secondary, terminological, issue.[228] Moreover, no satisfactory 'checklist' of fundamental ingredients of 'ownership' has ever been formulated, and that is it which 'sticks' in the bundle of rights that the person has that is pivotal. It is certainly the case that what principally matters in the context of both research and transplantation is who has the right to control the use of such materials. But even if this is convincing from an ethical point of view, it is crucial from *a legal* perspective to properly characterise such rights, as the remedies and entitlements one has will be structured as a function of this. It must be appreciated that property and personhood rights are juxtaposed in law and the requisite governing framework dictated by that *a priori* issue. The law necessitates such classification in order to invoke either jurisdiction or the availability of certain actions or remedies.[229] For instance, laws often classify bodily materials as 'products' in order to facilitate strict liability for those persons injured by harmful or defective items, etc.[230]

---

[227] Dr Ladyman, for instance, stated 'The fundamental principle that we must apply to interpreting the Bill is that material provided by people from their own body is theirs to control, and they must consent to how it is used', at House of Commons Hansard Debates, Standing Committee G, col. 059, 27 January 2004.

[228] B. Bjorkman and S. Hansson, 'Bodily rights and property rights' (2006) 32 *Journal of Medical Ethics* 209.

[229] See Campbell, 'On the general nature' at 80.

[230] In *AB* v. *National Blood Authority* [2001] 3 All ER 289, for instance, it was held that 'blood' was a product for the purposes of liability under the Consumer Protection Act 1987. However, by virtue of the very fact that it tends to generate strict- rather than fault-based liability, there is often a reluctance to construe legislation creating strict product liability to blood and other forms of human material supplied to others. In the US, the supply of blood has frequently been deemed to be a supply of services as opposed to goods; see, e.g., *Perlmutter* v. *Beth David Hospital* 123 NE 2d 792 (1954). But see *PQ* v. *Australian Red Cross Society* [1992] 1 VR 19. Some US courts have distinguished the provision of blood by hospitals and blood banks; see, e.g., *Carter* v. *Inter-Faith Hospital of Queens* 60 Misc. 2d 733, 304 NYS 2d 97 (1969). This in turn has spawned 'blood shield' immunity statutes in virtually all of the states.

As has been noted, personal rather than property rights tend to result in a (mere) right of compensation instead of restoration of the item and/or continuing control over it. This will be entirely inadequate where the person seeks to exercise physical control over, or recovery of, the requisite materials.[231] The California Court of Appeals in *Moore* asserted that the essence of a property interest is 'the ultimate right of control'.[232] Property rights may entitle a person to the return or recovery of tissue in certain circumstances, or to direct its intended or subsequent use.[233] In the absence of a contractual remedy there may be no other means of 'accessing' or controlling such materials in any of these situations. In that event, the tissue source's entitlement is converted at most to a potential right to compensation/reparation by way of a personal civil action. It might even be the case that, in some instances, no consent was initially obtained at all for the possession of such materials, let alone their subsequent usage. The laws in the UK appear to rely entirely on the function of criminal liability for non-consensual conduct as a *preventative* deterrent. In this context, the decision in *Yearworth* v. *North Bristol NHS Trust*, which not only endorsed liability in negligence for damaged sperm, but also bailment rights in the tissue (sperm) source, is highly significant.

The US authorities have tended to reject claims for conversion on the basis that the plaintiffs had no expectation of return of the donated bodily materials.[234] This was the basis upon which the District Court in *Catalona* rejected the applicability of bailment rather than the giving of an *inter vivos* gift.[235] However, these views ignore the potential conditionality of donated materials and proper continued 'directedness' in terms of use. It may have very well been that the plaintiffs in these cases had intended their gifts to be unconditional and absolute, and there was no intention ever to recover possession of the items. But that is a matter of fact and law in the context of each specific case, not a sweeping proposition applicable to all scenarios. For continuing control to be able to be exercised, we should rely on the concept of (gratuitous) bailment in respect of the living, and (constructive) trusteeship with regard to the dead. Such donation or 'gifts' are given for specific purposes and subject to specific conditions.

[231] As where a directed organ for transplant is misapplied or misdirected; see *Colavito* v. *New York Organ Donor Network Inc.* 438 F 3d 214 (2nd Cir. 2006).

[232] *Moore* v. *Regents of the University of California* [1988] 249 Cal. Rptr. 494 at 506.

[233] Even the majority in *Moore* did not rule out property rights where the donor could be anticipated to retain control of such materials following removal, e.g. for autologous bone marrow or cord blood grafting.

[234] See, e.g., *Greenberg* v. *Miami Children's Hospital Inc.* 264 F Supp. 2d 1064 at 1074 and 1076.

[235] See *Washington University* v. *Catalona* 437 F Supp. 2d 985 at 1001 (USDC Ed. Mo. 2006).

These exercise a continuing hold over the possessors or custodians of the tissue, and facilitate remedies to ensure continued implementation of the wishes of the donor.

Let us briefly reflect upon and anticipate the sorts of disputes which may relate to human tissue here. Firstly, (surplus) tissue consensually removed for therapeutic purposes may be used deliberately or unwittingly for research or other purposes (this was the gist of the issue in *Moore*) without consent.[236] Secondly, material donated for transplantation or research might be transplanted into a different patient or used for a different intended purpose, or no longer be able to be used for the original intended purpose.[237] The former would typically apply only to living donors, but in jurisdictions where directed deceased donation is permissible this issue might also arise in the context of misdirected organs donated after death, as occurred in the New York case of *Colavito*.[238] Alternatively, professionals may refuse to release material (e.g. banked cord blood or sperm) to the tissue source when it was originally given to them on the understanding that it would be made therapeutically available at a future time for that person or his/her child, i.e. for an autologous procedure/graft.[239] Compensation may also be sought for unintentional or wilful destruction or loss of tissue. It was asked rhetorically in *Yearworth* v. *North Bristol NHS Trust* 'Why, for example, should the surgeon presented with a part of the body, for example, a finger which has been amputated in a factory accident, with a view to re-attaching it to the injured hand, but who carelessly damages it before starting the necessary medical procedures, be able to escape liability on the footing that the body part had not been subject to the exercise of work or skill which had changed its attributes?'[240] These scenarios relate to the subsequent actions of professionals, but remedies may also be sought *by* professionals against third parties who have 'taken' or destroyed donated tissue without

---

[236] Patients may occasionally seek to recover diseased or other body parts removed by surgery, such as tonsils or their appendix, or even an amputated limb. An example is given of a person with a strong fear of fire who sustained psychological trauma on the discovery that an amputated limb had been incinerated; see L. Andrews and D. Nelkin, 'Whose body is it anyway? Disputes over body tissue in a biotechnology age' (1998) 351 *The Lancet* 53 at 56.

[237] For example, where an 'orphan graft' occurs following the death of an intended recipient after removal of the organ from the donor.

[238] See *Colavito* v. *New York Organ Donor Network Inc.*

[239] An autologous donation is where transplantable material is removed for that individual's own subsequent treatment, e.g. bone marrow, blood, ova. In some instances, contractual remedies may be available, i.e. if it was a private bank. See S. Munzer, 'The special case of property rights in umbilical cord blood for transplantation' (1999) 51 *Rutgers Law Review* 493.

[240] *Yearworth* v. *North Bristol NHS Trust* [2009] EWCA Civ 37 at [45].

requisite permission. In many instances, the actual return of the corpse or material is sought, e.g. the body upon which a post-mortem examination is planned by the coroner, or the organ to be transplanted into a waiting patient. Such a remedy may also be sought by an executor or other person dispossessed or denied possession of a corpse, to enable them to discharge their duty to dispose of a corpse by way of either burial or cremation.

In the UK the comprehensiveness of the regimes governing human tissue and assisted reproductive techniques based on consent significantly, but not entirely, obviate the need for recourse to property rights to resolve disputes. These statutes, however, work against the backdrop of property rights under the general law. Indeed, it is clear that there is no general antipathy toward users possessing property rights in human tissue, merely to such entitlements vesting in the human source of the tissue. Harris remarks that 'when rules are instituted governing the procedures to be followed when organs are transplanted from living or dead "donors" to patient recipients, it may not be necessary to fix ownership of the organ, during the transition period, in anyone'.[241] But even if property rights are not necessarily essential to protect the interests of the *user*, they may be indispensable from the point of view of the *donor*. Whilst Mason and Laurie maintain that 'there is arguably nothing inherently valuable in an appeal to property itself save when such an appeal can furnish rights or solutions to disputes which escape other legal concepts',[242] I would argue that accurate characterisation is also necessary to capture the essence of the right itself, the true nature of the entitlement. Indeed, these authors themselves assert that a consent model disempowers donors by framing their rights in terms of a unitary 'right to refuse'.[243] Laurie himself states that

A personal property paradigm could, in fact, serve an all-important role in completing the picture of adequate protection for the personality in tandem with other protections such as autonomy, confidentiality and privacy. However, the added value of a property model lies in its ability to empower individuals and communities and to provide the crucial continuing control over samples or information through which ongoing moral and legal influence may be exerted.[244]

Whilst access to materials from one's body can be controlled through the medium of consent, once materials have become separated from the body no straightforward rights to physical integrity are implicated and no clear

---

[241] Harris, 'Who owns my body' at 75.
[242] Mason and Laurie, *Mason and McCall Smith's Law and Medical Ethics*, para. 15.4.
[243] *Ibid.*, para. 15.19.
[244] G. Laurie, *Genetic Privacy: A Challenge to Medico-Legal Norms* (Cambridge University Press, 2002), p. 316.

threat to physical, as opposed to psychological, harm presents itself. Hence the necessity for property as opposed to personal rights.

### Square pegs and round holes

The Californian case of *Moore* which relied upon person-based concepts such as fiduciary duties – and in particular informed consent – illustrates the limitations of a non-property-based strategy to resolve the issues and protect the legitimate interests of the tissue source. Indeed, in *Greenberg* v. *Miami Children's Hospital* the Florida court rejected the informed consent claim on the basis that researchers as opposed to physicians had no duty to disclose their economic interests, i.e. in the absence of a therapeutic relationship.[245] Moreover, no duty would arise where the defendants had no intention to conduct research on the patient's cells at the time of removal, as his or her *medical* interests would not be affected. Assuming a duty existed, proving causation would be problematic in most instances in any event. Even 'consensual use', being a once-and-for-all event, may entirely fail to satisfy the very objectives and outcomes which the individuals themselves sought to achieve through donation, as the *Greenberg* and *Catalona* cases highlight.[246] In the first case, the providers sought to promote widely accessible and affordable carrier and pre-natal testing for Canavan disease, whereas ultimately the defendants patented the gene and diagnostic test for the disease, *restricting* access to them.[247] In the second, the researcher with the mission to examine the genetic factors associated with prostate cancer was denied access to the material (sought by more than 6,000 former patients) in favour of the former employer who owned the repository where the material was housed, but whose interest appeared to be primarily financial.[248] Property rights are essential to give

---

[245] *Greenberg* v. *Miami Children's Hospital Research Institute Inc.* 264 F Supp. 2d 1064 (SD Fla. 2003) at 1070. Likewise as regards all apart from Dr Golde in *Moore*; see Panelli J. in *Moore* v. *Regents of the University of California* 271 Cal. Rptr. 146 at 154. Neither informed consent nor fiduciary duties apply to organisations or individuals who receive tissues from researchers or who have no physician/patient relationship initially, nor to employing organisations.

[246] *Greenberg* v. *Miami Children's Hospital Research Institute Inc.* 264 F Supp. 2d 1064 (SD Fla. 2003); 208 F Supp. 2d 918 (ND Ill. 2002). *Washington University* v. *Catalona* 490 F 3d 667 (US Ct. App., 8th Cir. 2007) upholding *Washington University* v. *Catalona* 437 F Supp. 2d 985 (USDC Ed. Mo. 2006).

[247] See D. Gitter, 'Ownership of human tissue: A proposal for federal recognition of human research participants' property rights in their biological material' (2004) 61 *Washington and Lee Law Review* 257.

[248] See L. Andrews, 'Two perspectives: Rights of donors: Who owns your body? A patient's perspective on Washington University v. Catalona' (2006) 34 *Journal of Law, Medicine and Ethics* 398.

effect to, to control, the use intended, i.e. access to the materials and the development of technologies to help disease sufferers. These may be at odds with the goal of facilitating research on human tissue in the round. Hardcastle also points to the anomaly that would exist if the law provided a right of control to tissue sources who had consented to removal but not to those who had not.[249]

A further advantage of property rights in this context is their flexibility, sophistication and bifurcation, as well as their certainty. Different powers may be vested in different parties related to specific ends. Rights to possession may be separated from actual control, as where a pathologist performs a forensic post-mortem on behalf of the coroner/medical examiner/procurator fiscal. Personal rights are much less easily configured in such dynamic, malleable and interlocking forms. Whilst it has been alleged that the application of consent requirements would necessarily lack flexibility if property rights were conceded,[250] not only can consent come in various guises (e.g. presumed/tacit consent), but in some cases the *substantive* justification for allowing the use of such material based on collective need may simply override the need for consent at all.

Whilst actions to enforce property rights vested in donors, third parties and even relatives tasked with disposal of the corpse are essential,[251] personal actions nevertheless *also* need to be recognised to reflect relatives' rights to avoid *profound offence*. This may arise where non-consensual but potentially legitimate actions, or illegitimate actions *per se*, are performed upon the corpse. However, actions for injury or distress caused to surviving relatives by actions performed upon a corpse or parts thereof are currently problematic and difficult to properly classify and pursue in many legal systems. In England and Wales the common law typically requires proof that psychiatric harm resulted, constituting a substantial stumbling block to successful recovery.[252] A requirement of psychiatric harm seems unduly inflexible, though, especially when the action may be seen to reflect the denial of the deceased's will. Whitty contends that Scots Law properly incorporates an action for *solatium* for affront (the *actio iniuriarum*) in favour of the surviving spouse and next of kin. He describes such an action as the distinctive badge of an

---

[249] Hardcastle, *Law and the Human Body*, p. 148.
[250] See e.g. ALRC, *Essentially Yours*, para. 20.21.
[251] Nwabueze states that the concept of quasi-property 'merely embodies the next of kin's sepulchral rights, which do not sound in property, such as the right to possession and custody of the corpse for burial'; see Nwabueze, 'Biotechnology' at 31.
[252] The actions brought in *In re Organ Retention Group Litigation* fared in mixed terms on account of this requirement, see [2005] QB 506. See also *Devlin v. National Maternity Hospital* [2007] IESC 50 (Supreme Court of Ireland).

affront-based delict and that wounded feelings are distinct from psychological suffering. Moreover, the cause of action does not depend upon showing a right to possession of the body. Roman–Dutch law recognised a right of relatives to *solatium* for interference with the corpse of a relative. Under the doctrine of *injuria per consequentias* 'An *iniuria* directed at A becomes an *iniuria* against B because of the relationship of B to A'.[253] Such a right of action should be recognised across all jurisdictions, although a remedy of some analogous kind might perhaps already emanate directly from Article 8 of the European Convention on Human Rights by way of the Human Rights Act 1998.

## Directed/conditional donation

The directed donation of organs or tissues for transplant is a growing phenomenon, given impetus as a significant issue by growing organ shortages.[254] Sack J in the United States Second Circuit Court of Appeal in *Colavito* v. *New York Organ Donor Network Inc.*, stated 'And the reason for permitting it is to encourage her and others to make limited gifts rather than no gift at all'.[255] Directed or conditional donation of organs or tissue from deceased individuals is rarely addressed explicitly within transplant laws. The Human Tissue Act 2004 and the Human Tissue (Scotland) Act 2006 are both silent in this regard. But whereas directed donation to a specific person or institution from a deceased donor is explicitly permitted in all the US states,[256] in the UK there is a complete ban on such donations in guidelines issued by the Department of Health following the Report of the Panel, *An Investigation into Conditional Donation*, into an incident involving a racist condition occurring in 1998. The Panel Report asserted that 'Either the donor (or their relative) agrees to a part of his or her body being used for donation after death, or they do not'.[257] This policy was recently brought into stark relief in England, when Laura

---

[253] Whitty, 'Rights of personality' at 216. There would appear to be a distinct action for the wrongful removal and retention of organs in Scotland; see *Stevens* v. *Yorkhill NHS Trust and Anor* [2006] ScotCS CSOH 143 (13 September 2006).

[254] Highlighted by the recent spoof TV show in the Netherlands where a dying woman was allegedly going to direct her organs to one of three contestants on a live reality show, the *Big Donor Show*.

[255] *Colavito* v. *New York Organ Donor Network Inc.* 438 F 3d 214 at 228 (2nd Cir. 2006).

[256] Designated donees include: a hospital, accredited medical school, dental college, college or university, organ procurement organisation, other appropriate person for research or education, an individual, or an eye or tissue bank. See, e.g., section 11(a) 2006 Uniform Anatomical Gift Act.

[257] Report of the Panel, *An Investigation into Conditional Donation*, Department of Health, 2000, para. 5.3. Such an 'all-or-nothing' intention cannot be inferred from legislative silence, though, nor is there any necessary implication to this effect.

Ashworth, aged twenty-one, tragically died following an asthma attack. Her mother, Rachel Leake, aged thirty-nine, has end-stage renal failure secondary to diabetes mellitus. Laura was on the NHS Organ Donor Register and had told family and friends that she wanted to donate one of her kidneys to her mother. However, because at the time of her death she had not begun the formal process of becoming a 'living donor', the Human Tissue Authority (HTA) refused to let her mother receive one of her organs. Adrian McNeil, chief executive of the HTA, said: 'the central principle of matching and allocating organs from the deceased is that they are allocated to the person on the UK Transplant waiting list who is in most need and who is the best match with the donor'.[258] Thus, not only are issues of discrimination potentially implicated here but, as McNeil's remarks illustrate, concerns that organs and tissues should be directed, as a matter of justice, toward those with the greatest need.[259] But if organs are the property of the donor why is it not permissible to direct the destination of one's organs?[260] If Laura Ashworth was still alive she could and would have quite legitimately donated a kidney to her mother.[261]

Truog remarks that 'Many of the concerns raised ... regarding the directed donation of organs hinge on the question whether transplantable organs should be considered personal property or a societal resource'.[262] It is often glibly stated that organs from deceased persons are public resources to be distributed by relevant agencies on behalf of the state.[263] Indeed, there are frequently debates relating to whether organs belong to the nation as a whole or to the local transplant unit/centre responsible for retrieval.[264] But it should be questioned from where such dispositional

---

[258] http://news.bbc.co.uk/1/hi/england/bradford/7344205.stm. See also Human Tissue Authority press release 'HTA statement on directed donation of organs after death', 14 April 2008 and, later, Minutes of the thirtieth meeting of the Human Tissue Authority, July 2008, Item 8.

[259] D. Hanto, 'Ethical challenges posed by the solicitation of deceased and living organ donors' (2007) 356 *New England Journal of Medicine* 1062. See also A. Spital *et al.*, 'Solicitation of deceased and living organ donors' (2007) 356 *New England Journal of Medicine* 2427.

[260] A. Cronin and D. Price, 'Directed donation: Is the donor the owner?' (2008) 3(3) *Clinical Ethics* 127.

[261] See Comment, W. Rees-Mogg, *The Times*, 14 April 2008.

[262] R. Truog, 'Are organs personal property or a societal resource?' (2005) 5(4) *American Journal of Bioethics* 14 at 14.

[263] It has been alleged that most people would subscribe to this view; see W. Glannon, 'The case against conscription of cadaveric organs for transplantation' (2008) 17 *Cambridge Quarterly of Healthcare Ethics* 330 at 335.

[264] Rudge states 'A key issue in this respect is the extent to which cadaver kidneys are considered to "belong" to the local transplant unit responsible for retrieval , as opposed

authority over organs arises. How does the transformation from the 'gift of life' into public resource occur?[265] Morley argues that no-one has satisfactorily explained how an organ becomes community property upon separation from the donor's body.[266] Notions of collective/state property in body parts are anathema to most liberal as opposed to socialist societies. Lloyd Cohen asserts in the American context 'But, cadaveric organs do not belong to UNOS. UNOS is given custody and control of organs subject to the conditions placed on those organs by donors.'[267] He draws an analogy with charity trustees and argues that they are obliged to handle and deal with trust resources in accordance with the terms of the trust as drawn up by the settlor. It is inherently a conditional gift for which transplanters are rightly regarded as 'custodians' or even 'trustees'. If directed donation is permissible, specified donees *should* also be able to exercise some claim over the organ(s) concerned, apart from where, as in the case of *Colavito* itself, they are not clinically suitable for the donee in any event.

The permissibility of directed donation may be deducible from property rights. Walter Land once remarked 'The issue of ownership of transplantable organs is of utmost importance since the claim of making allocative decisions may be deduced from the issue of ownership'.[268] In like vein, James Childress, bioethicist and chairman of the Institute of Medicine Report[269] on transplantation in the US, has stated 'It took me some time to discern that our debates about "equitable access" and "equitable allocation" were, in part, debates about who "owns" donated organs'.[270] This would appear to be an *a priori* issue. Lack of resolution of this matter would seem to emanate from ambiguity. Lindemann Nelson

---

to "national" ownership of what can be considered to be a national resource'; C. Rudge, 'Transplantation of organs: Natural limitations, possible solutions – a UK perspective' (2003) 35 *Transplantation Proceedings* 1149 at 1149.

[265] Of course, a 'resource' is not necessarily an item of property – as the growth of the profession of human resource management testifies – but this appears to be the acknowledged implication in this context.

[266] See M. Morley, 'Increasing the supply of organs for transplantation through paired organ exchanges' (2003) 21 *Yale Law and Policy Review* 221 at 254.

[267] L. Cohen, 'UNOS: The faithless trustee' (2005) 5(4) *American Journal of Bioethics* 13 at 13.

[268] W. Land, 'The dilemma of organ allocation: The combination of a therapeutic modality for an ill individual with the distribution of a scarce valuable public (healing) good', in G. Collins, J. Dubernard, W. Land and G. Persijn (eds.), *Procurement, Preservation and Allocation of Vascularized Organs* (Dordrecht: Kluwer, 1997) 361. See also H. Kreis, 'Whose organs are they, anyway?', in W. Weimar, M. Bos and J. Busschbach (eds.), *Organ Transplantation: Ethical, Legal, and Psychosocial Aspects* (Lengerich: Pabst Publishing, 2008) 140.

[269] Institute of Medicine Report, *Organ Donation: Opportunities for Action* (Washington, DC: National Academies Press, 2006).

[270] J. Childress, 'Putting patients first in organ allocation: An ethical analysis of the US debate' (2001) 10 *Cambridge Quarterly of Healthcare Ethics* 368.

asserts 'We don't seem to know just what to make of organs for transplant. As things stand, organs aren't fully property as they cannot be sold. Nor are they fully public goods, as society may not use them at will. The problems about soliciting directed donation correspond to this ambiguity. Suppose my organs belong to me or to my estate. We would need an argument to block my providing them as gifts to whomever I chose. Suppose, on the other hand, at my death my organs became public goods. Then the appropriate way to distribute them would seem to be via a system of impartial, impersonal justice.'[271]

Directed living donation is of course not only accepted, but the norm. Kluge argues that donations by living persons 'create and sustain intimate personal relationships', and in particular family ties, and that the different approaches reflect (a) the (unique) privilege attaching to certain donations by living persons, which constitute *exceptions to the general rules of impartial allocation,* coupled with the fact that the involvement of society in deceased donation renders such gifts subject to societal standards and rules.[272] However, in so far as society is seemingly 'involved' in living donor transplantation also the latter rationale seems tenuous, and the former might suggest that *deceased* donation to family members at least should also be acceptable.[273] Fox remarks that 'directed donation, like living organ donation, offers the opportunity to make the notion of "gift" in organ donation coherent. That is, one can direct the gift to a recipient of his or her choosing – to a person in whom one has a particular interest.'[274] In any event, the deceased and living donor systems do not co-exist as separate and discrete, impartial and partial, systems. Living exchanges or 'swaps' are examples of hybrid-type arrangements, and whilst in all jurisdictions a living individual may donate organs or tissues to a person with whom they share a familial, genetic or emotional relationship, in the absence of such a relationship donation is typically required to be non-directed and offered to the first suitable candidate on the national

---

[271] J. Lindemann Nelson, 'Trusts and transplants' (2005) 5(4) *American Journal of Bioethics* 26 at 27.

[272] E.-H. Kluge, 'Designated organ donation: Private choice in social context' (1989) (September/October) *Hastings Center Report* 10 at 12.

[273] The American Society of Transplant Surgeons endorses the directed donation of cadaveric organs only to family members, friends and individuals with whom a relationship exists through community, but the Council on Ethical and Judicial Affairs of the American Medical Association has queried why donation should not be permitted even to individuals with whom one does not share a community bond.

[274] M. Fox, 'Directed organ donation: Donor autonomy and community values', in B. Spielman (ed.), *Organ and Tissue Donation: Ethical, Legal, and Policy Issues* (Carbondale, IL: Southern Illinois University Press, 1996) 43 at 47.

transplant waiting list, as is the case in all deceased donor scenarios outside the US.[275]

Even if one rejects the notion of ownership by the donor of their dead
body parts, one can nonetheless endorse the donor's right to control the
use of his or her body parts whilst either alive or dead. The notion that
organs are principally for donors to direct or control raises the possibility –
for some, spectre – of conditional donation based on membership of a
class. Hilhorst, however, notes that one may harbour feelings of 'belonging' within a community or group as much as one feels connectedness to
particular individuals.[276] He advocates class-directed donation based on
certain *positive* characteristics, and argues that the intention of partial
transplants is to 'include' not 'exclude'.[277] Certainly not every advantage
amounts to unfair discrimination, but to prefer one group is necessarily to
disadvantage another, e.g. donation to a local community or church group
would necessarily serve to deprioritise other groups with particular (e.g.
racial or religious) affiliations. Ankeny remarks as regards class-directed
donations as a whole 'In themselves, such motivations exhibit a failure to
respect individuals as equals, as worthy of equal respect and dignity'.[278]
She argues that the factors in favour of such donations do not trump our
typical concerns about partiality. Some would see any 'concessions' as
amounting to the thin end of the wedge, constituting a breach of formal
Aristotelian justice that equals be treated equally.[279]

One need not necessarily conflate directed and conditional donation,
though. Whilst the United Network for Organ Sharing (UNOS) accepts
directed donation it regards 'class-directed' donations as unacceptable,[280] neither do the Uniform Anatomical Gift Acts explicitly permit
conditional donations. Public policy may, and indeed sometimes must,

---

[275] For instance, under the scheme operated by UK Transplant. The US is exceptional in this
regard. See R. Gohh, P. Morrissey, P. Madras and A. Monaco, 'Controversies in organ
donation: The altruistic living donor' (2001) 16 *Nephrology Dialysis Transplant* 619.

[276] M. Hilhorst, 'Directed altruistic living organ donation: Partial but not unfair' (2005) 8
*Ethical Theory and Moral Practice* 197 at 205.

[277] M. Hilhorst, '"Living apart together": Moral frictions between two coexisting organ
transplantation schemes' (2008) 34 *Journal of Medical Ethics* 484 at 487.

[278] R. Ankeny, 'The moral status of preferences for directed donation: Who should decide
who gets transplantable organs?' (2001) 10 *Cambridge Quarterly of Healthcare Ethics* 387
at 393.

[279] It has been suggested that formulating policy rules may be so problematic that it would be
better perhaps not to embark on such a path at all; see G. den Hartogh, *Farewell to Non-
commitment: Decision Systems for Organ Donation from an Ethical Viewpoint*, Monitoring
Report Ethics and Health, Centre for Ethics and Health, The Hague, 2008 at 87.

[280] See UNOS, 'Directed Donation', at www.unos.org/Resources/bioethics.asp?index=11.
Nevertheless, it is reported that occasionally conditions that organs go to children, or to
'first-time recipients' only, have been accepted by OPOs. Surveys in the US reveal that

properly place constraints on donor autonomy and 'distribution' in the interests of society, and the enterprise of transplantation as a whole, even where it is thought that permitting such practices would result in an increase in donated organs. Whilst only Florida has specific discrimination provisions, prohibiting anatomical gifts on the basis of colour, religion, sex, race, national origin, age, physical handicap, health status, marital or economic status,[281] acceptance of certain types of conditional donation would infringe general anti-discrimination laws, such as the UK's Race Relations Act 1976, and human rights legislation and constitutional rights might be pertinent to some contexts. However, in so far as the organs themselves are (within the current legal framework) appropriately seen to be initially subject to the 'direction' of the person from whose body such organs are removed, there should be compelling reasons to restrict such choices. The burden of proof appears to rest with the state to justify limiting such choices. It is unclear why one should not 'prefer' one's close friends and relatives after death, even if no others. This ought not to tarnish the image of transplantation as a transparently fair system. There are nevertheless broad considerations relating to public trust and faith in the prevailing allocation system implicated in this debate.

whilst the public is generally disinclined toward conditional donation almost three-quarters are willing to allow a condition that organs go to children only, or first. See A. Spital [2003] 76(8) *Transplantation* 1252.

[281] By virtue of an incident occurring in that state relating to a Ku Klux Klan member who would donate only to a white person.

# Conclusion

It has been remarked that 'The history of transplantation itself is rooted in the era of bodysnatching'.[1] The legacy of non-consensual practices relating to both the living body and the corpse in the spheres of anatomical dissection and research are patent, in the latter case continuing right up to the present day.[2] Differing perceptions of the 'character' of human tissue have come to drive a wedge between prevailing professional practices and contemporary expectations. The Retained Organs Commission remarked in its Final Report that 'The research community struggled to see how what they regarded as work to advance medical science and promote better health could be wrong, whether or not it was done with consent. Human body parts, even human bodies, were perhaps to some scientists mere artefacts, no different from the instruments also utilised in their research.'[3] A seismic shift can now be seen, and a general crystallisation of the notion that individuals have a right to control the uses of tissues emanating from their living or dead bodies, reflected in the necessity for consent or authorisation. Audi contends that 'There is, I think, a moral presumption that one's relation to one's body is so intimate that the body should not be invaded, even after one's death, without at least one's prior tacit consent or at worst the consent of relatives or friends who can be assigned to speak authoritatively for one's interests (prior to death)'.[4] This is a matter of fundamental principle with permissions being linked to specific purposes. O'Neill, for instance, states 'Consent to removal of tissue for clinical reasons will not be viewed as entailing

---

[1] R. Richardson, 'Human transplantation and dissection in historical context', in M. Sque and S. Payne (eds.), *Organ and Tissue Donation: An Evidence Base for Practice* (Maidenhead: Open University Press, 2007) 4 at 18.

[2] As regards the living, this may be seen to be reflected in the use of the notion of 'waste' as regards surplus tissue.

[3] Retained Organs Commission, *Remembering the Past, Looking to the Future*, NHS, 2004, para. 1.25.

[4] R. Audi, 'The morality and utility of organ transplantation' (1996) 8 *Utilitas* 141 at 147.

consent to its use for research'.[5] The utility of the human body is now to be juxtaposed against notions of respect for persons. As the President's Council on Bioethics stated 'It is no exaggeration to say that our attitudes about organ transplantation say much about the kind of society that we are, both for better and worse'.[6] The same may be said as regards research.

There are common tensions in the spheres of both transplantation and research: the need for an ethically robust system for authorising the taking and use of tissue, and the pressure to ensure a sufficient supply of materials. The need for body materials is most immediately pressing in the sphere of transplantation but no less compelling for certain forms of medical research. An overarching legal and ethical framework is essential. A rights-based framework set against a dignitarian baseline reflects the most appropriate skeletal regulatory model, with individuals themselves having *prima facie* authority and control over materials emanating from their own bodies, best captured in the notion of property rights and donation in terms of (conditional) gifts. Such rights attach even to the use of one's corpse after death, and reflect posthumous interests deserving of protection.

In almost all societies the demand for body materials for research and transplantation is rising. Not only is there an escalating need for (*in-vitro* cultured) human tissue to replace animal models in laboratory testing, but deaths of patients with organ failure requiring transplants are increasing as are waiting times for transplant across the board,[7] exacerbating morbidity and fuelling unlawful transplant tourism and other efforts to evade 'official' constraints. The involvement of the EU in issues of organ supply as an aspect of 'public health' in this sphere bears testimony to the problems this shortfall generates. The recent Declaration of Istanbul stated that 'Unethical practices are, in part, an undesirable consequence of the global shortage of organs for transplantation. Thus, each country should strive to ensure that programs to prevent organ failure are implemented and to provide organs to meet the transplant needs of its residents from donors within its own population or through regional cooperation.'[8] This state

---

[5] O. O'Neill, *Autonomy and Trust in Bioethics* (Cambridge University Press, 2004), p. 153 [O'Neill, *Autonomy and Trust*]. One should not assume consent for non-therapeutic objectives from consent to therapy.

[6] President's Council on Bioethics, 'Organ Transplantation: Ethical Dilemmas and Policy Choices', Background Paper, 2006/7, at www.bioethics.gov/background/org_transplant. html.

[7] Averaging four to five years in the Netherlands, for example.

[8] The Declaration of Istanbul, 2008, Preamble. See 'Transplant tourists running out of destinations' (2008) 8 July *New Scientist*, at www.newscientist.com/article/dn14273-transplant-tourists-running-out-of-destinations-health-08July2008. It emphasised that

mandate of self-sufficiency exists even where no illegal transplant tourism occurs, as a function of the duty to care for the health of its citizens. As Noorani states 'Transplantation has now established itself as a first line treatment for end stage renal failure with excellent results. It is therefore the moral duty of governments to ensure that enough organs are available for transplantation.'[9]

The acceptance of a moral obligation of self-sufficiency may perhaps necessitate, in some contexts, a greater emphasis upon living donors.[10] Jakobsen states 'Aiming at giving as many as possible of the patients of ESRD [end-stage renal disease] the best possible treatment, without having to wait unnecessarily long and at the lowest possible cost to the community, Norway has succeeded better than other countries. The extensive use of living donation is an integral part of this success.'[11] Initially, though, a society should seek to optimise the use of available deceased sources of supply to achieve the requisite ends, apart from with regard to the use of *surplus* tissues from living individuals for the purposes of research. The Declaration of Istanbul also stated that 'The therapeutic potential of deceased organ donation should be maximised not only for kidneys but also for other organs, appropriate to the transplantation needs of each country. Efforts to initiate or enhance deceased donor transplantation are essential to minimise the burden on living donors.'[12] A shortage of available organs and tissues from deceased donors will exercise a correspondingly compelling effect on potential living donors relative to demand.

The subsidiarity principle promotes the preference for deceased sources for transplantation, certainly for substantial materials removed specifically for such purposes, and is reflected in various laws and official policy documents.[13] Although it may appear to hold little sway in the light of the dramatically expanding rates of living organ donation in Europe and

---

treatment of patients from outside the jurisdiction should only be performed where this was not detrimental to the nation's ability to serve the needs of its own population [Declaration of Istanbul].

[9] M. Noorani, 'Commercial transplantation in Pakistan and its effects on Western countries' (2008) 336 *British Medical Journal* 1378 at 1378.

[10] Indeed, the WHO has begun – in stark contradistinction to its traditional stance – to encourage living donation as a means of *avoiding* organ trafficking; see, e.g., Fifty-Seventh World Health Assembly Resolutions WHA40.13, 42.5 and 44.25 reported at (2005) 79 (6) *Transplantation* 635.

[11] A. Jakobsen, 'Living donor practices and processes in Europe', in D. Price and J. Akveld (eds.), *Living Organ Donation in the Nineties: European Medico-Legal Perspectives* (EUROTOLD, 1996) 1 at 10.

[12] Declaration of Istanbul at 1.

[13] Notably in the Council of Europe, Convention for the Protection of Human Rights and Dignity of the Human Being with regard to the application of biology and medicine, 1997, Article 19.

North America, this has invariably been a reluctant response to an unplanned on-going supply crisis. It may perhaps now simply be being recognised for the first time that a shortage of deceased materials is likely to be a long-term reality. Rates of supply from deceased donors are inadequate to meet demand even in nations with very impressively good rates of transplantation, such as Spain. Even novel, experimental and creative living donor strategies therefore have a clear role and justification in some societies at the present time, albeit that there is a need for rigorous procedural review to ensure what has been described as 'safety by procedure'.[14] But whilst the growth and variety of offers to donate organs whilst alive is a reflection of the richness of our moral world, all ethically acceptable donation strategies and policy options utilising deceased donors to enhance supply should be pursued to avoid over-reliance on living donors. There is a moral imperative to promote these as far as resources reasonably allow. Moreover, having regard to the longer term, research and development support should be provided to assist in the exploitation of xenotransplantation and stem cell therapies as potential future *alternatives* to human organ donation itself.

But whilst the quest for an increased supply of human material for such ends is crucial, it should not be regarded as ethically all-consuming. Consent (or authorisation) is presently perceived as a 'given' for organ and tissue donation, apart perhaps from the use of surplus or archived tissue for research. However, clear policy decisions need to be made with respect to the nature of the consent framework to be adopted and the infrastructural framework needed to be provided. At the present the role of relatives is not clearly articulated or illuminated as regards deceased donation in most explicit consent systems, creating a lack of clarity and a muddle at the heart of the process. It seems that their function is a conflation of separate lines of thinking, i.e. respect for the rights of certain relatives to manage the corpse for the purposes of burial or cremation and the role of relatives as conduits for conveying the will of the deceased. Two of the six objectives of the Human Tissue Act 2004 identified by the Department of Health relate to the improvement of public confidence anticipated to lead to increased rates of donation for research, transplantation, etc.[15] The strategy chosen appears to have been to attempt to involve and appease all of the involved parties on the donation side. But to the extent that relatives' decision-making powers in actual practice are

---

[14] A phrase coined by Gutmann and Land; see 'Ethics in living donor organ transplantation', at http://trans.klinikum.uni-muenchen.de/ethics.htm.

[15] M. Brazier and S. Fovargue, 'A brief guide to the Human Tissue Act 2004' (2006) 1 *Clinical Ethics* 26 at 26.

unfettered by the new law, this may actually serve to undermine the very objective of securing an adequate supply of organs and tissues for the requisite purposes.

There is, however, a clear move towards affording deceased adults exclusive decision-making authority. Cohen states 'But at bottom the moral authority for consent to donate organs lies only with the person whose organs they are, or were'.[16] But whilst the primacy of the wishes of the deceased over those of relatives is manifest in most laws and policies, the practice in most of these jurisdictions typically parts company with official policy. Although relatives have a crucial function in conveying further evidence as to the deceased's wishes, they have very often been afforded the right to make the decision for themselves, based on whatever grounds they choose.[17] As a function of a lack of information as to what most deceased individuals would have wished to take place, relatives face a potentially very difficult decision, at a time of extreme emotional crisis and stress, whether to allow a loved one to be 'cut up', or the 'wholeness' of the corpse compromised, for such ends.[18] As has been noted, relatives perceive this decision as involving a major sacrifice in many instances in the context of transplantation, leading to substantial refusal rates. Rates of relatives' objection are typically lower in presumed than explicit consent systems, due partially to the fact that they are not 'deciding' and at most are simply being afforded a discretion to refuse. Moreover, even when invited to decide, donation is more likely where the deceased person did not 'opt out' whilst alive, as there is some evidence of the person's lack of objection.

Emphasis on the wishes of deceased persons and the potential advantageous impact upon donation rates suggests that societies should at least consider the appropriateness of implementing a presumed consent framework for deceased persons. In presumed consent systems, the focus is principally upon the (deceased) donors themselves, and their own wishes,

---

[16] C. Cohen, 'The case for presumed consent to transplant human organs after death' (1992) 24(5) *Transplantation Proceedings* 2168 at 2170 [Cohen, 'The case for presumed consent'].

[17] Under the US Uniform Anatomical Gift Act 2006, although if the deceased is silent a relative may generally donate after death, a person may sign a refusal which would preclude a relative from having the power to donate. The 1997 Law of Germany is an exception, stipulating that the relatives should make the decision that they believe the deceased would have made him/her self. Kamm suggests that decision-making powers afforded to relatives after another's death reflect the delegation of state powers. F. Kamm, *Morality, Mortality. Volume 1* (Oxford University Press, 1993), p. 219.

[18] See V. S. Leith, 'Consent and nothing but consent? The organ retention scandal' (2007) 29(7) *Sociology of Health & Illness* 1023 at 1029–30.

although relatives are themselves entitled to object to donation in weak jurisdictions.

However, many consider that a real consent can only be founded upon a *factual* consent, i.e. cogent evidence of a *decision* to donate or not to donate. In certain circumstances, though, a *tacit* consent might be sufficient to this end. But in general this is not plausible in the absence of a direct approach and information at an individual level, supported by an extensive on-going public information campaign. Thus, most systems cannot at present aspire to reflect factual, tacit (silent) consent. The recommended systems proposed by den Hartogh and the German National Ethics Council, on the other hand, are not only well considered but would apparently suffice to establish a valid tacit consent. They differ in that under the former model the relatives would become superfluous to the decision-making process unless explicitly delegated the power to decide by the deceased. The latter would enable relatives to object when the deceased person had not actually positively recorded their wish.[19] The possibility of relatives being aware of wishes which might cast doubt on the 'decision' of a deceased person is a feature favouring the latter model, and in particular where the deceased person might have lacked decision-making capability when alive.

In the absence of any such direct approach, consent could only be regarded as *imputed* based on the evidence of the wishes of the majority of the populace, although some would carp at the use of the terminology of 'consent' here. It is this form of consent that is truly 'presumptive'. In any event, much hinges upon the available general and specific contemporaneous evidence as to individuals' willingness to donate after death in the community concerned. Where the available evidence supports the inference that a majority of citizens are willing to donate after death, such a system should be considered *in principle*. By dint of the failure of most individuals in explicit consent systems to communicate their wishes regarding donation prior to death, their will may not be currently being acceded to in many instances. The objective here is to reflect the wishes of the deceased in the greatest percentage of instances. But even in these contexts, public information and easy opportunities to object are essential. Whilst it is reasonable to assume a lack of objection in some instances on account of lethargy, it is not reasonable to do so on the back of ignorance. Such remarks are relevant also to research post-mortem,

---

[19]  Wilkinson notes that objections to presumed consent based on the exclusion of the family can only be properly aimed at strong systems which form a tiny fraction of the current schemes; see T. M. Wilkinson, 'Presumed consent and uncertainty about the wishes of the dead', unpublished Rotterdam conference paper.

although greater initial public education may be required to inform citizens of practices of which they were previously unaware.

There appear to be two different notions of autonomy at play in relation to the bodies of deceased persons. Firstly, a non-interference model requiring the integrity of the corpse to be left intact in the absence of consent, and secondly, a 'respect-for-wishes' model, as Gill has dubbed it, which gives sway to the wishes of the deceased broadly as regards the disposition of the cadaver and its parts.[20] Gill maintains that it is the last model which should be the dominant one here, and that this should drive a search for a system which best gives effect to the wishes of individuals who are subsequently deprived of life. If so, this lends support to presumed, imputed consent as a potential policy option.

Another question relates to the necessary degree of commitment to donation required. Wicclair asks

> If the premortem preferences and values of persons do matter ethically, is it sufficient to ascertain that proposed research is not incompatible with them? A stronger protection would be to require that the person who died would have consented. This stronger protection seems unwarranted and excessive however. First, the premortem preferences and values of the deceased person are respected in a significant sense; second, there is no risk of pain, suffering, morbidity, or mortality to the deceased; third, there is significant potential benefit to the living; and fourth, even when a deceased person would have consented to participate in a post-mortem research protocol if asked prior to death, it is unlikely that family members would have sufficient evidence to establish this conclusion.[21]

He argues that convincing evidence of an absence of an objection is all that is ethically necessary here. Once more, if this is accurate, presumed, imputed consent is a proper policy alternative.

Perception is as crucial as reality, however, and donation based on silence may be automatically conflated in individuals' minds with the state acquisition/appropriation of body parts:[22] 'Orwellian', in the words of the Church of Scotland's magazine.[23] It has been described as being at odds with the values at the heart of the democracy of the UK.[24] Goss asserts that 'Presumed consent runs counter to the principle of protecting

---

[20] M. Gill, 'Presumed consent, autonomy, and organ donation' (2004) 29(1) *Journal of Medicine and Philosophy* 37 at 44.

[21] M. Wicclair, 'Informed consent and research involving the newly dead' (2002) 12(4) *Kennedy Institute of Ethics Journal* 351 at 362.

[22] See, e.g., Comment, 'Matter of consent', *The Times*, 17 January 2008. The Institute of Medicine, however, rejects such a view; see Institute of Medicine Report, *Organ Donation: Opportunities for Action* (Washington, DC: National Academies Press, 2006) at 206 [Institute of Medicine, *Organ Donation*].

[23] See www.sundayherald.com/news/heraldnews/display.var.2156953.0.presumed_con.

[24] *The Times*, 18 January 2008.

patients' rights to fully informed agreement. It clashes with current thinking, which is moving towards the idea of involving patients fully in treatment decisions.'[25] Indeed, the very language of 'presumption' is
confounding and a hinderance here. Roseanna Cunningham stated in
the Scottish Parliament that 'A gift is not a gift if we attach the word
"presumed" to it. The proposal turns on its head the notion of organ
donation as a gift.'[26] During the passage of the Human Tissue Bill
through Parliament, the Minister of Health similarly remarked 'We
believe very strongly that we should not assume that someone wants to
make that gift'.[27] This has synergies with some of the reasoning of the
Organ Donation Taskforce (ODT) which was concerned that presumed
consent might undermine the concept of donation as a gift, and might
erode trust in NHS professionals and the Government, which might in
turn affect donation rates.[28] The relationship between clinicians and the
family of the deceased person was a particular source of anxiety. Whatever
the general merits of a policy, public perceptions are crucial. The ODT
received evidence that many of those who expressed disagreement with a
presumed consent law declared that they would remove their names from
the organ donor register in the event that such a policy became law.[29]

Healy observes that explicit consent systems are more associated with
liberal than corporatist (or conservative) regimes, i.e. more consistent
with a general orientation toward the individual rather than the state.[30]
Thus, whilst presumed consent is not at odds with a libertarian, individualistic framework it is not entirely familiar or 'at ease' with it either. The
Institute of Medicine Report remarked that 'It is important to note that
several possibly important differences exist between prominent U.S.
beliefs and values, particularly individualism, and the beliefs and values
of most of the countries with opt-out policies',[31] although it considered it
to be a mistake to presume that only explicit consent embodies altruism or
generosity.[32] But it is also erroneous to assume explicit consent displays a

[25] R. Goss (letter), 'Presumed consent further undermines medical ethics' (2000) 321
*British Medical Journal* 1023.
[26] Roseanna Cunningham, Debate on Motion S3M-483 (George Foulkes), col. 5546,
24 January 2008.
[27] Rosie Winterton MP, House of Commons Hansard Debates, col. 83, 28 June 2004.
[28] *The Potential Impact of an Opt Out System for Organ Donation in the UK: An Independent
Report from the Organ Donation Taskforce*, 2008 at 34 [*The Potential Impact*].
[29] Annex L, *ibid.*, Supporting Information.
[30] K. Healy, 'The political economy of presumed consent', 2005, at http://repositories.cdlib.
org/uclasoc/trcsa/31 at 12 and 22.
[31] Institute of Medicine, *Organ Donation* at 225.
[32] *Ibid.*, at 221. Childress maintains that presumed consent builds on 'passive altruism'; see
J. Childress, 'Some moral connections between organ procurement and organ distribution' (1987) 3 *Journal of Contemporary Health Law and Policy* 85 at 94.

greater orientation toward the individual when relatives are the usual decision-makers and frequently lack reliable knowledge of deceaseds' wishes. As Cohen declares 'We may presume one way, or presume the other, but presume we must'.[33]

Presumed consent is not, however, an ideal or universal panacea in any circumstances. One can anticipate higher 'conversion rates' (of potential to actual donors) simply from improved resourcing, infrastructure and systems. The Potential Donor Audit found that the conversion rate in the UK in 2005–6 was 49 per cent for heart-beating-deceased donors, but that the maximum achievable rate of donation was 23.2 per million population (p.m.p.) per annum, nearly double the existing actual rate.[34] But without a drastic reduction in 'refusal' rates, supply will still not come near to meeting demand. Ideally what is needed is for the wishes of individuals as to what they want to happen after their deaths to be made explicit in the overwhelming preponderance of cases. In that event, we could simply act only upon those cases where the deceased person him/herself consented to donation, hopefully leading to an even higher rate of donation.

But whilst it is crucial to seek to divine the wishes of individuals prior to their deaths, there are inherent problems pertaining to both voluntary and mandated choice systems in the context of a scheme where it is only the explicit consent of the deceased which will, legally, suffice. In voluntary systems it is unrealistic to anticipate the large majority of people explicitly recording their wishes, at least in the short term, although in the US requests to donate via driving licences appear to be rising rapidly. A reticence to confront or deal with our own impending mortality is not only understandable but inevitable in many instances. Mandated choice, on the other hand, is viewed by many as coercive, and the inherent pressure to decide could persuade many otherwise possible consentors to decide not to donate, i.e. coercion may distort responses. In other words, not only could either system result in *less* human material becoming available for research or transplantation than at present, but a 'first-person' consent system would *not in fact* be reflecting the real wishes of many individuals in any event. At least for the short to medium term it is therefore to be expected that relatives will continue to play a central role in cases where the wishes of the deceased are not directly recorded. But for the reasons explained earlier, rates of relatives' refusal will probably

---

[33] Cohen, 'The case for presumed consent' at 2172.

[34] K. Barber, S. Falvey, C. Hamilton, D. Collett and C. Rudge, 'Potential for organ donation in the United Kingdom: Audit of intensive care records' (2006) 332 *British Medical Journal* 1124.

remain at a relatively substantial level, again despite this not always being faithful to the views of the deceased.

The normal contemporary paradigm is for explicit consent systems to have opt in registers and for presumed consent systems to have opt out registers. The basic reasoning is that in explicit consent jurisdictions it is consent that justifies removal and use so it is consents that one needs to record and convey. Obversely, in presumed consent systems it is lack of objection that provides authority for removal and use so it is objections that one seeks to record and convey. Such reasoning is too simplistic. There is a need for registers to record both requests to donate *and* objections in all jurisdictions. In presumed consent systems it is still the case that an explicit stated wish to donate is stronger evidence of the desire to donate than is a failure to record an objection, so the additional recording of such positive consent would be a boon.[35] This preference for positive statements of intent can be seen in Belgium, whereby relatives may veto donation where the deceased had not objected to donation, but are not permitted to override the expressly stated wish of the deceased to donate.[36] Even more important is the ability to record objections in an explicit consent system. Not only is there no other means of communicating objections reliably in most instances apart from via relatives (and relying on their availability at the time of death), but many relatives refuse to agree to donation simply because there is no available evidence at all (not even a failure to object) as to whether the individual would have wished to be a donor. In a members' business debate in the Scottish Parliament, Mr Jamie Hepburn expressed scepticism as to the usefulness of a register for objections in an explicit consent system, stating 'In an opt-in and opt-out system, those who do neither effectively opt-out. There would be little or no improvement on the current situation.'[37] But this view is misguided. At least the failure to object is some evidence that there was no objection held, giving the family some indirect information upon which to base their decision. If relatives are perceived to have a substituted judgement function, the more evidence of the person's wishes the better. Thus, two-way registers should be universally established in the research as well as transplantation field.

Although consent is generally regarded as an essential pre-requisite of retention and use for research or transplantation, exceptions are made for

---

[35] Quite apart from providing better evidence to relatives in the event that they are tasked in practice with the ultimate decision.

[36] Law of 13 June 1986 on the removal and transplantation of organs, section 10(4).

[37] Debate on Motion S3M-483 (George Foulkes), Organ Donation, Members Business Debate, Scottish Parliament, 24 January 2008.

certain types of activity involving secondary use of tissue for research. The requirement for consent for the use of surplus tissue which has not been anonymised in the 2004 Act has nonetheless been criticised itself for being too indiscriminate. Furness and Nicholson state that 'There is evidence from surveys of public opinion that the majority of the public regard most "surplus" therapeutically excised tissue as having little or no emotional value. This clearly differs from the situation in respect of autopsy tissue.'[38] However, although surplus tissue from the living should be used in preference to tissue removed specifically for research from either living or deceased persons, the right to control the use of all tissue nonetheless inheres in the tissue source, albeit that 'proportionate' consent requirements may be justified in specific instances, including presumed consent. Whilst it is seemingly the case that the very large majority of individuals are indifferent to the fate or disposition of their tissues removed during therapeutic procedures, especially diseased tissue, this is not universally the case and fails to respect the individual's *prima facie* right to decide whether to contribute to any particular scientific initiative through the use of his/her tissue. Despite what are otherwise transparently valuable societal activities, some individuals may harbour personal objections based on profound as well as lesser beliefs, e.g. objections by orthodox Roman Catholics to research relating to birth control products.[39] This is the case whether such tissues are temporarily or permanently stripped of personal identifiers or not. Anonymised human materials are more than mere information.[40] However, assuming a right to record specific as well as general objections, it should be feasible to consent to research or transplantation in general, generic terms, despite a lack of detailed knowledge of such use(s). This is consistent with a shared, partnership approach. Where information is made available to all patients directly, informing them of such potential uses and of easy opportunities to reliably record any objections, presumed rather than explicit consent should also frequently suffice.

Generally the law concerns itself with 'takings' (i.e. removals) rather than storage or use. It is also generally pre-occupied with damage and harm. The Royal College of Pathologists has stated as regards surplus tissue from the living 'To some, it seems perverse to extend the law so that it creates an offence where nobody has been harmed, nobody wishes to

---

[38] P. Furness and M. Nicholson, 'Obtaining explicit consent for the use of archival tissue samples: Practical issues' [2004] 30 *Journal of Medical Ethics* 561 at 561.

[39] Traditional Jews might also require the return of surgically removed tissue to accompany their whole body at death.

[40] C. Trouet, 'New European guidelines for the use of stored human biological materials in biomedical research' (2004) 30 *Journal of Medical Ethics* 99 at 100.

complain and where the intention of the "offender" is to help the sick'.[41]
But as Quigley states

However, implicit in these approaches is the concept of a damaging act, and our
consideration of an individual's rights with regard to their body and our concerns
over the use and control of our bodies and of their parts and products are not
confined to considerations solely to do with damage.[42]

The proper entitlement of donors or their assigns to exert on-going
influence over body parts donated for specified legitimate medical or
scientific ends is not only a function of the avoidance of (physical or
psychological) harm but of rights of 'control' *per se*.

This *right of control* must be continuing, to ensure the 'faithfulness' of
the gift, and remedies should be available to execute this. Only rights of
property in isolated parts of living beings and corpses can adequately
ensure this, vesting rights originally in the donor. Beyleveld and
Brownsword assert that rule-preclusionary control is necessary to protect
the source's generic rights because 'The effect of not giving me such
control is that, in the absence of my having objected to a use, there
would be no necessary presumption against use by others where the use
did not appear to be specifically harmful to me'.[43] Nelkin and Andrews
have referred to the inappropriate 'finders' keepers' policy presently
endorsed by some public policy, allowing healthcare professionals to
exclude others from the 'patient's' samples.[44]

It is, however, a *non sequitur* to insist that property rights incorporate a
right of sale. It has been judicially observed that the Supreme Court has
'never held that a physical item is not "property" simply because it lacks a
positive economic or market value'.[45] This may simply be one of the
bundle of sticks/twigs missing in this context.[46] In any event, the core
idea of property is the right of exclusion. The view that a human interaction should only be removed from the market world where the transaction costs are too high (i.e. market failure) is an economists' view driven

---

[41] Response of the Royal College of Pathologists to *Human Bodies, Human Choices*, Royal
College of Pathologists, 2002, para. 9.
[42] M. Quigley, 'Property and the body: Applying Honoré' (2007) 33 *Journal of Medical Ethics*
631 at 631.
[43] D. Beyleveld and R. Brownsword, *Dignity in Bioethics and Biolaw* (Oxford University
Press, 2001), p. 187.
[44] D. Nelkin and L. Andrews, 'Do the dead have interests? Policy issues for research after
life' (1998) 24(2 & 3) *American Journal of Law and Medicine* 261 at 288.
[45] *Newman* v. *Sathyavaglswaran* 287 F 3d 786 at 797 (US Ct. App., 9th Cir. 2002).
[46] See E. Jaffe, 'She's got Bette Davis's eyes: Assessing the non-consensual removal of
cadaver organs under the takings and due process clauses' (1990) 90 *Columbia Law
Review* 528 at 549–56.

entirely by an efficiency and market philosophy.[47] Even moral aspects are subsumed into market rhetoric in such a paradigm, i.e. as external costs, whereas they are separate considerations.[48] This is a question to be tackled discretely and in the specific context, considering both intrinsic and extrinsic factors. Childress opines that 'The various available arguments do not convince me that the act of selling an organ is intrinsically immoral. However, there may be extrinsic reasons for prohibiting, or at least not encouraging, as a matter of social practice what is not intrinsically immoral.'[49] These might include – assuming they were justified – concerns about the impact on supply. Radin argues that to treat personal property as fungible property is to redefine and change the character of any act of 'giving'. It affects our understanding of ourselves as embodied and our understanding of the relationship between our selves and our bodies.[50] This may in turn be counterproductive in terms of levels of donation. Healy, however, argues that the role of money lies not in its instrumental qualities but instead in its *expressive* qualities.[51] Indeed, a recent Dutch Report considered that there were important ethical distinctions between types of reward in the transplant context.[52] It preferred payments to living individuals, and in particular an indirect reward such as life-long exemption from medical insurance, which would have a potential medical 'link' in people's minds.[53] In any event, proprietary market alienable rights vested in third parties should be universally available to items *derived* from human materials but *distinct* in character from them. These 'novel products' are continuing to expand in diversity, utility and character. Anderson and Bottenfield have remarked that 'Tissues

---

[47] The seminal source being G. Calabresi and M. Melamed, 'Property rules, liability rules, and inalienability: One view of the cathedral' (1972) 85 *Harvard Law Review* 1089. See also R. Epstein, 'Why restrain alienation' (1985) 85 *Columbia Law Review* 970.

[48] See E. Gold, *Body Parts: Property Rights and the Ownership of Human Biological Materials* (Washington, DC: Georgetown University Press, 1996).

[49] J. Childress, 'My body as property: Some philosophical reflections' (1992) 24(5) *Transplantation Proceedings* 2143 at 2144.

[50] See George, President's Council on Bioethics, Session 4: Organ Transplantation and Policy Reform, 7 September, 2006, at www.bioethics.gov/transcripts/sept06/session4.html.

[51] K. Healy, *Last Best Gifts* (University of Chicago Press, 2006), p. 36.

[52] See G. van Dijk and M. Hilhorst, *Financial Incentives for Organ Donation: An Investigation of the Ethical Issues*, Centre for Ethics and Health, 2007. Research conducted in the US has suggested that even as regards deceased donation support for funeral benefits, charitable donations, travel/lodging costs and medical expenses was higher than for direct payments; see C. Bryce, L. Siminoff, P. Ubel, H. Nathan, A. Caplan and R. Arnold, 'Do incentives matter? Providing benefits to families of organ donors' (2005) 5 *American Journal of Transplantation* 2999 at 3001.

[53] *Ibid.*, at 42. Although whether this would be sufficient in a national health service system is dubious.

have become increasingly processed, often closely resembling synthetic or metallic devices'.[54]

There is also a perception that allowing property rights will facilitate exclusive control and unfettered use and powers over such materials, including use for ethically unacceptable purposes.[55] However, there are limits to permissible uses of human tissue, and public health matters. After death, human tissue or whole bodies may only be donated for certain legitimate ends, or otherwise should be properly disposed of (whether re-united with the corpse as a whole or not) as part of the respectful disposal of human remains. It is not necessary for such items to be treated synonymously with other inheritable personal property. Thus, human materials are subject to property rights only for limited purposes. They do not have to form part of the deceased's estate.[56] It is also objected that property given 'binds', and to that extent is not desirable. But in fact no one is bound to hold anything as property or to accept any gift.

The notion of the 'gift' is undoubtedly exceptionally ambiguous and confounding; a 'vague notion'.[57] It is tempting to entirely abandon and replace it in this context. But whilst notions of what constitute a 'gift' emanating from legal, anthropological and sociological sources are generally burdensome rather than helpful, one must still agree with Laurie that 'The notion of the gift has a strong normative appeal in lay terms' in both the contexts being considered.[58] Whilst there may be an exception with respect to the use of surplus diseased tissue from living persons for research, where it is necessary to remove the tissue for therapeutic reasons, perceptions differ markedly even here.[59] The 'giving' of body materials for research and transplantation needs to be emphasised, unencumbered by the anthropological baggage accompanying 'the gift'.

---

[54] M. Anderson and S. Bottenfield, 'Tissue banking – past, present, and future', in S. Youngner, M. Anderson and R. Schapiro (eds.), *Transplanting Human Tissue: Ethics, Policy, and Practice* (Oxford University Press, 2004) 14 at 34.

[55] O'Neill, *Autonomy and Trust*, p. 153.

[56] Sperm left by will was held to form part of the deceased's estate in *Hecht* v. *Superior Court* 20 Cal. Rptr. 2d 275 (1993).

[57] G. den Hartogh, *Farewell to Non-commitment: Decision Systems for Organ Donation from an Ethical Viewpoint*, Monitoring Report Ethics and Health, Centre for Ethics and Health, The Hague, 2008 at 35.

[58] G. Laurie, *Genetic Privacy: A Challenge to Medico-Legal Norms* (Cambridge University Press, 2002), p. 312 [Laurie, *Genetic Privacy*].

[59] M. Dixon-Woods *et al.*, 'Tissue samples as "gifts" for research: A qualitative study of families and professionals' (2008) 9 *Medical Law International* 131. A charitable trust model was proposed here instead. Even here, though, more than half of respondents (relatives of children with cancer) were either happy with the 'gift' tag, or indifferent to it. The twenty-six respondents (out of fifty-seven) who were unhappy with it regarded it as inapt, patronising, implying the commercial nature of the arrangement, or designed to coerce authorisation. Many stressed the 'reviled' nature of the tissues in question.

Ordinary persons do not perceive the gift to create ties or expect exchange, even if certain 'basic' societies structure their relationships around patterns of burdened and obligated gift-giving. Indeed, to most lay people the idea of a gift emphasises the supererogatory nature of the gesture *without* any expectation of reciprocation. Whilst it is true that in some cases such donations do in fact 'burden' recipients with an unrepayable debt, this is the exception rather than the norm.

Regrettably, the use of such terminology has been conflated in the research context with the legalistic concept of gifts. Whilst gifts are intimately and crucially connected to the ownership of property,[60] *gifts* of property are usually taken to have been given with the intention that the property is given free of all claims, i.e. all rights have been relinquished. This has led to resistance in some quarters to the concept of the gift, particularly in the context of research. Tutton is concerned that such a notion, and the inclination to afford property rights to tissue users and processors but not to the sources of the tissues, separates the two, commercial and non-commercial, domains in an unacceptably opaque and illegitimate fashion.[61] In other words, as Laurie observes, the notion of the gift can serve to 'disempower' donors.[62] This may not only result in perceptions of inequity but could potentially jeopardise the trust of those who are being asked to freely donate to third parties who are then able to exploit such materials, including commercially, without constraints. It is therefore necessary to *translate* the fairly ubiquitous and popular concept of the gift into legal concepts which more faithfully and appropriately reflect and implement the wishes of donors.

'Gifts' of human material for research or transplantation are generally given for specific purposes and sometimes to specific recipients or users, and are sometimes subject to further additional provisos. These are the premises upon which the gift is based. It is a purposive gift equivalent to a donation for charitable ends. Whilst the donor may have no expectation of return of the material there is an expectation that it will be used in accordance with the 'terms' of the gift. It is necessary that control not be wholly surrendered in order for such terms to be respected and such permitted activities properly 'policed'. Whilst all control *may* have been deliberately relinquished this will be a function of the individual intentions and circumstances, and will typically be the exception. This may determine, *inter alia*, whether there is a right to withdraw samples (not merely results obtained

---

[60] J. Penner, *The Idea of Property* (Oxford University Press, 1997), p. 5.

[61] R. Tutton, 'Person, property and gift', in R. Tutton and O. Corrigan (eds.), *Genetic Databases: Socio-Ethical Issues in the Collection and Use of DNA* (Oxford: Routledge, 2004) 19 at 19.

[62] Laurie, *Genetic Privacy*, p. 312.

from their use) from a research facility once consent has been given, assuming that this is not dictated by contractual terms. Courts in the US in particular have seemingly been too ready to consider that donations of tissue for research were intended to be made entirely free of all future encumbrances or conditions, e.g. in *Washington University* v. *Catalona*.[63]

To this extent, as a matter of law, the conditional nature of such donations should be reflected in the generation of either a bailment of parts of the living or a trust relationship in parts of the deceased. The case of *Yearworth* v. *North Bristol NHS Trust* was a very recent and welcome endorsement of the bailment concept in the former context.[64] If a person acts inconsistently with the express or implied terms of the gift (*ultra vires*) then it fails and the property would then resort back to the *direction*, not necessarily the possession, of the original owner.[65] Alternatively, if the gift failed for legitimate reasons, such as where the organ could not be transplanted into the intended recipient, it could be explicitly defaulted to 'the normal distribution method', where this had been specifically provided. This should not be seen as lawyers' spin. It resonates with widely developing perceptions. The Medical Research Council has itself stated that 'While the status of human material is not clearly established under existing law, it is becoming clear that neither relatives nor the person removing the tissue from an individual becomes the owner. The transfer of such material may be viewed as a gift held in trust by the recipient.'[66] The notion put forward by the Supreme Court of California, that an informed person may simply withhold consent to any research plans he deems unacceptable, fails to allow for the possibility of later 'deviance' from the anticipated use and the vagaries of non-proprietary remedies able to secure compliance with such objectives.[67] Even the notion that informed consent may extend to dignitary harms as well as infringements of bodily integrity is constrained in reality.[68]

The Dutch Health Council observed that the general perception is of a tension between respect for the person and the interests of beneficence, but opined that there can be no moral basis for the taking of human tissues and

---

[63] *Washington University* v. *Catalona* 490 F 3d 667 (US Ct. App., 8th Cir. 2007) upholding *Washington University* v. *Catalona* 437 F Supp. 2d 985 (USDC Ed. Mo. 2006).

[64] *Yearworth* v. *North Bristol NHS Trust* [2009] EWCA Civ 37.

[65] L. Andrews, 'Two perspectives: Rights of donors: Who owns your body? A patient's perspective on Washington University *v.* Catalona' (2006) 34 *Journal of Law, Medicine and Ethics* 398.

[66] *MRC Guidance on Ethics of Research Involving Human Material Derived from the Nervous System*, 2003 at 8.

[67] *Moore* v. *Regents of the University of California* 51 Cal. 3d 120 at 141.

[68] See S. Perley, 'From control over one's body to control over one's body parts: Extending the doctrine of informed consent' (1992) 67 *New York University Law Review* 335.

organs than the voluntary gift.[69] It appears that the public also generally consider that medical research with human material is acceptable but only if accompanied by an adequate consent (which includes surplus tissues).[70] Of course, similar perceptions apply to transplantation. Generally, societies reject the notion that the common good trumps individual rights.[71] However, shortages of human materials for such purposes will test the limits of both ingenuity and policy. Brazier notes in the context of research that if there are an insufficient number of volunteers, a regulated paid vendor system may be the only way of meeting the needed supply, and this is equally pertinent to the supply of human organs for transplantation.[72] Alternatively, human materials may be taken either before or after death without any requirement for consent. In extreme circumstances of need this might indeed become a potentially viable public policy. However, I concur with Brazier that altruism has not yet been given a sufficient chance to prove its inherent capacity.[73] Trust is, however, the crucial issue with regard to supply, especially in relation to the deceased. Attitudes and decisions relating to donation will frequently be influenced by broader considerations, such as how the individual will be treated prior to death (would potential donors be treated less aggressively and appropriately simply in order to facilitate donations?), whether the person will be dead when body parts are removed, and how organs and tissues are allocated afterward (are they fairly allocated as between races, etc.?).[74] Even unrelated controversies may sometimes link in the public mind with issues relating to consent.[75] What is crucial is that the 'system' as a whole is perceived to be fair and transparent. 'Trust' and good will are multi-faceted in this connection. Where individuals wish to express such benevolence toward others we must ensure that their wishes are properly 'converted' and respected.

---

[69]  Report of a Committee of the Health Council of the Netherlands, *Proper Use of Human Tissue*, The Hague, No 1994/01E 31 and 34.

[70]  Report, *Qualitative Research to Explore Public Perceptions of Human Biological Samples*, 2000, Wellcome Trust and Medical Research Council at 15.

[71]  Etzioni describes the former as the authoritarian communitarian model. See A. Etzioni, 'Organ donation: A communitarian approach' (2003) 13 *Kennedy Institute of Ethics Journal* 1.

[72]  M. Brazier, 'Exploitation and enrichment: The paradox of medical experimentation' (2008) 34 *Journal of Medical Ethics* 180.

[73]  *Ibid.*, at 183.

[74]  In one US study, fairness in allocation was rated as the most important factor in willingness to donate; see B. Strock, 'Mandated choice and presumed consent: The silver bullets to solve the donor shortage?' (1996) 12(4) *UNOS Update* 14.

[75]  An example is the recent controversy in Singapore where relatives wished to have longer with the dead body prior to organ retrieval. They were aggrieved when removal took place immediately even though they had no objections to the deceased's organs being used for transplantation. The media were contacted by many individuals complaining about the presumed consent law in force, some even saying they would now opt out in protest; see www.reuters.com/article/latestCrisis/idUSSIN173241.

# Index